# the Complete Guide to Salt and Fresh Water Fishing Equipment

# the Complete Guide to Salt and Fresh Water Fishing Equipment

by Bill Wisner

*A Sunrise Book*

**Service Communications, Ltd.**

**E. P. Dutton & Co., Inc.**

New York

First Edition

Cover equipment courtesy of Abercrombie & Fitch Co., New York

10 9 8 7 6 5 4 3 2 1



Published by Service Communications, Ltd. and
Dutton-Sunrise, Inc., a subsidiary of E. P. Dutton & Co., Inc.
Published simultaneously in Canada by Clarke, Irwin & Company Limited,
Toronto and Vancouver

ISBN: 0-87690-212-3

Library of Congress Catalog Number: 75-42573

# Contents

# INTRODUCTION

Why go fishing?

A good question. Psychologists who are forever probing the whys of human behavior would probably suggest that fishing satisfies man's basic need to compete with his fellows—gives him an ego boost, so to speak. Others would point out that fishing can be traced back to man's basic need for survival—that fishing today is a lingering reminder of man's need to kill for food. Still others would interpolate that fishing is just another way for people in today's harried workaday world to release nervous energy and hostility.

It seems to us that the real reason is so obvious as to be lost in the shuffle: Fishing is fun. Basically, it is as simple as that.

There is more to it, however. Fishing does bring food. It is a relaxing pastime. You can fish with a minimal amount of equipment or with a wide range of specialized equipment, depending on the extent of your interest and thickness of your wallet. And last but not least, fishing is one sport that is enjoyed by folks of all ages—from preschool to old age.

To put icing on the cake, fishing is a healthy outdoor sport good for the mind, body, and soul. It can satisfy all the senses. The background of fishing is music to the ears. Listen to the restless song of the surf as it hurls breakers on a beach, the gurgles of a stream hurrying through weeds and over rocks, the screeching of gulls over a patch of surface-feeding tuna, the throaty "bee-ohh" of a lonely hooter buoy dancing in a chop, the soft slap of waves against a boat's hull, the splash of a marlin as it returns to the sea from a skyward leap.

There's just one thing. To derive the most enjoyment and realize maximum success in fishing, you must be properly equipped. Mind you, we say *properly*, not expensively. And the prime purpose of this book is to guide you to that proper equipment.

It can be assumed that prehistoric man started fishing when it occurred to him that those things swimming around in the lake might also be a kind of food. Since his tools were limited, we can also assume that man then employed the equipment most readily available—his hands. Thus was born the first fishing "rod," the human arm, and the first "hooks," human fingers. As man evolved, he probably began to use stones to throw at fish (after all, it worked with birds). Spears would be a logical successor to stones and were undoubtedly more successful. Crude nets fashioned from vines would have been another development.

Although it is pure speculation, we figure that the very first tackle had to be a simple hand line. The reasoning of the first hand line's inventor might have gone something like this: "I see that those things swimming around also eat. Now if I could tempt them with food of some sort, maybe I could catch them more easily. But how and with what?" Here our friend hit a temporary obstacle, but eventually, by patient reasoning, he came up with a hand-line arrangement, probably fabricated from vines or, perhaps, animal sinews. He had also invented bait.

And so man evolved and developed; so did fishing equipment develop to the point where now there is equipment to handle every conceivable assignment—from extracting a half-pound sunfish from a quiet pond to hauling in a 1,000-pound black marlin on the rolling briny. Fishing equipment today is highly specialized, with outfits designed for particular kinds of service. For this manufacturers deserve a lion's share of the credit—but not all of it. The unending procession of individual fishermen (and women—Dame Juliana Berners of the fifteenth century is credited as the first to write about fishing rod construction) from prehistorical days to the present—all are responsible, through experimenting and field testing, for the superb equipment each and every one of us enjoys as we pause on the long road to wet a line.

We have tried to include in this book the broadest range of equipment possible and the most up-to-date information on each item. However, because manufacturers change their prices on various items from year to year, and because stock and prices vary from region to region and from dealer to dealer, please keep in mind that the prices given in this book are *approximate* retail prices.

Good fishing!

Main display room at Gladding International Fishing Museum.

A far cry from today's superb reels, the early Billinghurst was named for its creator, a Utica, New York clockmaker. This is one of many collectors' items on display in the famous Gladding International Fishing Museum in South Otselic, New York.

This is a Hendryx casting reel from a long-gone era. See those coins? They represent its cost in its heyday—15c. America's angling past is reflected in many such collectors' items on exhibit at the Gladding International Fishing Museum in South Otselic, New York.

# Basic Angling Methods 1

There's an old saying in the sport: Fishing is easy. All you have to do is be there *yesterday* when the fish were biting like crazy.

Despite the fact that situations work out that way sometimes, that old fragment of wit, probably authored by a cynic, is tongue-in-cheek stuff. Fishing actually *is* easy—when you familiarize yourself with some simple procedures and the reasons behind them.

Maybe you're asking, "But how come some fishermen are better than others, or at least seem to have more luck?" Again—familiarity with procedures and understanding the logic behind them. To that you can add one word: *experience*! The best anglers are those who fish regularly. As for that vague intangible called luck, some of it does enter the picture (via chance selection of good or poor locations, for example), but fishermen create most of their "luck" themselves, and it's invariably in proportion to personal knowledge and ability to capitalize on it.

Rod-and-reel talent is within grasp of everyone who remembers that it's based on these details: (1) Some knowledge of a species' general habits—places it commonly frequents and when, whether sluggish or aggressive; (2) the what, where and when of a fish's feeding habits; (3) what natural food to present as bait, or how to approximate it with an artificial; and (4) how best to present that offering in an irresistible manner. When you come right down to it, fishing is merely a matter of appealing to a fish's stomach. As some wag remarked, even a fish wouldn't get in trouble if it kept its mouth shut.

## The Keystone . . .

. . . is methods.

After all, the most effective bait or lure available can't operate if it isn't presented to the quarry and offered to best advantage. This presentation is sport fishing's know-how, a detail that separates the men from the boys. It's also a detail that strongly influences tackle selection.

There are several basic methods, each applicable to several, even many, kinds of fishes. These fundamental techniques, in turn, are subject to multiple variations. This shouldn't alarm newcomers, for learning the basics is easy and variations are added along the way.

Further, basic angling methods cover all species of marine and freshwater species throughout the world. Flycasting, for example, snares trout in Ireland, Argentina, and New Zealand as readily as it does in Colorado or New Mexico. This writer has used the same basic method for black marlin along Australia's Great Barrier Reef as he employed to catch yellowfin tuna off Cape Town, South Africa, and bluefin tuna off Montauk, New York—even precisely the same artificials for the two kinds of tuna.

These are the basic angling methods. Remember that they have application in both salt water and fresh water:

*Bottom fishing,* also known as *sinker-bouncing*: Many angling targets are what we call ground fishes. That is, they reside or spend a lot of time searching for food on or near the bottom of the lake, bay, stream or ocean. Catfishes are among the many examples in fresh water. Flounders are among the even more numerous examples in salt water.

The extent to which they spend time on the bottom varies considerably, according to species. Some are exclusively residents of the floor, seldom venturing more than a few feet above it. Certain kinds—sturgeons, for example—have mouth parts suited only to feeding right on bottom. Other species, such as the northern weakfish, seek food along a bottom when the larder is skimpy upstairs. These fish shop for food wherever it happens to be most abundant. Still others are bottom feeders at certain times, such as at night, when they know little creatures come out of hiding in sand or mud, or perhaps after rough water has dislodged them.

So bottom fishing is designed to bring a bait or lure down to these citizens. According to species, baited hooks may be right on the floor or a couple of feet above it. When a species is known to range at varying levels above bottom, the smart procedure is to rig high and low hooks to cover those possibilities.

Tackle for bottom fishing often has to be sturdy. Not only is the size of the fish sought to be considered, but also these details: (*a*) Rigs may be heavy, since sinkers are needed to keep them on bottom against the upward thrusts of currents (as much as eight ounces or more of sinker may be required); and (*b*) bottom angling frequently is in fairly deep water, which increases water drag on the line and adds strain on a rod when cranking in a customer.

*Trolling:* We might call this the reverse of bottom fishing, since it was created to contact fishes that cruise or food-shop near the surface. Trolling consists of towing some item of natural food, such as small whole fish, or an artificial astern of the boat at a speed compatible with the species sought. Some fishes respond only at a very low speed, the craft barely making headway. At the other extreme are battlers such as wahoos and barracudas that zero in on offerings being towed at a fairly lively clip. In the main, trolling is best suited to the more active, aggressive feeders. But there are exceptions to every man-made "rule" in fishing. Sharks are active and agressive enough, but for some reason (possibly poor eyesight) are seldom caught on a trolled offering.

In addition to being tailored to the feeding *modus operandi* of the likes of tunas, marlins and several fresh-water gamesters, trolling offers an advantage by covering a lot of territory, especially important when the targets tend to be loners. On the other hand, it's the least economical technique because a boat is in constant motion, burning fuel all the time.

Much trolling is done at the surface or just beneath. However, there are times and/or species that necessitate going deeper. In summer, for example, certain marine battlers (bluefish, for one) and fresh-water fishes (bass) take to lower levels to escape heat. Use of wire line, trolling sinkers, or a device known as a downrigger takes rigs to those desired levels. Some cold-water species, notably lake trout, may be trolled at 100 feet or more down. Sometimes trolling is so deep that it becomes a kind of bottom fishing too, the bait or artificial being made to bump or hop along the bottom. A variation of trolling is the so-called *mooching*, employed for salmon in the Pacific Northwest. This is a kind of interrupted or spasmodic trolling in which a bait is made to dart upward from the bottom on a slant by alternate surges and pauses of the boat.

Rods designed primarily for trolling offer a wide latitude, and choice is a matter of personal taste.

*Drifting:* Offers the same advantages as trolling—covering ground and keeping a bait alluringly in motion; and since current or breeze propels the boat, no fuel is wasted. This is not a substitute for trolling, however. A kind of intermediate between that technique and fishing at anchor, it can attract fishes that like their prey "on the hoof," so to speak, but for which trolling would be too fast. (Drifting is excellent for sharks, by the way.) Natural bait, not artificials, usually is employed, although there's no law against trying the latter, alone or in combination with bait. In standard drifting, bait may be dead or alive. Because of its attraction action in the water, live bait often is favored. Small live fishes—minnows, shiners, eels—are candidates and sold for that purpose.

Drifting has only two drawbacks. It can be impractical if the propelling current or wind is too fast. And it can be tricky, if not dangerous, on busy waterways and in areas where there are rocks just below the surface.

Tackle wielded in drifting is the user's choice, spinning or conventional, and varies considerably. Any kind, except flycasting, will do. There's no specific type for this method. If there's any criterion, it's a matter of gauging the gear to sizes of fishes hunted.

*Fishing at anchor or still-fishing:* This is employed when it's desirable or necessary, because of a species' habits, to concentrate on a given area: a hole or channel, for instance, or in the vicinity of rocks or a wreck, or over a reef, or near a patch of aquatic vegetation in which the fish lurk. Many fishes feed or seek haven in such places. Some believe in togetherness when they feed. They may concentrate in one small area, and only yards away water will be devoid of them. All the foregoing are reasons why the depth sounder has become a popular fishing tool. Often it's an advantage to anchor off to one side of a tide rip, tumbling water of a fast-moving river or other similar location where fishes may be feeding, then drift or cast a bait or lure to them.

Much still-fishing is done on or near the bottom, especially in salt water. But the levels worked depend upon the feeding habits of the species sought and may be anywhere from the bottom to the top. The same species may be encountered at different levels, requiring some experimentation at the start of fishing. Atlantic mackerel are a good example. An anchored boat also is a platform for casting to near-surface objectives.

Again the choice of tackle is wide and runs the gamut of conventional and spinning outfits. Its caliber—that is, whether light, medium, or whatever — is influenced by such factors as sizes of fishes anticipated, weights of rigs and water depths. As in any method, many anglers like to "go light" for maximum action, but this demands an appraisal of one's ability and a willingness to lose fish on occasion. At an extreme are bottom fishes whose bulk tips a scale at 100 pounds or more, like California's giant sea bass and Florida's largest groupers, for which sizes up to 500-plus pounds are recorded. Needless to add, these require heavy-duty tackle. For most still-fishing a conventional or spinning outfit in a light to medium class serves nicely. (For weight-rating of gear, see tackle section.)

*Boat casting:* This is really a subdivision of both still-fishing and drifting, with the boat serving as a platform. It's designed primarily for surface- and near-surface-feeding targets. Sometimes it's better to pause and cast to a school of fish rather than risk scaring them by trolling. In any case, it's one of the most exciting methods because you see your opponents and may even get to watch them grab your offering.

Boat casters are invariably light-tackle buffs, so their equipment is either the fly fishing type or light baitcasting or spinning gear.

*Flycasting:* To the fresh-water purist, this is the only way to fish. Certainly it can be one of the most exacting. To place a lure like a tiny dry fly, that weighs practically nothing, in precisely the right place and proper fashion to entice a fish to seize it requires a well-learned skill. This challenge is fly fishing's greatest attraction. In fresh water, much flycasting focuses on the trout family; but it also is employed for salmon, bass and just about any species you could name. Because of the tackle's extreme lightness, it affords lively sport even with little panfishes.

In recent years flycasting has branched out to include salt water, and now this is one of the fastest growing facets of angling. It's also one of the most exciting salt-water techniques. Marine flyrodders are daring souls, not at all awed by the sizes of their opponents. The range of their catches goes from cero mackerel and bluefish to tarpon and tunas. Samples on the books of the Salt Water Fly Rodders of America, International: 75¾-pound amberjack; 136-pound Pacific sailfish; 154-pound tarpon; 272-pound shark (species not given).

Caliber of tackle wielded in fresh-water and salt-water flycasting naturally differs. The latter is heavier. The main reason, of course, is the generally larger opponents. Too, the artificials are larger, bulkier and more wind-resistant, and frequently breeze is a problem on open water.

*Surfcasting:* The traditional portrayal of a surfcaster shows a solitary figure on a lonely oceanfront beach, his long rod bent in combat with some unseen adversary as breakers curl shoreward and gulls wheel overhead. "Surfcasting" remains exclusively a salt-water term, but its use has broadened to include shoreside casting in general. Thus the participants can be on the shores of inlets, bays, lagoons and channels, as well as along an ocean coast—on the beach or on jetties.

With that in mind, these are factors influencing selection of tackle: (*a*) casting distance required; (*b*) weights of rigs involved; (*c*) locally prevailing conditions, such as strong currents or frequent wind; (*d*) size and combat nature of opponents—whether long-running, degree of stamina; and (*e*) combinations of any or all those factors. They're all variables, and sometimes they pose problems. That's why it isn't possible to recommend one "all-purpose" outfit. While a single rod-and-reel combination will perform satisfactorily under a fairly wide range of conditions, it can't be expected to be all things at all times everywhere. That's why your true surfcasting *aficionado* possesses more than one outfit.

Spinning tackle originally was designed for casting assignments, and casting is still its forte. For that reason, many salt- and fresh-water fishermen favor it over conventional-type gear. Further, with it beginners can realize distance quicker and easier than the older kind of tackle. However, there is surf fishing equipment of both types, and in a range of weights.

Casting distance isn't always a prerequisite of shoreside fishing success. Catches are commonly made within 100 feet of where an angler is standing, even closer in fresh water and on oceanfront jetties and along inlet channels. On the other hand, there are shores whose makeup demands appreciable casting distance. Perhaps a beach slopes very gradually into deeper water, or a productive slough or hole or sand bar is some distance out. Reaching such places becomes doubly difficult, if not impossible, in the face of a strong breeze.

Incidentally, surf boat casters and trollers often have an advantage over their shoreside brethren in being able to contact fish out of casting range.

*Jigging:* In its standard form jigging is done from a boat at anchor or drifting, and it's intended to cover several levels at which fish may be cruising. Depending upon species sought, it may be confined more or less to one plane or wander through several, bottom to near-surface. The most common form of jigging consists of lowering a fish-attractor to the desired depth, reeling it upward, letting it drop back, reeling it upward again, and so on. Keeping the come-on in motion is another idea behind jigging. There are all-metal lures in shapes suggestive of small bait fishes designed for jigging. Often they're chrome plated for the added attraction of glitter. Natural bait also is used, alone or in combination with a metal jig.

A modified form of jigging is employed in conjunction with trolling. Here it consists of continuously jerking the bait or lure with the rod to impart even more action to it.

Another variation, called snagging, is mostly done in fresh water, notably for fishes that do not readily take a baited hook. Two, three or more treble hooks are attached to a weighted line, and the wielder continually jerks the rig upward with the hope that one of those hooks will snag in the body of a passing customer. Snagging is frowned upon by anglers as not being true fishing. It is even prohibited by law in some areas.

*Chumming:* Strictly speaking, this is not a fishing method in itself, but a supplement to several methods. It consists of distributing overboard some item of food that will attract fishes to the vicinity of waiting hooks. Since currents carry chumming material outward, it's a means of contacting fishes that otherwise wouldn't come anywhere near the baited hooks. It has wide application in salt and fresh water for still-fishing and drifting (drifting and chumming comprise *the* method in shark fishing). It can be used by pier and shoreside anglers too, so long as there is some current to distribute the chum, but not too much to dissipate it prematurely. The list of items that have been used for chum is long and includes: assorted fishes, usually ground into a mushy pulp for better, more economical distribution, but also in pieces or even whole when very small; clams and mussels, minced, in pieces or whole; whole small shrimp or pieces of large ones; canned fish food for pets; and such quaint items as bread crumbs, uncooked oatmeal, kernels of corn and, in a pinch, even bits of shells from hardboiled eggs.

No money-back guarantee with chumming, but it often perks up otherwise slow fishing and can make good action even better. In some instances, notably for large marine gamesters such as giant bluefin tuna and sharks, it's practically a must because they tend to be wandering loners. Its drawbacks are that it adds to the cost of angling and sometimes the more popular chumming materials are in short supply or unavailable.

*Ice fishing:* This fresh-water method is gaining more and more followers every year in northern states all across the U.S. and now takes in suitably cold mountain regions of California. There are ice-fishing tournaments and festivals. On some of the larger lakes, such as those in the Midwest, communities of small, portable shanties mushroom in winter on the ice. Some even lay out "streets," with names, and elect mayors. The reason for ice fishing's growing popularity is simple: it provides fishing in winter, which otherwise would be a long recess. Northern pike, yellow perch and pickerel are among the species caught under the ice. The sport has become so popular that now some states have regulations governing kinds of fishes and seasons.

The equipment involved—a gadget called a tip-up, an auger for cutting a hole in the ice, some other items—is specialized. (See Fresh-Water Tackle.)

Comparatively little through-ice fishing is done in salt water. The kinds of fishes available at that time of year in northern latitudes are very limited, to put it mildly, and consistent very cold water is required to form salt-water ice that is safe to walk on. Much of what fishing *is* done is confined to eels and involves special spears, not rods and reels. Eels winter in bottom mud. To find them necessitates repeated blind jabbing of the bottom. It's frosty work.

*Wading:* It isn't a method *per se*, but it is a very helpful supplement, a kind of intermediate step between shoreside operation and fishing from boats. It's a standard procedure in fresh-water angling for flyrodders after trout and other battlers and for bass fishermen working the shores of lakes. It's also employed by marine anglers for certain species on sand and mud flats and in very shallow water of bays and lagoons. Wading flats and casting are a popular method of stalking bonefish in Florida and elsewhere.

*Miscellaneous methods:* These are less-used techniques, often localized. Some may be limited or banned by law in certain areas. We include them here in the interest of completeness.

*Dipnetting:* This is a procedure for fishes too small to catch on hooks, such as smelt, and usually concentrates on species traveling in dense schools. It's fishing for the table. Although it has its enthusiasts, dipnetting is not sport fishing in the accepted sense of the term. As its name hints, it involves a long-handled net with which fish are dipped out of the water. Dipnetters work from shore and often capitalize on migratory runs of schools in and out of estuaries and river mouths.

*Spearfishing* doesn't come within the scope of this book, since it is a sport more closely allied with skin and scuba diving. Employing hand-thrown and powered weapons, it accounts for a wide variety of species, from small reef dwellers up to huge groupers and dangerous sharks. Most of the time no love is lost between spearfishermen and their rod-and-reel brethren, but many members of the former group perform such valuable services as tagging fishes and reporting on the productivity of artificial fishing reefs.

*Jugging:* This quaint procedure has advocates in the U.S. South and is used for large catfish. Its basic rig is a glass or plastic jug, to serve as a buoy, to which a length of line and a baited hook are secured. The jug is set adrift, whereupon its bobbing signals that a customer has taken the hook. Following the bobbing buoy in a boat, the angler retrieves it and lands his catch by handlining the "cat." In a sportier refinement, provision is made for detaching the jug and switching the rig to a rod and reel.

*Grabbing:* There's no better name for it. "Grabbing" means seizing fish with the bare hands. It too has practitioners in the South and concentrates on catfish. Grabbers take advantage of the fact that during the egg-incubation period male catfish belligerently stay by the nest to guard it. In one version of grabbing they also capitalize on the willingness of the males to attack any intruder. In this technique the bold grabber extends an arm, the fish "charges," and the invader tries to thrust his hand through the cat's mouth and out the gill covers. If he succeeds, he has the makings of a fish fry. If he doesn't, he has a scraped arm. Less confident grabbers use a large, hand-held hook.

An easier, less hazardous form of grabbing was popular years ago on oceanfront strands in northeastern states in autumn and winter. It was called frost fishing and involved one species, northern whiting. These fish sometimes pursue smaller prey into a surf with such vigor that they are stranded on the beach by an outgoing tide, thereby providing a bonanza for residents who simply picked them up.

The famous grunion hunts in California are similar. Grunions are unique in the fish world in that they come ashore to spawn. These strange breeding migrations out onto the sand are precisely timed with the tides; and since tides can be predicted within minutes in advance, so can the grunions' appearance. The upcoming event is duly mentioned in local newspapers so that anyone who is interested can gather fresh fish for the table.

*Hand-netting:* A first cousin of dipnetting is practiced along some open stretches of California beach to gather small fishes such as surfsmelt for home use. In one procedure the gatherers work in pairs, a small net between them, to trap little smelt wandering through shallow water close to shore. It isn't as much sport as battling a hard-fighting opponent on the end of a line, but it requires know-how and agility and the participants have fun . . . and candidates for frying pans back home.

These next procedures frequently are frowned upon—even considered unsportsmanlike by rod-and-reelers. Nevertheless, they have their fans. We won't editorialize.

*Jacking or gigging:* Essentially it consists of sighting fish in shallow water and spearing them by hand. Gigging is practiced in many areas around the rim of the Gulf of Mexico. Jacking is a night version, employing a lantern whose light not only reveals the presence of targets but also attracts little creatures that draw fishes. Although some of them probably participate at times, most tackle anglers usually hold jacking in low regard.

*Trotlines:* A trotline consists of a long main line, heaviest in the outfit, from which shorter, lighter fishing lines are suspended at intervals. Spaced a couple of feet apart, these shorter lines carry baited hooks. A trotline is positioned in a strategic place—across a stream from bank to bank, or perhaps buoyed and anchored in a channel—and checked for catches from time to time. Basically it's a commercial fishing method, a trotline being a scaled-down version of the infamous longline; but there are recreational fishermen who use the device.

## Let the Tools Fit the Job

Theoretically at least, there is a kind of middle-of-the-road fishing tackle. An angler conceivably could get through his or her piscatorial career with only one outfit (somewhere in the light-medium to medium range) and catch just about all the finned rascals one would be likely to encounter, especially as ability increased. Many a rod-'n'-reeler did it in the old days.

But that was yesteryear. Old-timers didn't have much choice. Today's serious fishermen, those who want to enjoy their sport to the hilt, realize that there is no one outfit to satisfactorily handle *all* assignments. While this doesn't mean your home should resemble a tackle shop, it does demand *some* variations in equipment to broaden fishing potential. Today's serious anglers have a wide variety of equipment from which to choose. Those rod-'n'-reelers in the old days had an excuse for making one outfit do. Modern fishermen do not.

---

# Types of Tackle 2

## TACKLE CORNERSTONES: BASIC KINDS

All marine and fresh-water sport fishing tackle is classified according to three major categories: conventional, spinning, and flycasting. If we want to stretch our scope we can add the specialized gear employed in ice fishing and say that there are four basic types. But for now we'll hold that last in abeyance.

Presumably, seniority inspired the appellation "conventional tackle," to distinguish it from the younger spinning equipment. In any case, conventional tackle is characterized by a reel whose spool revolves. That's the main feature separating it from spinning gear, whose reel has a fixed or stationary spool. Whatever subdivisional designation a reel may be given—baitcasting, surf fishing, and so on—if it has a revolving spool it comes under the group heading "conventional tackle." With one outstanding exception: fly fishing equipment. By revolving-spool definition it fits into the conventional classification, but is not included when one thinks of conventional tackle. Because of its specialized techniques and artificials, it's always considered separately under its own heading.

We can best define spinning tackle by comparing it with the conventional kind, and the comparison mainly concerns the reels. A conventional reel's spool turns to allow line to play out, as in casting or when playing a fish, and also to retrieve line. It's a simple, very serviceable arrangement. Only trouble is, a revolving spool gains momentum when line pays out rapidly. What can happen then is that its turning speed reaches a point where it exceeds that of line going out, creating loose coils of line in the process. So instead of cooperating with the outgoing line, the fast-turning spool literally overtakes it and begins winding line back onto itself. Coupled with any loose coils, the result is the most gosh-awful tangle you ever saw. Polite names for this mess are "backlash" and "bird's nest." Backlashes occur chiefly during casts. They also can be caused by casting that is too forceful, unevenly spooled line, and casting into a strong wind, but the biggest culprit is spool over-running. Along with causing aggravation and ruining casts, they consume precious fishing time to untangle—and a few yards of line if the caster becomes frustrated and whips out his knife.

Backlashes are not without a touch of humor. Although the victim doesn't chuckle, there is something funny in watching a dignified guy wind up for a cast, real experienced-like, then see his rig stop abruptly in midair about six feet away. We can afford to laugh. It happens to all of us.

Conventional reels once had heavy spools, the idea being that their weight added casting momentum. It did, but too much, once they got rolling. Too, there was appreciable inertia to overcome at the start of a cast, making it difficult to toss the lighter artificials. In all, some horrendous snarls resulted. Today's lighter spools lessen inertia (thereby broadening the range of lures reels can handle) and to a certain extent cut down on backlashes. There are anti-backlash mechanisms built into some reels, but even they can't eliminate bird's nests entirely, and many casting regulars disdain them because they do to a degree cost casting distance. Those regulars prefer to prevent over-running of the spool by light thumb pressure to brake it.

## Opposing Principles

The first man who dreamed up the idea of a fixed spool reel conceivably was a fisherman plagued by backlashes. In any case, one of spinning tackle's biggest virtues is the impossibility of backlashes—but not "tangles." Under certain conditions, such as windy days, they're a possibility even with this kind of gear. But over-running of the spool is impossible with a spinning reel for the very simple reason that its spool doesn't turn.

Here is a simple experiment to illustrate the major difference between a conventional reel and its spinning counterpart.

Hold an ordinary spool of sewing thread between thumb and forefinger. To demonstrate a conventional reel's operating principle, hold the spool with its long axis parallel to your body, loosely enough so that it can turn, the free end of its thread aimed outward. With your other hand pull the thread away from you. Your hand's pull represents that of a lure or bait being cast, or a fish demanding line. The spool turns, just as a conventional reel's does when line goes out.

In retrieves a conventional reel's crank causes the spool to revolve in the opposite direction, bringing line back on it. Those old-fashioned "knuckle-dusters" mentioned earlier had a knob for a crank, mounted right on their large wooden spool. Consequently, their relative ratio was 1:1, one revolution of the knob equaling one turn of the spool. Multiplying reels, the kind we use today, have a gear system that "multiplies" each turn of the crank. According to a model's retrieve ratio, its spool's revolutions per turn of the crank may be anywhere from 2½ to 3½ or 4, over 5:1. Higher gear ratios in that range may be desired for faster working of lures or reduce retrieve time between casts.

Now hold that spool of thread with its long axis at right angles to your body, but this time simulate a spinning reel's spool by holding it firmly so it can't turn. Again pull the thread away from you, *slowly*. You'll see that it leaves in coils, without aid from the spool. This radically different manner of departure is the core of spinning reel operation.

Since a spinning reel's spool is stationary and obviously can't wind in line, there has to be a radically different way of retrieving. As in the case of a conventional reel, retrieving is effected by activating a gear train with the crank. But there the similarity stops. The spinning reel utilizes an arrangement called a "pickup" to gather in the returning line and redeposit it on the spool.

Over the years, three basic kinds of pickup mechanisms were devised: manual, automatic pickup arm, and bail, also called full bail. The manual type is a curving arm which gathers in the line. In casting it lies out of the way, must be snapped into position manually for retrieves. Many casters have liked this arrangement, but it has a drawback in that the arm can be bent accidentally, impairing its function. The automatic pickup is substantially the same as the manual, except that it automatically swings into position when the crank is returned to retrieve line. It can have the same drawback. Another objection, shared by the manual type, is that a strong breeze can cause the line to catch on the pickup arm. In the bail type, gathering of line is effected by a curving half-hoop that extends across the spool's outer face and is secured at both ends. For casting, the bail is out of the way and a flow of line can be controlled by a finger. For retrieving, the bail automatically swings into its pickup position when the crank is turned. The bail type is the most prevalent today.

In all three instances there has to be some part of the reel that revolves so line can be redeposited on the spool. The part that turns is a cup-like housing surrounding the spool and bearing the pickup. To further aid in redepositing, the spool has a short back-and-forth shuttle motion, along the rod's axis.

Reels of the manual and automatic pickup types have a roller over which incoming line glides. Some rollers turn, others are fixed. Any objection to the former is that they can become sticky and "freeze." Both types can become grooved in time, increasing line wear. With a bail type, line simply slides along the metal hoop, back onto the spool.

Spinning reels are divided into two main groups, *open-face* and *closed-face*, the latter also called spincasting reels. On the former the spool is exposed. On the latter it's concealed by a cone-shaped housing, with line leaving and returning through a hole in its center. Both kinds operate on the fixed spool principle, the line leaving in coils. On the closed-faced reel these coils are gathered inside the cone before leaving. Of the two, the open-face is probably the more popular. Many spinning veterans favor it because a certain amount of line friction inside the housing of a closed-face reel can cut down on casting distance. On the other hand, the closed-type face often is a choice of baitcasters when distance isn't of prime importance. Too, there's an advantage in that a strong breeze can't interfere with coils of line leaving the reel because they're contained inside the cone.

Not to confuse you, but closed-face spinning reels are subdivided into two kinds. Although they operate on the same principle, one mounts underneath the rod in usual spinning reel fashion, whereas the other goes atop the rod like a conventional reel. Both types are often called spincasting reels and have the most popular application in baitcasting.

All spinning reels and conventional models worth their salt are outfitted with an adjustable drag or brake system as standard equipment. A drag's sole function is to provide resistance to line being pulled from the spool, and its degree of resistance can be regulated from zero (fully off) to maximum for that particular reel. "Tightening" and "loosening" are the terms for increasing and decreasing the amount of drag, and tightening a drag often is spoken of as "putting pressure on a fish." That tells the purpose of a brake. Various situations may indicate tightening the drag—to better control a long-running fish, for instance. Long-distance runners such as bonefish, permit, mako sharks and marlins could strip a reel of line if given half a chance. Tightening the drag also tires a fish more quickly. Sometimes that's desirable after a long argument with a particularly obstreperous opponent. At other times it isn't desirable because it cuts the action short.

A drag is a definite asset, if used properly. The common error is to set up too tight on a drag. But this mistake usually is corrected quickly, especially after a few popped lines and maybe a fractured rod. With larger opponents the usual procedure is to set the brake at what we call striking drag—just enough to set the hook, after which it's tightened further if needed. Frequently it's necessary to alternately tighten and loosen a drag during combat to adjust to conditions at the moment. The idea is to find a medium between two extremes: a drag that is too loose, permitting a fish to peel off more line than is necessary, and one that is too tight, risking a broken line and lost fish. Obviously, drag adjustment is a wide variable. It comes through experience and "feel."

*Tip:* What many fishermen do not realize is that, because of a physical principle, the lower a supply of line becomes on a reel, the greater an automatic drag effect. This may reach a point where it's necessary to slack off a bit on the brake manually or risk consequences. It's another good reason to keep spools adequately filled with line.

The most common drag mechanism is comprised of discs of some tough material—one called Teflon is used a lot today—which creates the spool's resistance by pressure and friction on each other, functioning like a slip clutch. Pressure and friction are increased or decreased by tightening or loosening the drag. Even with the drag tightened, enough pull on the line will cause the discs to slip (the slip clutch idea). This is arranged purposely as a measure of protection against a snapped line—up to a point. Slip clutch or no slip clutch, it's still possible to break a line because of an over-tight drag.

Drags are activated and regulated by hand. Except on more expensive models, the universal means of adjustment from full-off to full-on among conventional reels is effected by a star-shaped wheel mounted on the crank's shaft. This so-called star drag has been popular for many years. Some of the more expensive reels—the Fin-Nor is one—have what is called a quadrant brake. Here the drag is adjusted by means of a lever on the side of the reel's housing. It moves through about 90 degrees of drag. In a hurry the quadrant lever is easier to operate than a star wheel, but its greater advantage is that it's calibrated so that you can see what you're doing. That also makes it possible to adjust the drag more precisely and return to a desired setting. There's no calibration on a star wheel, and setting is sometimes by guess and by golly. But then, you're paying more for a quadrant brake.

Among spinning reels there is a wider assortment of drag-adjustment arrangements; whatever the type, it is positioned within convenient reach. A model lying on this writer's desk could be called typical. It has what it's manufacturer calls a "spring-loaded drag," which gives a clue to its mechanics. The drag is adjusted by turning a large, triangular-shaped knob mounted on the spool's outer end. Like some others, this particular reel has a drag calibration, numbers 1 through 10. That's a help in setting a drag beforehand, but isn't always easy to see when battling a very busy opponent.

Another distinguishing feature of a conventional reel is its free-spool mechanism. This is a clutch, activated by a lever on the spool's end plate. When in the *on* position, the reel's gears are disengaged and the spool is free to turn in either direction, with no influence on the drag. This is for casting and when it's desirable to pay out line quickly. Flicking the lever to *off* re-engages the gears and the drag is in effect. Terrible tangles can result when line pays out fast, uncontrolled, in free spool. Light thumb pressure serves as a brake. A conventional reel also has a "clicker" or ratchet mechanism that can be thrown on or off by a small sliding button on its end plate. A clicker provides a certain amount of resistance to line going out if the reel is in free spool, and also serves as an audible warning of a fish tinkering with the rig.

A mechanism peculiar to spinning reels is the anti-reverse. This too is activated by a convenient lever. In a way it's a counterpart of the free-spool arrangement. When on, the anti-reverse lock immobilizes the crank, except for retrieving line, and pits the reel's drag against the pull of a fish. The anti-reverse is left on right up to the time a fish is landed. It's also left on in trolling to prevent line from being pulled off the spool by the boat's motion. Once a fish is on, the drag takes over. Additionally, an anti-reverse lock is handy when transporting tackle. By winding in excess line, putting the lock on, and mooring the hook somewhere on the rod or reel, there's no dangling rig to catch in clothing or underbrush.

## Other Points of Difference

A spinning rod is as obviously different from a conventional cousin as its reel. To better point up the dissimilarities we'll put rod and reel together.

The biggest noticeable difference is that a spinning outfit is "upside down" in comparison with a conventional ensemble. That is, the reel is mounted underneath the rod instead of on top. An exception to this is a certain kind of closed-face spinning reel which you will encounter elsewhere in these pages. Another glaring difference is that the reel's crank is on the user's left (for right-handed people).

To explain the upside down business we have to return to the fixed spool principle. As you now know, line leaves an open-face spinning reel in coils—large coils. If the reel were atop a rod, gravity would cause those coils to slap against the rod and possibly foul up the operation. With the reel underneath, they have complete freedom. Also because of those coils, there has to be another alteration. The standard guide on both spinning and conventional rods is the ring type. But those on a conventional "stick" are too small to gather in the coils of line properly, so the guides on a spinning rod, notably those closest to the reel, are much larger. Additionally, spinning rods generally are longer and more willowy than their conventional equivalents, and so may carry more guides.

Anyone used to conventional tackle will find the "opposites" of spinning gear a little awkward at first, but this evaporates quickly. Perhaps the most awkward detail at the start is the positioning of the reel's crank on the left for right-handed users. This is based on the idea that it's better to have the favored hand free to operate the pickup mechanism and control the flow of line with a finger. There are spinning reels with their crank on the right for left-handers. Some manufacturers—Feurer Brothers is one—sell spinning reels that can be flipped for either right- or left-handed cranking. There are also southpaw conventional reels, but none that can be flipped.

## Which Is For You, Conventional or Spinning Tackle?

Alas, no one but you can answer that. There are too many variables. For someone else posing the query it's rather like asking, "Which is for you, a blue suit or a brown suit?"

Angling procedures, prevailing conditions—those under which you'll do most of your fishing—and the finned game involved have a lot to do with selection. But in the final analysis a choice also hinges heavily on acquired personal preference. And that, of course, comes only with use. All we can do here is cite a few points as general guidelines. You'll have to take it from there.

First off, spinning tackle was designed primarily for casting. That doesn't rule it out for other methods, but in casting it stars. Credit goes to its overall makeup: the comparatively longer, more willowy rod and the very nature of the reel. Achieving casting distance is easier than with regular tackle. Further, since there's no spool inertia to overcome in casting, spinning gear permits use of much lighter lures, thereby increasing the equipment's scope. Frequently there are situations—like trying to tempt wary trout in a small stream or stalking even warier bonefish on a sand flat—that demand rigging of small, very light aritificials. For spinfishermen there are lures weighing one-quarter ounce or less. Such featherweights couldn't get a conventional reel's spool turning in a cast.

Another big plus in spinning, as we've already mentioned, is the absence of backlashes.

Most important to beginners and new converts from conventional tackle, it's much easier and quicker to become a proficient caster. Whether or not it remains easier and more comfortable under a wide range of conditions, once a wielder really gets the hang of it, is an individual proposition. All we can say is, there's a flock of faithfuls who prefer spinning tackle.

In short, you should try both in similar circumstances. Until you decide, maybe you can borrow a friend's outfit.

Spinning tackle is available in a wide range of calibers, from extra-light fresh-water gear to heavier-duty equipment for surf fishing and offshore bouts with larger species. With this range it can accommodate a very wide assortment of fresh-water and marine sport fishes. The medium- to heavy-duty outfits have accounted for a lengthening list of battlers, from big salmon and striped bass, through albacore, tuna and sailfish, to marlin (not the giants) and sharks. A New York friend of this writer, veteran angler Charles R. Meyer, racked up a 261-pound 11-ounce mako, the most active and hard-fighting of sharks, with spinning tackle. That happened to be light gear—twelve-pound line, since Chuck is a fisherman of vast experience, and it set a twelve-pound-line world record which, at this writing, still stands. It should go without saying that such light weapons are not for greenhorns.

Although spinning tackle is used in certain fishing assignments by some fishermen, your writer prefers conventional gear for these activities. These include bottom fishing, surfcasting and trolling with the bulkier rigs (such as heavy sinkers, whole natural eels, and bunker spoons and other big artificials). *As a personal opinion,* here the length and inherent flexibility of spinning rods works against them. Heavy rigs, compounded by an objecting fish, can be difficult to reel in. In surface trolling, a spinning rod's flexibility can make a lure too active, causing it to leap from wave to wave, even into the air.

If there's any quarrel with spinning tackle, it usually lies more with the user than with the equipment. And that comes back to the old story of an angler expecting one outfit to be all things at all times. By rights, a serious fisherman should have outfits of both kinds. He can start with a single outfit of one type or the other, but sooner or later he supplements it. Chances are, if he does an appreciable amount of fishing, he will *have* to.

## Fly Fishing Equipment

As mentioned previously, this is in a class by itself and because of its nature has to be catalogued as ultra-light to light tackle. Lightness is a key detail of both rod and reel. And you can add lures too. The equipment's overall lightness is both an asset and a liability. It's an asset because it provides maximum action with a fish of any size. In this respect the only outfit approaching it is extra-light fresh-water spinning tackle. It's lightness is a liability because just that much more angling skill is demanded. Don't misunderstand—the rankest beginner can take up fly fishing from scratch (remember, experts once were neophytes too). What we're saying is, to become really proficient at it requires practice, experience and a lot of patience. If you're the very impatient type you might better leave fly fishing alone and stick to spinning gear for light-tackle action. On the other hand, if you stay with it you will sample some of the most exciting fighting there is.

The equipment's extreme lightness—like that of an outfit whose rod and reel together weigh less than half a pound—takes a bit of getting used to, especially with some of the fly rods' lengths. So do the various flycasting techniques, which require hand-stripping of line from the reel. Casting here is peculiar to fly fishing. But the sport's biggest challenges are: (*a*) properly placing and working of lures, and (*b*) successful playing of a fish on a rod that seems to have about as much substance as an umbrella rib.

Fly fishing tackle—rod, reel and line—all relates to the lures. Among those rigged in flycasting are the smallest and lightest of all. Grouped under the heading Artificial Flies, these are fashioned—"tied" is the correct word—to simulate in size, shape and perhaps color various kinds of aquatic or terrestrial insects upon which trout and other fresh-water fishes feed. At the lowest end of the size scale they're tiny, carry wee hooks, and are next to weightless. There are larger, heavier artificials, such as those designed to imitate minnows and the so-called streamers and bucktails used in marine flycasting, but they're all characterized by lightness.

It requires adapted equipment to cast these little rascals. And that brings us to a very important component of the ensemble: the line. Reels used in fly fishing have revolving spools. It would be impossible to cast those extremely light lures with them, were it not for the line. Fly line in itself supplies the weight needed in casting to get itself off the reel and take the lure to its target area. In this respect fly tackle is unique among all angling equipment. It's also the reason that seasoned flycasters match their rods to their lines, rather than the other way around. Matching of rod and line is very important for proper balance of tackle, more so than with any other kind of gear. Remember that when you go to buy either line or a rod. Improperly balanced fly tackle will not give optimum performance.

Over the years fly rods have been marketed in a wide range of lengths, from about 5½ to 9½ or 10 feet; at the extremes are a 4-foot 4-inch "bantam" to extra-long, two-handed-casting models going to 11 and 12 feet and even longer, designed for "big water" and the heftiest salmon. Weight often is a more important criterion than length for fly rods. Within their own group they can be classified from ultra-light to extra-heavy, with a range from only 1 ounce for that aforementioned bantam, up to 10 and 15 ounces and more among those big, two-handed salmon rods.

Like other kinds of rods, those wielded in flycasting may be classified according to their action in use. This is as good a place as any to define the terms "fast action" and "slow action," which you'll run across in your reading. Essentially, "fast" means that a rod quickly returns to its normal posture after bending. "Slow action" is the reverse. A fast-action rod returns to normal more quickly because there's less bending throughout its length. Another classifying method employs the terms "dry fly action," "wet fly action," and "bass action." Broadly speaking, dry-fly-action rods are faster; the other two are slower. There are variations and overlapping.

In addition to length and slenderness, distinguishing characteristics include snake-type guides and comparatively short handle and butt sections. Although fly rods usually have one ring-type guide on the butt section and a tiptop guide like conventional-style rods, the other guides are of the so-called snake design, which is a simple loop of wire, not closed like a ring. These save some weight, a factor in fly tackle. Also saving weight are the shorter handle and butt sections. Because of the nature of fly-casting, a longer handle-butt section for leverage isn't needed.

Today fly rods have joined their conventional and spinfishing cousins in being made chiefly from fiberglass. Split-bamboo models are still available —some hard-nosed "purists" won't wield anything else—but they cost like the dickens.

Fly rods are marketed in two-piece and three-piece models, mainly for easier transportation and storage. There are some that disassemble into four sections for owners who do a lot of traveling. A common feeling among fishermen is that the fewer sections any rod has, the better. Some believe that the stiffness of metal ferrules connecting the sections—their "joints," so to speak—can impair the smooth movement of casts. Or they suspect that ferrules are potential weak spots under stress. The former problem is really of little consequence to the average fisherman, whatever kind of rod he's using. As for potential weakness in the "joints," that should be no headache with a well-made rod in normal—as opposed to abusive—service.

Lightness is followed through in fly reels. Weight is saved by using light metals and alloys and by generally simpler construction. Three kinds are offered: *1.* Single-action. In design this is like those old "knuckledusters" mentioned earlier. The crank is a knob mounted directly on its spool. No gears or multiplying mechanism—a 1:1 ratio, hence the term "single-action." *2.* Automatic. Here line is retrieved by a spring-driven mechanism.

*3.* Multiple-action. A gear system turns the spool more than once (it may be up to three or four times) per revolution of the crank handle.

Choice among the three is largely a matter of personal preference. The single-action fly reel is the simplest, and therefore the lightest, easiest to use and least likely to go out of whack. It also offers an economy factor. It's probably the best choice for novices. The more complicated automatic saves effort in retrieving line, but adds weight, which is why some regulars favor the single-action type. Some also like the latter's simpler, freer action. Further, an automatic must be of good quality to withstand repeated use, otherwise it will develop "bugs." The same things are true for a multiple-action model as for an automatic. An advantage of the multiplying type is that it combines a single-action "feel" with faster retrieves, and therefore comes into its own when long casts are involved.

All except the cheapest fly reels have some sort of drag mechanism. It may be only a clicker ratchet arrangement or adjustable. A brake of some kind is a highly desirable feature, and ideally it should be adjustable. Applying drag pressure may be necessary to slow a larger or harder-running fish to prevent the reel from being denuded of line and backing.

Due to the nature of casting in flyrodding, involving hand-stripping of line from the reel, no free spool mechanism and clutch are needed. (That also saves weight and some cost.) For the same reasons, the reel is mounted on the rod's underside. Although the spread is not as great as among other kinds, fly reels do vary in size and weight, according to types, specific models and intended use, whether fresh water or salt. Thus spool diameters can range from just under 3 inches to 4-plus, with weights going from 3 ounces to 10 or so.

Desirable features in fly reels include: (*a*) strength in lightness; (*b*) corrosion- and wear-resistant parts and finishes; (*c*) interchangeability of spools for easy switching from one type of fly line to another; (*d*) simple disassembly for cleaning and repairs; (*e*) ready set-up for right- or left-hand operation. The last is for single- and multiple-action models. Automatics are activated by a trigger mechanism that can be reached with either hand.

*Tip:* An important item frequently overlooked by new purchasers of fly rods is a good case. Although a fly rod is not as fragile as it appears, it nevertheless must have suitable protection when idle, stored or in transit. And that goes double if it's to be subjected to the not-so-tender mercies of baggage handlers. A tough case of fiber, aluminum or plastic is an excellent investment if one doesn't come with the rod. This writer favors either fiber or impact-resistant plastic. He has seen aluminum cases dented by careless handling.

## Greeting a "Newcomer"

Up until recent decades, fresh water was the sole bailiwick of flyrodders. Then, along about the 1930s, some adventuresome pioneers began taking marine battlers with fly tackle. At first they confined their efforts largely to species that could be sighted in shallows, such as bonefish and permit. In due course they discovered the other salt-water gamesters also responded to flies—and provided the wildest kind of action on such light tackle—so they began going after fish such as snook and tarpon. Lacking statistics, we can only imagine the mortality rate of tackle.

These daring souls, crackerjack fishermen mostly, remained a small, select group for a long time. But eventually the gospel spread, and a salt-water version of fly fishing began to mushroom into one of angling's fastest-growing methods. An inevitable consequence was the development of fly rods, reels and lures for this new sport. Essentially the equipment is the same as its fresh-water counterpart, except that it's understandably sturdier. It has to be, considering the greater sizes of the opponents tackled. Even the artificials are larger, not only because of the fishes, but also because breeze frequently is a problem on open water. Differences in the equipment will be seen in our "showrooms" exhibiting them.

Salt-water fly lines are unique and will be discussed in their own section.

---

# Tackle Selection 3

## PERSONAL ASPECTS OF TACKLE (and Some Pitfalls)

In the previous chapter we facetiously compared selection of fishing tackle with a choice between a blue suit and a brown suit. That comparison isn't quite as outlandish as it sounds. You'll see as we progress.

First, by way of review, let's briefly recount the general factors influencing selection of equipment:

1. *Kind of fishing to be done.* This was detailed in the chapter titled "Basic Angling Methods."

2. *Sizes of fishes sought.* By this we mean an approximate range. You know the kinds that interest you most. Learn how big they generally grow in the sport fishing theater. It's good to know commercially caught weights too, but generally they're greater than those hooked by rod-and-reelers.

You should know something about the food and feeding habits of your targets to help in selecting bait and lures. It also will help to learn about the fighting characteristics of the fishes sought. Because of these, a comparatively small fish may be much trickier to play than a heavier, more sluggish opponent.

3. *Equipment size in relationship to fish size.* Unless you're a determined light-tackle buff, a devotion not recommended for beginners after game of any real size, stay with equipment more in line with the sizes and combat characteristics of the species involved. At best this gauging will be approximate, but it will have latitude to handle oversized specimens and particularly tough mavericks within that range. Later you can graduate to light weapons for heavier opponents.

4. *Prevailing local conditions in places where you'll be doing most of your fishing.* Examples: (*a*) strong currents—even more of a tackle factor in deep water—or fast-running rivers; (*b*) frequent strong breezes—if you plan to do a lot of casting; (*c*) presence of rocks, reefs, wrecks, coral heads and other underwater masses into which your hooked fishes can run and from out of which you'll have to argue them—a circumstance that can require stouter tackle than usual; (*d*) in stream fishing, the abundance of trees and underbrush along shore—such obstructions can demand shorter rods than for open water; and (*e*) if you're primarily a caster, whether or not there will be appreciable distance between you and your target spots.

Although they won't be solely determining factors, you should give thought to those local conditions. Some are variable and unpredictable—they may even change in a matter of hours within the same locale. But don't let that throw you; you'll be able to size them up well enough for gauging your tackle. And equipment suited to factors in your area will be serviceable under similar conditions elsewhere. You also should give thought to whether most of your fishing will be done from a boat or shore, for reasons outlined in "Basic Angling Methods." Depending upon fishes sought and local conditions, this could become important if you must make one outfit do for a time. A single outfit may suffice for both boat and shore angling in your neighborhood, or you may have to figure on two.

## Getting Personal

Cardinal rule No. 1 in selection of tackle is: Get the right equipment for the assignments at hand. Despite the sheer, bewildering mass of gear available, this isn't difficult. Keep in mind the things we say here; observe and talk with other fishermen (never hesitate to ask questions); and always keep in mind that *tackle shop* people invariably are anglers themselves and are standing by to help you—they're among the finest guides of all.

Cardinal rule No. 2 is frequently overlooked, especially by novices: Buy tackle that "fits" you personally. That's important. To derive maximum enjoyment—and become proficient—you should have tackle you can handle comfortably and without undue fatigue. This phase of selection isn't at all difficult, thanks to the gigantic inventory of gear on the market.

Ease and comfort in handling are based on two main details: caliber of tackle involved, and the wielder's general physical characteristics. Obviously, a spinning outfit is easier to handle than a big-game rod carrying a 12/0 reel. Along the same lines, a husky six-footer is better able to wield the heavier equipment, like a big conventional surf combo, than a smaller person. Since this book has no way of knowing whether you're six-feet-six, weighing 275 pounds, or five-feet-one, weighing 120, the guidelines have to be broad. In this department we'll put degree of skill aside and concentrate on personal physical details.

Much of the selection of tackle for ease and comfort of handling centers about the rod. And here there *is* a parallel with buying a suit.

Take the easily overlooked detail of butt length, for instance. Fly rods have a relatively short butt-handle section. On other types this section varies considerably in length. It's in proportion to overall rod length among most models; but those designed for heavier casting assignments (bulkier rigs, greater distances) are outfitted with longer butts for necessary leverage. Here's where arm length plays a part. A caster with short arms may find a long-butt rod awkward and tiring.

Personal build is a factor only in that it can determine the maximum weight of tackle that can be handled over periods of time without fatigue. For the vast majority of fishermen this isn't of paramount importance, due to the species and methods involved. But if an outfit is fatiguing to use it will blunt the edge of fishing pleasure. Arm, shoulder and back muscles are assets in arguing with the larger game fishes, not only because of the opponents' sizes, but also because of the equipment's weight. However, big-game tackle is wielded from a fighting chair, which supports much of its weight. (Unless you're constructed like a gorilla, you could have problems handling heavy-duty gear standing up.) In all, personal height is probably less a factor than build, although taller folks may be better able to handle the longest rods.

A detail that may be overlooked at purchase time is how a rod's grip fits the hand. Modern rods have grips in a variety of contours, so there's a choice. The grip is a detail that contributes to comfort and pleasure in use.

The overall "feel" of a rod as you wield it is understandably important. This is an intangible for which only you can be the yardstick. Fortunately, it's like love (but without the drawbacks): You'll recognize it when you find it. We'll elaborate on that later. Generally speaking, a rod that "feels right" to you will perform well for you.

In performance, much of a rod's feel depends upon its inherent action. For simplification we can consider "action" to mean its degree of flexibility. The range is from moderately stiff ("fast action") to soft ("slow action"), with all degrees in between. Extremes are represented by extra-supple fly rods at one end of the scale and the rugged weapons of big-game fishing at the other. The concept of an ideal rod combines just the right amounts of sensitive flexibility and stiffness or "backbone," but not necessarily in a 50:50 ratio. According to intended service, it often is essential to favor one over the other. Thus among bottom-fishing rods and big-game sticks the accent is likely to be more on "spine" than on flexibility to better handle heavy rigs and larger battlers. Not that they're as rigid as hoe handles; they must have flexibility too—otherwise they would drastically limit the action. Among casting rods people tend to want more flexibility. But casting rods also must possess a certain amount of backbone to set a hook and help wear down a fish's resistance.

Years ago, the flexibility of rods often was in proportion to their lengths—increasing on the longer models. Today, rods within each classification—baitcasting, surf fishing, etc.—tend to be more standardized in length. This is because their material is the same, most of them being made from fiberglass, and manufacturers can vary their action by the degree of taper—that is, the rate of increase of diameter between the skinny outermost section and the thickest portion where the handle begins. Accordingly, we come close to that "ideal rod" mentioned a minute ago. There are models whose uppermost quarter is slender enough to provide sensitive flexibility for casting some of the lighter rigs and detecting nibbles; then the rod rapidly becomes thicker toward its lower end to furnish "muscle" for handling heavy rigs and fighting assignments. Selecting rods for their action, therefore, is a detail that ties in with intended angling methods.

## Balanced Tackle

All tackle, within each group—conventional, spinning, and fly fishing—can be graded by the terms ultra-light, light, medium, heavy and extra-heavy. Only trouble is, at best this is an arbitrary and unprecise, even vague, arrangement. Another serious flaw is that it can't possibly have all-inclusion application as a standard. For example, a fresh-water fly rod designated as "heavy" within its group would be called light in the conventional tackle category. And, because of this grading's flexibility, there's frequent overlapping within a given group because of an individual's ideas of what constitutes "light," "medium," and the other categories. A rod that feels light to Charley is a medium to Fred; light for Bertha might be heavy for Hortense.

In the days of linen lines, whose strengths were measured in numbers of threads, and before the appearance of spinning tackle in the United States, someone devised a conventional-tackle grading system that was fairly precise. It was based upon the number of threads in lines and the weights of rods' tip sections: different classes were indicated with designations such as 2/3, 4/6, 6/9, etc. A 2/3 outfit was one what combined a 2-ounce rod with a 3-thread (9-pound test) linen line. The first figure represented tip weight in ounces, the second indicated the recommended line for that tip. While this was mainly a system for balancing tackle, it had merit. The only trouble was, not all fishermen heeded it. And when linen lines gave way to synthetics, strengths no longer were measured by numbers of threads. The system went up the flue.

That ultra-light to extra-heavy grading still is used and suffices as a broad, general guide within each type-group. But now the tendency is more to grade tackle—except fly fishing equipment—according to line strengths. It involves the rods and goes according to the maximum line strengths they can handle. You'll hear terms such as "20-pound tackle," "50-pound tackle," and so on. Those figures refer to the strongest lines the rods can accommodate without risking possible damage. Naturally they can and do fish lighter lines.

On many rods today is a decal stating their maximum safe line strength, or at least the heaviest lines they can handle satisfactorily. When a rod lacks such a label it's wise to ask the tackle dealer for the information at the time of purchase. Exceeding the limit could mean a fractured rod.

As we have noted, the vast majority of all fishing rods marketed today are made from fiberglass. Some are solid; others are tubular or hollow. By virtue of having more glass, the solid models are generally sturdier, although somewhat heavier. These can be more suitable to handling the heavier rigs and artificials. We should add immediately that the tubular type also is strong and offers an advantage in being more adaptable to a wider range of lures. Both are durable and tough, and choice becomes a personal matter, influenced by opinions and differences in price. Both types serve novices well.

Although they share the assets of ruggedness and durability, not all fiberglass rods are alike. Much depends upon such details as kind and quality of raw materials, proportion of glass to bonding agent, method of manufacture, and thickness of the wall in the case of tubular models. Those—along with the quality of other components and workmanship—account for differences in price tags. However, good fiberglass rods are manufactured by established brand-name builders at prices within ready reach of all anglers.

In your fishing education, you'll encounter the term "balanced tackle." A synonym is "matching tackle," and its definition goes according to type of gear involved. "Balancing" implies precision in mating reels and rods. The process isn't that exact. "Matching" is a better name for it. For conventional and spinning equipment it means matching reels to rods. For fly tackle, a much more precise matter, it means balancing lines and rods primarily, with reels more or less secondary. For now we'll confine ourselves to the conventional and spinning categories.

Since it's obvious that a conventional reel isn't going to be mounted on a spinning rod, or a spinning "mill" on a conventional stick, matching involves reel *size*. Logically a reel should be in proportion to its rod, and the matching is quite simple because there's latitude. The flexibility doesn't include outlandish extremes, but it does allow for a size or two in either direction without mishap. At worst, a slightly oversized reel contributes some extra weight and maybe takes more line to fill it properly than is needed. A somewhat undersized reel could be a more serious disadvantage by not holding enough line for the assignments at hand. Although it isn't critical (in fact, many anglers fish in blissful ignorance of it), reasonable balance is desirable because it does contribute to ease and pleasure of wielding. But the matching often comes down to personal preference. Because of it, some experienced fishermen have been known to purposely "mismatch" reels and rods to a degree. An angler might like the feel of a somewhat smaller-than-usual reel on his favorite rod; conversely, the extra spool capacity of a larger-than-usual model may be a boon to another fisherman. Anglers don't always go by the book. A good thing, too, or we might not have a lot of the gear we have today.

There can be no absolute formula for matching, but an approximate one goes like this: With fishing methods and kinds and anticipated sizes of opponents as starting points, expected maximum line strength equals caliber of rod (light, medium, etc.), which in turn equals general size range of reel. The result should be about the right size to accommodate sufficient yardage of the lines involved and sturdy enough to handle their strengths.

That may sound intricate, but you'll learn that it isn't. Besides, you can always play it safe by asking your tackle dealer for guidance. You should seek his advice anyway.

Conventional-type reels are graded for size numerically like this: 1/0, 2/0, 3/0, and so on up to young winches labeled 14/0 and 16/0 (uncommon). The figure preceding the zero doesn't represent any unit of measurement, but is merely for comparison purposes. The larger that figure, the bigger the reel and the greater its spool capacity, and in well-made models, the more rugged its gears and other innards (important with heavier lines and bigger fishes).

For some reason, a similar numerical system has yet to be devised for spinning reels. Instead, they're graded simply as light, medium and heavy based upon their weight and spool capacity. Manufacturers extend and elaborate on this grading, according to models they produce for specific uses—ultra-light fresh-water spinning, general salt-water use, offshore fishing, etc. Thus the range of sizes is broadened to extend from midgets of about 4 ounces for ultra-light fresh-water angling with lines of 3-pound test or less (some so fine they're called "hair lines") on up to muscular units of 25 and 26 ounces for heavy-duty surfcasting and offshore service with some of the huskier game fishes. Accordingly, spool capacities range from under 200 yards up to 600, 800, depending upon diameters (strengths) of lines used.

The majority of fresh- and salt-water spinning reels in service fall within the range of 8 to 20 or 25 ounces, with line capacities of 200 to 400 yards. There's flexibility, but, generally speaking, those of 8 to 12 ounces in the light class are intended for lines to 8- or 10-pound test; the mediums of 12 to 18 ounces are for lines to about 15-pound test; and the heavier models over 18 ounces for fish lines to 30- and 40-pound test.

Other factors, such as rod size and ease of handling, being compatible, spool capacities are often more of a criterion than weight in determining proper reel size. Examples: (1) For general fresh-water use, a maximum of 200 yards of line to 8-pound test usually does nicely, indicating a spinning reel in the light category. (2) In surfcasting, where the need for some distance requires 250 to 300 yards of, say, 20-pound line, a medium-size reel is in order.

Conventional reels are similarly gauged. Use the smallest, a 1/0, for fresh-water and marine angling involving the lightest lines to 6-pound test or so, and situations where relatively little yardage, 100 or less, is required, as in shallow-water action. From there the matching goes up through 20- to 40-pound lines and 200 to 300 yards, to heavyweights in the 10/0 to 14/0 category handling 80- and 130-pound lines in yardage of 1,000-plus.

But let's emphasize again: *there's latitude in selection of both spinning and conventional reels.*

There's a certain variation among models of different manufacturers of the same designated size class. That is, a 4/0, we'll say, by builder "A" might be slightly larger or smaller in some dimensions than the same-classed model of manufacturer "B." But don't bite your nails over it. Quality being equal, such dimensional disparities don't mean beans. The same is true of spinning reels.

Reel spools vary in diameter and width, according to types of reels, models, sizes and manufacturers, and these details naturally affect spool capacities. When a model is selected for assignments at hand, spool diameters and widths are satisfied by necessity. We need only add that among conventional surf reels the spools are wider than usual to aid in casting.

*Tip:* Any reel functions best when its spool is filled properly. Don't overload or underload. The former will cause hideous tangles. Underloading—an insufficient amount—could leave you embarrassingly short of line in the middle of playing a long-running fish . . . and there's that automatic drag effect mentioned earlier. Because of physical variations, there's no blanket rule for proper filling of conventional and spinning spools. It's usually recommended that a spinning spool be filled to within 1/16- or at least 1/8-inch of the outer edge. Greater latitude is allowable with conventional reels. On the smaller models filling may be to within about 1/8-inch of the edge of the flanger, whereas on the big reels it may be to within a ¼-inch or so.

Even distribution of line on a spool is important, otherwise bad tangles can result when it pays out. On a spinning reel even distribution is more or less taken care of automatically by the combination of its pickup mechanism and shuttle action of the spool, but distribution should be checked periodically. On conventional reels new line should be loaded evenly. Later, in use, simple guiding with a finger of the free hand will deposit line back on the spool evenly. Certain conventional reels incorporate a level-wind mechanism. Geared to the crank, this shuttles back and forth to automatically distribute incoming line evenly. Many fishermen consider it well worth whatever little it may add to a reel's cost.

On the other hand, many seasoned anglers do without it because it does cut down on casting distance and must be kept free of sand or other foreign matter to function properly.

## General Notes on Lines

As you can imagine, lines today are legion, marketed under excellent manufacturer labels such as Cortland, Ashaway, Garcia, Newton, Gudebrod, Gladding, and Ande (German), for every conceivable kind of fishing. And they come in strengths ranging from spider-web-thin 1-pound test, up to 130- and 200-pound test. Included are the most specialized of lines—those employed in fly fishing. These will be detailed separately elsewhere.

Among conventional-tackle and spinning lines are four basic types: braided; monofilament; solid wire; and metal-core. All except the solid-wire type share one detail: they involve synthetic materials.

Granting our acknowledged respect for linen lines, the synthetics have been an enormous contribution to sport fishing, for reasons linen lines don't match. (*1*) Being practically impervious to water, they're not susceptible to rot, mildew, or appreciable swelling when wet (the last can cut down on yardage accommodated by a spool). (*2*) They have greater strength in finer diameter. This means more yardage on a spool; less water drag on the line, which can cause appreciable strain when trolling and deep-water bottom fishing; and less visibility in water, a factor that can be of importance with fishes that "spook" easily. (*3*) Being tough and durable, they have good service life and therefore are economical. (*4*) They can be mass-produced readily, which means some cost saving to consumers.

Nylon was the first synthetic fishing line material, but at the start it had a serious drawback: excessive stretch. A certain amount of "give" in a line isn't harmful. Sometimes it's even helpful, acting like a long rubberband to maintain tension on a hook and keep it planted. But an excess is bad because it absorbs much of the force exerted by a rod when setting a hook. In cases of opponents with leathery mouths or concrete-hard jaws there may not be enough force left to sink the point. Nylon still stretches to a certain extent, but excesses have been largely corrected. Dacron has proved a favorite synthetic because it incorporates about the highest degree of the virtues of synthetics with less stretch than nylon.

The major difference between monofilament and braided types is in construction. Like linen lines, braided synthetics consist of strands twisted upon each other. "Monofilament" is a coined word meaning literally "single-strand," and that's precisely what a monofilament line is, a single strand. To produce monofilament lines manufacturers devised extrusion, a process whereby the synthetic material is forced through holes of suitable diameters, like making spaghetti.

Each type, braided and monofilament, has its own set of assets and a "liability" here and there. These assets and drawbacks vary among the products of different manufacturers, sometimes according to type or diameter and often according to anglers' personal opinions. Fishermen develop preferences in lines just as they do in their automobiles both in type and manufacturer. You'll do the same.

Here are a few general comparisons. We preface them by saying that the more serious "bugs" in synthetic lines have been chased away for the most part. It depends upon specific use to a great extent, but any existing drawbacks among mono and braided lines in good brands usually are relatively minor.

(*1*) Mono lines naturally have a smoother surface than braided types. Because of this they are somewhat more abrasion-resistant and therefore favored for fishing around rocks, coral reefs and other underwater obstructions. For the same reason, monofilament line may be rigged as a leader in combination with a braided line. Or when the main line is monofilament and abrasion is a threat, anglers will interpose a generous length of somewhat heavier monofilament as a leader between rig and main line.

(*2*) Also because of their smoother surface, mono lines are somewhat less prone to wear generally and specifically on rod guides. Since they're less likely to fray than braided lines after considerable use, they're more economical. But today the difference in wear on rod guides in average use is minute, particularly on such hard materials as Carboloy.

(*3*) Some mono lines, notably the larger diameters, have an inherent stiffness. If stiff enough, it can cause the line to literally spring from the spool when paid out slowly, or lie in loose coils on the spool if not retrieved under proper tension. Either way, tangles are a possibility. Refinement has reduced much of the stiffness. In some mono lines it's offset by a flatter, oval line instead of a completely round one. Excessive stiffness is to be avoided, not only because of the reasons given, but also because it makes the line harder to handle and it can interfere with the proper working of the smaller artificials.

(*4*) On the plus side for braided lines, they're a bit more supple, due to the way they're made. This makes them somewhat easier to handle, for example, when working a lure. For the same reason, some fishermen find them easier to cast than mono when the larger diameters are involved.

(*5*) Because it is a single strand, a monofilament line is less visible in water than a braided type. But this difference is of consequence chiefly when easily alarmed species are sought, and of debatable importance otherwise. Besides, lines come in colors purposely designed to lessen their visibility. It should be added that minimum visibility isn't always an advantage to *fishermen*. In certain trolling and casting situations it helps to be able to see the line, and there are colors to aid that too.

Its lesser visibility is also a reason many anglers like mono as leader material; but here again the importance of that difference is debatable in many common situations. Incidentally, monofilament is gaining popularity as a substitute for wire in big-game fishing requiring greater strengths.

Here the mono may be 100- to 200-pound test. It's favored over equivalent wire because it's easier to handle and doesn't kink. It cannot be substituted for wire at all in shark fishing, however, because of those creatures' teeth and abrasive skin.

As their name implies, metal-core lines have a center or core of metal, such as lead, and this is surrounded by an outer covering of synthetic material. These lines are designed for deeper-than-average trolling, the metal core being a built-in "sinker." But since there is a certain amount of buoyancy in the synthetic coat, these lines do not take rigs as deep as the solid-wire types. The latter are consequently more in use where deeper trolling is necessary. Both types come in varying strengths.

Stainless steel and a nickel alloy called Monel are the most common wire line materials. They do their job admirably, but have one major drawback: They tend to kink. Since kinks are weakened portions and potential breaking places under stress, wire lines must be checked frequently for kinks. Those little zigglies can also snag in a rod's guides . . . and make believe that can't cause problems when a fish is on! Badly kinked sections of wire always should be replaced. Give 'em the deep six. Attempting to straighten them could turn out to be false economy by weakening the wire further. As they say in Ecuador when a marlin gets away, *"¡Adios, pez!"*—goodbye, fish.

If you plan on doing an appreciable amount of fishing with wire lines for deeper trolling, you should have a rod with at least a top guide of the roller type. Better is one with roller guides throughout. Wire line will groove ring-type guides.

Wire line is not to be confused with wire leader material. A wire leader is interposed between rig and fishing line for protection against (*a*) the dental armament of toothy rascals like pike and bluefish, (*b*) the rough exteriors of tarpon, sharks, others, (*c*) the file-like weapons of marlin and other billfishes, and (*d*) razor-sharp gill covers of species such as snook.

Two kinds of wire are used. One is stainless steel. The other is a carbon steel, commonly called piano wire (presumably from original use in that instrument) and sometimes music wire. It comes plain, tinned and galvanized. Piano wire is a bit stronger than stainless in any given diameter, usually costs less, but can rust. Piano wire leaders made up beforehand should be protected against dampness and checked for rust after use. Needless to say, rusty wire is weakened wire and should be discarded. A big-game charter skipper, a friend of this writer, keeps his made-up piano wire leaders in light oil until used, then discards them after one use.

The two kinds of wire are sold in handy coils so fishermen can fashion their leaders in desired lengths. They come in graduated strengths, with progressively large numbers indicating increasingly stronger material. Numbers range consecutively from 2 through 15, and this abbreviated table shows some strength differences:

| Size No. | Gauge (Diameter in Inches) | Stainless Steel (Pounds Test) | Piano Wire (Pounds Test) |
|---|---|---|---|
| 2 | .011 | 27 | 28 |
| 5 | .014 | 44 | 46 |
| 8 | .020 | 86 | 93 |
| 9 | .022 | 104 | 114 |
| 12 | .029 | 174 | 198 |
| 15 | .035 | 240 | 288 |

Choice between the two types of wire for leaders becomes purely personal. Both do their job well. If rusting is bothersome, preference can be given to the stainless variety. The difference in strength between it and an equivalent gauge in piano wire shouldn't be a key factor; but if it is a cause for concern the angler simply goes to the next largest number in stainless.

As they become longer or stronger, wire leaders become a bit harder to handle, due to the metal's inherent stiffness. That's why anglers try to keep lengths and strengths to a practical minimum. Wire leaders to 20 feet and longer are rigged for the likes of giant bluefin tuna (to 1,000 pounds), larger sharks (tigers, up to 1,750 pounds for a U.S. specimen; and white sharks, up to 2,664 pounds—an Australian beast and the largest fish ever taken on rod and reel), and huge 1,500 pound black marlin. But world-record-minded fishermen have to keep in mind that the International Game Fish Association imposes limits on leader lengths (but not on strengths): No longer than 15 feet for lines through 50-pound test; a maximum of 30 feet for 80- and 130-pound lines.

Commonly these wire leaders are a single strand. Some are tobacco-colored for fishes that might become suspicious or shy at glints of metal. In any case, when a fish is brought to gaff, whoever handles the wire leader should be wearing cotton work gloves to avoid severe hand lacerations. Single-strand wire can cut like the dickens—and there you have another reason why many big-game anglers substitute strong monofilament for wire whenever possible.

Both kinds of wire can and do kink, like wire line, and must be checked at intervals. Your writer once lost a superb mako shark in the 300-pound class when the rascal leaped three or four times, causing the leader to kink and snap. *¡Adios, pez!* That couldn't be helped, but it shows what a kink can do. There are some braided wire leaders, plain and plastic-coated, that are more flexible because of their construction and therefore less apt to kink, but they're somewhat heavier per given strength and require metal sleeves and a crimping tool for fashioning into leaders.

While we're on the subject we should also mention cable leaders. These are intended for the largest game fishes and come in great strengths. They come plain or with a plastic coating for some protection in handling, and can be bought "loose" or already rigged. But they're stronger than necessary in most instances and are rather bulky, and so are being rigged less and less, being replaced by single-strand wire or muscular monofilament.

## Choice of Lines

So many variables are involved in line selection that each angler is an individual case. It's impossible for us to make specific recommendations. After all, we have no way of even guessing what you'll be fishing for, or where or how. However, here are some general guidelines that will assist you.

Keep these influencing factors in mind: (*1*) weight ranges of fishes sought, with an eye to any possibilities of heavier species being in the same area; (*2*) notable or special combat characteristics of opponents—exceptionally hard-fighting, long-running, deep-going or rock-hiding; (*3*) angling methods, which may involve heavy rigs; (*4*) your tackle, including the maximum strength line your rod can handle safely and the spool capacity and general sturdiness of your reel; and (*5*) in casting from shore or boat, how much distance may be required.

Find yourself a good tackle shop. Get to know its personnel and rely on them for guidance and advice. Invariably they're fishermen themselves and very familiar with conditions in your region. With due respect to fine department stores and their equally good sporting goods departments, a sales clerk might be a skiing buff—or a recent transfer from corsets, girdles and brassieres, second floor.

Among comparable lines by different manufacturers, there may be certain variations in such particulars as suppleness, strength per diameter, wear- and abrasion-resistance, general life, degree of stretch, knot strength, visibility (to fishes or fishermen), handling ease, and the way they lie on a reel spool or come off it. In the overall picture, these differences among quality lines by reputable manufacturers usually are minor and of no great consequence. Sometimes the differences also include certain extras, such as lubrication incorporated in a braided line, or a trolling line that is color-coded every so many yards to let you know how much you have out.

Anglers commonly find certain combinations of the foregoing details more to their liking in lines by specific manufacturers. Such preferences are based on personal opinion, which in turn evolves from experience.

Generally, you can't go wrong with name brands. Try their various lines. Along the way ask questions of other fishermen. If you find a brand that seems to suit your purposes better than others, stick with it. It's as simple as that.

Those five factors outlined in our quick review are your general guides to the amount and strength of line you'll need for angling assignments. Again, it's impossible to guess your specific needs, but obviously you're going to need more line for, say, deep trolling at 100 feet for lake trout than for dunking a sinker in a shallow bay. Here you also can be guided by proper filling of your reel spool.

Wire line is a kind of specialized case when it comes to amount. Some anglers fill their reel with it. This is not only unnecessary, it's also unnecessarily expensive. As we said, wire is harder to handle than regular line, can cause some awful tangles if not spooled properly and tends to kink. Why increase the chances of tangles by filling the reel with it? Besides, much of that wire may not be in action and therefore be wasted. Also, in salt-water use, unused portions on the reel may become corroded. And too, wire can in time undergo metal fatigue, become brittle, and necessitate replacement.

The solution is to "back" a practical length of wire line with the regular stuff, Dacron or monofilament. This means that so many yards of Dacron or mono go on the spool first, to which is connected the desired yardage of wire, and together they fill the spool properly. Now only that working length of wire need be replaced when it becomes "tired" or badly kinked, and the backing stays on, where it will keep practically indefinitely with a little care. How much working wire you'll need will depend upon the depths at which you want your lure or bait to travel.

Water depths enter the picture here if only because you'd have the devil's own job trying to troll working wire 40 feet down in 20 feet of water. The amount of wire required to take your rig down to desired levels may demand some experimentation from area to area. This is because in fishing we always have to reckon with variables, not the least of which is the fishes themselves. Trolling speed is a factor. Faster or slower, it can raise a lure or cause it to sink deeper. When there are strong currents, they exert an upward thrust on a rig. And the nature and weights of the lures and baits are also influential. But for openers try this approximate "formula": 8 to 1, the first figure representing the amount of wire required, the second being the depth at which the lure or bait will travel. In other words, if you want the attractor to ride at, say, 10 feet down, let out 80 feet of wire; at 15 feet down, 120 feet of wire out. Remember, though, that those figures are for the amount of wire actually in use. You should have a few extra yards still on the spool.

## Purchasing Points

There's more to successful fishing than just plopping a baited hook into the water. And when it comes to buying equipment, all of us from greenest tyro to seasoned veteran are faced with a mind-boggling array. If you get confused, take heart. All the seeming intricacies will iron themselves out. Don't let buying errors jiggle your nervous system. Every angler worth his salt makes mistakes: buying the wrong type of line, or too little or too much; or even when knowing better, falling for an off-brand "bargain" reel that sounds like a coffee grinder the third time out; or collecting so many lures it becomes impossible to use them all—and maybe picking up some freakish models designed to catch fishermen instead of fish.

But you can go a long way toward avoiding pitfalls if you follow a few simple procedures.

1. Place an accent on quality. Dependability, good performance and your money's worth will follow automatically. Nowadays quality tackle doesn't have to be expensive, and it will pay for itself many times over in fishing enjoyment and success. If you're going in for a sport, do it with the idea of getting the most out of it. Chintzy equipment is a very bad start; and junk, if it doesn't discourage you altogether, is in the long run more expensive.

2. To repeat, stay with name-brand manufacturers. Penn, Gladding Garcia Corporation, Fenwick/Sevenstrand, and Shakespeare are a few of the good ones. When you buy name-brand products you buy years of research, field testing, technical knowledge and solid production methods. Most important, you buy a reputation that has to be maintained in a highly competitive field, and they back their reputations with warranties. Further, these manufacturers offer service for repairs and worn-parts replacement. In cases of obscure manufacturers, domestic and foreign, the reverse of all this may turn out to be the awful truth, and you wind up with a pile of junk.

Take advantage of sales of name-brand tackle items. But beware of "bargains" in unknown-name equipment that offer "complete fishing outfits" consisting of rod, reel, line, a couple of lures, 100 assorted hooks, all for some ridiculous price like $7.98. Can you buy a suit for that kind of money? No one gives anything away, not even fishing tackle.

At this point we should qualify what we said about staying with name brands. That's always a safe policy. But it would be unfair not to mention the fact that there are many small firms, some of them only one-, two- and three-man outfits, that produce quality equipment—not lines, to our knowledge, although there may even be a couple of those, but rods, reels, lures and assorted accessories. They're obscure in that they're little known or even completely unknown to the greater segment of the sport fishing public. They're not obscure in the connotation intended earlier—little known and manufacturing junk. The only trouble with these smaller firms is they do not advertise extensively, and so they become known chiefly by word of mouth or local inquiry. You learn about them on your own.

Along the same lines are the custom rod builders. These usually are very small, often one-man operations. They construct rods to customers' specifications, personal ideas, or whatever. The rods understandably tend to be more expensive than equivalent stock models, but they can be beautiful pieces of work, giving pride of ownership. Numerous tackle shop owners build custom rods as a side activity.

3. If you're new to the game or unsure of your ground, take an experienced angler with you when you do your buying. In our various "showrooms" of tackle later on we'll indicate quality details to look for. Your companion can help you to check them with a more appraising eye.

In passing we should mention the situation in which a beginner receives tackle as a gift from a well-meaning but uninformed relative or friend. It's very nice, except that all tackle looks alike to non-anglers, and unless the buyer visits a tackle shop and gets some guidance, it's anyone's guess what the recipient will wind up with. The error could be worsened if the equipment happened to be on sale or was bought by mail order.

Chances are fairly high in such instances that the recipient will receive gear unsuited to his or her intended fishing. If so, instead of trying to get along with the outfit, the recipient should find out diplomatically where it was purchased, seek the advice of a more experienced fisherman regarding replacement, then arrange an exchange. (An aside to non-fishing donors of tackle items: You might be safer giving a gift certificate and leaving selection to the lucky recipient.)

4. Actually "heft" various rods in the store, preferably with a matching reel in position. Notice how an outfit feels in your hand, and give attention to the rod's handle and butt length. This is primarily to get an idea of its weight and overall length as suited to *you*. While you're at it, see if the reel's crank and other controls are easy for you to reach. Notice the feel of the crank's handle. Many reels have contoured handles for more comfortable gripping. Carrying the procedure a step further, have your companion or the tackle man seize the free end of the line in simulation of a fish, then lean back a little on the rod to get an idea of how the outfit will feel to you in action. See how comfortable it is for you to hold the rod, bent under tension, with one hand while cranking in line with the other.

If casting equipment is involved, ask the shop owner if he has an area where you can make a few practice casts. Some shops have space set aside just for this, and provide a dummy casting lure. Or perhaps you can take the outfit outside. If the combination feels right to you, but you're not quite sure of your appraisal ability, let your more experienced friend make a few casts with it. This won't be the same as your doing it, but at least your friend will be able to appraise its overall action for you.

The foregoing doesn't add up to a sure-fire criterion to indicate how you and a given outfit will get along as a team. Nor is it any barometer of fishing success—that lies with *you*. But it will help considerably in getting you properly outfitted, and it could prevent your coming away with tackle that proves to be awkward for you to handle.

5. You may be asking, "How can I tell beforehand if tackle will stand up under the stresses and strains of actual use?" The answer is simple: You can't—not with 100% certainty. And if you think about that a minute you'll understand why. To begin with, fishing gackle is like an automobile in that its performance and life are in its owner's hands. There are anglers who use tackle, and there are those who abuse it; and even a fine piece of machinery like a Rolls-Royce can be beaten to death. Further, there's no foretelling what angling situations will be encountered. In sport fishing the unusual is often commonplace. For example, you might very well tie into a battler that is much too heavy or tough for your equipment. What frequently happens here is that the engagement terminates abruptly when the line breaks. If it doesn't, you play your opponent as best you can, avoiding excessive strain on the rod imposed by such antics as trying to "horse" the fish in by force (here too the line probably will pop, but you never know).

You have every assurance that well-made tackle—not necessarily expensive tackle—will stand up very nicely indeed. And with freedom from abuse and outlandish situations, and just a little care, it will give you many years of service.

6. This note is for newcomers and other less-experienced anglers: You'll hear much about the delights of light-tackle fishing—its heightened excitement, intensified thrills, greater action, and satisfaction in victory. What you may not hear about so frequently are losses of rigs, lures and substantial line yardage, tackle casualties, and lost fish. Those are all calculated risks in light-tackle fishing, which means purposely wielding weapons appreciably lighter than ordinarily necessary. Unless you're prepared to face such calculated risks, we suggest that you stay away from

lighter-than-usual equipment until you're qualified to handle it. Until then the results could be too discouraging. You can always graduate to progressively lighter gear.

7. There are literally thousands of lures for fresh- and salt-water fishing. An introductory word about their selection and purchase is in order here.

In time you'll amass a collection. Every fisherman does. Depending upon the lures and how you use them, they will turn out to be variously "killers," poor producers, versatile (able to rack up several species), or specialized. And you'll develop favorites.

Build a collection sensibly. Don't try to do it all at once. That can be unnecessarily expensive, and you could wind up with models that aren't really useful to you. Instead, go about it like this:

Through reading and talking with other anglers, learn about the food and feeding habits of the finned game you seek. Keep in mind that any lure, whatever kind it may be, is designed to imitate in appearance, action or both some item of natural food.

Familiarize yourself with the basic types of artificials—plugs, jigs, spinners, flies, etc.—and learn why they work. Discover which of those basic types are most effective in *your* region—and, very importantly, when. Other anglers will help you with this pinpointing. So will tackle shop personnel. Tackle shops are especially helpful because their cash registers tell them which lures are getting the best results—and when.

Start your collection with a nucleus consisting of a few standard, locally proven models. Choose discriminately, trying to select as much as possible lures that are "versatile"—that is, can be used under a variety of conditions and for different species. As a for instance, there are types—like plugs—that prove deadly in more than one angling method. Within the type groups—spoons, etc.—are specific models that are lethal to three, four or more kinds of fishes. There are also artificials that can be rigged interchangeably for salt and fresh water, with equal effectiveness. Sometimes fishermen discover additional versatility unknown even to the lures' makers. (That brings up a *tip*: Artificials frequently are accompanied by manufacturers' suggestions as to how to best fish them. Follow those directions, but don't let them prevent you from experimenting. Remember that it was through experimentation that artificial bait came about in the first place.)

Around this nucleus you build your collection in similarly selective fashion. Here and there along the way you also add a model that is specific for a kind of fish, a technique, or an area—or time of year. When you go on a trip or vacation that will involve fishing in a strange area, take along a suitable representation of your own lures. Often attractors that are effective in one place work in many others too. In the strange area you can seek out a tackle shop to determine the best local lures. They may also work in your home locale, and they're a practical souvenir of a trip.

Not that you would, but don't try to keep up with all the new lures that emerge. It isn't necessary and too many are being developed for you to hope to keep up with them. Let it hastily be added that we're not against large individual collections. Far from it. If selected with some thought, the more different kinds of lures on hand, the greater an angler's scope. It's just that collecting lures for the sake of collecting isn't financially or piscatorially practical.

We have to tell you a little story to underscore a point:

One of the most intense fishing nuts we've ever known was a close friend named Joe who would rather fish than eat. He owned an unbelievable collection of rods and reels. He needed them—well, some of them, anyway. An electrical engineer who spent a lot of time in the field, Joe traveled considerably and fished wherever he went, participating enthusiastically in every method known to man, short of longlines and trawls. A couple of outfits were as much a part of his car as its wheels. Even in the dead of winter he was likely to be wandering around with a reel bulging his overcoat pocket: not to use—there was just a certain pleasure in having it with him. His collection of rods and reels was awesome to behold, but it was nothing next to his personal inventory of lures. Joe's "hangup" was lures. He had them by the hundreds, at least. Artificials were to Joe what booze is to an alcoholic. He couldn't resist them. When a lure caught his eye he bought it, whether he needed it or not. There's little doubt that collecting had superseded use. Point is, he amassed so many that he couldn't have used them all if he had lived to be a hundred, and he'd spent a small fortune in the bargain.

That was Joe. At the other extreme is skimping on lures. Except for costing less, this is worse. A smart angler goes to neither extreme.

Among lure manufacturers you'll encounter many well known, respected names. Fred Arbogast, Lazy Ike, Greek Chub, Heddon, Eppinger, Mepps, Tony Acetta, Lisk Fly Manufacturing Company, Bill Norman, Burke Flexo-Products, Rapala, and numerous others comprise a lengthy list. Added to those are models marketed under the house labels of tackle builders. Still further, there are many reputable small firms throughout the nation that specialize in lures only, producing artificial flies, lifelike plastic imitations, etc. For those you'll have to scout ads in fishing publications, notably the regional kind.

Apart from the way they perform, there are several facets to lure quality: rugged construction; permanence of colors and finishes; the hooks and the way they're attached, etc. While there can be some variations in these departments among manufacturers, it's reasonably safe to say that any lures sold by reputable manufacturers, large and small, are good and will give purchasers their money's worth. Such are the bonuses of modern materials and production technology—and competition. None can be guaranteed to catch fish. Manufacturers turn out the best products possible. The rest is up to users.

## Reassurance

What we've endeavored to do here is to point up details to serve as general guidelines in selection of tackle. Hopefully we haven't made the process sound complicated. It isn't, really. On the other hand, it shouldn't be a lackadaisical, random affair. In between is a sensible course. You'll find that it all boils down to merely giving the matter some thought. Then look around and ask questions. And the more you fish, the easier selection of tackle will become.

As you progress through this book you'll find still more assisting details. Our objective is to get you well outfitted at a price you can afford. Make good outfitting *your* objective too. It will pay enormous dividends in sport fishing fun and success.

---

# Salt-Water Tackle Showroom 4

## SALT-WATER TACKLE

Now that you have an overall view of the different types of equipment in service and selection guidelines, we will show you representative equipment found in the market today. The first showroom will exhibit marine tackle. For display of their wares in this book we have concentrated to a great extent on the larger or better known manufacturers. This is not to snub any small or lesser known companies that also turn out quality products, but rather to accent the fact that you can't go wrong with name brands. These people have been in business for years for a very simple reason: they turn out good stuff.

For easier browsing, this showroom will be divided into two main departments, conventional or revolving-spool tackle, and spinning gear. You'll find salt-water fly fishing gear in the chapter titled "Fly Fishing Tackle Showroom."

### Some Preliminaries

Grading any tackle for "caliber"—that is, light, medium, heavy, etc.—can become a complex matter, confusing even to seasoned anglers. To begin with, it's a flexible arrangement. It can vary from manufacturer to manufacturer, according to rod design and construction. It's stretched this way and that even more among fishermen. As we already pointed out, a rod that might be classified as "medium" by one user could be called "light" by another, according to the kinds of fishing each does and his own ideas on the subject. And fishermen sure do develop ideas.

In broad calibration, the maximum line strengths rods can handle often are a prime factor in classifying tackle as light, medium or whatever. If that were the only factor, grading would be simple, but all kinds of variables jump into the scene to complicate things—rod taper and action, fast or slow; weights of artificials or rigs that a rod can accommodate; and the greatest variable, the kinds of fishing done, size ranges of species sought, and the ability of the individuals involved. Obviously, a rod rated as medium or just right for, we'll say, battlers to 20 or 25 pounds would become light when wielded for 100-pound species.

Overall, salt-water conventional and spinning equipment is classified as ultra-light, light, medium, heavy and extra-heavy or heavy-duty. But even here there are differences in grading the two types, influenced by extremes. At one end are big-game conventional rods rated to take lines up to 130-pound test and handle the bulkiest rigs, like whole-fish bait up to 10 pounds and more trolled for giant black marlin. You'd be hard put indeed to find spinning tackle rated to handle such lines and rigs. At the other extreme is ultra-light spinning gear, designed to fish lines of 3-pound test and finer, and to cast very light artificials up to ¼-ounce.

Because of the variables involved, there should be caliber-grading according to fishing methods—in other words, each should have its own. And to a certain extent they do. You'll encounter grading differences in tackle employed for surfcasting, trolling, bay fishing, deep-sea bottom angling. One example is that devised for shark fishing, where even the lightest gear would be considered heavy for some other kinds of action.

If you're a novice you should become acquainted with these various calibrations, but not lose any sleep over them. In the final analysis you'll be doing your own rating as to what constitutes light, medium and heavy, as suits *your* procedures. And always you can find a tackle dealer to give you assistance.

## Quality Check List

There are certain details you'll want to look for when buying your basic equipment—rods and reels.

*Rods:*

1. Materials: Unless you're shopping specifically for a split-bamboo model, which isn't likely unless you're an experienced "purist" with up to $100 or more to invest, the conventional or spinning rod you buy will be of fiberglass. You'll have a choice between solid and hollow, or tubular, types. The former, by virtue of containing more glass, is essentially sturdier and somewhat heavier, and better suited to casting the heavier lures and working the heavier rigs used in bottom fishing. Quality being equal, a solid-glass rod usually costs less than a hollow one. Conversely, a tubular type is lighter to wield and a bit more versatile because of somewhat greater flexibility. It has the strength to take care of many of the assignments for which solid rods are brought into play, yet has that extra flexibility for fishing the lighter artificials. A selection between the two types is largely a matter of individual preference, based on experience. For novices, or even anglers of average experience, differences in flexibility are not all that great. For beginners, however, a practical choice as a starter might be the solid type. In any case, difference in price shouldn't be a criterion. In the long run it's insignificant.

But price differences, supplemented by a tackle dealer's recommendations, are a workable guide to quality. As pointed out earlier, quality hinges upon the grade of raw materials, proportion of glass to bonding agents, and overall workmanship. Skimping in any one of those details is bound to produce an inferior product. However, you do not need to be an authority on fiberglass to be assured of quality. Stay with name brands. They're all competitive—they have to be—when it comes to materials and workmanship. You can get a quality rod at a price you can afford.

*2.* Guides—number and construction: very important. Again, you don't have to be an expert to detect inferiority.

One of the first details to check is the number of guides. Builders of inferior rods often skimp here. On good rods the number of guides varies according to type (conventional or spinning), length and model. A minimum is about four or five on the short conventional and spinning rods, and there can be more on longer models. Here's a simple test for an adequate number of guides on a conventional rod: Bend the rod by applying pressure to the line, as when playing a fish. Nowhere should the line touch the rod. If it does, that rod doesn't have enough guides and is probably inferior in other respects. Since guides are mounted on the underside of a spinning rod, a line isn't likely to touch it. But spacing is important, most especially that of the guide nearest the reel, the largest one, whose job it is to collect coils of line leaving the spool. You won't have to worry about this on a well-made rod.

Here's something else you won't have to worry about with a properly constructed rod, but it's a point of information you might want to file with your lore: Too few guides on a spinning rod can cause a sag in the line that adds friction in casting. Similarly, it's possible to create unnecessary friction and wear on a line by having too many guides on a conventional type rod. A rule of thumb followed by some home rod builders in one guide for each foot of overall rod length.

Poorly constructed guides betray their inferiority by their appearance. They look poorly made, even to an unpracticed eye. These are details to check: (*a*) How well the rings are secured to their frames. (*b*) Frames may be made from nickel silver, brass or stainless steel. They should be sturdy looking and chrome-plated or otherwise resistant to corrosion. (*c*) The rings should be of Carboloy or tungsten carbide or some other hard material to resist wear by lines. Agate once was used for good guides, but it is fairly heavy and expensive. Now there are lighter ceramic rings that accomplish the same purpose. (*d*) Adequate wrappings. This is another place where makers of cheap rods economize. Their wrappings are skimpy. Those on good rods vary in width, but extend well to either side of the frame, are neatly applied, and well secured with varnish or an epoxy compound.

You won't be concerned with roller guides unless you're shopping for a conventional-type rod for use with wire lines or for big-game fishing. In the former case, a good rod has at least a tiptop guide of the roller type. Big-game "sticks" generally are outfitted with roller guides throughout. In any case, when roller guides are indicated, the most important one is the tiptop. Second most important, from the standpoint of line wear (this is not a factor with wire), is the one immediately adjacent to the tiptop, and from there on toward the reel they become increasingly less important. Nevertheless, their number is important in distributing strain evenly throughout the rod. (Because of their height, line isn't likely to be able to touch the rod.) Their number varies according to manufacturer, model and length, and runs to about five or six. Understandably, roller guides add more to a rod's price tag than the ring type. Construction generally is of a lightweight metal throughout, although there are less expensive roller guides made from synthetic materials. Many anglers favor metal because of its inherent sturdiness. Details to check include wrappings as well as rollers that turn freely and are made from a hard substance to minimize wear on both line and themselves.

You won't find roller guides on spinning and other casting rods because of the guides' design, size and weight. Lightweight plastic roller guides were tried on those rods some years ago and were found unsatisfactory for one reason or another. Besides, the heaviest lines and wire are not used with those rods.

Another important detail of guides is their alignment. Here again an inferior rod often betrays itself. Simple eye-sighting along the tip section can reveal guides sloppily mounted off-center to the right or left. The differences may not seem like much, but imperfect alignment creates unnecessary line (and guide) wear, a certain amount of binding when fighting a fish, and impairment of casting. On a properly constructed rod the guides are aligned perfectly, from the one closest to the reel out to the tiptop.

*3.* Other rod hardware: The reel seat is important; it should moor the reel securely. Few things in fishing are more awkward than having a reel work loose during combat. The most common arrangement consists of a fixed band into which one foot of the reel fits snugly, while the other foot is locked in place by a sliding collar with a gnurled ring. Some rods calling for larger reels have two such locking rings instead of the fixed collar and one ring. This arrangement is recommended for the heavier reels.

Most reel seats are metal, and so must be protected against corrosion, a sneaky invader that can impair a gnurled ring's operation, even cause it to "freeze," by fouling up its threads. Long in use, especially among salt-water rods, are reel seats of brass, with corrosion protection provided by chromium plating. For lightness, some rods have aluminum reel seats. They're strong as well as light, but they can develop a drawback in prolonged salt-water service. Even when anodized against corrosion, aluminum can begin to deteriorate after repeated exposures to salt water and salty air. Also, in the interest of lightness, some rods nowadays have reel seats of high-impact plastic. On rods by quality manufacturers they serve well.

Put a suitably matching reel into the seat and lock it in. Check its security. It should be tight, with absolutely no play in any direction. Its gnurled ring or rings should work freely, yet tighten securely. *Tip:* Junky rods have junky reel seats, evident in the poor quality of their plating and the sloppy way their locking arrangement functions.

Other components of rod hardware are its ferrules, where tip and butt sections join, and it's essential that the two parts of each ferrule must fit properly. They're held together by friction, and there should be neither too little nor too much. Only a hair's looseness will cause the tip section to turn in use, throwing the guides out of alignment. On the other hand, excessive snugness means you have to wrestle with the rod every time you put it together and disassemble it. You can tell by feel whether or not ferrules unite properly.

Most ferrules are metal, commonly aluminum or plated brass, and so should be protected against corrosion by anodizing or chroming. Their fitting tolerances are so close that even a small amount of corrosion—or particles of sand—will raise hob with them. They also should be checked after appreciable use for signs of wear. It doesn't take much of it to produce looseness, and that becomes a real nuisance. If it's bad enough, the ferrules should be replaced. *Tips:* After each salt-water use it never does any harm to separate the ferrules and clean them. While you're at it, do the same thing for the reel seat, paying special attention to the gnurled ring's threads.

The corrosion problem is eliminated (but not the problem of sand) with glass ferrules. If you recall, we compared these with metal ferrules earlier.

*4.* Taper and action: These are tip section characteristics. "Taper" refers to that increasing diameter between the slender outermost portion and the thickest section adjacent to the handle section. There are various kinds and degrees of taper. In one, for example, the rate of increase in diameter is uniform throughout. Another has a slender, very flexible tiptop section for handling lighter lures, after which the diameter quickly increases to provide muscle to cope with heavier rigs and hard-fighting opponents. In short, type and degree of taper determine a rod's action.

As we said earlier, rod actions frequently are spoken of as being "fast" or "slow," fast defined as quickly returning to normal after bending, while a slow tip, of course, is the reverse. These details are indicative of a rod's flexibility and the location of maximum flexibility, as determined by its taper. To put it another way, a rod's action is the curvature it assumes under stress. Accordingly, we come up with the following categories: *extra-fast* equals bending in the uppermost one-quarter; *fast* equals curvature in the upper one-third; *medium* equals bending in the upper half; and *slow* equals curvature throughout, from tiptop all the way down to the start of the handle.

Any and all of these actions can be used in any and all kinds of fishing. However, particular types of rod action may be better suited than others to bottom fishing involving fairly heavy rigs and husky opponents. In still another adaptation, fly rods generally have slow to medium action, better suited to fly fishing's peculiar casting requirements. And so it goes. Desired rod action is influenced by kinds of fishing done and personal preferences that come with experience. So if you get down to the finer points there can be no all-purpose taper. Unless you have preconceived notions on the subject, discuss taper and action with your tackle dealer. And if you're a novice don't be overly concerned about them at this stage.

*5.* Rod handles and grips:

Handle sections, terminating in the butt, vary in length according to requirements and models. On surf rods they're exceptionally long, 21 inches or more, to supply the leverage needed to fling lures appreciable distances. Double-handed spinning rods are similarly outfitted. Handles become proportionately shorter on smaller rods. Wood is the classic material. Over the years handles have been fashioned from hickory, ash and oak because of their toughness and near indestructibility. Cheap rods have handles of pine or other soft wood that can crack or snap under strain. Nowadays some models have handles of aluminum for lightness or, for economy, high-impact plastic.

The number of grips on a rod varies according to type. Light spinning and conventional rods, together with less expensive models, usually have one, as do fly rods. Longer and heavier-duty models, notably those in marine service and two-handed spinning rods, have two. One is ahead of the reel as a foregrip for better support of the rod. Its mate, the rear grip, is behind the reel and longer.

The best grip material is specie cork. It's light, durable and provides a good gripping surface. It's also more expensive than other materials.

Because of its weight, specie cork still is favored for fly rods and other light types.*

Among some rods, where added weight isn't critical, grips now are being fashioned from foam-rubber synthetics such as urethane and neoprene. These materials feel good to the hands and are very durable, and they save purchasers money as a substitute for the increasingly more expensive cork, which has to be shaped. Many salt-water rods have grips made from wood. If a rod is to be used in trolling, where it's frequently thrust into a holder, the foregrip is better made from wood than synthetic material, which could be worn by repeated rubbing against a holder.

The handles and butts of big-game rods rate mention. Fashioned from wood, they contribute substantially to total rod weight because they must be stout and especially strong. Stresses and strains imposed by the likes of a giant bluefin tuna, hard-charging mako shark or bulky marlin are tremendous. That punishment and the weapons' weight require that big-game tackle be operated from a fighting chair equipped with a gimbal to receive the rod butt. In combat with a big opponent this end of a rod has its own share of stresses and strains, since it becomes one end of a lever, with an irked fish at the other end and an angler in the middle as fulcrum. Accordingly, it has to be reinforced. This is accomplished by a metal cap with a cross-shaped nock which fits into a gimbal's retaining pins—they prevent a rod from turning in the fisherman's grasp. Available for big-game rods is a special, tubular-metal butt section. It curves at an angle so that the rod is in a somewhat lower position in action. This can help lessen strain on arms and shoulders during long battles.

## What to Look for in Reels

There are legions of reels. They cover every conceivable angling assignment. In the spinning and revolving-spool divisions they range from 4-ounce midgets up to burly, heavy big-game "winches" in the 12/0 and 14/0 classes. Their range of price tags is equally wide, according to size, model, maker, and any special features such as a level-wind mechanism or anti-backlash device. But collectively all those by reputable manufacturers have one thing in common: They make it possible for every one of us to own a good reel at a cost we can afford.

We'll give you a check list of details to keep in mind. *They apply to reels in general.* Special pointers concerning fly reels are discussed in *their* showroom.

*1.* Follow this rule and you'll be off to a substantial start:

Steer clear of cheap or "bargain-price" reels. They're likely to be bad news. More frequently than not, they reward purchasers with poor

*A charter skipper friend of the writer stored some quality rods with specie cork grips at home during the off-season. He also had a pet raccoon that was given the run of the house in winter. That fool animal gnawed the cork off every one of those rods. Moral of the story is: If you want to own rods with cork grips, fine. If you want a pet raccoon, that's okay too. But never the twain should meet.

performance, unreliability, breakdowns and short life. This makes them expensive in the long run, with aggravation as a surtax. Further, there probably won't be any comeback, and it may be impossible to get parts for repairs.

Don't misunderstand. By "bargain-price" reels we mean *junk*. You'll find genuine bargains when there are special sales of name-brand reels.

*2.* Rule No. 1 above is doubly important because a reel is like an automobile's engine in that there's no way you can inspect its inner workings before you buy. Poor reels are very likely to contain hidden defects that will make themselves known later, when it's too late. Frequently they show at the worst possible time because it takes action to reveal them. Figure it this way: If a reel looks junky or doubtful on the outside, what must the inside be like, where you can't see?

Fortunately, you can rely on the know-how and integrity of reputable makers for the quality of a reel's innards. You must remember, though, that even among name brands there are grades of good quality so that there can be a spread of prices for the market. Difference in price tags are a yardstick, aided by descriptions in catalogues and talks with tackle shop personnel.

There are several desirable internal features you can ask about. You may not find them all in a given reel—except, maybe, among the more expensive models—but they occur in combinations, according to builders, models and price tags. You won't find any of them among inferior reels. Gears are a criterion separating reels, being variously made from stainless steel, brass and other metals. Good gears are machined or machine-cut. Cheap gears are stamped out like cookies, often assembled with burrs and all. Some of the less expensive models have acceptable combinations of nylon and brass gearing. Other desirable internal features include: (*1*) ball bearings and roller bearings of hard steel; their number varies among models, and cheap reels generally have none; (*2*) self-lubricating bushings; (*3*) stainless steel crank shaft with its own bearings or bushings; (*4*) ready lubrication or sealed, self-lubricating bearings. And among salt-water reels, the greater the internal protection against corrosion (through materials), the better.

*3.* An internal mechanism of great importance is the drag or brake. There are various designs; some are there manufacturers' exclusively. The most common type works on a friction and slip-clutch principle, so it's important that drag washers and discs be made from tough, durable material. Teflon is one in use today. For its brake discs the Garcia Corporation uses a material called Ferodo, which goes into racing car brakes.

A drag must work smoothly and dependably, and show no signs of stickiness or "chatter." With some line on a reel you can get a preliminary idea of its smoothness by pulling it from the reel at different settings. This can't be a positive guarantee for the future, but it can reveal poor functioning; and again you usually can rely on the integrity of reputable manufacturers. Remember that some of the responsibility will be on *your* shoulders in the way you care for a reel.

*4.* Notes on spools: A favored material is solid aluminum. It's light and strong. Plastics have been used in spools, and while they too are light and strong, up to a point, they have a drawback. Synthetic lines can build considerable pressure when packed tightly, and pressure has been known to fracture plastic spools. On conventional reels, aluminum spools offer advantages over those of steel. Being lighter, they will start to turn quicker in casting, making it possible to use lighter rigs, and when revolving they won't gain as much momentum, the factor that creates backlashes.

Spool construction is reasonably uniform among reels of comparable quality, so line capacity becomes a prime guide. This is governed by the kinds of fishing done and the line strengths (diameters) and yardage involved.

Interchangeability of spools is a very handy feature. It enables you to switch from one line strength to another in short order. Not all reels have it, so inquire.

*5.* Spinning reels' bail or pickup mechanism must function smoothly and be reached readily. Try it. Stainless steel is a good material, and if the bail has a roller it should be hard-chromed against wear.

*6.* Exterior finishes: Good looks are a bonus, and manufacturers pay attention to eye appeal. But durability, which includes resistance to chipping in normal use and protection against rust and corrosion are more important criteria. For this the sideplates of conventional reels and major areas of spinning models are given finishes of epoxy or hard-baked enamel, while all metal parts usually left bare are of stainless steel or are chrome-plated. Exposed aluminum is anodized.

*7.* General features: Check a reel under consideration for how it "feels" to you. Can you easily reach all the controls—drag adjustment, free-spool lever (conventional models), clicker button, and anti-reverse (spinning reels)? Can you grip the crank handle comfortably? If those questions sound trivial, remember that you'll be spending a lot of time with the reel you select.

*8.* Specials and extras: (*a*) These include a level-wind device and a quadrant brake, both confined to revolving-spool reels and discussed earlier. (*b*) Some conventional reels incorporate an anti-backlash mechanism of one kind or another. The Ambassadeurs produced by Garcia, for example, incorporate an exclusive centrifugal brake (in addition to the regular drag) to cut down on backlashes in casting. (*c*) Among conventional and spinning reels, retrieve ratios go up to 4:1, even 5:1. You might inquire about models with a clutch that permits switching from "high gear" in retrieves to a lower ratio when playing a fish. (*d*) A special feature among some spinning reels (the firm of Feurer Brothers has offered it) is an arrangement whereby the reel can be flipped from one side to the other for operation with either hand.

Such features contribute to price tags, but if they appeal to you they're worth the added cost.

You don't buy tackle every day. That's another substantial reason for getting good equipment. Besides, considering its long life, dependable service, and the pleasure it gives, good tackle, even the expensive kind, is a modest investment.

## A Note on Custom Tackle

When we say "custom tackle" we mean rods alone, rods made to order for specific individuals. *They* cost enough. Made-to-order reels would be out of sight.

Along with their respective prices, the big difference between a custom-built rod and a comparable model such as you might heft in a tackle shop is similar to that between a custom-tailored suit and one that you'd take from a rack in a men's clothing emporium. In fine designing and quality of materials they might be equal, but the custom model fits better. (Or at least it should. This writer once splurged with a custom-tailored suit that fit like a ten-dollar shroud. In the boondocks. A poorer section. Back around 1900.)

We use the word "fit" advisedly in the case of custom-constructed rods because the most common reason for ordering them is to incorporate personal ideas, notably variations not encountered among stock models. These may involve special tapers, more or fewer guides, unusual proportions between handle and tip section lengths, etc. Maybe the customer has some private theories to test. What's more likely, he feels that he will be able to handle this made-to-order rod better—it will have a better "fit," in other words. Further personalizing is effected by specifying the color of the fiberglass blank from which the rod will be fashioned, the type and lengths of grips, and color combinations of guide windings. He also can have his signature reproduced on the rod. And to put icing on the cake, there's pride of ownership. After all, this rod was made for *him*. There isn't another one exactly like it in the whole world.

Custom construction doesn't necessarily mean proportionately greater quality of materials. Fact is, the builder probably gets his materials from the same sources as do manufacturers—or even from rod manufacturers themselves. And there are stock models whose components are every bit as good. As a general rule, quality of materials is assured in a custom rod by the very nature and cost of the transaction, especially when the purchaser dictates specifications. Workmanship may be something else again. By rights it should be the best—and usually is, among established builders. Price is a factor, of course, and there are degrees of craftsmanship. A yellow light of caution is flashed by chances of fly-by-nighters and something-less-than-skillful builders. So if and when you're ready to order a custom rod, heed the advice of the old Romans who went around shrieking *"Caveat emptor!"*—Let the buyer beware! Personally, we wouldn't order a custom rod from out of state without learning something about the builder beforehand.

A custom rod in itself won't catch any more fish for its wielder. Not unless the wielder's skill improves, in which case a stock model probably would serve just as well. Nevertheless, there's no denying that certain extra pleasure afforded by a personalized rod.

Custom models come considerably higher than those in stock, and among the likes of split-bamboo fly rods and big-game "sticks" they're downright costly. Unless they have more money than they know what to do with—a description that doesn't fit many around at the moment—novices and less-experienced fishermen can forget custom rods for the time being. Even if they could afford them, it seems foolish to lay out that kind of money until they learn how serious they are about the sport. There's plenty of time later, when experience and fancy—and the old pocketbook—so decree.

Okay, now we go into the showroom proper.

## SALT-WATER RODS

### Skippers Specials (Garcia)

These rods orginated as a joint effort of Garcia and Conolon Corp., in about 1963, then were field tested for years by skippers and expert anglers. During testing they whipped virtually all sport species encountered in Southern California and Mexico, including swordfish and giant black sea bass. They're a rich brown color, hand-assembled, beautifully wrapped. Other features: Neoprene handles and foregrips; heavily chromed Varmac brass reel seats, with two locking rings for added reel security; Varmac stainless steel guides, hard-chromed. The series offers eight rods. All are one-piece except model **B572**, which is two-piece. Guides number 5 to 7, plus tiptop, according to models.

Lengths: 6'4" (model **B573**) to 8' (**B576**—medium action, fast taper; 15- to 40-lb. lines, 1½- to 4-oz. lures). Actions: Light (**B571**—8- to 15-lb. lines, ¾- to 1½-oz. lures) to heavy (**B570**—7' trolling rod with 5 guides and Aftco roller tiptop; 30- to 80-lb. lines).

**B573:** 6'4", medium action, fast taper; 5 guides, tiptop; for 12- to 25-lb. lines, 1- to 2½-oz. lures.

**B574:** 6'10", medium action, fast taper; 6 guides, tiptop; 12- to 30-lb. lines, 1- to 2½-oz. lures.

**B575:** 7', medium action, fast taper; 6 guides, tiptop; for 15- to 40-lb. lines, 1½- to 4-oz. artificials.

Price range: $30.00 to $35.00.

### Solid-Glass Salt-Water Rods, by Garcia

All in smart black, there are thirteen models in the series: Two 5½' boat rods; 7' popping rod; 7½' spinning and trolling model; nine boat and trolling rods, 6' to 6'5". They're all one-piece, with actions ranging from light to heavy. They carry 3 to 5 guides, all hard-chromed—carbon steel on eleven models, stainless steel on the other two. They're rated for lines from 20-lb. test up to 80, and for lures from ½ oz. to 5 oz., according to models.

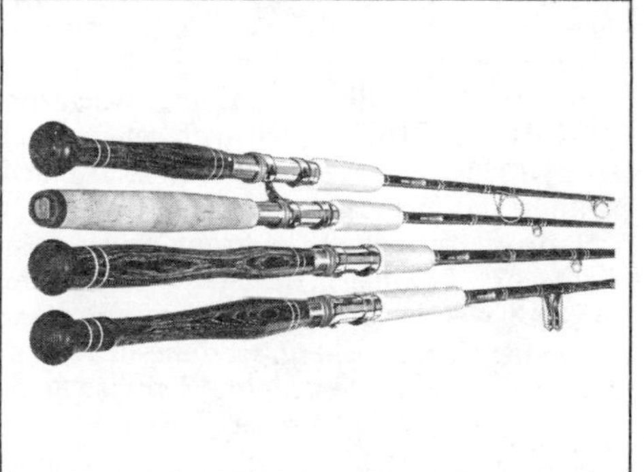

Representatives are:

**2877:** 5½', light-medium action boat rod; 20- to 35-lb. lines, 1¾- to 3½-oz. lures.

**2887:** 7', light-action popping rod with detachable butt, trigger reel seat; 12- to 20-lb. lines, ½- to 1½-oz. lures.

**2879:** 6½', heavy-action boat and trolling rod, with one-piece shaft continuing through hardwood butt; 4 guides and roller tiptop; 30- to 80-lb. lines.

**2889:** 6'5", heavy-action boat and trolling rod; one-piece, with detachable hardwood butt; 4 hard-chromed roller guides and roller tiptop, all stainless steel; for 30- to 80-lb. lines.

Price range: $16.00 to $28.00.

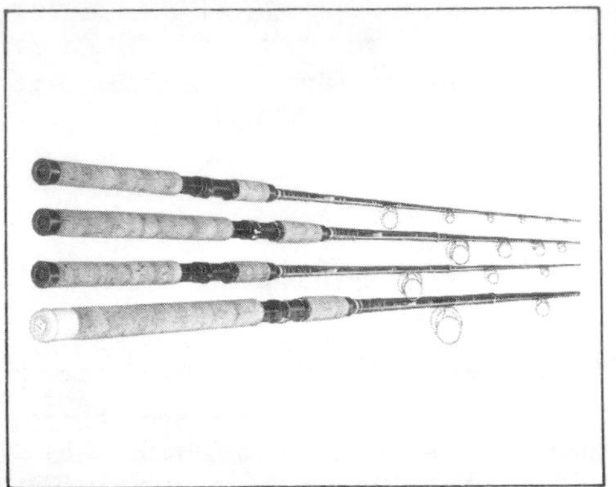

**Salt-Water and Fresh-Water Spinning Rods (Garcia)**

In this group in its rod family Garcia places eleven models: Three worm-spinning rods; two with an ultra-fast taper; four steelhead and marine spinning rods; and two salt-water spinning jobs. Collectively, they go from 6' to 10' long, have 5 to 7 hard-chromed Varmac guides, plus tungsten carbide tiptop, handle lines from 10- to 40-lb. test, and will cast artificals weighing 3/8- to 4½-oz. Their rich brown color forms an eye-pleasing contrast with the cork handles and foregrips.

Representatives of the group are:

**2506:** 7', two-piece, fast-taper steelhead and salt-water spinning rod; rated light-action for marine fishing, medium-heavy for fresh water; 5 guides, tiptop; handles 8- to 15-lb. lines, 5/8- to 1-oz. artificials.

**2553:** 9½', two-piece (with Allan chromed brass ferrule), medium action, fast taper; 6 guides and tiptop; 12- to 30-lb. lines, 1- to 4½-oz. lures.

Price range: $23.00 to $32.00.

**Garcia's Blue Salt-Water Rods**

Eleven handsome conventional and spinning models in blue glass: Three conventionals; two salt-water spinning rods; four designated as steelhead and spinning rods; and a special coho salmon rod. The group's length range: 6½ to 10'. Actions range from light, through medium, to heavy. Guides number 4 to 6, plus tiptop, and are hard-chromed carbon steel or stainless steel, all according to models.

Examples are:

**2662:** 6½' boat rod, one-piece tip section, heavy action; 4 guides, tiptop; detachable wooden handle; white neoprene foregrip contrasting with blue of tip section; heavily chromed, front-locking reel seat. For lines to 50-lb. test.

**2653:** 7'4", medium-action, one-piece marine spinning rod with detachable wooden handle, neoprene foregrip; 4 guides, tiptop; rated for 10- to 20-lb. lines, 1- to 4-oz. artificials.

**2650:** 8', light-action, two-piece steelhead and salt-water spinning rod; 5 guides and tiptop; 8- to 15-lb. lines, 5/8- to 1¼-oz. lures.

**2654:** 10' spinning rod with medium action, fast taper; two-piece tip section with 6 guides and tiptop. Designed for 12- to 30-lb. lines, 1- to 4½-oz. lures.

**2656:** a special coho rod: 7'9", two-piece, medium action; 5 guides and tiptop; made for 10- to 30-lb. lines, 1- to 3-oz. artificials.

Price range: $16.00 to $23.00.

**True Temper's 9500 Series**

Here's a versatile group whose nine members cover a wide range of marine and fresh-water assignments—fishing at anchor, trolling, casting, bottom bouncing, dock and pier fishing. They're also smartly designed, with white blanks and contrasting maroon windings and black striping. And these are major features: Solid glass construction; stainless guides throughout, all windings with Tempercote; hard, tough, straight-grained ash handles and upper grips; chromed brass reel seats with double locking rings.

In length they range from 5' (**No. 9500**) to 7½' (**9545**), with lower handles going from 18" to 21". All except **9545** are one-piece. Model **9545** has a two-piece tip section. Actions range from light through medium to heavy.

Random samplings:

**9500:** 5', handle 18", 4½" upper grip; light action; 2 guides and tiptop.

**9510:** 5'10", handle 21", 4½" upper grip; medium action; 3 guides and tiptop.

**9530:** 6', handle 21", 4½" upper grip; heavy action; 3 guides and roller tiptop.

**9545:** 7½', two-piece tip section, 18" handle, 4½" upper grip; 4 guides and tiptop.

Price range: $10.00 to $22.00.

**Uni-Spin Series, by True Temper**

Under the banner Uni-Spin are offered several versatile rod and reel combinations. The following is a good example:

Uni-Spin **No. 63LC:** The manufacturer bills this one as the "Universal fresh-water and light salt-water outfit." Designed for spinning and spincasting fishermen, its unique feature is that the reel, although removable, is an integral part of the reel.

The reel is literally built in, and in its latest model has a rear gear support (to eliminate gear stripping) and stronger, quieter anti-reverse mechanism. The rod is True Temper's own Holloglass, 6½' long, two-piece, with an intermediate taper. It carries 4 stainless guides and tiptop, and they and the ferrule are wrapped fully with Tempercote windings. The overall disassembled length is 40". Uni-Spin **63LC** has a lefthand crank, but the same outfit is available as **No. 63RC** with a right-hand crank. Comes in a fully zippered, fleece-lined vinyl carrying case.

Approximate retail price ranges of the various Uni-Spin combinations go from $12-$33 on the low side to $16-$47 on the high side.

**Green Pal Salt-Water Rods, by Heddon**

Here's a new group that has taken its place in the big family of marine and fresh-water rods produced by an old and well-known manufacturer. Generations of anglers have known the name Heddon.

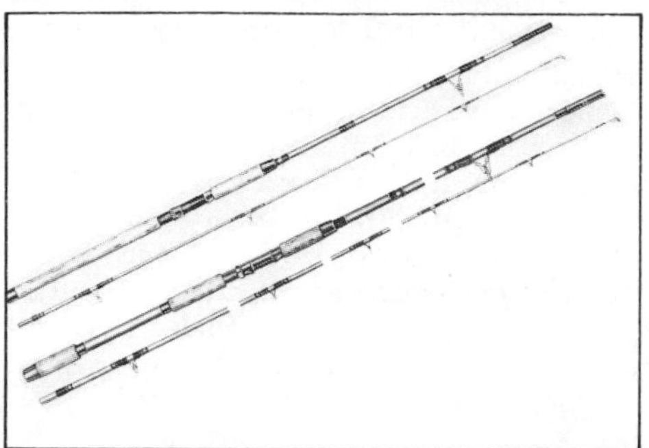

The Green Pal series embraces eleven models, of which six are designed for surf spinning, two are popping rods, two are engineered for salmon and steelhead action, and one is for mooching. They all share these construction qualities: Heddon's fiberglass and workmanship; striking green color with contrasting wrappings; corrosion-resistant guides, slides and ferrules, as well as a highly corrosion-resistant reel seat; specie cork butt and foregrip; and positive-locking ferrule-slide combination. They're offered in lengths from 8' to 11', all with a fast taper. All except two—**Nos. 7535** and **7536**, the popping rods—are two-piece. The exceptions have one-piece tip sections.

Samples from the group:

**Nos. 7505, 7510, 7515, 7520, 7525** and **7530** are surf spinning rods. Their lengths go from 8' for **7505**, through 9' for **7515**, to 11' for **7530.** The two single-piece popping sticks are 7' long. The mooching rod, **No. 7538**, is 8½'. The two salmon-steelhead models, **Nos. 7540** and **7542**, are 8' and 8½', respectively.

Price range: $25 to $30.

**Fenwick's Offshore Trolling Rods**

Fenwick divides these into four categories, with a total of fifteen models. Together they have tip sections of 65" (thirteen rods) and 72" (two models), butt lengths of 16" to 20", and are designed to handle lines from 12-lb. test to 130. All are in rich, dark brown, double-wrapped for extra durability in action. According to models, other features include: Neoprene foregrip; Hypalon-covered stainless steel handle; roller guides throughout, or carbide ring-type guides with roller tiptop.

Deluxe series, six rods, for offshore big-game trolling: **Nos. 610, 620, 630** and **640** are rated for 12-, 20-, 30- and 50-lb. lines, respectively. Tip lengths are 65", butt lengths are 16". All four have Aftco roller guides throughout, including a double-roller lead guide. The other two deluxe models, **660** and **670**, are for 80- and 130-lb. lines, respectively, have 65" tips, 20" butts, and Mildrum double-roller guides throughout. And all six rods have Hypalon-covered stainless steel handles, guaranteed unbreakable, with gimbal nock, and heavy-duty machined reel seat components. They come in a padded, black vinyl case.

Standard series, five models, for general ocean trolling: **Nos. 611, 621, 631, 641** and **831** (same as **631**, except one-piece construction—handle doesn't detach). Starting with **No. 611**, they're designed for 12-, 20-, 30- and 50-lb. lines. Shared specifications: 65" tip; 16" butt; tiptop roller guide, other guides of carbide ring-type; double-locking, chromed brass reel seat; Hypalon-covered stainless steel handle.

Offshore series, two rods, for general ocean service: Models **663** and **673**, both new for 1975, and rated for 80- and 130-lb. lines, respectively. Both have: 65' tip section, 20" butt; double-locking reel seat; Hypalon-covered stainless steel handle; Mildrum guides throughout—a double-roller tiptop.

Price range: Deluxe series, approximately $150.00; standard series, approximately $00.00 to $75.00.

### HRH Glass Rods by Tycoon/Fin-Nor

Any fishermen who have been on the salt-water scene for a spell usually look on the combination of a Tycoon rod and a Fin-Nor reel as the Rolls and Royce of tackle. These HRH glass rods are in that Tycoon/Fin-Nor tradition. They're magnificently crafted, built from the best white spun glass in tubular construction, each rod tapered to the manufacturer's rigid specifications. There are nine models in all, as follows.

In one group are three, designated as plug casting, lightweight spinning, and medium-heavy spinning models. All three have cork handles and foregrips. The HRH plug casting rod features a heavy action, trigger grip. The other two models have Perfection ring guides and tiptop, are available in one- or two-piece versions.

In the second group are six rods, designated as **Nos. 12, 20, 30, 50, 80** and **130**, which figures also show the pounds-test lines they're rated to handle. All have butt sections turned from solid aluminum, anodized, with special heavy-chromed fittings, plus heavy-duty, screw-locking seats to assure perfect alignment of guides and reel. All have roller guides throughout: Aftco and stainless tiptop on **No. 12**; Tycoon/Fin-Nor nylon rollers and stainless tiptop on **Nos. 20, 30, 50**; Tycoon/Fin-Nor aluminum rollers and tiptop on **Nos. 80** and **130.** Available for **No. 30** on up is a curved aluminum butt, an optional extra.

Approximate prices: HRH spinning rods, $75. The other HRH models: **No. 12**, $140; **No. 20**, $145; **No. 30**, $150; **No. 50**, $175; **No. 80**, $300; **No. 130**, $350. Curved butt for **Nos. 80** and **130**, $25 additional.

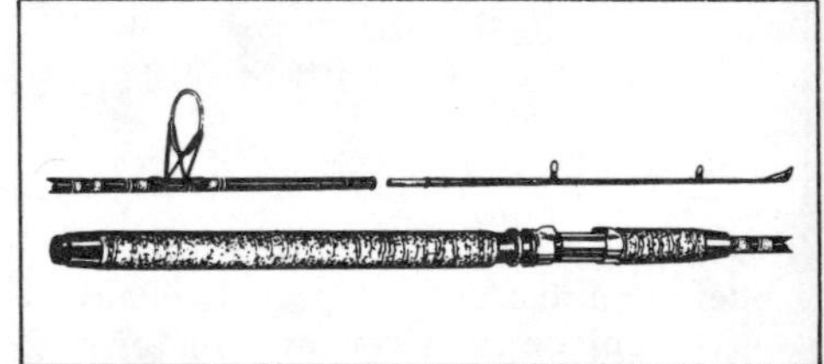

### Daiwa Rods

Maxi Power salt-water spinning rods: five models, all of tubular glass, 2-piece construction, fast taper, with five to six hard-chromed, bridged, stainless steel guides and tiptop, specie cork grip, double locking reel seat of brass, hard chrome-plated, epoxy finish with polyurethane undercoating. Models **3024N** through **3026N** are 7½' to 9' long, with medium light action. **No. 3024N** takes 8- to 17-lb. lines; the other two, 10- to 20-lb. lines. **Nos. 3027N** and **3029N** are 9' and 10' long, respectively, both with medium action.

Model **3027N** is for 10- to 27-lb. lines. **No. 3029N** takes 10- to 30-lb. lines. Prices go from $21.88 to $30.63.

Ventura Big Game Rods: Their series designation is **8083**, followed by a model number indicative of the IGFA line-class that rod is rated handle. There are six models, **Nos. 20**, **30**, **50**, **80**, **130** and **U** (IGFA unlimited class). All are 6'8" long, 2-piece fiberglass, triple wrapped, with roller guides throughout. Prices go from $96.25 for **Nos. 20** and **30** to $165.75 for **No. 130** and $210 for **No. U**.

Among many other Daiwa rods: (1) Surf-Spin Stick Series: Glass-jointed surfcasting

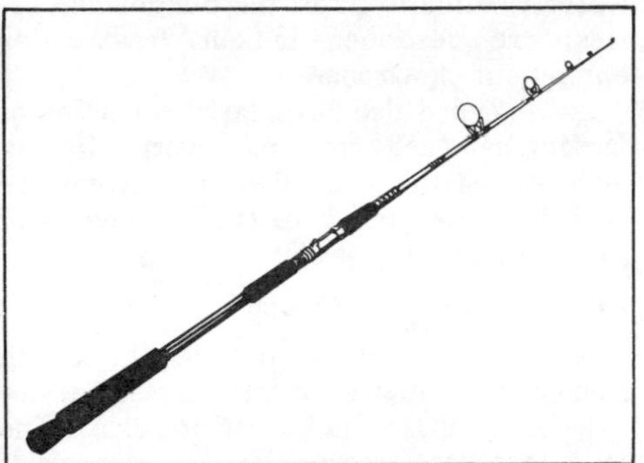

rods with neoprene grips, fifteen models, 9' to 13' long, with action from medium to medium-heavy to heavy, $35 to $71.75. (2) T.T.W. Tournament Rod Series: six power-packed models, 6' to 8', rated for lines 15-25 lbs. up to 20-60 lbs., featuring extra-heavy-duty fiberglass (3 layers at tip to 40 layers

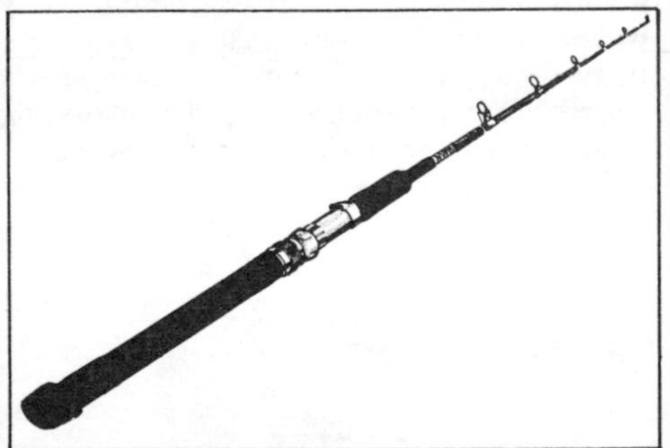

at butt) and one-piece rod blank extending all the way to butt end. Price range, $43.75 to $100 (for ocean trolling, aftco guides throughout).

**Rods by Quick Corporation of America**

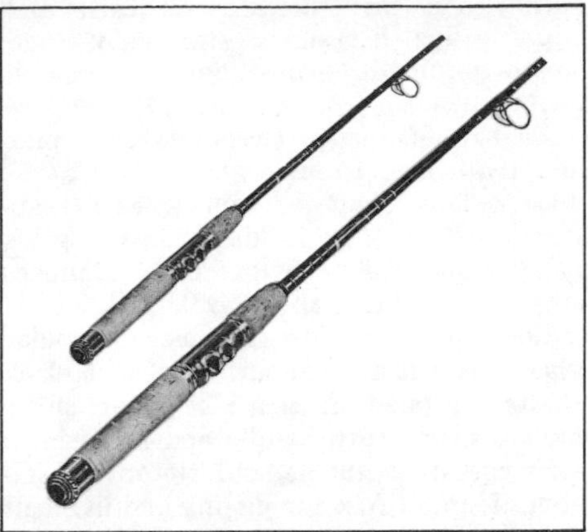

**Nos. 6066** and **6071**: two-piece spinning rods with medium-heavy action, Neo-Grip handle, suited to light salt-water fishing and fresh water's more rugged assignment. Quick suggests both for 6- to 15 lb. lines. Model **6066** is 6½' long. **No. 6701** is 7' Approximate price: $25.00.

Quick spinning rod **No. 6080R** has two-piece fiberglass for light salt-water duty and fresh water's rambunctious rascals. It classifies as a good rod for steelheads and coho salmon. For it Quick recommends 8- to 15-lb. lines. Approximate price: $27.00.

**St. Croix Salt-Water Rods**

St. Croix offers a sizable selection, among which are these:

Coastal Series: Newly expanded for even greater scope, with rods for spinning and spincasting (and both in the same models), medium- to heavy-action boat fishing, fly-casting, and gimbal-nocked models with Aftco roller guides for IGFA 20-, 30-, 50- and 80-lb. line classes. As a group their lengths go from 5½' to 13'. Also according to models, they're either hollow glass or solid, two-piece or one-piece.

Representatives include (1) Coastal 500 series, one- and two-pieces, 7' to 13', featuring mahogany-colored shafts, double-wound stainless steel guides and Carboloy tiptop, cork grip, chromed reel seat. Approximate price range, $12.95 to $29.95. (2) Five two-piece fly rods, 7½' to 8'9", with 4 to 6 snake guides, stainless steel stripper and fly tip. Prices, $6.99 to $34.99. (3)

Medium-action boat rods, one-piece, 6½' and 7', solid glass—black—with scarlet and white wraps, 3 stainless steel guides and tiptop, chromed reel seat, detachable handle of hard wood. Prices, $6.99 to $24.99.

Foul-Proof Series: twelve models, one- and two-piece, tubular glass, 6½- to 8', with yellow shafts, chromed reel seats (some with double-locking rings), glass handle, and foul-proof guides of stainless steel. Price range, about $9.99 to $29.99.

Commander Series: two-piece, tubular glass, extra-fast-taper surf rods, with black shafts wrapped in sea blue over silver mylar, specie cork handle and foregrip, 5 stainless steel guides and tiptop, nickel-silver ferrule. Also for jigging and live-bait fishing. Three models, 8' to 10'. Price range, $14.99 to $29.99.

Regulation Tackle: Among St. Croix's top-line rods for IGFA line classes, 20-lb. through 130-lb. and unlimited class. Features include jet black tubular shafts wrapped in garnet and white, Aftco roller guides and tiptop (except two models, 20- and 30-lb. class, available with roller tiptop and double-roller stripper, but with 6 stainless steel ring guides in between), 18" hardwood handle, detachable, 8" Cushionite foregrip, chrome-plated brass Universal gimbal nock. Price range, $69.00 to $199.00.

**Zebco Rods**

The Centennial series: This is a new group of rods in Zebco's tribe. It's comprised of six spincasting sticks whose collective capabilities go from light to medium marine angling to medium-light to heavy fresh-water fishing, worming and deep jigging. Plus three spinning rods, 5½' to 6½', for light to medium-light sweetwater action. The six spincasting models measure 5½' to 7'. All are characterized by strength in lightness, thanks to high-density tubular glass, which adds sensitivity too. Other details are hard-chromed steel guides, wrapped with contrasting nylon over gold foil, light and strong aluminum handles with butt grip and foregrip of select specie cork, and permanent, flared ABS butt caps for comfort (on most rods). Centennial series price span, about $8.00 to $14.00.

Other Zebco rods with fresh- and/or salt-water capabilities, like the Sundowner series, are described in our fresh-water equipment showroom.

*Note:* Zebco also has a large collection of factory-balanced spinning, worm fishing and spincasting combinations, complete with rod, reel and line, ready to go—and priced to suit any wallet.

**From Gladding-South Bend**

Among the groups of Gladding-South Bend rods for marine or fresh-water service—or both—is the Outdoorsman series. The manufacturer presents it as "America's finest low-priced rod series." Purchasers will have to be the judge of that, but we can point up some features: Extra-strong metal casting handle with spiral-drive reel lock; fixed-seat spinning handle of two-toned anodized aluminum, with locking ring; cork grips; braced and standard wire-frame guides and tiptop, hard-chromed; fully wrapped ferrules; new, fast tapers; high-luster epoxy finish. Their fiberglass shafts are a warm shade of brown with contrasting guide wraps and darker brown reel seat.

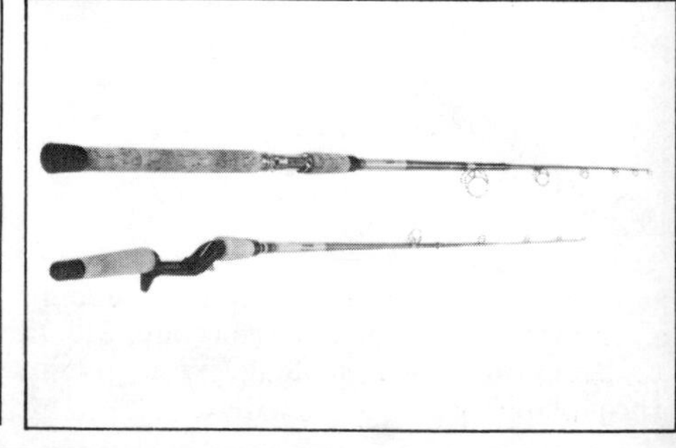

Members of the Outdoorsman series:

Three spinning models, two 6½', one 7', fast taper on the 6½-footers, GSB's Powerflex action in the 7-footer. Priced about $12.95.

Two ultra-light spinning rods, 5' and 5½', ultra-light action, with 4 hard-chromed guides and tiptop. Priced about $9.98 to $21.98.

Two spincasting models, 6' and 6½', two-piece, medium action, 5 hard-chromed guides and tiptop. Priced about $5.95 to $25.00.

Fly rods: 8' and 8½', two-piece, 5 snake guides, hard-chromed stripper and tiptop. The 8-footer is designed for 7-weight fly line. The 8½-footer is balanced for No. 8 line. Priced about $9.98 to $28.00.

In fresh-water fishing the Outdoorsman series carries GSB's Magnum Bass Rod classification, which means they're designed for lunker-size bass.

**Matched Fishing Outfits from Martin Reel Co.**

Under the banner Martin Bretton are offered four Matched Spinning Sets which balance a U.S.-made Martin rod with a France-made Bretton reel. Joining two ultra-light fresh-water outfits (**Nos. 817** and **814**) in the quartet are two for light surf angling and light salt-water fishing in general. They also can be used for fresh water.

Spinning Combination **818** teams the following: two-piece, 7' tubular glass rod with stainless steel guides and tiptop, and backbone for tough opponents; 400M reel with 3.8:1 retrieve, tough 6-plate drag, helical gear system, ball bearing mounted, and capacity of 300 yds. of 8-lb. line. Approximate retail price is $45.95.

Spinning Combination **827** matches these components: A muscular, two-piece, 9' surf spinning rod, Martin No. 1-129; and an equally strong Bretton 807M reel with a 4:1 gear system and a capacity of 175 yds. of 20-lb. line. Total weight of the outfit, exclusive of line, only 26 oz. Approximate retail, $77.95.

Shown is Another type of Martin Balanced Rod & Reel Combination is **No. 851**, a spincasting outfit economically priced at about $23.95. It rod is a two-piece fiberglass 6-footer, Martin No. 5-102, on which is mounted a Martin 500 reel.

## SALT-WATER REELS

**Penn's Surfmaster Reels**

It seems safe to say that the name Penn is known to fishermen all over the world. It also seems safe to state that Penn Surfmasters are seen on all U.S. coasts. Popular pricing, Penn dependability and proven long life are reasons. Other reasons are construction features: Rugged, reliable star drag with white-oak leather washers; 3:1 gear ratio; hand-fitting torpedo handles; one-shot lubrication; rod clamps; and ready take-apart.

Surfmasters are offered in eight models. **Nos. 100, 150, 200** and **250** have reinforced plastic spools, widths 1-5/8" to 2-7/16", plate diameters from 2¾" to 3-1/16". Their respective weights and capacities (30-lb. Dacron), starting with **No 100:** 16 oz., 125 yards.; 17½ oz., 150 yds.; 18 oz., 175 yds.; 20 oz., 250 yds. They take about the same yardage of nylon squidding line. An extra spool is included.

**Nos. 100M, 150M, 200M** and **250M** have the same spool widths and plate diameters as their counterparts above, but their spools are chromed brass (extra spool not included). Weights and capacities (30-lb. Dacron or 36-lb. nylon squidding line), beginning with **100M:** 17 oz., 150 yds.; 18 oz., 200 yds.; 19½ oz., 225 yds.; 22½ oz., 300 yds.

Approximate prices: $25.00 to $30.00.

**The Penn Senators**

At the risk of sounding like stockholders in Penn, which we're not, we have to say that these are probably the best known big-game fishing reels in the world. The writer has used or seen them on boats from South Africa to Australia, Nova Scotia to Ecuador. Many a world record has been set with a Penn Senator.

These "senior statesmen" of the Penn family come in sizes from 4/0 (450 yds. of 30-lb. Dacron) up to the whopping 14/0 (850 yds. of 130-lb. line) and 16/0 (1,000 yds. of 130-lb. Dacron). Shared specifications, all models: (1) One-piece, machined bronze spool, strongest ever produced; those on the 9/0 through 16/0 turn on aircraft-quality ball bearings; (2) full-range, adjustable drag system with tough, heat-resistant brake lining discs; (3) stainless steel gears, with ratios specifically suited to reel sizes; (4) double nickel-silver rings on rugged sideplates; one-shot lubrication system; suitably sized torpedo handle; and fishing harness lugs. Forward rod braces are standard on the 9/0 through 16/0. The 14/0 and 16/0 have double braces.

Price range: $50.00 to $225.00.

**"Junior" Senators**

You might want to know that the famed Penn line also is represented by Special Senators, engineered for light-tackle game fish action. These are six models, with their weights and sample capacities (Dacron line): **No. 110**, 1/0, 18 oz., 200 yds. of 30-lb.; **No. 111**, 2/0, 22 oz., 275 yds. of 30-lb.; **No. 112**, 3/0, 26 oz., 350 yds. of 30-lb.; **No. 112H**, 3/0, 25 oz., 350 yds. of 30-lb.; **No. 113H**, 4/0, 34 oz., 450 yds. of 30-lb.; and **No. 114H**, 6/0, 52 oz., 400 yds. of 50-lb.

Gear ratios range from 2¼:1 to 3.7:1 for fast retrieves, important when taking in slack created by a fish changing direction. Other features include: Moly-coated steel gears; sideplates reinforced by inside and outside rings; one-shot lubrication system for long life; oversized torpedo handles for better gripping and leverage; Penn clutch premitting instant counterbalanced shifting between free spool and engaged positions without stripping gears; one-piece, solid, perfectly balanced spool; rod clamps on all models for extra reel security.

Approximate prices: $30.00 to $80.00.

**Penn Squidders**

One-screw take-apart is a prime detail of these casting reels, made to take both plastic and metal spools. Lightweight, rugged frames, ball bearings, and a fast 3⅓:1 retrieve ratio are among other assets. **Nos. 140, 145** and **146** come with two plastic spools. Models **140M, 145M** and **146M** are the same except that they come with one metal spool. An interesting feature of the plastic spools is air brake fins to make casting easier. Weights are 16 to 18 oz., with capacities going from 275 to 400 yds. of 20-lb. monofilament. An anti-reverse is available as an option. **No. 140** has a left-hand version.

Approximate price: $40.00.

**Mariner Series, by Penn**

Although they will handle all lines—mono, braided, etc., these reels are characterized by narrow, deep spools for wire and lead-core lines. Among other features are synchromesh gears, double-leverage handle, and full-range, adjustable drag. The series starts with Penn Mariner **No. 149**, the simplified version, and goes on to offer the Super Mariners **49** and **49M** and three models of the Master Mariner **349**. Specification ranges: Weights, 29 to 37 oz.; gear ratios, from 2.1 to 3½:1; capacities, 200 to 245 yds. of Monel (0.024), 250 to 350 yds. of 30-lb. Dacron. All spool widths are 1 5/8".

Approximate price: $50.00.

**Penn's Small-Budget 70s**

They're Penn's least expensive revolving-spool reels, yet they incorporate reinforced plastic sideplates and spool, sliding click, free spool action, and all exposed metal parts of solid brass. (*Note:* They do not have a star drag.) There are three models. In addition to meeting small budgets, they're designed for general salt-water and fresh-water fishing—bays, ponds, piers, lakes, rowboats, rivers, etc. They can be mounted atop a rod or underneath, for right- or left-hand operation.

Sea Hawk **No. 77:** Two-knob handle, multiplying gears, weight 9 oz. Holds approximately 125 yds. of 36-lb. line, appreciably more in lighter lines. Approximate price, $4.50.

Sea Scamp **No. 78:** Weighs 10 oz., holds approximately 150 yds. of 36-lb. nylon, more yardage of lighter lines.

Approximate price, $6.50.

**The Internationals, by Penn**

These are Penn's top-of-the-line, luxury game fishing reels, superbly styled in a golden finish, beautifully engineered. A sampling of their features: (1) Unique drag system with powerful, full-floating disc design, activated by a quadrant lever moving through 120 degrees of arc for a wide selection of brake settings; (2) pre-set drag automatically keeps tension within safe limits to minimize broken lines; (3) strike-set stop for instant setting of drag at strike tension without fumbling or guesswork; (4) perfectly balanced frame, distributing weight evenly for control of reel and rod; (5) shielded, stainless steel ball bearings; (6) one-piece pinion and spool shaft, machined from stainless steel and hardened—won't rust or wear; (7) stainless steel drag gam that holds exact tension adjustment set by angler; (8) double-dog design for maximum security and long, wear-free life.

There are five models of the Internationals: **No. 20**, 2½/0; **No. 30**, 4/0; **No. 50**, 6/0; **No. 80**, 10/0; and the biggest, **No. 130**. Specification ranges: Spool widths, 1 5/8" (**No. 20**) to 4" (**No. 130**); plate diameters, 4" (**No. 20**) to 6½" (**No. 130**); and gear ratios from 1.6:1 )**No. 130**) to 3½:1 )**Nos. 20** and **30**). Approximate capacities (Dacron lines) range from 1,200 of 12 lb. and 700 yds. of 20 lb. on **No. 20** to 1,200 yds. of 80 lb. and 850 yds. of 130 lb. on **No. 130**.

Approximate prices: **No. 20**, $225; **No. 30**, $240; **No. 50**, $300; **No. 80**, $425; **No. 130**, $700.

### Spinfisher Spinning Reels, by Penn

Penn has expanded its line of Spinfisher reels for marine and fresh-water service with two new models:

**No. 706** (**707** for left-handers): A rugged, strong reel with simplified construction. Features include: Manual pickup; line roller on stainless steel ball bearings; Penn drag system; ball bearing pinion gear; fast 3.8:1 ratio. It holds 300 yds. of 20-lb. line, 350 of 17 lb., sells for about $40.00.

**No. 716:** Not much larger than a man's hand this is the smallest and lightest (only 8½ oz.) of the Spinfishers. Some features: High-speed gears for very fast 5.1:1 retrieve; multi-drag system of Teflon; push-button-removable spool. For light, limber rods and lures as small as 1/8 oz., the bantamweight **716** holds about 225 yds. of 4-lb. mono, 175 yds. of 6-lb. mono. Approximate price: $28.00.

Other Penn Spinfishers are the **720**,**710**, **712**, **722** and **704**, in graduated weights from 9½ oz. (**720**) to 21 oz. (**704**). Features among them include tough Teflon drag system, anodized solid aluminum spool, tungsten carbide line roller, and main shaft, bail and shielded ball bearings of stainless steel, gear ratios up to a fast 4.1:1. Approximate capacities go from 300 yds. of 4-lb. mono (**Nos. 720, 722**) to 22 yds. of 12-lb. mono (**710**) and 285 of 15-lb. mono (**704**).

Approximate prices: **No. 720**, $16; **No. 710**, $32; **No. 712**, $30; **No. 722**, $25; **No. 704**, $40.

### Shakespeare's Marina Green Spinning Reels

There are ten models, three of them for southpaws. Their finish is dark green enamel over a light but strong aluminum alloy body, with chrome-plated bail. Marina Green specifications include a level wind system, multi-disc drag, on-off reverse lever. All are numbered in the **2200**s and in capabilities range from extra-light up to heavier salt-water duty. Here are representatives:

**2200 II:** Smallest and lightest, 7 oz., 5:1 gear ratio for rapid retrieves, push-button-removable spool holds 170 yds. of 6-lb. mono.

**2210 II:** A medium, "all-rounder," 11 oz., 3.75:1 retrieve ratio, push button for spool removal, capacity of 270 yds. of 6-lb. mono or 180 yds. of 8 lb.

**2240 II:** Bridges heavy fresh-water and medium salt-water assignments, 4:1 retrieve, weighs 16.5 oz., holds 260 yds. of 12-lb. monofilament.

**2260 II:** At 22.5 oz., the huskiest Marina Green, rated for heavier chores in both salt and fresh water, 3.5:1 gear ratio, takes 260 yds. of 20-lb. mono.

Price range: $20.00 to $35.00.

### New 2400 Spinning Reels, by Shakespeare

Four models—**2400**, **2410**, **2430**, **2450**—featuring Shakespeare's "wrap-around" skirted spool design for long, smooth casts, "completely elminating the possibility of annoying line tangles." Dual ball bearing construction, precision gears, multi-disc drag system, and convertible crank handles for use by either hand are starred details.

**No. 2400** is for all-around spinning, has a super-fast 5.2:1 retrieve, holds 180 yds. of 6-lb. mono. **No. 2410** is model **2400**'s somewhat bigger brother, has a 4.5:1 gear ratio, takes 270 yds. of 8-lb. mono. **No. 2450** is engineered for salt-water action, with a

4.1:1 retrieve, and a capacity of 400 yds. of 12-lb. mono. **No. 2430** is for heavy fresh-water or light marine service, winds in line at the rate of 4.2:1, accommodates 300 yds. of 10-lb. monofilament.

Price range: $30.00 to $45.00.

### Quick's 550-N Salt-Water Spinning Reel

The manufacturer's billing for the **550-N** describes a rugged, dependable husky "mill" designed to absorb a lot of punishment along the surf and elsewhere in marine service. It's corrosion-resistant, with bail and other parts engineered to withstand sand and salt water. Specifications include: Precision-machined gears; ball bearing drive on main shaft; self-lubricating handle bearings; stainless steel bail with tungsten carbide line guide; adjustable bail release mechanism for softer or harder operation to better suit special situations; anti-reverse on reel flange for easier operation; fold-away handle of stainless steel. The **550-N** weighs about 19 oz., has a 3.22:1 gear ratio, takes 330 yds. of 20-lb. line.

Approximate price: $32.00.

The **440-N** Finessa is the 550-N's "younger" brother. Weighing 13½ oz., retrieving line at the ratio of 3.55:1, and accommodating 325 yds. of 12-lb. line, the **440-N** Finessa is designed for general salt-water use, as well as for such husky fresh-

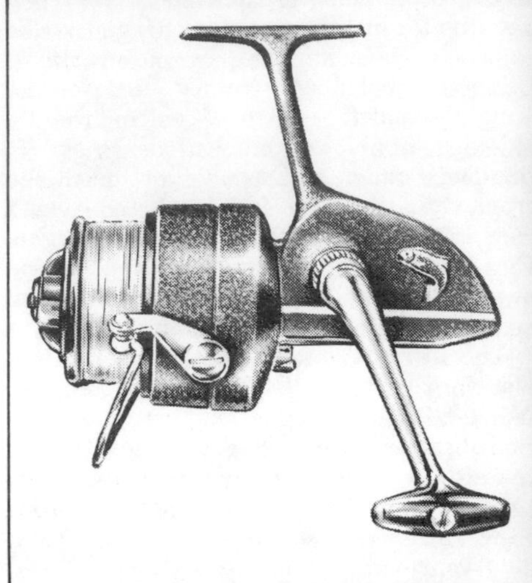

water opponents as steelheads and coho salmon. Its other specifications are the same as for the **440-N**. There's also a push button release on the spool for fast changes. Approximate price: $28.00.

### The Fin-Nor Family

Borrowing a phrase from show business, Fin-Nors are a legend in their time. And they have been called "the Rolls-Royce of reels." Prices have something to do with this, we suspect, but the real basis of the nickname is a quality of construction that places them on a Rolls-Royce level in their field. No two ways about it, they're magnificent pieces of machinery. This statement from Tycoon/Fin-Nor will give you an inkling: "An automated machine tool could turn out a reel spool in minutes. It takes our master craftsmen three hours to do it by hand." Further, all Fin-Nors are individually registered—a personally engraved nameplate is included—and are guaranteed for their life against defects of materials and workmanship. Each comes in a custom, shock-proof carrying case. Fin-Nors, by the way, have their share of IGFA world records.

All the features of Fin-Nor are notable. On the outside they include a very distinctive golden finish and a quadrant lever that activates a brake of incredible precision, smoothness and dependability.

Inside, out of sight, are gears and other components backed by that reel-lifetime guarantee. You have to handle a Fin-Nor to really appreciate it.

There are six sizes:

**2½/0:** A compact bundle of muscle, very fast—4:1 retrieve, perfect for 62 to 203 lb. lines. Capacity is 1,200 yds. of 12 lb., 850 yds. Its retrieve ratio is 4:1.

**4/0:** Ideal for 30-lb. line, which it can accommodate to the tune of 800 yds. Its retrieve ratio is 4:1.

**6/0:** An excellent combination of medium size and big-reel features. Retrieves at 3:1, holds 650 yds. of 50-lb. line.

**7½/0:** A reel in the 50-lb. line class with greater capacity than a 6/0. It takes 1,000 yds. of 50 lb., winds it back on at a ratio of 3:1.

**9/0:** Comparatively new in the family, this dual-geared model has been called the ultimate 80-lb. line reel with the versatility of the Fin-Nor 12/0. It was tested in Australia on the Great Barrier Reef's giant black marlin going 1,000 lbs. and better. It holds a full 800 yds. of 80-lb. line, has a 2 3/4:1 retrieve.

**12/0:** This is the classic Fin-Nor in big-game angling. There are probably very few, if any, sport fishing arenas around the globe where it hasn't tangled with giant opponents, and world records it helped establish include those for blue marlin, swordfish and black marlin. An instant-change gear gives a choice of take-up drives. Standard retrieve ratios are 2:1 and 1:1; the special offers 3:1 and 2:1. Its huge spool takes 850 yds. of 130-lb. line.

Approximate prices (hold on to your hat): **2½/0**, $375; **4/0**, $400; **6/0**, $425; **7½/0**, $580; **9/0**, $600, and **9/0 Special**, $775; **12/0**, Standard or Special Ratio model, $875.

### Other Fin-Nors

**No. 3** spinning reel: Holds 300 yds. of 8-lb. line or 225 yds. of 10 lb. Features include Fin-Nor full-circle drag disc, ingenious automatic pickup finger that eliminates a bail, very distinctive golden finish. Price, $125. The larger **No. 4** spinning reel incorporates the same Fin-Nor quality features but holds 400 yds. of 8-lb. line or 300 yds. of 15 lb. Price, $130. A Fin-Nor Presentation Series offers both reels, in a handsome, hand-rubbed walnut case, with the recipient's name on an engraved plate on each reel and the case. Approximate price, $350.

Also available are three revolving-spool trolling reels in the Golden Regal series: The **12-20**, a light but powerful reel that holds 1,000 yds. of 12-lb. line or 800 yds. of 20 lb., $175. The **30** incorporates big-game reel features in a smaller model, takes 800 yds. of 30-lb. line, $200. And the Golden Regal **50** is engineered for bigger game on lighter tackle, accommodates 600 yds. of 50-lb. line, sells for about $225.

### Spinning Reels by Feurer Brothers

From their native Switzerland the Feurer Brothers, Roger and Walter, brought their considerable watchmaking talent to the United States—North White Plains, N.Y., to be exact, where they established a factory to make parts for such high-quality watches as Omega, Rolex and other expensive timepieces, as well as for U.S. Government space age devices. It has been part of American angling history that a number of watchmakers and clock builders eventually turned their attention to construction of reels. The result of Roger and Walter Feurer's passion for precision are seen in some sixteen spinning reels and fly reels.

**The Mastereel,** model **FB450,** combines watchmakers' precision with huskiness for all-round marine service. Your attention is

called to its quadrant-drag brake, activated by a lever conveniently located near the crank. A Feurer Brothers exclusive, it takes the guesswork out of drag setting and can be preset for any strength line. Without releasing the handle, the brake can be adjusted from free spooling to maximum line test with a flick of the finger. The free spooling feature is handy for paying out line without opening the bail or touching the line. Further, spools can be changed without disturbing the drag setting. Other specifications: Full bail pickup (manual type available); full anodizing to prevent corrosion. Weighs 19 oz., has a fast 3.88:1 retrieve ratio, holds anywhere from 350 yds. of 10-lb. line to 185 yds. of 20 lb.

Approximate price of the Mastereel, $37.95.

**The Larchmont, FB412,** weighs 12 oz., has a 3.44:1 retrieve, full bail, exclusive Feurer Brothers quadrant-drag brake, and is designed for both light salt-water and heavy fresh-water duty. Its large-spool capacity goes from 200 yds. of 8-lb. test to 125 yds. of 15 lb. With its smaller spool it holds 140 yds. of 8-lb. or 125 of 10 lb.

Approximate price, packed with two spools, $35.75

**Heddon Reel**

New from Heddon are four salt-water trolling reels. Two of them are the **445** and **450,** both with a double frame for extra strength, sturdy star drag, metal spool and free spool action. **No. 445** has a 3:1 gear ratio, 2-1/8" spool, 3-1/16" plate diameter,

weighs 20 oz., holds 200 yds. of 20-lb. mono. **No.450** has a 2½" spool width, 2-5/8" plate diameter, weighs 19 oz., takes 200 yds. of 36-lb. nylon or 30-lb. Dacron.

Approximate list prices: **445,** $19.39; **450,** $20.93.

The other two new marine trolling reels from Heddon are **409** and **499.** They share these specifications: Level-wind mechanism; metal spool; smooth star drag; free spooling; 3:1 retrieve. The **409** has single-frame construction, 2-1/8" spool, 3-1/16" plate diameter, holds 300 yds. of 20-lb. monofilament, weighs 20 oz. **No. 499** has double-frame construction, 1-3/4" spool width, 2-5/8" plate diameter, takes 250 yds. of 15-lb. mono, weighs 14 oz.

Approximate prices: **409,** $28.42; **499,** $22.40.

**Zebco XRL80 Spinning Reel**

The "RL" in its name indicates that it's convertible to right- or left-hand use. It's designed for surf, boat and pier duty, including heavy assignments. Among its features: Die-cast aluminum body and cowl;

precision, heavy-duty gears; oil-retaining bronze bearings; spring-loaded, multiple-disc drag; selective anti-reverse; stainless steel bail arm with hard-chromed roller guide; strong aluminum alloy handle with torpedo grip; removable spool of anodized aluminum, parafin-impregnated against corrosion; and corrosion resistance throughout. Weighs 19-3/4 oz., holds 220 yds. of 20-lb. line.

Approximate price: $18.00 to $20.00.

**The Ambassadeurs, by Garcia**

Garcia offers several series of these revolving spool reels for baitcasting and a range of other marine and fresh-water assignments. They call their Ambassadeur **10000C** a light-tackle big-game reel for any kind of boat or surf action. Its extra-wide

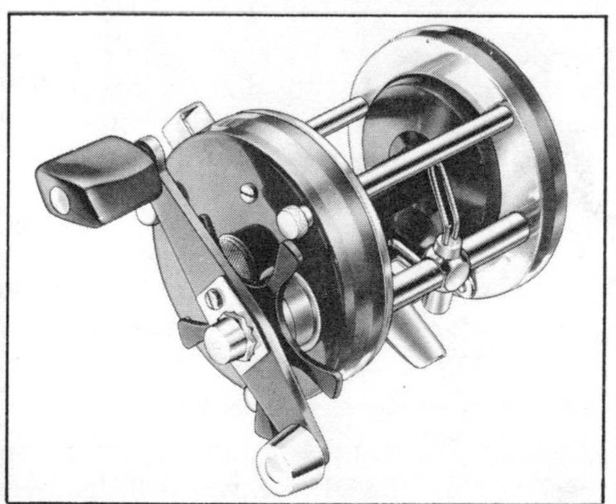

spool rolls on Swedish, precision, stainless steel ball bearings for casting distance, takes up to 475 yds. of Garcia' s 30-lb. Royal Bonnyl line. A big feature is the dual retrieve rate. Its high gear retrieves line at a rapid 4¼:1, but with a fish on it it automatically shifts to a lower 2½:1 for muscle. Also a feature is Garcia's exclusive centrifugal brake to cut down on backlashes in casting.

Approximate price: $80.00.

**Garcia's Ambassadeur 7000**

A husky "mill" rated for hard fighters in either salt water or fresh—kingfish, yellowtails, striped bass, tarpon up to 100 lbs., lake trout, salmon and steelheads.

Equipped with a level wind, its solid aluminum spool on an axle of Swedish stainless steel evenly distributes up to 350 yds. of 25-lb. Royal Bonnyl, brings it in at a fast 4:1. Other bonus features: Free spool that automatically re-engages in retrieves; star drag; four-block centrifugal brake working with its adjustable mechanical brake to virtually eliminate backlashes. Like other Ambassadeurs, the **7000** features no-tool takedown.

Approximate price: $65.00.

**Mitchell Spinning Reels**

The manufacturer of Garcia and Mitchell reels offers a sizable family of these reels for salt water and fresh water.

Representing the tribe here is the Mitchell **330**. An automatic bail that swings out of the way in casting, closing the instant a retrieve is begun, heads a long list of

features including: Teflon drag; constant-cycle gears with a 3.7:1 retrieve ratio; brash bushings. The **330** comes with two spools, each with a drag built in, that change quickly by merely pressing a button—without disturbing the drag. Also with an automatic bail and oilite main shaft bushings, but with a rapid 4.8:1 retrieve and two sets of roller bearings, is the Mitchell **440** (also available as the **441** for left-handed fishermen).

Approximate prices: Mitchell **330**, $24.00; Mitchell **440**, $26.00.

### Daiwa's 8000 Series Spinning Reels

One representative in the series is model **8600**, weighing 17 oz., with a retrieve of 3.7:1 and a capacity of 250 yds. of 15-lb. line. Features include: One-piece, drop-forged, machine-cut spiral gears for strong, smooth retrieves; three sealed, stainless steel ball bearings; spring-loaded drag with Teflon washers; hard-chromed stainless steel line roller, supported by a magnesium alloy cam; non-corroding spool. Price about $42.

Also in the 8000 series, at $35 each, are: **No. 8100**, a light 9 oz., with a sealed stainless steel ball bearing, spring-loaded snap-off spool. Some of the other features of the **8100:** fast 4.6:1 retrieve, spool capacity of 200 yds. of 6-lb. line; and the **No. 8300,** incorporating two sealed stainless steel ball bearings, several 8100 features, 3.7:1 gear ratio, and capacity of 200 yds. of 12-lb. line.

### The 7000 Series by Daiwa

It offers five models, budget-priced from $5.25 for the 7-oz. **7270** to $25.03 for the 22-oz. **7700.** The **7270** features simplicity of design, "trouble-free command action,"

single-piece bail, 3.2:1 retrieve, a capacity of 220 yds. of 8-lb. line. Model **7700** specifications include: Swedish steel bail with lifetime Permalast line guide; anodized spool; crown face gears; 3.4:1 retrieve; capacity of 225 yds. of 25-lb. test. It weighs 22 oz. In between those two, each with its list of Daiwa features, are the 8½-oz. **7280** ($8.05), 12-oz. **7300** ($14.53), and 15-oz **7600** ($22.75).

### Electric Reels by Miya Epoch U.S.A.

Would you believe an electric spinning reel? New is this Miya Epoch **500**, fed by a

12-volt (d.c.) rechargeable battery. It's balanced to be operable with one hand, holds 164 yds. of 30-lb. nylon line or 220 yds. of 25-lb. test. Its retrieve is described as fast. Its hoisting power and "fishing power" are given as 20 lb. and 55 lb., respectively.

Price of the Miya Epoch **500**, with switch and battery cord, $165. Battery comes in its own shoulder case, with a mini-tester, $39.99. Compact charger for 6- or 12-volt batteries, $19.99.

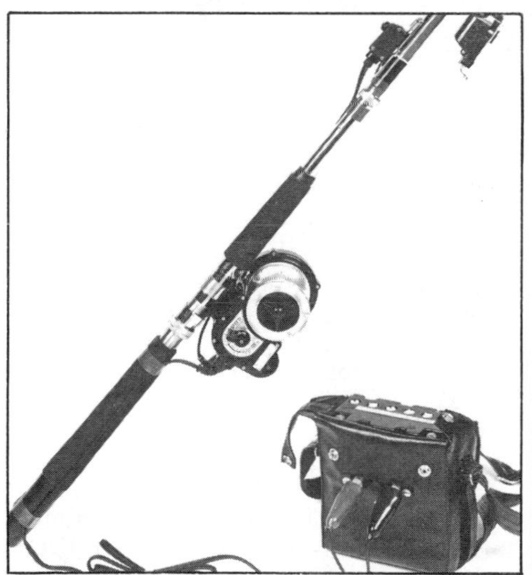

There is also an electric-driven (12 v.) revolving spool reel designed for boat fishing, salt water or fresh (heavier assignments). It features a two-stage, variable speed, high-torque motor in a black housing, with a specially constructed transmission for strong-hoisting power. The motor has a maximum high speed of 500 r.p.m., maximum low speed of 335 r.p.m. Hoisting power is 7.7 lb. maximum in high speed, 13.2 lb. maximum in low. Fishing power is listed at 44 lb.

Prices, including battery cord, switch and handle: $99 with plastic spool, $109 with metal spool.

## Line Department

For half a century quality fishing lines have been the name of the game at Cortland Line. And there isn't a kind of angling, from ultra-light flyrodding to heavy-duty off-shore ocean action, for which Cortland doesn't have lines. It need only be added that they wouldn't have stayed in business for fifty years if they didn't turn out good products.

Cortland turns out so many salt-water lines that we can't possibly display them all here, but we'll show a representation just to give you an idea.

There's the long-popular Greenspot trolling line, made from braided Dacron, with all the inherent advantages of that material. Greenspot has taken its share of world records, and—this is important for record-minded hopefuls—meets IGFA strength-class specifications. Its color is sand, with distinctive green spots. It comes in strengths from 12/10-lb. test (first figure is IGFA class, second figure is minimum wet test) to 130/117, and in spools from 50 to 1,200 yds.

**Cortland's Cam-O-Flage Monofilament**

A limp line that changes color every foot or so to be "the sneakiest monofilament

ever," with controlled stretch and high tenacity. In strengths from 4- to 60-lb. test, in 100-yd. spools and bulk spools.

**Squidding Line, by Cortland**

Many anglers are divided according to preference for braided or monofilament lines. Many others use both, according to conditions. Cortland's squidding line is braided nylon, offered in two colors, dark green or sand, with the manufacturer's Dry-Seald finish, Therm-Set for low stretch. You can get it in strengths from 18-lb. test to 108, on spools from 50 yds. up, including bulk lengths. Offered with the same choice of colors, strength range and spool lengths is Cortland's trolling line.

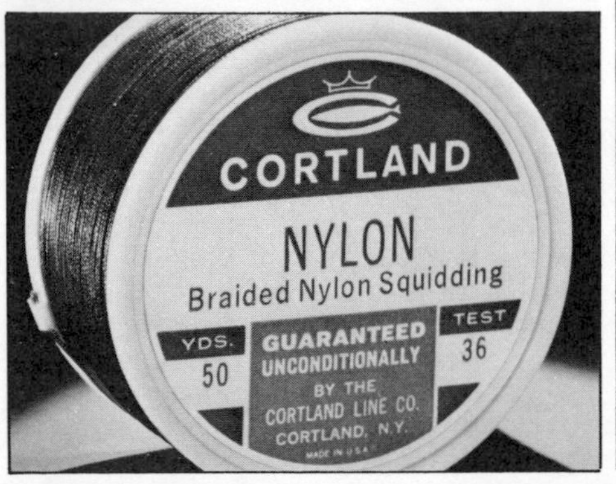


Among this producer's many other lines, in strengths ranging collectively from 10-lb. test to 50, are: Heart-O-Gold nylon casting (braided); Monowire, a solid, stainless steel kink-resistant alloy; Micron (mini-diameter fiber) casting and trolling, also Micron braided spinning line; 7-Star monofilament and, from France, Nylorfi mono.

Cortland also manufactures a full array of fresh-water and fly lines.

**Newton's Ghost Dacron Line**

Made for surf fishing and big-game trolling, Newton's Ghost line meets IGFA specifications in all strengths, 20- to 130-lb. test. Low stretch (a Dacron asset), the manufacturer's extra-hard finish for abrasion resistance, and a diameter that is consistent and small for the lines' strengths are important details. On spools from 50 yds. up.

**Newton Monofilament Lines**

They include the Master, E.S.P. and Miracle labels. All three have controlled limpness for casting ease and accuracy, controlled stretch for maximum hook-setting power and strength. Master mono is low-visibility platinum gray, in strengths from 4- to 40-lb. test. Newton's E.S.P. mono comes in bronze or blue, 4-lb. test to 50. Miracle mono offers a choice between aqua or mist color in twelve tests, 4-lb. to 60-lb. Among the three, yardage per spool starts at 100, goes up into bulk lengths.

**Laker Lead-Core Line, by Newton**

For deep trolling, it features a soft lead center inside braided nylon, with a smooth, tough plastic coating for easy handling, lengthy life, prevention of core break-through. The line is color-coded at 10-yd. intervals so you can tell how much is out. In 18-, 27- and 40-lb. tests, packed two 100-yd. spools to a box.

**Sevenstrand Stainless Steel Wire**

For leaders. Twisted from the highest quality stainless steel wire. Each size is twisted into the "proper lay" for its diameter, heat-treated for greater flexibility, more uniform strength throughout and a bronze camouflage finish. Extremely small diameter for its strength.

In tests from 8-lb. up to 250-lb., in 30-ft. coils and on spools of 300 ft. and more.

**Sevalon Nylon-Covered Sevenstrand Wire**

With amazing diameter for its strength (thinner than monofilament of equal rating), this wire has added flexibility and kink-resistance provided by a thin covering of nylon. Available in the same strengths and lengths as Sevenstrand stainless steel wire.

**U.S. Line Company**

In 1975 U.S. Line Company marked its fifty-third anniversary. And since fishing lines have been its specialty all along, it goes without saying that this manufacturer produces a great assortment. Here are some representatives:

**U.S. Mahogany King-Oval:** Oval monofilament designed specifically for free-spooling conventional reels. Lies flat on a reel, has high knot strength. In tests from 12-lb. to 60-lb.

**U.S. Mascot:** All-around line, braided DuPont nylon, in 15- and 24-lb. tests.

**U.S. Beach King:** For surf and shore fishing, in a natural sea-sand color. Rated as easy to cast. Smooth-braided nylon, deep treated with anti-friction, salt-waterproof dressing to cut down on thumb burns, provide minimum friction in casting and retrieving. In tests from 18-lb. to 96-lb., with minimum diameter for strength.

**U.S. Dacron Troll-A-Line:** For light- to heavy-tackle sea duty, in 20-, 30-, 50-, 80-, 130-lb. tests. Made from DuPont Dacron polyester fiber, whitish in color with an identifying strand of black. Also available in tan. Also in bulk spools, same tests, for filling bigger reels.

U.S. Line also offers these deep trolling and wire labels, ranging in strengths overall from 10-lb. to 60-lb. test: Deep Water Lead-Core; Almet 304 Wire; Dark Monel; Bright Monel; SS305 Nylon Coated Stainless Steel.

**Monofilament Lines by Ande Inc.**

You can get Ande monofilament in tests from 2 lb. through 300 lb. They come in two finishes, premium and regular. Quality of the lines in the two finishes is identical, the only difference being that the premium has a sheen, whereas the regular has a matte (dull) finish. Ande Tournament Mono is available in IGFA 6-, 12-, 20-, 30-, 50-, 80- and 130-lb. line classes. Line colors include gunmetal, blue, pink, clear and tournament green. In support of the ever-widening popularity of Ande monofilament lines is the manufacturer's claim that they have figured in the establishment of seventy-five world records around the globe.

**Sunset Lines**

Sunset Line & Twine Company produces a wide range of lines to cover marine and fresh-water assignments, including flyrodding. Here are some representatives:

**Troll Queen:** Spliceable, braided Dacron trolling line in IGFA class sizes, 12- to 130-lb. test, plus an unlimited class that tests out at 165 lb. wet. It has Dacron's abrasion resistance (a factor in fishing among rocks), as well as exceptional knot strength. Colors are green and sand.

**707 Unifilament Oval Nylon:** Sunset calls it the first single-filament, ribbon-shaped nylon. It's designed to combine the best features of both braided line and monofilament. It's flat, so it won't dig in on a reel, and it has the smallness of round monofilament, but won't coil in casts. Also has excellent knot strength. In silver gray, packaged as 2 connected 50-yd. spools. In tests from 12-lb. to 50-lb.

**Surf King Squidding Line:** Sunset's best nylon surf-squidding line. A small-diameter, coreless braid that flattens on a reel spool to increase its capacity and to cast smoothly. Other features: Pre-stretching to keep elongation at a minimum; tough silicone treatment for reduced wear, increased casting distance. In tests from 12 lb. to 110 lb., packaged as six connected 60-yd. spools in a plastic utility box.

**Tel-A-Depth Weighted Trolling Line:** A braided jacket of no-stretch Dacron over a special core of soft lead alloy, soft and pliable to resist kinking. This line has a color change every 30 feet, ten colors, to aid in judging yardage. Comes as two connected 10-yd. spools in a box. Four strengths—18-, 27-, 36- and 45-lb. tests.

**Micro-X Dacron Trolling Line:** Braided Dacron in all IGFA line classes, 12- to 130-

lb. test, guaranteed not to exceed classification standards and so jeopardize potential records. Also available in an unlimited class (165-lb. test, wet). In sand, greenspot and bluespot colors. In spools from 50 yds. to 1,000 and 3,000 yds.

Sunset also markets a family of monofilament lines whose collective strengths range from 2- to 60-lb. test. Look for these labels: Flexon; Marked Flexon (red marker every 10'); Limpy; Crystal Polished Monofilament; TX-50; and Special Dependable Monofilament. Budget-minded anglers will find that last one interesting. It comes in strengths from 4-lb. to 40-lb., mist blue color, twelve spools per carton.

### Gladding-South Bend Lines

One hundred sixty years is a long time to be in the fishing line business—or any business. That's Gladding's record, which should make it just about the oldest line maker in the U.S. Gladding has amassed considerable expertise in 160 years, and now produces a huge family of lines for every assignment from flipping a featherweight fly to whipping a half-ton marlin.

**Gladding Trident Greenspot:** Braided Dacron and billed as having the smallest diameter per pounds-test of all braided salt-water lines—thus, giving the greatest reel capacity. Other features include the maker's Fiberlubed process and heat-set finish. It comes in IGFA 12- through 130-lb. classes, packaged as six 50-yd. spools and six 150-yd. spools, in hinged plastic boxes either way. It's also available in 600- and 1,000-yd. spools, individually boxed.

**Super Squidding Line:** Sand color, in 18-, 27-, 36- and 45-lb. tests, on 150-yd. spools.

**Gladding Depth-Finder Mono:** Supple, strong, yet extra-soft. In eight strengths, 6-lb. tests through 30 lb. And it's color-metered every ten yards to help show payoff levels. Comes on 100- and 200-yd. spools.

Among its monofilament lines Gladding offers these six labels: Mercury; Gladyl; Clearon; Super; L-B Nylon; Champion. Overall their strengths range from 2-lb. test to 60 lb. They're available in lengths from the popular 100-yd. spools on up to bulk quantities.

### Garcia's Braided Dacron Trolling Line

Now made from DuPont's newly developed high-tenacity Dacron for finer diameter than ever (meaning more line on a spool) and minimum stretch. Each strand is lubricated **before** braiding to eliminate internal friction, a big cause of line wear. It also allows knots to be drawn snug and tight, without piling or binding. This line

can be spliced too. It comes in all IGFA classes, 6-lb. through 130-lb., and 162-lb. test. It's guaranteed to break within 5 percent **under** its labeled strength, so there can be no IGFA disqualification on that score. Available as six connected 50-yd. spools and in single bulk spools of 500 to 1,200 yds.

### Royal Bonnyl

Royal Bonnyl represents a formula in monofilament research that required years to develop and test. The results are these starred features: Thinner, pound for pound,

than standard monofilament; increased spool capacity and casting distance; consistently uniform diameter, micrometer-measured; extra-hard finish; highly abrasion resistant, chip-proof, can't cut into itself; a balanced combination of limpness and springiness to make it lie firmly on a spool, yet handle nicely in casting. Available in strengths from 2-lb. test to 80. Packaged as two and six connected 100-yd. spools in boxes, also on long-length spools.

**Garcia's Nylon Squidding Line**

A popular surfcasting line with braided-in lubrication to minimize internal friction, special waterproofing to reduce absorption,

smooth suppleness, and proper amount of stretch, heat-set. In 18-, 27-, 36- and 45-lb. tests. Comes on two or six connected 50-yd. spools and on 1,000-yd. spools.

**Garcia's Lead-Core Trolling Line**

For deep trolling. It carries a flexible lead core permanently sheathed in a strong,

tightly braided nylon sleeve, and is color-coded every ten yards so you know how much is out. In 18-, 25-, 40-, 60-lb. tests. Comes on two connected 50-yd. spools and two connected 100-yd. spools.

**Invisible Monofilament**

Garcia's Invisible Monofilament, a popularly priced mono, has a specially formulated color that is highly visible in air

yet virtually "disappears" in water—a big advantage in very clear water and with "spooky" fish. And it knots well, minimizing poor knots, the biggest single cause of monofilament breakage. Available in 13 strengths, 2 lb. to 60 lb. Packaged as two and six connected 100-yd. spools, also on long-length spools of 1/8 lb. to 1 lb.

**Lines From Shakespeare**

**No. 5000 Braided Mono:** Yes, you read it right, this is **braided monofilament,** a new concept that combines a braided line's manageability with the casting quality and toughness of monofilament. Noted for Shakespeare's 5000 are lack of stretch, extreme softness, freedom from twist, long wear and strong knots. Pure white, it comes on a 200-yd. spool in 12-, 15-, 20-, 25- and 30-lb. tests.

**No. 4477 Thin Troll Wire Line:** An extremely supple, 7-strand, stainless steel wire line in extra-fine diameters. About it Shakespeare says: "It sinks fast, runs virtually drag-free, and resists kinks like crazy." In strengths from 20-lb. test to 125. For regular trolling and downrigger use it comes on 200-yd. spools, but also is available in bulk.

**No. 6000 Salt Water Mono:** A premium grade monofilament with great shock power, minimum stretch, and a tough finish. It also incorporates Shakespeare's Guide-Glide formula for smooth flowing and casting distance. Color is a pale greenish. Comes in 12 strengths, 8 lb. to 100 lb., on ¼- and 1.7 lb. spools.

**No. 4499X Braided Dacron:** A soft-braid, small-diameter line designed for all-around sea duty, including bottom bouncing. Available in 12-, 20-, 30-, 50-, 80- and 130-lb. tests. Sold on 50-yd. connected spools and on 1,200-yd. bulk spools.

**Tycoon/Fin-Nor Lines**

Although designed for all-around service, Tycoon/Fin-Nor lines are made especially for tournament fishing. Each spool is break-tested 3 times, recorded on the label, individually numbered; thoroughly tested for uniformity of strength and diameter, with results recorded with a serial number and affixed to the spool.

**Tycoon/Fin-Nor Gold Bond Dacron:** Resistance to abrasion, uniformity of test and accuracy in stretch control make this an excellent tournament line. Comes in five strengths, 20- to 130-lb. test, and lengths of 500 to 1,200 yds.

Tycoon/Fin-Nor also offers Tournament Monofilament, 6- to 80-lb. test, in lengths of 600 to 1,000 yds.

## FISHING LINES BY ASHAWAY

Founded in 1824, then incorporated as Ashaway Line & Twine in 1883, the Ashaway people started bending their efforts to the manufacture of quality fishing lines back in 1903. Since then the firm has claimed several firsts, like the first commercial use of monofilament nylon (1939), the first heat treatment of lines (1946), and introduction of the first Dacron fishing lines (1952). As you can imagine, Ashaway has developed a sizable family of lines. Here are some representatives of the salt-water group:

**Green Back:** Braided, spliceable, coreless, Dacron trolling line with low elasticity, high knot strength, rot-resistance. Green Back comes in 12- to 130-lb. tests, is guaranteed to be within IGFA line classes. It's available as six connected 100-yd. spools and on 500- and 1,200-yd. spools for big-game reels.

**1319 Squidding Line:** Waterproof, lubricated, abrasion-resistant, needs no drying, sand color. Made for both squidding and heavy fresh-water action. Semi-flat construction prevents over tight packing on reels. Wet tests: 14-, 18-, 25-, 36-, 54-, 63-, 72-, 90-, 108-lb. Comes as six connected 50-yd. spools.

**Griffin Sport:** This is a lead-loaded, multicolored, deep trolling line, pliable but with a strong nylon cover. Comes in wet-test strengths of 18-, 25-, 40- and 60-lb., with 10-yd. color separations. Also available as four connected 50-yd. spools with 5-yd. color separations.

**Gudebrod Line**

Another old, widely known and highly respected producer of marine and fresh-water lines is Gudebrod Fishing Tackle, a division of Gudebrod Brothers Silk Company, Philadelphia.

Among their labels is the **G-6** Trolling Line, a tournament-quality line for all salt-water and fresh-water trolling. Features: Dacron's low stretch for more sensitive contact and instant striking power; precision braiding for a smooth finish, strength in fine diameter, low water drag; proofed against mildew and rot, requires no drying. In bluespot and greenspot colors (and white, 6-lb. test only). All IGFA line classes and 180-lb. unlimited, and meeting IGFA specifications. Comes as six connected 100-yd. spools, also in 500- and 1,200-yd. spools individually boxed, those long lengths in 20-lb. test and up, with a free splicing needle.

**Gudebrod Green Dart Monofilament:** For spinning, casting trolling, all types of spinning and casting, reels. Ultra-soft and limp, it handles well, lies snug. Conventional-reel users will like its easy thumbing. Other details: Thin, uniform diameter; high knot strength; special translucent green color that becomes almost invisible in water. In strengths from 4- to 50-lb. Packed as two and six connected

100-yd. spools, also as 500-yd., ½-lb. and 1-lb. spools, boxed individually. (In case you're toying with the idea of getting a 1-lb. spool of 4-lb. Green Dart, maybe you ought to know that it contains about 13,500 yards.)

Gudebrod also offers its budget-priced Silver Crest Monofilament and, at even lower cost, Gem Monofilament.

Gudebrod's G.T. Dacron Lines for casting (**No. 603**) and trolling (**No. 604**) have a particularly interesting detail in that they are Teflon-coated to reduce line friction and guide wear and eliminate

mildew and rot problems. Both are greenspot color.

**No. 603:** For plugging and surfcasting, a slick line with all of Dacron's assets, plus the Teflon coating to keep it drier and lighter. In tests from 5-lb. to 45-lb., 100-yd. connected spools in a two pack and six pack, as well as 500- and 1,200-yd. spools boxed individually.

**No. 604:** Gudebrod calls it their finest trolling line. Braided with great care to meet IGFA specifications. For all marine and fresh-water trolling assignments, with the inherent advantages of Dacron and the Teflon coating as a bonus. No. 604 is available in IGFA classes from 6- to 130-lb. test. Comes packed as six connected 100-yd. spools, and in 500- and 1,200-yd. spools boxed individually with free splicing needle and instructions for use.

# Fresh-Water Tackle Showroom 5

In broad classifying we split all tackle—conventional kind, spinning and fly fishing —into salt-water and fresh-water divisions. About the only purpose this serves, really, is to indicate an overall difference in weight or "caliber" of equipment between the two. Marine tackle is heavier than that employed in freshwater fishing simply because it is aimed at larger opponents. Otherwise the two divisions are the same. That is, the components in a spinning rod, in one division, are indentical in nature to those of its counterpart in the other; a fresh-water revolving-spool reel possesses the same fundamental anatomy as its marine contemporary; a salt-water fly rod is merely a big brother to a fresh-water model; and so on.

Conditions being within reason, tackle can be wielded interchangeably, fresh water and salt-water. The only possible major difference, all other factors being equal, is that some fresh-water equipment may not be as heavily protected against salt corrosion. This doesn't prevent interchangeability. It just means that its owner should clean corrosion-vulnerable parts after exposure to salt water.

Most important, details to check and quality criteria are the same for comparable tackle in both divisions. Those for conventional-type and spinning equipment are pointed out in the beginning of the "**Salt-Water Tackle Showroom**".

## ICE FISHING EQUIPMENT

It seems that no matter what we humans do, other humans are sitting on the sidelines trying to figure out why we do it. Fishing through the ice is no exception. "Analysts" have offered assorted explanations—take your pick of these: It's good sport and gets food for the table. For active anglers it bridges a long gap between regular seasons, helping to lessen winter tedium. It's just something to do, a healthful activity that gets one out in the sun and air at a time of year when one otherwise might be cooped up. Or, in the opposite direction and less kindly, it must be some odd compulsion that makes people brave frigid temperatures and polar winds. The ice adds a special aura of mystery and suspense. It's an opportunity to walk on water, a feat otherwise impossible for mortals and therefore strangely attractive.

Then there's the simplest, most logical explanation of all, one often overlooked by non-participating observers: People just like ice fishing.

Well, so much for "analyses." Whatever their motivations, increasing numbers of new ice anglers are out on the ice every year.

### The Techniques

Broadly speaking, there are two principal methods, jigging and using a device known as a tip-up or tilt, and there are the usual regional variations. Both methods call for simple, inexpensive equipment.

**Jigging:** This is usually employed for species an angler can expect to hook in fair numbers—yellow perch, bluegills, smelt, other panfishes. So the technique is based on trying different spots until a school or "pocket" of fish is encountered. This means some work, since a hole must be cut through the ice at each place tried, but a good catch is realized when contact is made.

In shallow-water jigging for panfishes such as bluegills and crappies the angler feels for nibbles before trying to plant his hook. Natural bait—worms, live minnows, grubs, etc.—is the attractor. In deeper-water operations the fisherman doesn't wait for bites, but employs what is known as a jig-and-snatch procedure. This consists of jigging the bait repeatedly, literally making it "dance" for eye-catching action, then suddenly jerking it upward, the idea being to "snatch" or hook a passing fish. Experienced jiggers can work fast enough to extract quite a few fish from a school with this mehod. A certain amount of speed is important because the rig must be returned to the water quickly after a fish is unhooked, before the others move off. Also to save time, bait in this deeper jigging should be tough as well as attractive, so it doesn't have to be replaced frequently. A bait commonly used is a piece cut from a local species.

Regular rod and reel combos are often wielded in jigging, but the traditional badge of the regular is a jigstick. As its name hints, this is merely a short stick. It has a handle on which line is stored and at its outer end is an eye or simple guide through which the line passes. Rig depth is determined by counting the turns of line as they leave the jigstick. The device is crude, but it works.

There are conventional-type rods designed for ice angling. These usually are short, under 4½ feet, since the wielder must be close to the hole in the ice. Typically, they're fairly stout in the section adjacent to the handle, to manage rigs and larger fishes at depths, but have a sensitive tip to feel the lightest nibbles and afford action with small pan species. Ice rods of this type usually do not carry reels, as their moving parts could freeze in bitter weather. Instead, they have a simple line-winder -- just two arms of wire -- from which line can be unwound as needed and for storage of line when not in use. They have one to three guides, according to length, and a tiptop. Wooden handles are standard, and some are outfitted with a cork grip.

They're simple in design because the wielders frequently are wearing gloves. And because of their simplicity they're quite inexpensive. The choice between a rod of this type and a jigstick is a matter of personal preference. It depends upon their respective models, but because of its construction an ice fishing rod can provide more action, especially with the smaller panfishes.

Monofilament line generally is favored. On an average, strengths do not exceed 10-pound test, and amount naturally depends upon depths fished. Hooks are scaled to the bait and sizes of the targets, and usually are small. A sinker of suitable weight, one to get the bait down fast in deeper-water action, completes the rig. Often the sinker is scraped to make it shiny and lend attraction. Flashy artificials and the so-called ice flies also are rigged, but usually in conjuction with natural bait.

**Tip-up or tilt fishing:** Whereas a jig angler is looking primarily for quantity, since his targets are small, the tip-up user generally is out after larger game, like walleyes, northerns, chain pickerel and, where permitted by law, trout and salmon. He usually sets out a number of tip-ups or tilts, again in compliance with any state laws governing their use, in what he believes are potentially productive locations. Then he sits by and waits for response, unlike the jigger who roams the ice to probe different places. In other words, the jig fisherman tries to go to the fish, while the tilt angler waits for fish to come to him. In this respect tip-up fishing demands more patience than the other. It also calls for more protection against cold.

Tip-ups vary a bit among models, but they all share similar essential components and the same manner of functioning. A tip-up's major parts are a spool to hold line and an arm—carrying a little flag on some models -- which is triggered into flying upward to signal a bite. There are two basic designs. Probably the most widely used is the above-ice type, whose line comes out through the hole in the ice to the arm-triggering mechanism. The other design has its line spool below the surface, where a bite causes it to turn and trigger the signal arm. Both kinds have their advantages and drawbacks. The above-ice type is much more convenient to handle when a fish is hooked. Further, it can be more sensitively adjusted to light nibbles. On the debit side, in very cold weather it requires frequent checking to be sure the hole hasn't refrozen around the line. Freeze-overs are not as much of a headache with the underwater type, since the line doesn't come up through the ice; but it has to be lifted from the hole before its line can be grasped, a hand-chilling chore.

Lines employed with tilts run heavier than those in jigging, not so much because of the larger fishes sought, although that's part of it, but because they're easier to handle when fingers are cold. The amount of line on a tip-up spool goes according to depths fished. After a rig has been lowered to its desired level there has to be sufficient additional yardage on the spool to handle any runs. A short leader of fine wire is added when toothy species such as pickerel and northerns are involved.

The most widely used tip-up bait is a live minnow, 2 to 5 or 6 inches long, even larger sometimes, according to the intended opponents. And because the bait is alive, hook sizes are gauged proportionately so as not to injure or kill it. A common practice is to tie a small snap-swivel on the end of the line to facilitate changing hooks. Like their salt-water brethren, tip-up fishermen carry sinkers in assorted sizes, using only enough weight to take a rig to the desired depth and hold it there.

## Accessory Gear, Other Equipment

Obviously, some means of cutting through ice is a necessity. This is accomplished with either a spud or an auger. The former is a long-handled implement with a sharp metal end for chopping. It is hard work, but effective, and for years a spud was **the** tool for the job. Then the ice auger was developed. It drills a hole in fairly short order, and many ice fishermen favor it over the spud because it bores a smoother hole, without jagged edges that could snag lines or hamper landing of fish. Ice augers are marketed in various diameters. Most of them are hand-operated, but there are powered models for those anglers with the price.

Once a hole is chopped or drilled, it must be kept free of ice. Designed for the task is a long-handled skimmer or scoop, another essential. Helpful is a brush or broom for sweeping away any snow at a hole site.

After making a hole through the ice, the next step in either jigging or tilt fishing is to determine water depths so rigs can be dangled at the proper levels. A simple sounding-line is all that's needed to measure depths. It's merely a length of stout twine or line carrying a heavy sinker. Marking it at intervals is a good idea. Often experimentation at different levels is required to find the payoff zones, by the way.

Ice fishing frequently lures its buffs some distance from shore, especially on large lakes, so it's important that they have everything they need for the day's activity with them. High on the list is an ample supply of bait, along with one of those carriers designed to keep minnows alive. In addition to required equipment, ice anglers carry spare hooks, line and sinkers, plus extras of any line hardware they may use. Regulars add a hand gaff for dealing with the large fishes. It can spell the difference between a catch and a loss when lifting a husky, lively fish upward through the hole.

A portable, self-contained depth sounder can be useful in fishing through the ice, just as it is in open water. (More on this in the chapter "Electronic Aids to Fishing.")

How is all this stuff transported out on the ice? No problem. Participants improvise with assorted vehicles. Simplest is a sturdy wooden box, with or without crude runners that has a short length of rope for towing. There are youngsters' sleds and some homemade jobs, too. The going is tricky, but on large lakes with thick enough ice it wouldn't be startling to see automobiles.

Most important for enjoyment of this sport is protection against cold and wind—and stress the latter. In few other kinds of angling— indeed, in few other winter sports—is proper clothing so important. Ice fishermen often are at the mercy of a frigid wind sweeping across a lake, and in tip-up tending there's relatively little moving around.

Thermal underwear is important. Insulated garments provide warmth without bulk or excessive weight (See "Clothing for Fishing"). Particular consideration should be given to items that keep the wind out. Wind contributes greatly to the chill factor. Protection of head and face also is an important consideration. A ski mask is practical. So is a parka with a warm, insulated hood, and it's even better if the hood has a drawstring to tighten it around the face. A hat with ear flaps is just about minimum head protection—but none at all if a breeze sends it skating across the ice.

Get the right footwear. It should be insulated and completely waterproof —accent the latter. Sooner or later, shoes that are not waterproof will get wet on the ice from slush, snow and water, and soggy shoes mean miserably cold feet. Best is all-rubber footwear. Recommended are hunter's boots, fully waterproof because of a rubber exterior, warmly lined, and reaching above the ankles. Keeping the ankles warm is part of the battle too.

And don't forget sunglasses. Glare from ice and snow can be rough on the eyes.

Veteran ice fishermen devise additional protection. Many construct their own portable windbreaks, which can be set up and moved when the wind shifts. More elaborate are the little one-room shanties seen on northern comparative comfort,snug against the wind. Portable stoves make things even warmer and snugger.

Ice fishing isn't for everyone. But the sport does have a lot going for it and lots of popularity. If you're still skeptical, take a winter swing through the Midwest sometime.

## THE ROD DEPARTMENT

Berkley & Company turns out a very versatile range of conventional and spinning rods for fresh water and salt. One series is the Cherrywood Series for spinning. Lengths: 5' and 5½' for ultralight fishing, 5'3" and 5'9", featuring Berkley's "powerlite" action, for lures from 1/16 oz. to 3/4 oz. Also available in 7- to 8¼-ft. lengths. Construction details include specie cork grips, chrome-plated stainless steel guides and tiptop, anodized aluminum reel seat. Overall prices, $26.95 to $34.50.

Other Berkley series names are: Para/Metric Curt Gowdy Signature; Para/Metric Custom; Buccaneer; Tri-Sport; Fiber-Flex; Regulation-Thread Class. Among them are more conventional and spinning models, fresh-water and marine, for boat spinning, popping, trolling, steelhead/mooching, baitcasting, ultra-light action, etc. Berkley also offers a selection of fly rods.

**Berkley Rod & Reel Weekender (No. BRR-30):** The manufacturer bills it as an "all in one fishing outfit." Components are: Buccaneer 6½' tubular spinning rod, 5-piece pack rod model; Berkley 412 spinning reel carrying 250 yds. of 8-lb. Trilene XL line; 2 extra spools of Trilene XL in a

molded-polypropylene, 4-compartment lure box; ½-oz. marabou jig; booklets of fishing tips and knots. All in an impact-resistant carrier with a green, textured, non-glare finish. Overall size, 18" by 6½" wide by 5" deep. Price about $69.95. Also available at the same price is the **BRR-10** Weekender, equally complete but with spincasting equipment. Berkley markets several other rod travel packs and deluxe rod-reel travel pack outfits, from $35.95 up. King is item **No. PC8C**, an 8-rods-in-1 combination that contains four spinning, two fly fishing and two baitcasting/spincasting outfits, $250.

**Zebco Rods**

New in the Zebco family is the Sundowner rod series. Twelve models. Six for spinning: **No. 7050**, 5'6", light action, for light fresh-water spinning, through **7550**, 7'6", medium/heavy action, for heavy fresh-water and medium salt-water use, to **No. 7950**, 10', a heavy-action surf rod. Also six spincasting models: **No. 6300**, 6', deluxe, medium action, for all-round fresh-water fishing, through **8877**, 7', heavy action, for heavy fresh-water/medium salt-water, to **No. 8810**, heavy action, for all-round bassing. Sundowner features include: Zebco's exclusive Transa-Coil tubular glass—light but extra-strong, combining tip sensitivity with magnum power in the butt section; hard, chrome-plated stainless steel guides and tiptop; anodized aluminum reel seat; grips of specie cork; flared ABS butt cap for cushioning comfort. Color is an attractive brown. Price range: $14.00 to $23.00.

**Zebco's Pro Staff Rods:** The series was expanded for 1975, now offers eleven models—four spincasting, five spinning, two fly rods. Among their shared features: Transa-Coil to dissipate line friction heat, tubular glass with tough epoxy finish Slipstream guides, tiptop aluminum oxide with ABS shock ring inserts; anodized aluminum reel seat and reel seat hardware; grips of select burnt cork in a darker shade of brown for a rich-looking contrast; Zebco's unique flared ABS butt cap.

Spincasting: **PS10,** 6', medium action. **PS12,** 6'6", medium/heavy action; **PS30,** 5', deluxe worm rod; **PS32,** 5'6", worm action.

Spinning: **PS20,** 5'6", light action. **PS21,** 6'6", light/medium action. **PS22,** 6'6", medium action. **PS24,** 7', medium/heavy action. **PS29,** 5'9", worm action.

Fly fishing: **PS42,** 8'6", deluxe, bass action. **PS40,** 8', deluxe, trout action.

Price range of the Pro Staff series: $20.00 to $23.00.

**Fenwick HMG Graphite Rods**

Claimed as a first by Fenwick and introduced in 1974, these rods have been billed as "the greatest technological advance in fishing rods since fiberglass," "the ultimate," and "for fishermen who must have the finest rod made." Other plaudits include "near-incredible action and power characteristics" and great capabilities.

In simplified explanation the HMG rods' material could be called a happy wedding of Fenwick's advanced design technology, graphite, and the manufacturer's own resin systems. The result is a rod unlike either fiberglass or bamboo. Its action is unique. Then there's the weight—or, rather, lack of it. An HMG rod is exceptionally light, yet extremely durable. Also very noticeable is the vibration-dampening factor, important in casting. HMG rods cease vibrating almost at once. Further, they have been acclaimed for their sensitivity, and this, coupled with their dampening factor, means a clearer message telegraphed along the shaft to the angler.

General price range of the Fenwick HMG rods is: $90.00 to $150.00.

**Rods by Pflueger**

These long-time tackle builders offer several versions of their Powerods. Among them is a series for baitcasting.

**Powerod 104BC:** Designed by professionals for all plugcasting and worm fishing. Starred features are a new, deluxe, extra-light pistol grip handle—detachable, with anodized gold collar—all Fuji guides and tiptop, smooth fiberglass cloth finish with gold trim and simulated gold, diamond-style wrap. Designated as **No. 104BC,** it

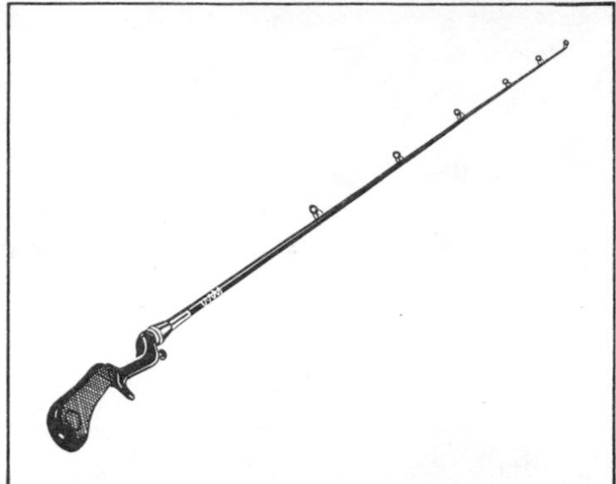

comes 5'6" and 6', each with 5 guides and medium-heavy action. They match and balance Pflueger's **610-B** and **611-B** Supreme reels. Priced from $20.00 to $30.00.

Another Pflueger Powerod for baitcasting is in the Medalist series, **No. 202BC,** in lengths from 5' to 6', with medium-fast tip to heavy action, cork grips, stainless steel guides and Carboloy tiptop, one-piece tubular construction. For plugs, spoons, worm fishing. Approximate price: $15.00 to $25.00.

**Pflueger push-button Powerods for spincasting: No. 202PB** is in the Medalist series. Specifications include: 6' and 6'6" lengths, 6 3/4 and 7 oz., light action, tubular fiberglass, stainless steel guides and Carboloy tiptop, nickel-plated, wrapped and double-coated brass ferrules, cork foregrip and new, oversized cork rear grip. Approximate price: $15.00 to $25.00.

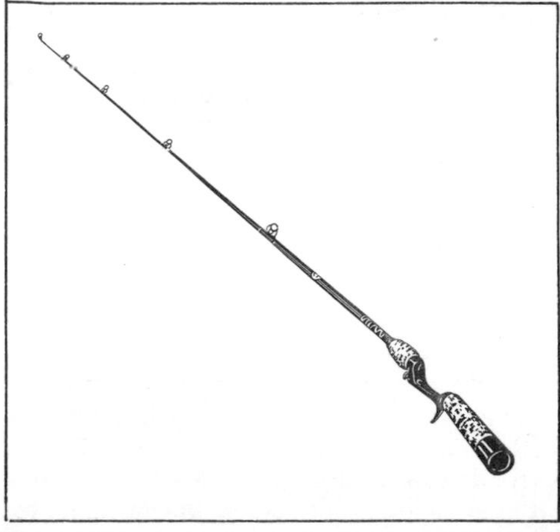

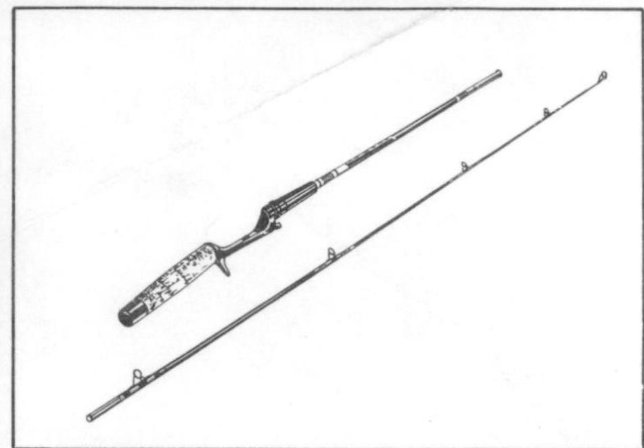

**No. 481PB** is a new, budget-priced tubular glass rod with such quality features as wrapped ferrules, deluxe double offset handle with select specie cork grip. This push-button Powerod is 6' long, has medium-light action, 4 guides. Approximate price: $10.00 to $20.00.

**Stillfish Equipment**

**Panfishing rod-reel combination by Stillfish Corp.:** Reel is built in, rod telescopes for easier carrying. According to model, lengths extend to 8', 10' and more, and telescope to either 55" or 63". High-impact styrene reel is 3½" long, comes pre-spooled with 48' of 12-lb. monofilament. Fold-away crank handle locks line. Rod is gold color, reel is green, Approximate retail prices for from $12.50 to $24.50. Line is inside the rod, incidentally. If it breaks, it can be rethreaded in five minutes with wire threader provided.

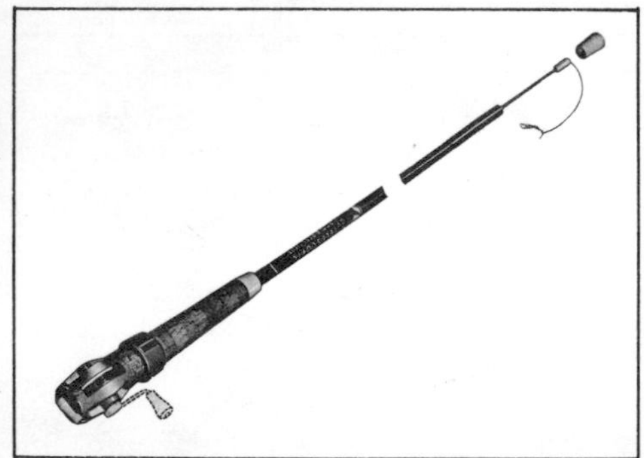

The outfit also is available in a child's model, a two-section fiberglass rod that extends to 4' and floats. Telescopes to 26", weighs 4 oz. Line being inside the rod prevents it from tangling. High-impact styrene reel. Comes complete with 48' of 12-lb. line, bobber, swivel, fishing instructions, about $6.50, retail.

Also comes in an ice fishing version, three models, one or two-section, extending from 26" to 48", telescoping to 15" or 19", about $6 retail, all models.

**Martin Reel Rods**

Martin Reels Company, "The fly Tackle People," produces several cleverly conceived travel sets. Model **9264** Sovereign Travel Set will outfit you for action in both fresh-water and salt-water arenas. Among

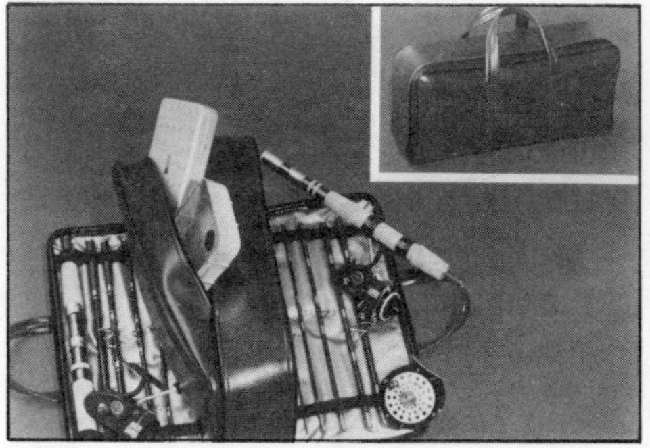

its components: Martin tubular rods **No. 31-666**, 6½', for spinning/fly action, and **No. 1-666**, 6½', for salt-water spinning; **Model 104** spinning reel, with ball bearings, helical gears, Teflon drag, 5:1 retrieve; Martin's **804SRM** salt-water spinning reel, 4.75;1 retrieve, ball bearing-mounted helical gears; **No. 66** single-action fly reel with push-button spool release, click drags; **No. 641** fly box; **99002** lure box. All in a good-looking Naugahyde case, 16½" by 7½" by 4½" with room for extra spools, and more. About $199.95, retail.

Martin's **No. 8570** spincasting Portage series travel set is tailor-made for fresh-water buffs: 5½' tubular rod with locking reel seat and matching Martin **700** closed-face reel with star drag, tough steel gear system, 8-point, chromed pickup, quick-change spool. Comes in a trim Naugahyde case that fits into an attache case or back pack. Approximate retail price, $60.95.

Also available as travel sets are Martin's Portage rods, in Naugahyde cases, as well as Bretton and Portage series rods

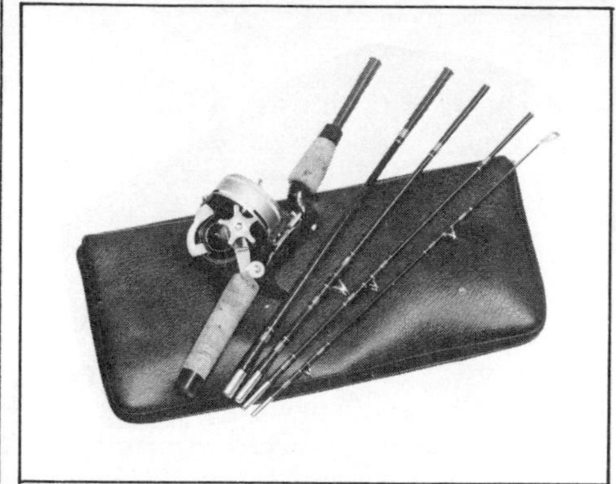

available separately. The rod range includes models for flycasting and worm fishing to salt-water spinning.

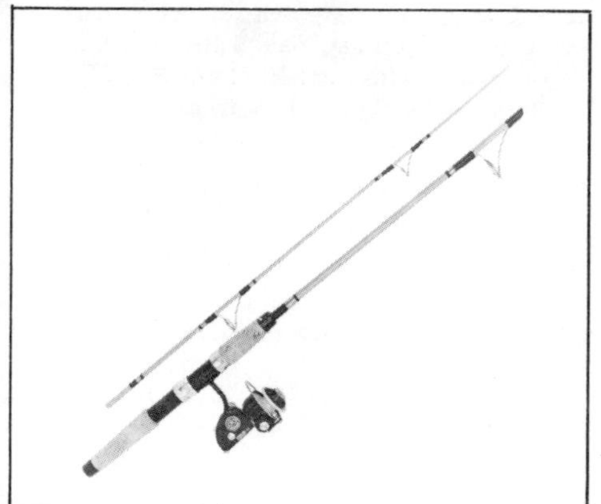

Martin Reel Company offers an array of rod-reel combinations for fresh- and/or salt-water fishing. Available are **No. 814,** with matching Bretton 104 reel (5:1 ratio, made in France) and Martin **No. 1-125** ultralight spinning rod (U.S.A.). Designed for lures to about 1/16 oz. Approximate price, $52.95. Model **No. 818** Martin rod/Bretton reel combination is for general fresh water fishing and lighter salt water action, including bonefish. Reel holds 300 yds. of 8-lb. line, matches the two-piece, 7', tubular glass rod. Approximate price: $45.95.

**Rods by Heddon**

Heddon Special Purpose Worm Rods: Engineered with a special action to fish plastic worms effectively. Features include Heddon's Rugged Pal Mark special construction and all-glass ferrule.

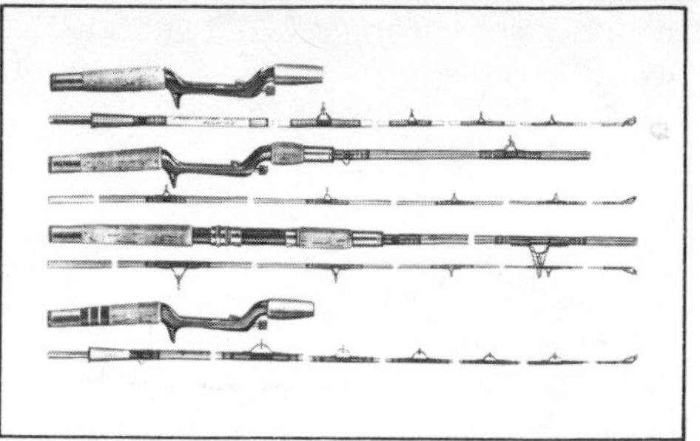

**No. 6277** for casting, 5½', one-piece, $16.87.

**No. 6275** for spincasting, 5'8", two-piece, $17.92.

**No. 7444** for spinning, 6'3", two-piece, $23.24.

**No. 6322:** New in Heddon's top-of-the-line Mark V series. Stainless steel wire/wraps, walnut and Tenite inlaid handle, other distinctive features, for casting, 5¼', one-piece, $35.21.

Heddon's Starcast series is priced for budget-conscious anglers.

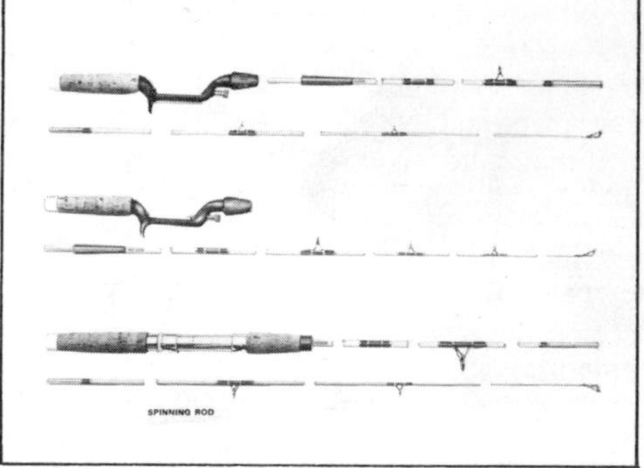


**Nos. 3551** and **3553:** 5½', 6', two-piece, solid fiberglass, specie cork grip, chrome V-frame guides, ferrule and slide. Both rods have Heddon's Universal Action. For spincasting. Each, $7.49.

**No. 3335:** For casting. Detachable offset handle with Heddon's new "speed grip," solid fiberglass, V-frame guides and tiptop, strong nylon wrappings, specie cork grip. This Starcast is one-piece, 5½', with Universal Action. Approximate price, $7.49.

**No. 3771:** A Starcast for spinning, 6', two-piece, Universal Action. Solid glass, with aluminum reel seat, specie cork fore and rear grips, chromed V-frame guides and tiptop, nickel-silver ferrule, nylon wraps. Approximate price: $7.49.

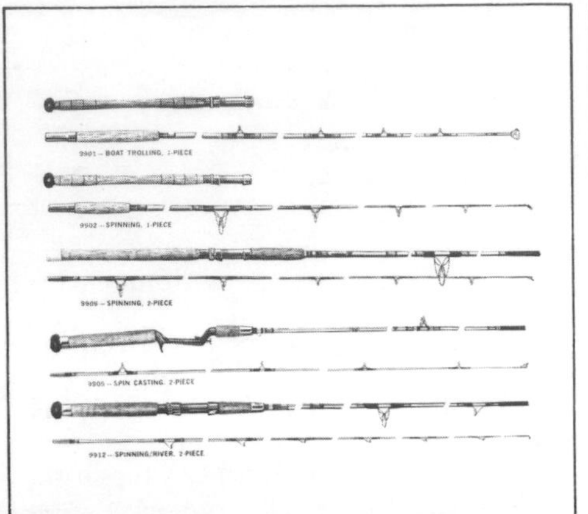


Heddon's Silver King Coho Rods: Four models, crafted from special Heddon glass for strength and power, field tested and proven with steelheads, Great Lakes cohos, other salmonid fishes. Models and approximate prices include: **No. 9902,** 7½', one-piece, spinning, $20.23; **No. 9908,** 8½', two-piece, spinning, $29.26; **No. 9909,** 9', two-piece spinning, $29.26; **No. 9912,** for spinning and river fishing, 9', two-piece, $29.26.

**Powerscopic Rods**

These telescoping rods are offered in two series. The "P" series has five models for spinning, spincasting and fly fishing, with 7' spin/fly combo (**No. P4000**). Telescoped, they measure 15½" to 19", according to models. Extended, they go 6' to 8'. The other series is the "G," with six models for ultra-light fishing, spinning, spincasting, fly fishing, including a 6' spin/fly combination (**No. G508**). Collapsed, they're 12" to 16", according to models. Extended, they go from 5' to 8'. Approximate prices range from $20 to $35 but are subject to change without notice.

**Finessa Rods by Quick**

The Finessa line includes rods for salt water as well as for fly fishing and fresh water. Those mentioned here are among the models designed primarily for fresh water.

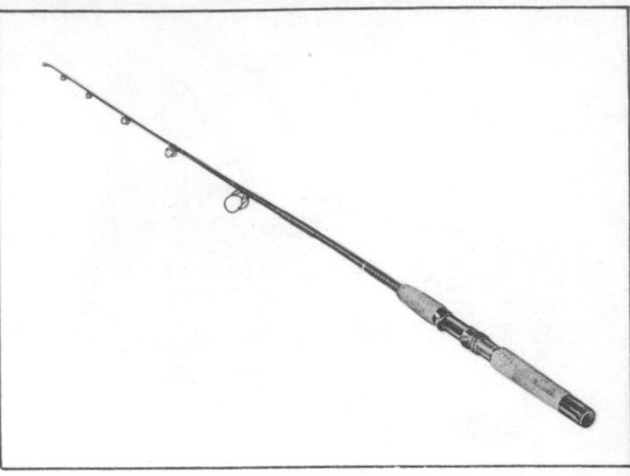

**Finessa No. UL6056R:** 5½', two-piece, ultra-light, recommended for 2- to 6-lb. test lines. Quick's 110-N reel balances it.

**Finessa No. 6070:** 7', two-piece, fast taper, with Neo-Grip handle, recommended for 4- to 12-lb. lines. Takes any Quick fresh-water reel, including 330-N and 331-N.

Price range: $20.00 to $25.00.

**Rods by Gladding-South Bend**

Two old, highly respected names in tackle manufacture are united by a hyphen in production of a veritable forest of tubular and solid glass rods for fresh-water and marine angling.

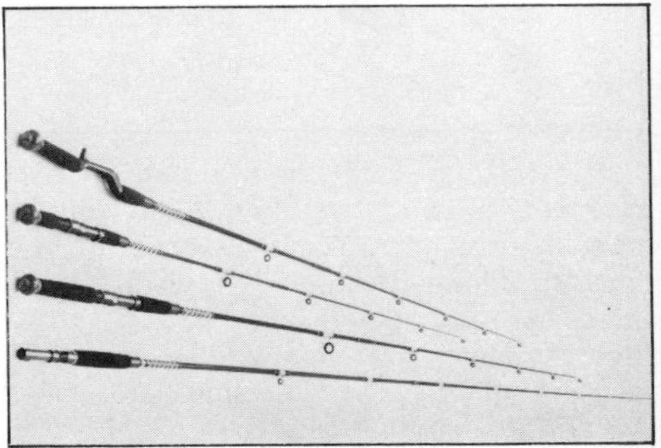

**Gladding-South Bend's Classic IV series:** was completely redesigned for 1975 to accent the series' slogan, "True custom quality at production prices." There are four basic models, nine versions. Shared specifications: Tuflex fiberglass construction; jam-proof Ferrule-Flex fiberglass ferrule with glass-weld reinforcement; manufacturer's exclusive Gladcoat finish; heat-dissipating Speed Guides to encourage casting distance, each guide double wrapped against slippage; elegant new cushion grips—soft, tough, non-skid; hard plastic protective butt cap. On the spinning models the reel seats are of extra-deep, anodized aluminum with double-locking hoods. Spincasting models have a die-cast aluminum handle with chip-resistant epoxy finish. Rod colors are rich mixture of shades of brown. Examples are:

**No. 1-146-260:** Spincasting and light to medium baitcasting, 6'.

**No. 1-246-150:** Featherweight for ultra-light spinning, 5'.

**No. 1-246-866:** Spinning, big bass or salt water, wide range of lures.

Fly rods: Five versions in the Classic IV series, starting with **No. 1-446-170,** 7', for No. 6 or 7 fly line, to **No. 1-446-493,** 9'3" for bass, salmon, salt water, lines Nos. 9 and 10.

Approximate Classic IV series price: $27.95.

**Gladding-South Bend's Classic III series:** Features include tubular (hollow) Tuflex blanks, carbide guides and tiptop, specie cork grips, good looks—rich brown color and contrasting gold-colored wrappings. Examples are:

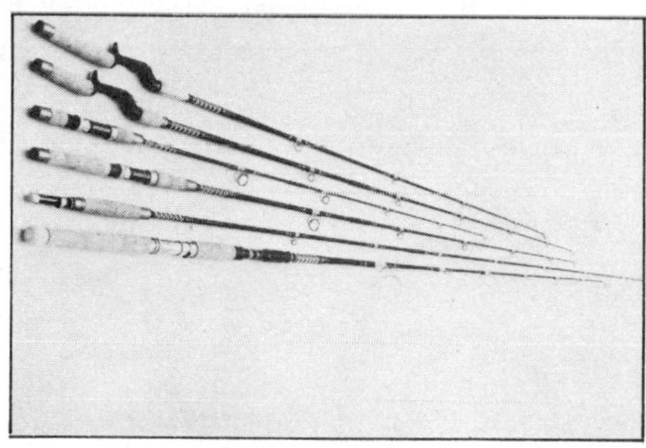

**No. 1-042-460:** A Gladding Magnum Bass Rod, 6', 1-piece, Power-Flex action, spiral drive reel seat fastener, detachable handle.

**No. 1-142-860:** Two-piece spincasting, 6', Gladding-South Bend's Veri-Flex action, extra-strong handle.

**Nos. 1-242-050** and **1-242-866:** For spinning, 5' and 6½', with ultra-light action and Veri-Flex action, respectively.

**No. 1-442-280:** Two-piece tubular glass fly rod, 8'. Fitted with duo-lock, anodized reel seat, carbide stripper, 6 stainless steel snake guides. Balanced for No. 7 line.

**No. 1-243-870:** For salt-water spinning. Tubular fiberglass, two-piece, fast taper, with Gladding-South Bend's double-built construction, heavily chromed brass reel seat with double locking rings, stainless steel guides, carbide tiptop, specie cork foregrip, oversized rear grip with protective rubber butt cap.

Approximate Classic III series price: $19.95.

Among other Gladding-South Bend rods: Solid and Tubular Pack models; Solid and tubular Rainbow Rods; Bassin' Man series; Outdoorsman series; White Knight series; Forester series; and for marine fishing, the Harnells, Outdoorsman Saltwater Rods, and the Salt Water Specials.

### St. Croix Tackle

The output of St. Croix Corp. is varied. Not only does it include rods but also reels of all types and items of terminal tackle hardware. Particularly impressive is its inventory of rods, which cover every facet of angling from flyrodding to surfcasting and ocean boat fishing.

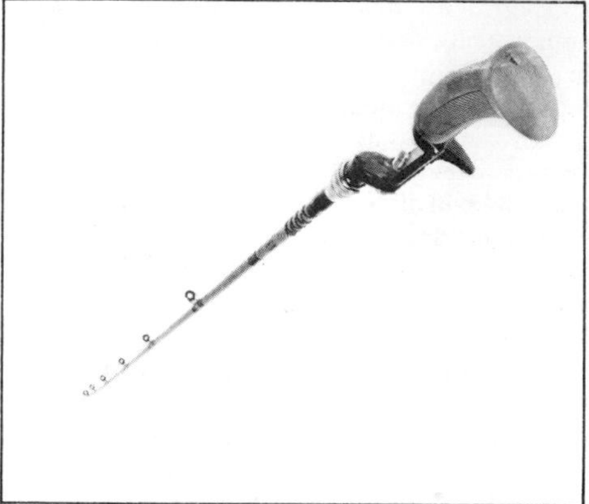

Of particular interest to fresh-water Izaak Waltons are St. Croix's Stud Stix. Ten models comprise the Stud Stix group: four for plugging, four for worming, two for ultra-light fishing. All are one-piece, tubular, with construction featuring St. Croix Ultra-Lite XL glass—"camel brown" shafts with dark brown, black trim wrappings. Spincasting models have a brown, pistol grip handle for all-weather gripping. Spinning models have specie cork grips, with brown reel seat, gold-colored double locking rings, gold butt and foregrip caps. The plugging and worm fishing modela measure 5½' or 6', have either Carboloy guides and tiptop or Fuji guides throughout. All are designed for spinning or spincasting. The two ultra-light models, **Nos. 588** and **689**, are for spincasting and spinning, respectively, are 5½' long and fitted with 5 stainless steel guides. Price range of the Stud Stix: $24.99 to $34.99.

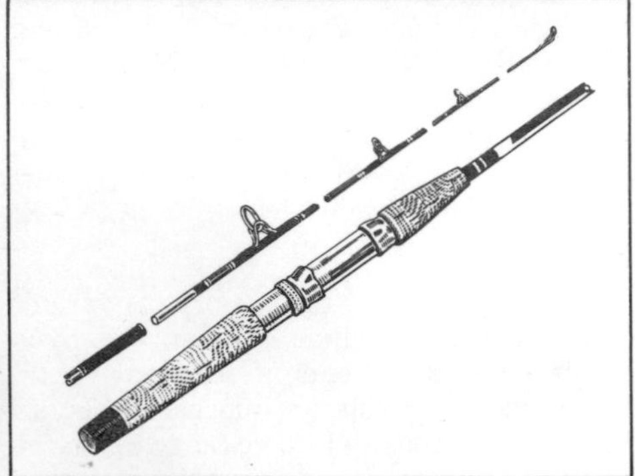

St. Croix's Green Grabber series spotlights six models, five for spinning and spincasting, one for fly fishing. **No. 82,** 6'6", is styled in the new Green Grabber look—environmental green, with forest green wrappings and yellow accent ("a tested background color scheme for the spookiest of fish," says the manufacturer). Rod has 3 chromed guides and tiptop, wrapped ferrule. For lures through 3/8-oz. Approximate price $6.99 to $9.99.

Other St. Croix rod series names you might want to investigate include Imperial XL (ultra-light), Blue Bandit, Golden Galaxy, Premier, Magna-Taper (progressive taper), Blue Demon, Viking, Coastal, Raider, Mariner, Commander, Captain.

**True Temper's 5800 Series,** featuring non-slip pistol grips: 5½' and 6', all one-piece except **5802** (two-piece), with strong, ultra-light magnesium handle (non-detachable). Model **5808** is solid glass. All have tungsten carbide tiptop, durable poly-foam foregrip, Tempercote windings,deluxe anodized aluminum cap, black blank with white accent stripes, decorative spiral butt wind. Choice of guides: **5800 series,** stainless steel wire frame; **5800A series,** tungsten carbide. Either way, 4 guides per rod, plus tiptop. For worm fishing, spinner baits, plugging. Action ranges from ultra-light (**No. 5809**), through medium (**5800, 5802, 5808**), to heavy (**5801**). Price range: $17.00 to $23.00.

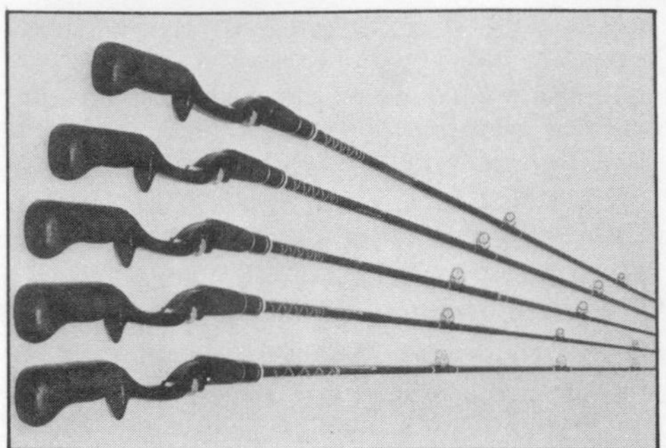

**True Temper's 8000 Series,** for steelhead, salmon and special-purpose fishing: eight models, seven for casting or spinning, one for popping. **Nos. 8000** through **8006** are two-piece rods for casting or spinning. **Nos. 8005** and **8006** are designed especially for salmon, **8000-8004** for steelheads. **No. 8510** is a one-piece popping rod. Features of **8000-8006:** True Temper's Holloglass construction; 5 or 6

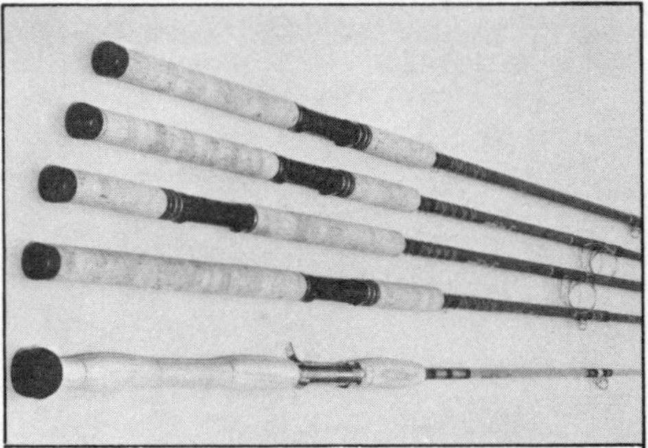

hard-chromed stainless steel guides (tungsten carbide tiptops on **8003, 8004**); Tempercote on all windings; anodized aluminum reel seat; keeper bar; Temperglas ferrule—strong, light; balanced lightness. **No. 8510,** the 6½' popping rod with medium action, is solid glass, has four stainless steel guides and tiptop, chromed brass, finger hook reel seat, hard, strong, white ash handle. Lengths of the other rods go from 7½ to 9' (**8004**). Price range: $19.00 to $26.00.

**Balanced Fishing Outfits from Garcia**

Here are four from which you can choose:

**Kingfisher GK-32 Spincasting Outfit:** The Kingfisher spincasting and spinning reels are fairly new in the Garcia family. This particular outfit is named for the GK-32 spincasting reel, weighing only 8 oz., operable with either hand. It comes spooled with 100 yds. of 8-lb. monofilament and matching rods. Approximate price: $15.00.

**Garcia 120 Spincasting Outfit:** Running mate of the **GK-32** combination, this outfit stars Garcia's famed Abu-Matic reel, Model 120, with its Syncro-Drag. Reel has its drag setting pre-set at the factory comes with 8-lb. Royal Bonnyl. Its line-release trigger fits either right-handers or southpaws Matching the reel is a Garcia Rod. Approximate price: $16.00.

**Kingfisher GK-10 Spinning Outfit:** It's GK-10 spinning reel, with 3.1:1 retrieve and capacity up to 200 yds. of 8-lb. mono, matches the outfits Kingfisher rod. Line is included. Approximate price: $15.00.

**Garcia 320 Spinning Outfit:** Components of this combination are a Garcia-Mitchell 320 reel (holds about 190 yds. of 8-lb. monofilament), ideal for most fresh-water spinfishing, balanced Garcia rod, and mono line. Garcia 320 Spinning Outfit sells for about $16.00.

Also from Garcia for fresh-water fishing: (**1**) Brown Series of spinning rods, 5' to 7', for ultra-light, light and medium action; (**2**) Brown Series, baitcasting and spincasting rods, 5½' to 7', including special worm rods, light to heavy action; (**3**) Avocado Series for spinning, worm/spinning, spincasting, baitcasting, worm fishing, plus one model (**No. 8220**) with special muskie design, very heavy action–5' to 7' range, all models except muskie rod with light to medium action; (**4**) Blue series, a good-looking group, 5' to 7', for spinning, spincasting, baitcasting, plus four fly rods, 7'3" to 9', three with dry fly action, one with bass bug action.

**Among the Rods from Shakespeare**

**Woodgrain Wonderods, Series 608:** In the group: two pushbutton models, 6' and 6½'; three spinning rods, 6½' to 7'; four fly rods, 7½' to 9'. Fiberglass rods with a smart, teak woodgrain finish, select specie cork grips, carbide tiptop, gold-anodized appointments. Approximate price: $30.00.

**Presidential Wonderods, Series 508:** Two baitcasting models, 5½ and 6'; three pushbutton rods, 6 and 6½'; 5 spinning models, 5-7'. All are one-piece, built from Shakespeare's Kwik Taper blanks, with cork foregrip and handle, black butt cap. Collectively they handle lures to 5/8-oz. Rod blank color is white. Also in the series, white with contrasting black trim, is an 8½' fly rod, 4 oz., two-piece, with 7 guides and cork grip, designed for No. 8 line. Approximate price: $25.00.

**Eye-Crosser Worm/Bass Wonderods:** Ranging in lengths from 5½ to 6' are models for spinning, handling lures to 5/8 oz. Series also includes: 8½', 5-oz. heavy-duty spin/fly combination rod for artificials to 5/8 oz. steelheads and other husky opponents; a heavy-duty fly rod, 9', 6.2 oz., for No. 11 line; and a closed-face spinning rod, 7', light action, for lures to 3/8 oz. Colors are white blanks with black-over-yellow winds. Price range: $23.00 to $25.00.

**Rods by Daiwa**

Daiwa fresh-water spinning rods, with chrome-plated stainless steel guides and tip top, in lengths from 5' to 7', cost about $16.10.

Daiwa Ultra Power rods in lengths from 5' to 7' run from $16.80 to $24.07.

**Lew Childre Speed Sticks**

"Speed Sticks" is a Lew Childre trademark, and there's a flock of models: one-piece, two-piece and telescoping, in a range of lengths from 5'2" to 7' and in calibers from extra-light to heavy, for spinning, baitcasting and spincasting. Among them features include the assets of fiberglass construction, hard Fuji ring guides, non-corrosive stainless steel hardware, and flotation because of the lightweight Lew-Fuji component parts system.

**Telescopic Tackle Box Speed Sticks:** In spinning and casting models, closing to 19", extending to 5'9", guaranteed unconditionally for a year. Closed, they fit into attache cases and aircraft carry-on luggage too. They range from extra-light, for medium-short range accuracy and baits to

½ oz., to heavy, for long-range accuracy, deep baits to 1¼ oz. Price range is about $24.00 to $32.00.

Other Lew Childre Speed Sticks include a large assortment of one- and two-piece models in a full range of actions from extra-light, through medium, to heavy.

## FRESH-WATER REELS

### From Feurer Brothers

The same Swiss watchmaking experience entering into production of their marine spinning reels goes into their fresh-water versions.

**Feurer Brothers' Masterspin:** Weighing but 7 oz., its retrieve ratio is 2.75:1, with a line capacity to about 100 yds., according to line strength. Major features include automatic feathering (helpful in accurate casting), automatic anti-reverse, hardened steel pickup, smooth and fully adjustable

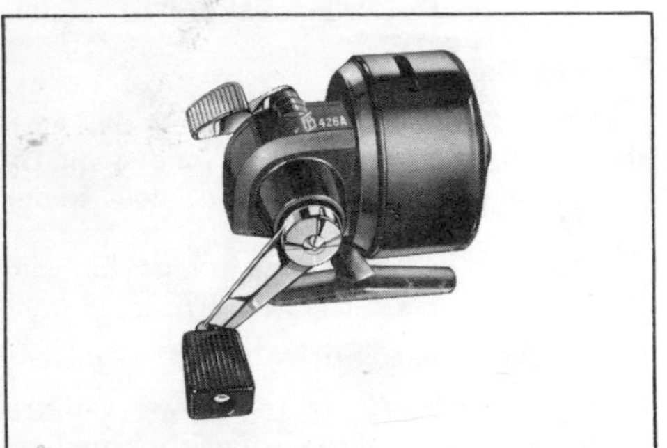

drag, easy spool change, and all-metal construction. Designated as model **FB 426,** Masterspin lists at $16.45. It's also available in a deluxe version, **FB427**, with chrome finish, for $18.65.

**Feurer Brothers Spinster:** Its builders call it a "work horse of spinning reels," time-proven for dependability, a choice if one reel must serve as several. **FB417** has a stainless steel pickup with roller, rugged insides, fingertip anti-reverse control, patented nylon expansion drag with precision adjustment for smooth, positive braking. The Spinster weighs 9.6 oz., has a 3.44:1 gear ratio, holds anywhere from 140 yds. of 10-lb. line to 240 of 6-lb. Price about $17.55.

### Heddon Reels

**Heddon Model 112 Spincasting Reel:** A popularly priced (about $6.23) reel with all-metal construction, including gears and spool, star drag, 7-point metal pickup for iine flow lever operated with either hand, weighs 7 oz., comes spooled with 100 yds. of 6-lb. monofilament. This is but one model in the Hedliner series, which includes a fly reel, four spinning models.

**152 Spincasting Reel, in Heddon's Pal series:** 10 oz., a quality reel in its price range, about $10.43. Features include: Precision all-metal gears; strong all-metal housing; wide thumb trigger; star drag; optional anti-reverse; hard epoxy finish for corrosion resistance. Comes with 100 yds. of 8-lb. mono line and practice plug.

**Heddon Model 282 Spinning Reel:** A fresh-water reel that can handle light salt water assignments too. Weighs 13½ oz., holds 200 yds. of 8-lb. mono. **No. 282** features fast 4:1 retrieve ratio, 2-race ball

bearing system, helical gears, folding crank, chenille line guard, multiple-disc drag. About $20.93. With the same features, but weighing 9 oz. for ultra-light spinning and holding 100 yds. of 6-lb. monofilament, is **No. 281**, about $19.39.

### Johnson Reels

**Sabra 130B:** This is one of the models starring Johnson Reels' patented Automatic Transmission. When you turn the crank forward, the reel shifts into a strong, hook-setting, direct drive retrieve. When a fish runs, you release the handle and the reel down-shifts automatically to its drag. **Sabra 130B** also has Permalloy gears, oil-impregnated bronze bearings, stainless steel crank and drive shafts, rotor nut/snubber for extra line-snubbing action with heavy lures, safety lock, and oscillating spool to crosswind line for even distribution and smooth casting. Colors are an attractive combination of dark green, black, white. Comes with 310 feet of 15-lb. mono, can accommodate up to 230 feet of 20 lb. Extra spools available. Recommended for 6' or 6½' rod with medium to heavy tip. Approximate price: $26.00.

**Johnson 710B:** Classified as an all-around closed-face spinning reel. Model **710B** details include Automatic Transmission, stainless steel line guide, Permalloy gears, safety lock, Dia-Chrome rotor. Color scheme same as Sabra 130B's. Recommended for 6' tubular glass rod with medium tip. Comes with 280' of 10-lb. mono. Optional spools are available with 6- to 15-lb. test line. Approximate price: $21.50.

**Johnson Century and Citation models:** Nicknamed "The Convertibles," they're at home on either a casting rod or a spinning stick. Mounted topside on the former, they're casting reels with push-button accuracy, no backlashes. Mounted underneath, they provide the tangle-free casting of closed-face reels. This switching also provides a choice of right- or left-hand operation. **Century 100B** comes with 200 feet of 10-lb monofilament. Citation **110B** is Century's bigger brother. All the same features but with double the line capacity—410 feet of 10-lb. mono. Both reels have Selecto-Dial multiple-shoe drag, Dia-Chrome rotor, dual anti-reverse, tungsten carbide pickup pin, attractive green-white-black color scheme. Approximate prices: Century **100B**, $12.00; Citation **110B**, $17.00.

**Johnson Executive Travel Pack:** 5-piece tubular glass rod, choice of one of Johnson's three most popular reels—Century, Commander 150, or No. 710, plus extra reel spool—all in fleece-lined leather-like vinyl case. Approximate price, $40.00.

### Zebco Reel Family

Zebco bills its famous Cardinal series as the end product of Old World craftsmanship and finest quality materials. Among their shared specifications are Swedish stainless steel worm gear, precision aligned with the bronze drive gear; exclusive stern-mounted drag control, with multi-disc system; stainless steel ball bearings; positive anti-reverse; corrosion-proofing. All come with an extra spool.

**Cardinal 3:** New, ultra-light, super-fast 5:1 retrieve. Capacity, 178 yds. of 4-lb. line.

**Cardinal 4:** All-purpose fresh water reel, fast 5:1 gear ratio, line capacity of 200 yds. of 8-lb. line.

**Cardinal 6:** For heavy fresh water/light salt water action, a popular bassing model. Capacity, 180 yds. of 17-lb. monofilament.

**Cardinal 7:** For heavy fresh water fishing and medium marine assignments, engineered for husky, hard-walloping opponents. Easily holds 180 yds. of 20-lb. line.

### Reels from Daiwa

This California outfit offers a wide range of spinning reels—open- and closed-face—as well as revolving-spool types, for fresh water and salt, with approximate prices from as low as $5.25 for the **No. 7270** open-face spinning reel and **No. 2100** closed-face model to $67.20 for the Millionaire **6H** high-speed (5:1), wide spool baitcasting model. Here are some representatives:

**Millionaire 3H Baitcasting Reel:** Fast 5:1 retrieve; smooth, spring-loaded drag with Teflon washer; stainless steel main drive gear; calibrated spool tension brake system, capacity of 165 yds. of 15-lb. mono. Price, $37.80.

**No. 7280 Spinning Reel:** 8½ oz., 3.2:1 retrieve, pre-balanced rotor unit, one-piece metal master gear, anti-reverse, automatic positive bail, capacity of 200 yds. of 8-lb. mono. Price $8.05.

**Daiwa 24:** Heavy-duty fresh-water spincasting model, 11 oz., with 3:1 retrieve, positive Dialoy pin pickup, twist-free star drag, automatic side pushbutton line release, die-cast master and pinion gears, chrome-plated carbon components, corrosion-resistant finish on front cover, $15.40.

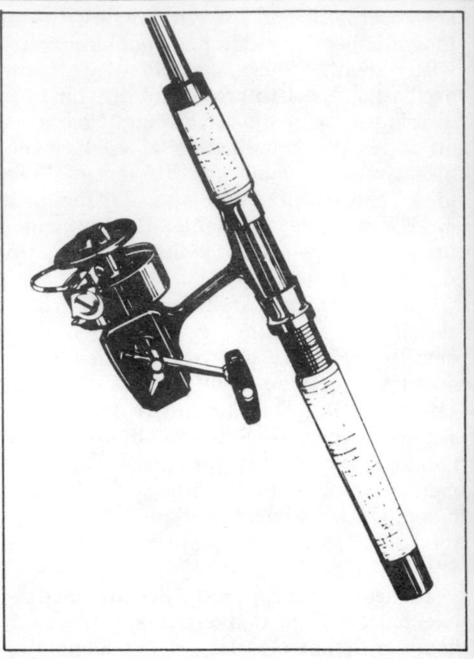

New in 1975 were Daiwa's pre-mounted tackle combinations. Rods and reels are selected and balanced at the factory. All outfits except one (**No. PMC-5,** for worm fishing and spincasting, $57.75) come with Daiwa's premium Mon-Dex line. Sample outfits: **No. PMC-1,** fresh-water spinning, $20.30; **No. PMC-3,** salt-water spinning, $43.75; **No. PMC-6,** Silver Reel Spinning Combo, $52.50.

**Reels by St. Croix**

**No. 33 Baitcasting Reel:** Feather-light (only 4 oz.) with these features: Double handle; quadruple multiplying gears; level-wind mechanism for automatic even distribution of line; fingertip drag and anti-backlash adjustment screw; on/off clicker; maroon color, with anodized aluminum sideplates; capacity of 100 yds. of 15-lb. line. Price range: $4.99 to $6.99.

The St. Croix Americana Series: American-made, closed-face reels with models for beginners and experienced anglers. They include:

**SC-1 Colt:** Ideal for beginners. Solidly made, practically break-proof. Has 3:1 retrieve through flash-hardened Permalloy gears, steel drive shaft. Other features:

Multiple-point pickup; special pushbutton safety lock; adjustable star drag and anti-reverse; Cycolac gear case and anodized aluminum cover. Handles 6- to 12-lb. lines, comes with 240 feet of 10-lb. mono. Price range: $9.99 to $12.99.

**SC-2 Charger:** Work horse of the Americana group. Specifications: 3:1 gear gear ratio; flash-fired Permalloy gears; die-cast metal spool; audible, adjustable drag; special safety lock; Zamak alloy frame, Cycolac gear case, anodized aluminum cover. Handles lines from 6- to 12-lb. test, comes with 200 feet of 10 lb. Price range: $12.99 to 14.99.

Other models in the Americana Series: **SC-3 Mustang,** with features that include double the line capacity of the Charger, diachrome rotor, dual anti-reverse, tungsten carbide pickup. Handles lines to and including 15-lb. test (260 feet). **RF-76 Range-Finder:** Has all the quality features of other Americana models plus St. Croix's exclusive Strike-Release Ranger-Finder mechanism. With a finger flick its Memory Lok can be set for a constant casting distance or uniform depth, yet is ready to handle a snag or unexpectedly hard strike. Handles lines through 12-lb. test, comes with 180 feet of 10 lb. Approximate prices: Mustang, $17.99; the RF-76, $9.99.

**Pflueger Reels**

**Pflueger's No. 511B Supreme Casting Reel:** 1¼" light-arbor spool, with free spooling for casting; smooth star drag; machined bronze and steel gears; oversized power handle; capacity, 100 yds. of 15-lb. monofilament. Price range: $25.00 to $35.00.

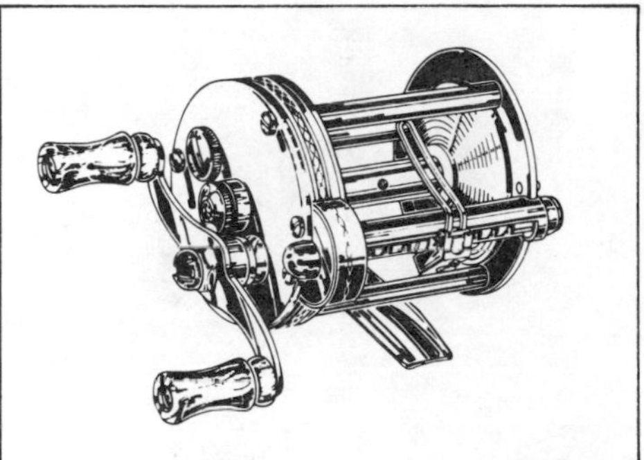

**Pflueger's No. 1893L Akron Casting Reel:** Chromed and polished frame; brass gears, bronze bushings; light aluminum spool; capacity of 175 yds. of 15-lb. braided line. Price range: $20.00 to $30.00.

**Pflueger's No. 681 Spinning Reel:** Fast 4.5:1 retrieve; new skirted spool; deluxe folding crank; easily reached anti-reverse lever; converts from right- to left-hand retrieve in seconds; rich metallic gray finish; weighs 13 oz., holds 250 yds. of 10-lb. mono. Price range: $15.00 to $20.00.

Pflueger produces a long parade of revolving-spool, spinning and spincasting reels. You might want to look into their International group of open and closed-face spinning reels, as well as the Trump model and other Supremes among the revolving-spool types.

**True Temper Reels**

**True Temper 327 Blue Heron Spincasting Reels, 300 Series:** Long list of specifications includes: All die-cast aluminum housing; ball bearings; precision metal gears; brass bushings; anti-reverse; anodized aluminum shroud cover; hard-chromed, stainless steel, free-running-roller pickup pin; detachable metal spool, oscillating to wind line evenly. Weighs 9½ oz., has 3.2:1 retrieve, comes prespooled with 100 yds. of 10-lb. mono. Price range: $11.00 to $28.00.

**True Temper Blue Heron Spinning Reels, 700 Series:** Ball bearing drive is a key feature. Others include: Stainless steel bail with hard-chromed stainless steel roller pickup (tungsten carbide roller); folding handle; positive lock on bail to prevent premature release; built-in shock absorber to cushion bail release. Blue Heron **737** sells in the range of $21.00 to $29.00.

Also from True Temper: 5 Uni-Spin factory-matched rod and reel outfits for spincasting, designated as combinations **Nos. 63, 633, 636, 638, 66.** For all-round fresh water to rugged fresh water/general salt water.

**Garcia Reels**

Anyone at all familiar with The Garcia Corporation knows that it manufactures a very large family of fresh-water and marine reels of all types, revolving-spool to closed-face spinning. Here are just a few representatives:

**Ambassadeur 5000/6000 Series Baitcasting Reels:** Perfect materials, precision machining and flawless craftsmanship are Garcia's claims for all the Ambassadeurs. Distinctive features include: Two sets of brakes—centrifugal to control spool speed in casting to minimize backlashes, plus a mechanical brake adjustable to any lure weight; free spooling with convenient thumb control; enclosed level wind with stainless steel pawl; quick, no-tool take-down; corrosion-resistant anodized finish. Each comes with its own hand-fitted case, plus tools, spare parts, oil. Additionally, the Ambassadeur **5000, 5000A, 5000B** and **6000** have hand-fitted floating bushings supporting the spool axle. Color is a rich burgundy red. Spool capacities of 15-lb. monofilament range from 130 yds. (**No. 5000**) to 220 yds. (**No. 6000**).

New in the 5000/6000 Series is the Ambassadeur **5000D,** designed for bass fishermen and incorporating an anti-backlash centrifugal brake and other Ambassadeur features. The "D" stands for "direct drive," combining the power of direct retrieve with a smooth, adjustable drag and free-spool casting ease. Color is rich emerald free. Also grouped with the 5000/6000 series is the **1750,** also with Ambassadeur features, an ultra-light baitcasting reel accommodating 100 yds of 15-lb. mon.

Approximate retail price range of the foregoing Ambassadeurs is $40.00 to $60.00.

**Abu-Matic 170:** Abu is an old name in the Garcia family, and the builder calls this Abu-Matic **170** "the most sophisticated spincasting reel in the world." Among the reasons are its self-lubricating bushings, smooth and fully adjustable star drag, positive anti-reverse, no-twist oscillating spool, and corrosion-resistant finish. Another detail of sophistication is the exclusive Sincro-Drag, which gives instant drag reduction when needed, simply by backing off on the handle, then returns to the original brake setting immediately on resuming the retrieve. Comes fully wound with 15-lb. Royal Bonnyl, for about $25.00.

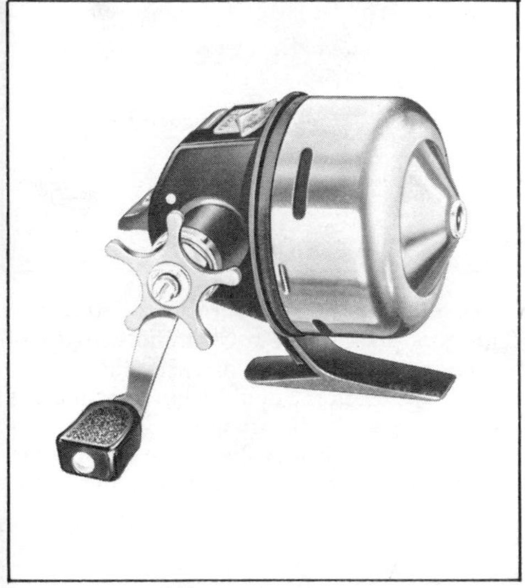

**Abu-Matic 120:** Incorporates several of the Abu-Matic features, with a tamper-proof drag, but is budget priced at about $15.00. Comes spooled with Garcia's 8-lb. Royal Bonnyl.

**The Garcia-Mitchell 300:** Rated among the most popular spinning reels in the U.S. because of its versatility. Pushing a button changes spools from line strong enough to land a hefty bass to line light enough to make a 6-inch brook trout a sporting proposition. Teflon drag, thermo-baked, corrosion-resistant finish, one-spot lubrication, convenient anti-reverse, and folding handle to save space are among its Garcia-Mitchell assets. And it's one of the maker's handsomest reels in the bargain.

Also available as **No. 300C** with ball bearings, and as **300DL**, a presentation model (for tournament awards) with gold-plated trim, packed in its own smart wooden case. All three versions of the **300** can be had as either right- or left-hand models. Approximate price $19.00.

**Martin Reels**

**Bretton 500 Spincasting Reel, from Martin Reel Co.:** 9 oz., in distinctive mist green. Specifications: New Monocon spool for longer, smoother casts; patented "dimple" brake to prevent line squeeze; extra sensitive 8-point pickup; fast retrieve—one turn of handle brings in 15" of line; multi-disc star drag; no-tool take-down. With 100 yds. of 8-lb. Martin Tuff mono, about $14.95.

**Martin Bretton 807S Spinning Reel:** Made in France, weighs only 12 oz. but is engineered for king salmon, cohos, steelheads. Has fast 4:1 retrieve, holds 175 yds. of 20-lb. line. Other specs: Precision machined helical gears; two ball bearings on main shaft; smooth multi-disc drag; stainless steel bail equipped with shock absorber, carbide line roller; push-type on/off anti-reverse click; folding handle; coin-slotted take-down. Priced at about $37.95.

**Quick's 220-N Finessa:** All-round fresh water spinning reel—light (about 11 oz.), compact, with lively 3.55:1 retrieve, capacity of 220 yds. of 8-lb. monofilament. Also has: Ball bearing drive on main shaft; stainless steel bail with tungsten carbide line guide; self-lubricating handle bearings;

all precision-machined gears; adjustable bail release mechanism for softer or harder operation to meet special situations; space-saving folding handle; galvanic treatment against corrosion. Approximate price is $22.00.

### Reels From Quick

**Quick's Microlite 110-N:** Another in the Finessa line. Details include those listed for the Finessa 220-N and a pushbutton release on the spool for rapid changing. Weighs 8½ oz., has a fast 4.75:1 gear ratio, holds 220 yds. of 6-lb. line, goes for about $22.00.

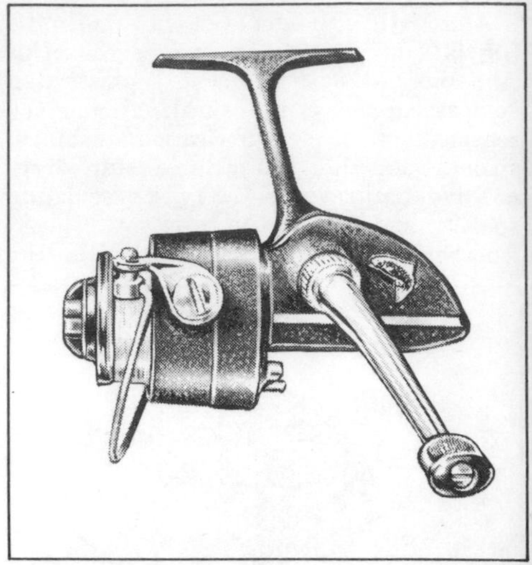

Also from Quick Corporation of America: The good-looking new Champion series of revolving-spool reels, all resistant to salt water corrosion for doubling in light marine assignments. Four models, all with star drag, multiple-disc brake, silent level wind, counterbalanced handle, chromed fittings:

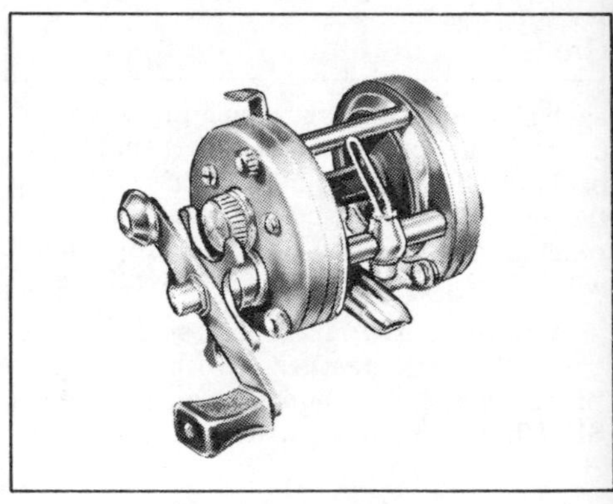

**No. 700:** 8.4 oz., 3.65:1 retrieve, 250 yds. of 12-lb. test, about $45.00.

**No. 800:** 11 oz., 3.65:1 gear ratio, 275 yds. of 15-lb. line, about $48.00.

**No. 700-B:** 8.4 oz., rapid 4.65:1 retrieve, 250 yds. of 12-lb. line, centrifugal anti-backlash brake in addition to calibrated spool tension drag, about $55.00.

**No. 800-B:** 11 oz., 4.65:1 ratio, 275 yds. of 15-lb. line, stainless steel ball bearing drive, wider spool, about $60.00.

**Zebco Reels**

**Zebco US76 spincaster:** "For the 'reel spirit' of fishing." It's easy to cast with the **US76**, and it has strong metal gears, continuous anti-reverse, husky star drag, interchangeable spool filled with premium Zebco monofilament line. Price range: $2.60 to $3.00.

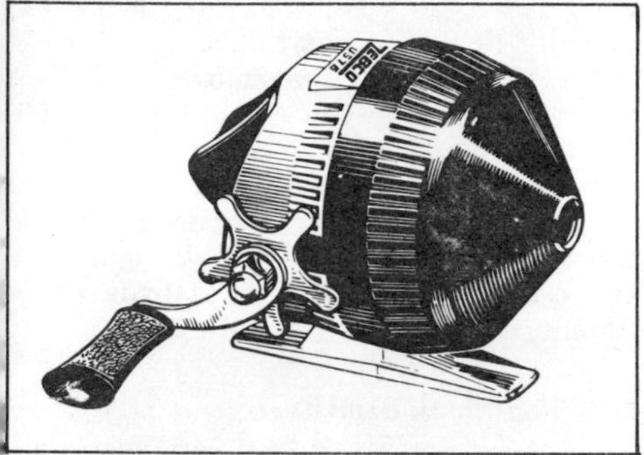


**Note:** Zebco offers a flock of spincasting reels and spinning models for fresh-water and marine fishing, including its famous Cardinal group.

Also from Zebco is a large selection of balanced rod-reel combinations. The **Combo 1176** is designed especially for young hands.

Components are a **US76** spincasting reel, Zebco **4076** rod (4'6", high-density fiberglass, light action, clip and screw reel lock). About $5.00. There are several combinations for grownups too, spinning and spincasting.

**Shakespeare Representatives**

Esthetics are not the most important detail of a reel, but still there's pride of ownership with good looks. . . and Shakespeare's reels sure have them.

**Model 1767 II:** Recommended by noted professional caster Bill True. Among the reasons: Fast 4:1 retrieve; permanent non-reverse star drag preventing line twist; extra-strength gear and pinion system; positive anti-backlash control. Add one-piece, die-cast spool, carbide line pickup pin, aluminum crank, tough epoxy finish in two-tone gray over rugged aluminum case. Comes filled with 70 yds. of 12-lb. Shakespeare 7000 mono, plus extra spool carrying 100 yds. of 8-lb. No. 7000 mono. Sells for approximately $23.50.

What we mean by Shakespearean good looks, the **No. 1960:** For big-water action, fresh or salt, with tough customers. Accented features include: Guts where they count—precision drive gears of copper-infiltrated steel for brute strength, long service . . . stainless steel pinion for big-fish punishment . . . solid, one-piece frame . . . heavy-duty star drag with oversize washers . . . lever-controlled free spool of reinforced, glass-filled ABS to take extreme pressures of packed monofilament . . . oversize carriage screw on level wind for a long wear, plus easily removed stainless steel pawl . . . precision 3-piece construction for easy cleaning and lubrication. Holds 375 yds. of 20-lb mono or 200 yds. of 30-lb. Goes for about $35.00. Also available as **No. 1961**, same specifications otherwise, but without level wind, $32.00.

"Tough-minded, budget-priced" (about $7.50)—Shakespeare's **998** spincaster: Frame of molded Cycolac (Borg-Warner Corp.), metal pinion on aluminum alloy gear, stainless steel guide ring, removable spool, black frame and cone. Filled with 85 yds. of 8-lb. mono.

New among the Shakespeareans: **No. 2500** fresh-water spinning reel. Cited quality features are ball bearings, extra-strong precision gears, multi-disc, spring-loaded drag system, 4.3:1 retrieve, capacity of 170 yds. of 6-lb. line, smart black finish. Sells for about $14.00. Its companion model, **No. 2510,** embodies the same features but accommodates more line, 160 yds. of 10-lb. mono.

### The Berkley Family

Along with rods, lines and terminal tackle for fresh and salt water, plus fly fishing gear, Berkley markets a versatile collection of spinning and spincasting reels. Included are 4 spincasters with strong metal construction, star drag, and retrieve ratios of 3:1 or 3.5:1 that come spooled with 80 to 125 yds. of 8- to 17-lb. Trilene XL line Approximate prices: Model **56,** $9.95; Model **290,** $12.95; Model **300,** $16.95; Model **350,** $30.95.

Berkley **604:** A first-rate ultra-light spinning reel. Has Berkley's exclusive cam-operated bail system, die-cast face gear, anti-foul grad knob, hard-chromed line pickup, fold-away handle, coin-removable side plate, 3.6:1 retrieve. Comes with 200 yds. of 4-lb. Trilene XL, about $22.95.

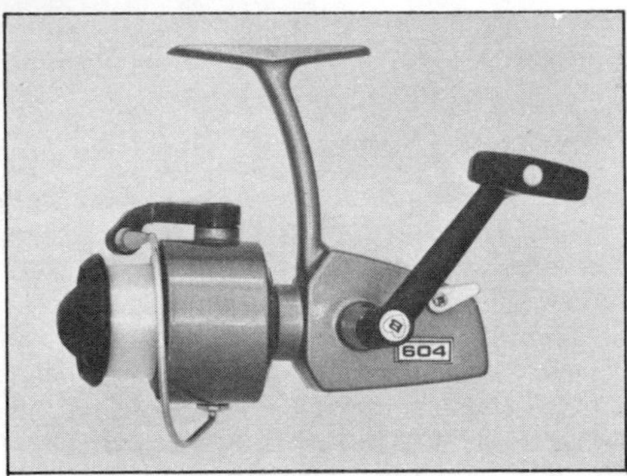


Ask to see Berkley's Castamatic **1,** billed as the only fully automatic spinning reel made. Projecting above the reel within easy grasp is a long, fingertip-action trigger. You pull it at the start of cast, cast in usual fashion, then release it. You never touch the line or bail. Great for night fishing, and in cold weather you can cast with gloves on. Castamatic **1** comes spooled with 225 yds. of 8-lb. Trilene XL, about $55.

### From the American Import Co.

Under the L. M. Dickson label: Samson series of spincasting reels. Maroon die-cast housing with contrasting spool cup in metallic gold; heavy-duty gear train; complete anti-rust, anodized undercoat. Three models, with guarantee card:

**No. 998:** Zamak gears; nickel-plated, rolledge rotor; steel pin pickup; wheel drag; 2.7:1 retrieve. Weighs 8.5 oz., holds 110 yds. of 8-lb. test. About $12.95.

**No. 997:** Basically the same details as No. 998's, but with line capacity of 100 yds. of 6-lb. test. About $10.95.

**No. 999:** Heavier-duty. Stainless steel rotor, brass pinion gear, star drag, ceramic pin pickup, level wind spool. Weighs 12½ oz., retrieves at 3.5:1, holds 200 yds. of 16-lb. line, sells for approximately $17.95.

### Gladding-South Bend Reels

**Gladding-South Bend's Classic Series Spinning Reels:** Four models, ultra-light (Classic **925**) to heavy salt water model (Classic **960**). Thirty-one features are listed Highlights: Exclusive Magnum Drag—14 braking surfaces, wide adjustment; all ball-bearing construction; rust-resistant materials throughout, with double epoxy finish coat; precision, machine-cut helical gears; anodized folding crank; selective anti-reverse—positioned ahead o gear system to take strain off gears; Dynamic bail system, stainless steel, with very hard line roller on Teflon (DuPont material) inner sleeve. Approximate prices salt water $24.95; others: $14.95.

**No. 730-A by Gladding-South Bend, fo fresh water service:** Newly designe member of the popular 700 Series Corrosion-resistant metal construction stainless steel bail, positive anti-reverse wide-range, multiple-disc drag. **No. 730-A** also features die-cast spool, folding crank Gear ratio is 3.5:1. Holds 225 yds. of 8-lb line, sells for about $9.95.

**Gladding-South Bend's Spin Cast 95** Sturdy, precision-cut metal gears o stainless shafts; oscillating level-win spool; strong multiple-disc drag; selectiv anti-reverse; ceramic pickup pin; rubbe line snubber to grip line tightly without damage; 3.1:1 gear ratio. Comes filled with approximately 100 yds. of 15-lb. monofilament for about $2.95.

**Reels from Eagle Claw [Wright & McGill]**

**Eagle Claw Blue Pacific Spinning Reels:** Don't be misled by that "Blue Pacific." The series has fresh water models too. It encompasses six models, **No. 125** (ultra-light, 8.5 oz., 4.1:1 retrieve) to **No. 625** (heavy salt-water reel, 24 oz., 3.5:1 gear ratio). Features of the Blue Pacifics include: Ball-bearing construction; rugged, heavy-duty

bail (folds for easy storage, locks securely in casting) of chromed stainless steel with special hard-chromed roller; anti-reverse; multiple-disc drag with a wide range of adjustment; fold-away aluminum handle; chemical treatment against corrosion; brown epoxy finish, scratch- and mar-resistant. Price range from about $16.00 to $32.00.

**Eagle Claw Mediterranean Spinning Reels:** Again, don't let the name fool you. The series includes fresh water models. Range is from the ultra-light Model **ECO** (6 oz., extra-fast 5.5:1 retrieve) to marine Model **ECU** (21 oz., 3.5:1 gear ratio). In the Mediterranean series are light, medium and heavy fresh water reels—Models **ECQ** and **ECP**, Models **ECR** and **ECRU**, and **ECS**, respectively. They go from 9½ to 11 oz., with retrieves from 4.25:1 to an extra-fast

5.5:1. All are handsomely designed/ and epoxy-finished in a distinctive shade of brown. On their list of specifications: Extra-durable frame; metal parts treated against corrosion and oxidation; full-range, adjustable friction drag; collapsible handle and bail (fresh-water models only); anti-reverse; heavy-duty bail with rugged, chromed line roller. Spool capacities of the fresh-water Mediterraneans are from 250 yds. of 4-lb. test (Model **ECQ**) to 225 yds. of 12-lb. (Model **ECS**). Approximate price scale: $30.00 to $50.00.

Eagle Claw also offers Blue Pacific reels in three spincasting models, all with push-button control, chemically treated against rust and corrosion, in a good-looking brown and gold epoxy finish. **No. 102** for light lures, **No. 103** for light to medium, **No. 104** for medium to heavy. Prices are about: **No. 102**, $12.00; **No. 103**, $20.00; **No. 104**, $22.00.

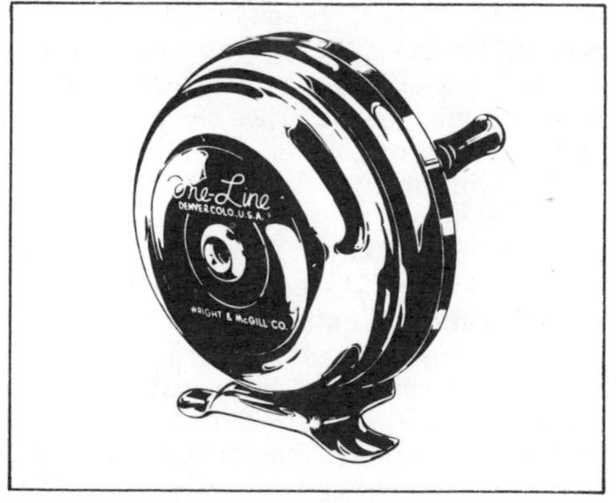

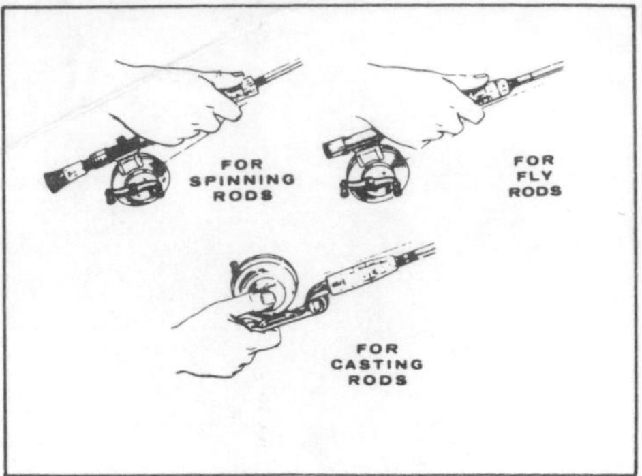


**Eagle Claw Model 10BS Freline:** Designated as an all-purpose spinning reel, adaptable to casting, spinning and fly rods, quickly adjustable to either left- or right-hand operation. Very easy to use, recommended for novices and youngsters. Capacity is from 150 yds. of 4-lb. line to 90 yds. of 10 lb. Attractively finished in burgundy red. Sells for about $16.00.

## MORE ABOUT LINES

Today's fishing lines are "ambidextrous," interchangeably used in salt water and fresh, thanks to the assets of their synthetic materials and production technology. We already have spotlighted many brands in our "Salt-water Tackle Showroom." Those will give you a comprehensive idea of their great availability in various types and broad range of strengths. We need only add some random samplings here to round out our coverage.

Many tackle manufacturers market lines under their own brand labels. Among comparable lines, basic construction (**i.e.**, braided, monofilament, metal-corded, wire) is the same, and so may be their basic materials (Dacron, nylon, etc.). But line and tackle manufacturers add their own features, such as special finishes, low-visibility color, built-in lubrication, and so on for utilitarian distinction. All reputable manufacturers maintain high standards of quality—they must in a highly competitive field. So it invariably turns out that any preference for a particular brand is an individualistic thing, shaped by the angler's ideas and experience (and success), and by what he or she considers bonus features. Differences of opinion, therefore, do not reflect on the quality or serviceability of other lines.

As you browse through our fresh-water tackle showroom keep in mind that equipment wielded in sweetwater angling may be designed for marine use, too, or at least is adaptable to it. (The reverse also is true, of course.) In any case, under reasonable conditions it probably will perform equally well in both arenas. But it also must be remembered that tackle earmarked primarily for fresh-water service may or may not have adequate corrosion protection for extended marine fishing. Lacking it, frequent cleaning is required to fend off salt sabotage.

### Berkley and Company

One of Berkey's monofilament labels is Trilene. It comes in the following versions, 2-lb. test to 80: "Standard" Trilene; Trilene XL; Dura Tuff; 5000 Series Worm Fishing Line; Tensimatic (heavy-duty).

Among other lines marketed by Berkley: A group of nylon monofilaments—Spin Chief (4- to 150-lb. test), Depth-O-Matic (color-coded trolling line, 15- to 40-lb.), Dew Flex (4- to 150-lb.), Mill Ends (assorted colors, 2- to 40-lb). Braided lines for baitcasting, trolling, surfcasting, etc. —Medallion brand (nylon baitcasting, 10- to 50-lb., Dacron trolling and surfing, 10-117 lb.), Crusader nylon lines for bait-casting, squidding, 10- to 50-lb. and 18- to 110-lb; Crusader Canepole Line (assorted weights and colors).

Additionally, Berkley produces a large array of leaders in nylon, Steelon and cable and many ready-made rigs for fresh- and salt-water fishing.

### Zebco

This company spools many of its reels with DuPont Stren, a fluorescent monofilament. (Fact ia, DuPont Stren has been on the U.S. marine and fresh water fishing scene for a long time and is widely used.) The unique property of this line is that the sun's ultraviolet rays make it "glow" out of water so that the angler can better see and control his line. Underwater the glow disappears because ultraviolet rays are absorbed by water, so there's low visibility to fishes. DuPont Stren fluorescent line comes as clear blue (blue glow) and Golden Stren (bright golden glow). The glow, by the way, is seen from early light until dusk, on bright days or under cloudy skies. Stren is sold in a wide range of strengths and lengths.

**Gladding-South Bend**

Gladding's Bassin' Man All-Pro Line was developed as a magnum line for lunker-size black bass. Comes in strengths from 10- to 22-lb. test. Color is a near-invisible smoke gray, in spools from 150 to 300 yds.

You'll find other lines under the Gladding-South Bend banner in the salt water tackle department. To those you can add these labels: Dreadnaught (nylon casting line); Beachcomber (striped bass special); and South Bend Black-Oreno (midnight blue, braided nylon casting and trolling line—Oreno is an old name). Plus special purpose lines, and leaders in nylon, monofilament and Vinylsteel.

**Sunset Line & Twine Co.**

Many Sunset lines are spotlighted in our salt water tackle section. Add to those: The Specialist label (soft-braid nylon casting line particularly suited to black bass fishing, in mist green or camouflage, 9- to 35-lb. test); Black Magic Casting Line (medium-priced, braided nylon, silicone-treated, 10- to 30-lb.); and Flat Braid Nylon Surf Line (sand or green, 18- to 90-lb. test).

**Shakespeare**

Among its lines are Presidential Braided Casting Line, in black or camouflage, strengths from 10- to 40-lb. test. Soft, supple, extra-strong when wet.

**Gudebrod Lines**

Although Gudebrod also markets a sizable fleet of lures, it is primarily a line company, and its great assortment shows it. Some Gudebrod labels that can be appended to those already mentioned:

Catfish Line: Braided nylon, minimum stretch, for rugged service. Sand color, 35- to 108-lb. test.

Real Strike Nylon: Budget-priced, for fresh or salt water use, casting, trolling, etc. Braided nylon, 10- to 108-lb. test.

Silk Casting Line, **No. 500:** "No-stretch" braided silk of premium quality material, with a twisted core inside a braided jacket, waterproofed for minimum absorption, 9- to 42-lb. test.

Bee Line: Extra-fine diameter, braided nylon casting line, originally created for East Coast distance tournament surf-casters, also popular among New England striped bass fishermen using large plugs. Somewhat less stretch than mono, good knot strength. In tests from 10 to 108 lbs., **No. 516.**

Metered Lead Core Trolling Line: For deep lake or ocean trolling. Durable, tightly woven nylon jacket for finer diameter, color-coded, 18- to 45-lb. test.

Tournament Casters' Line: Made especially for casting, long popular in distance and accuracy tourneys. Untreated, soft nylon (**No. 513**) or silk (**No. 514**) braids, red/white combination, 4½- to 9-lb. test.

**The Garcia Corporation**

**Platyl Monofilament Spinning Line.** Mist-colored for minimum visibility in water, with great knot strength. In tests from 1 lb. to 40 lbs.

Also from Garcia, two braided casting lines with braided-in lubrication to virtually eliminate external and internal friction for longer life. One is designated as Sinking Dacron, the other as Floating Nylon. Both come in ten strengths, 10 to 50 lbs.

**Cortland Line Company**

Along with a complete inventory of fly lines and many others for fresh and salt water service, Cortland supplies:

**Nylorfi:** Billed as the most popular monofilament line in France, from where Cortland imports it. Super-strong and nearly invisible in water. Cortland reports that in tests with five other topflight 20-pound mono lines Nylorfi had the smallest diameter, greatest straight-pull breaking strength per diameter and greatest knot strength. This premium monofilament comes in tests from 4 to 30 pounds, on 100-**meter** spools, which means 109.3 yards, or almost 10 percent more line per spool.

More Cortland labels (see also marine tackle section):

**Cortland Wormer:** Braided expressly for fishing plastic worms with free-spool reels. Two-tone green color to help signal strikes. Controlled stretch. Ten to 35-lb. test.

**Mono-Worm:** A new oval or flat shape to lie snugly on a reel, not dig in. For revolving-spool reels only. In two-tone green, 12- to 35-lb.

**Tournament Grade Monofilament:** Uniform diameter for uniform strength throughout, with certified tensile strength to meet IGFA specifications. In mist green, 6- through 80-lb. test.

**Cortland Kerplunk:** Lead-core line for deep trolling, braided nylon jacket over special lead core. Changes color every 10 yards for easier depth-finding. Five strengths, 18 to 60 lbs.

**U.S. Line Co.**

**U.S. Black Knight Nylon:** Hard-braided, non-absorbent nylon, with waterproof treatment against moisture infiltrating braiding. Recommended equally for fresh, salt or alkaline waters. Great flexibility, extra-smooth for easy-on-the-thumb baitcasting or surfcasting. In tests from 9 to 45 lbs.

**U.S. Castfast:** Black nylon, "precisionized" for maximum striking resilience, smooth-braided with frictionless waterproof impregnation, 9- to 45-lb. test.

**U.S. Duo-Chrome:** Budget-priced camouflaged line to break up visual continuity in water, 10 lb. to 30 lb.

**U.S. Westfield Monofilament:** An improved mono, softer and smaller in diameter, mist green or powder blue, in eleven strengths from 2 to 40 lb.

**U.S. Braided Monofilament:** Developed in 1959 for closed-face reels and improved thereafter. Green-colored, smooth-braided mono designed to be more pliable than one-strand extruded mono, with less stretch. For all spinning reels, 4-, 6-, 8-, 10-, 12-lb. tests.

**U.S. Mighty-Mono:** A light gray extruded monofilament, budget-priced, in twelve strengths from 4- to 60-lb. test.

**U.S. Da'N'Nyt:** DuPont "miracle" fibers, non-absorbent, unaffected by salt or brackish water or grease. Exclusively a U.S. Line development, tension-braided for strength, compactness, smooth casting. In a traditional "salt and pepper" pattern to reduce visibility to a minimum, 9- to 30-lb. test.

**Ashaway Line & Twine Mfg. Co.**

As with other manufacturers, we've listed a number of this outfit's lines in the salt-water tackle department. Other Ashaway lines include:

**Extra-Strength Nylon Bait Casting Line:** Waterproof, heat-treated, minimum wear. In ten strengths, 6- to 45-lb, wet test. Color is black.

**Original Nylon:** For baitcasting. Smooth, pliable, in a black, waterproof braid, 6- to 45-lb. wet test.

**Ande Inc.**

This West Palm Beach, Florida, firm specializes in monofilament lines.

## ICE FISHING GEAR

Normark Corporation is inspired and qualified in more ways than one to produce ice fishing equipment. To begin with, it's located in Minneapolis, which, with its twin city St. Paul, is in the heart of the great Midwestern ice angling country. For another thing, its ice fishing equipment comes from Europe, where the sport has been pursued for centuries.

To fish through the ice you naturally have to create an opening first. To facilitate this, Normark offers **Fin-Bore II**, an auger that bites its way through in less than one minute. It comes from Sweden, features blades of top-quality alloy steel, electrically tempered for uniformity of cutting edges, removable for sharpening. The new double offset handle (removable for carrying) is for high-speed cutting (tested up to 25 inches in 15 seconds). And Fin-Bore II makes the job still easier by pushing chips out of the hole. Plastic scabbard protects the blades. Overall assembled length is 61½". In three diameters: **No. FB11-6**, 6"; **No. FB11-7**, 7"; **No. FB11-8**, 8½". Respective prices are approximately $37.75; $42.45; and $44.15.

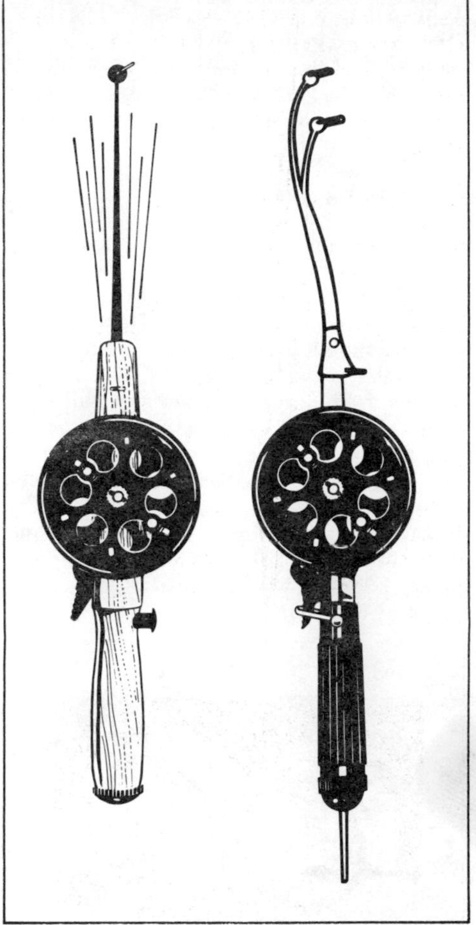

Suggestive of a hand drill, but anything but, are thrumming rods, actually rod-reel combinations. They come from Finland and are designed specifically for vertical fishing at deeper levels, through ice or in open water. The term "thrumming" stems from the fact that the outfit causes a lure to thrum or vibrate for added attraction. Simply pushing a button on the handle does it.

Normark offers two models, **Teho 2** and **Teho 3**. Both have these specifications: Overall rod length, 19"; rod tip of high-tensile, impact-resistant plastic; molded reel with adjustable drag tension button; a depth meter built into the reel; spring tension reel brake. **Teho 2's** handle is northern hardwood, with storage space.

**Teho 3** has a double tip for feeling light strikes and fighting heavier fish, and it folds for carrying compactness. Its handle is high-impact plastic, also with storage space. Prices go about $8.50 for **Teho 2,** $8.95 for **Teho 3.**

### Gudebrod Equipment

Designed for ice fishing in particular and vertical angling in general by the Rapala lure people in Finland are the Pilkki jigging lures, designed to vibrate, flutter, swim to one side in imitation of a wounded minnow. Will take a wide range of fresh-water species, from perch, crappies and sunfish to lake trout, walleyes, northerns. Choice of four colors, four sizes, 1½" and 3/16 oz. to 3½" and 3/4 oz. Prices about $.99 to $1.25 each. Also for vertical fishing are the Rapala balanced jigs. In various combinations of nickel, copper, brass, red, black, 1-3/8" and 1/8 oz. to 2¼" and ½oz., about $1.95 to $2.95.

Ice fishing line from Gudebrod: G-T Dacron offers special advantages to ice anglers. Its special Teflon coating resists water and therefore freezing, keeping the line limp. It also has a minimal stretch factor at any depth for strike sensitivity and good hook-setting. Color is greenspot. Comes in tests to 45 lbs, two connected 100-yd. spools. Prices start at about $3.15 per spool.

### Ice Fishing Equipment from the Worth Company

**Worth's Pop-Up, a magnetic tip-up:** Among its several accented features:

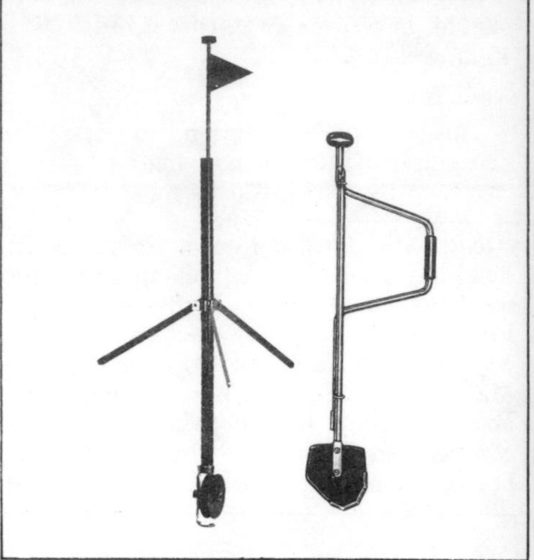

Freeze-proof, even in subzero temperatures; no exposed line or trip mechanism, three-point suspension stays put even in a 50-mile wind; snow-proof—drifting snow can't plug mechanism; positive signal, shows only when a fish hits. Other specs: Rugged construction of space age plastic, feels "warm" even in subzero weather; magnetic trip adjusts from light for panfishes to medium for walleyes, and heavy for lake trout and northerns; spool winder—Worth design for easy winding in of line; spool lock—easily gripped gnurled knob adjusts tension on spool, locks it for storing; easy to operate. Model **MTV**, about $6.50.

**Worth/Mustad Ice Auger:** Features a new concept in ice cutting, a straight-edge blade. Can be resharpened by owner, instructions included. Two-piece handle of 5/8" solid steel, cadmium-plated. Threaded bracket on handle locks unassembled sections for easy carrying or storage. **No. SA6** has 6" blade, **No. SA8** has 8" blade; blades are interchangeable on same handle, can be bought separately. Approximate prices: **SA6,** $21; **SA8,** $26.75.

**No. IC9 Hub-Bub:** An artificial designed specifically for ice fishing, but effective in other angling too. Two spinner blades create a hubbub, red fluorescent beads add attraction. Treble hook in size 16 only. **No. IC9N** has nickel finish; **No. IC9G** has gold finish. About 75c.

**From Feldman Engineering & Mfg. Co.**

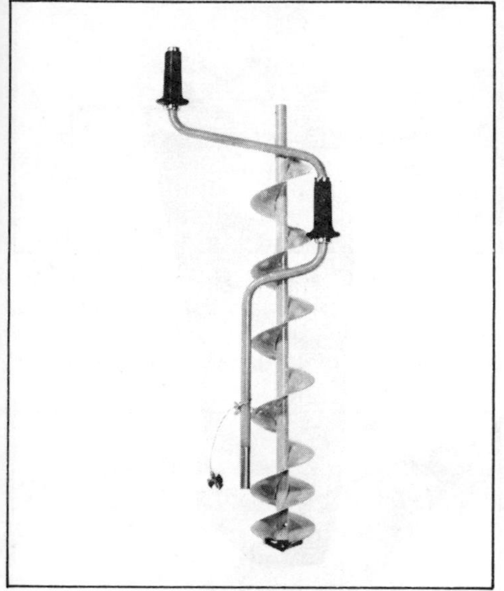

**Jiffy Power Ice Drill:** Lightweight, just 19 lbs., plus bit. A 3 hp. gasoline motor drives its 7-, 8-, or 9-inch bit through the thickest ice in seconds, with easy chip removal by spiral auger. A great time and effort saver. Has centrifugal clutch, low gear ratio, sturdy construction. Completely portable, safe, simple to operate. Fully guaranteed. From $129.95.

**Feldman Hand Ice Drill:** New design with drop forge cutter for maximum drilling power and speed, aided by handle brace and bit with long leverage. Handle detaches for transportation, compact storage. Weighs 7 lbs. **No. HID-5** with 5" cutter, about $29.95. **No. HID-7,** with 7" cutter, about $35.95.

**Jiffy Ice Skimmer:** A needed accessory to keep hole clear. Jiffy features an easy removal of any ice buildup—just tap its bottom on the frozen lake surface. All-steel construction, plated against rust, strong rivet handle. Bluegill Model, **No. 1321,** 4-3/4" ladle, about $1.59; Pike Model, **No. 1322,** 6" ladle, about $1.75.

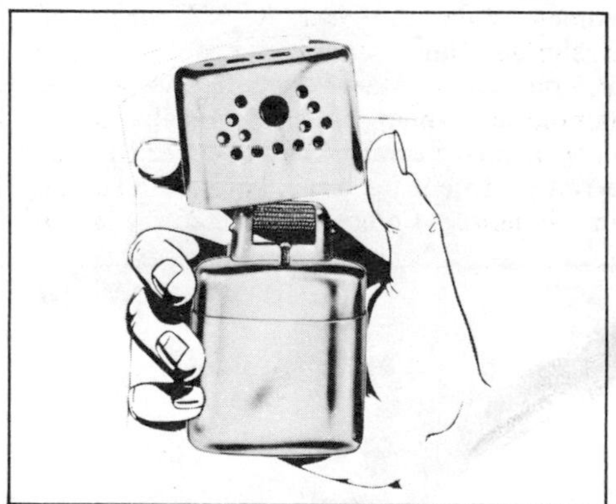

**Aladdin Laboratories, Inc.,**

**Jon-E Hand Warmer:** Gives comforting hand warmth all day on one filling (1 oz.) of Jon-E Fluid. Use it as a cigarette lighter too. New, improved burner for fast, easy start. Made from chrome-plated steel, polished, with drawstring carrying bag. In two sizes, approximate prices: Standard, **No. 700**, $4.50; giant size, $5.50. Also as Jon-E twin pack, **No. 700** warmer and 8 oz. can of fluid, $5.09. Fluid separately, 8 oz. for 59c, 16 oz. for 95c; lighting wicks, 10c. Replacement burners for the 2 sizes, $1.50 and $2.

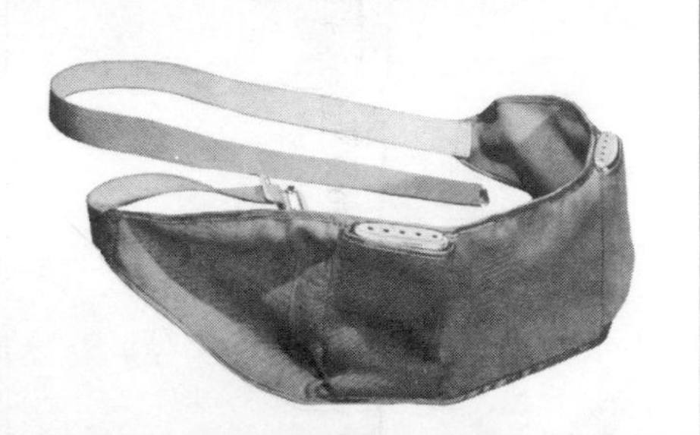

**Jon-E Body Belt:** Fits snugly, warmly across the kidney region, where shivers often start. Made from durable, color-fast, scarlet twill. Adjustable to fit everyone, over all clothing, holds two standard size Jon-E Hand Warmers. Approximate retail price, $2.95.

**Bay De Noc Lure Co., Gladstone, Mch.**

**Pimple Pole:** A compact, rigid rod—14" overall, folds to 10"—for ice fishing, drifting, jigging, still fishing. Odd name comes from the fact it was originally designed for manufacturer's Swedish Pimple lures. Made from basswood with laminated veneer tip, protected by double coat of float varnish. Sliding cover conceals a compartment for lures, hooks and sinkers in handle. Comes with 25 yds. of

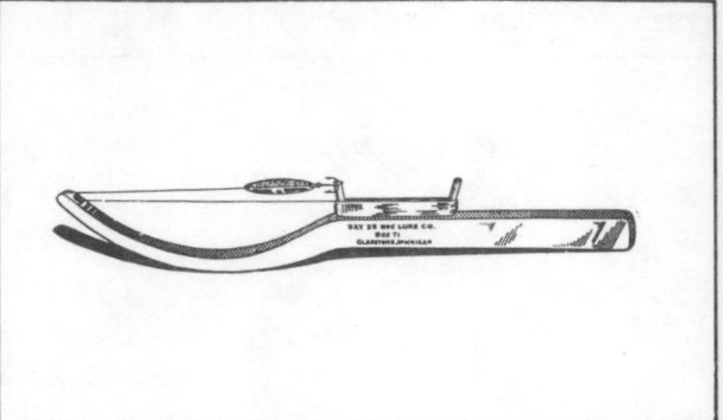

monofilament line. **No. 16WL**, about $2.25. **No. 10225**, Folding Pimple Pole, is essentially the same, but 16" and comes with 25 yds. of 12- to 25-lb. mono, about $2.65.

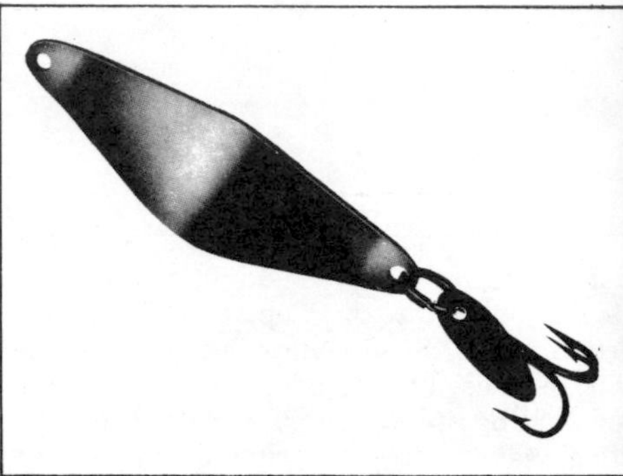

**Do-Jigger:** A shad-action jig for ice fishing and warmer weather spinning and jigging as a spoon. Effective on trout, perch, walleyes, northerns. Unique "wing" design flashes in a lazy fluttering action. Used with bait, it's reported very effective in winter. In various finishes, including nickel, gold, metal and color combinations, 1/6 oz. to 1/3 oz., approximately 89c to $1.25.

# Fly Fishing Tackle Showroom 6

Long ago a wit remarked, "There's no greater love than that of one drunk for another."

True, but he should have added, ". . . except, maybe, that of a chronic fly fisherman for *his* sport."

The book *There's No Fishing Like Fly Rod Fishing** neatly dissects this uniquely intense devotion in its lead-off chapter, titled "Philosophy of Fly Fishing" and penned by Roger Latham, one of the volume's ten author-experts. He starts by drawing an interesting parallel, akin to something we just said:

> Becoming a fly fisherman is little different from falling in love!
>
> The love of fly fishing is much like the love of a man for his one special woman. Over the years, an admiration and devotion develop that are as endless and timeless as the sands and tides.

Fly fishing's magnetism is a multifaceted thing. The biggest attraction unquestionably is its challenge. The word "challenge" is overworked in participator sports, but not here. To place a tiny lure, with practically no real weight of its own, in precisely the correct manner and spot to cause a fish to rise to it, then play the rascal successfully with the skinniest, most willowy kind of rod imaginable calls for one of angling's highest degrees of skill. And it's the degree of skill that dramatically separates the inept from the good flycasters and, at the top, masters of the sport. Which of those three levels is achieved is entirely up to the degree of tenacity of the beginner.

Roger Latham reminds us that every fly fisherman starts out as a clumsy, green initiate. Even for Izaak Walton, the sport's first *mahatma,* there had to be a beginning—and he wasn't nearly as well off in the tackle department and reference literature as today's neophytes. For those intent upon becoming good at it, fly fishing becomes a virtual course of study, right from the initial kindling of interest, complete with textbooks and field classrooms. Each student prepares his own tests, takes them, and grades himself accordingly. For novices the old International Correspondence Schools motto comes to mind: *Patience, Perserverance, Practice.* Accent that last. With it, skill can be attained.

The rewards of proficiency in fly fishing are many. Perhaps the greatest is the satisfaction that comes with doing something well.

In few other kinds of angling do genuine devotees become so thirsty for knowledge. Like their brethren in other phases of sport fishing, they devour books and magazine articles, like dedicated chess players, reviewing the works of masters. They command a knowledge of equipment. They learn all they can about their intended targets—trout or tarpon, bass or bonefish. But it's in the investigation of lures that they often go beyond the rest of the fishing fraternity. Not only do they familiarize themselves with the anatomy and how-to of their artificials, but also the why. They even delve into the life cycles of the insects and other creatures their lures are designed to imitate. Many become amateur entomologists and zoologists in the process. And in few other kinds of angling do so many participants fashion their own lures. Fly tying is an integral part of fly fishing.

**Preliminary Notes on Tackle**

In *There's No Fishing Like Fly Rod Fishing,* author-expert Leon Chandler comments:

> An important factor in the great surge of interest in fly rod fishing in recent years is that equipment is better and easier to use than ever before. Manufacturers have devoted much time, money, and effort to design and produce rods, reels, lines, lures, and accessory items in all price ranges to meet all fly fishing needs. The problem that faces most novice fly fishermen is to know which of the many available items will best serve his purpose.
>
> For the person choosing his initial outfit I strongly advise that contact be made with retailing sales personnel who are knowledgeable about fly fishing equipment. Properly balanced equipment is a very important part of the enjoyment of the sport, and far too many beginners have been disillusioned and frustrated because they tried to start fly fishing with mismatched gear.

To carry Leon's advice a step further, we'll add that the most important phrase in fly fishing for all participants is *properly balanced tackle,* and that means line, rod and reel. Accent balance between line and rod. In no other kind of fishing is this relationship so critical. Simplified, balancing fly tackle means matching the *weight* of a line to the *action*—stiffness or flexibility—of the rod with which it's to be used. It has been said that hard-nosed purists have been known to select a particular fly line they like, then match a rod to *that,* rather than the other way around. But that isn't a recommended standard procedure, at least not for the less-experienced.

Line quality is very much a part of balanced fly tackle too. The best, most expensive rod turned out by a firm such as Orvis in Vermont can't function properly with inferior line. Conversely, in the right hands a quality line can make even an inferior rod do a passable job.

Why all this concern about balancing line and rod? You could say that it's because of the nature of the beast—(the "beast" being fly fishing). Among all forms of casting, fly fishing is unique. In those other kinds the weight of an artificial or rig supplies casting impetus, with the line being pulled from the reel. In fly fishing many of the lures are essentially near-weightless, so forward impetus must be supplied by the line. Without it you couldn't cast those flies. With their extreme lightness they wouldn't be able to move the line, much less overcome the inertia of a reel spool. Even aided by the lines' weight, it was necessary to develop specialized casting techniques to propel them to target areas.

As he gains lore and experience—and confidence—the once novice progresses to better, more sophisticated gear. There's time enough for this. At the outset a newcomer can get his act together with a less-expensive outfit. Note that we didn't say *cheap* outfit. In no other kind of angling is it more of a mistake to launch a career with junky gear. Besides, there's no excuse for it. Thanks to fiberglass, there is a complete range of good fly rods with price tags everyone can afford.

If you follow the path trod by most of your predecessors, you'll become more critical of tackle and more discerning in proportion to your experience. The rod that got you started may no longer be completely satisfactory. It probably won't be, because you will have branched out. Maybe you'll keep that as a spare or for particular situations, but chances are you'll be looking for more sophisticated tackle. One day you may even be shopping for one of those superb split-bamboo instruments. Hopefully, you'll be able to plunk down the $100-plus. As we said, there will be time enough for that.

Of all the tackle items acquired by fly fishermen, the object of greatest affection is the rod. To say that it's cherished is an understatement. It's treated almost like an offspring, exhibited to other anglers and brought out to be admired even when no fishing is in prospect. And why not? If its owner has been in the game any length of time, chances are that it's a handsome piece of work representing a respectable cash outlay.

When fly fishermen gather for scuttlebutt sessions the chatter invariably focuses mainly on rods as the chief implement. But this overshadowing doesn't lessen the importance of the other two major items, reel and line. Actually, reels come in for their share of affection too; and no matter how many a veteran may acquire over the years, he usually has one or two that remain long-standing favorites. You won't be surprised to hear that fly reels come with a wide range of price tags. They do not go as high as those on quality rods, if we include the handcrafted split-bamboo gems that can't leave a store for less than $150, $200—and up. But again it's the old story of getting what you pay for.

Three types of fly reels are offered: Single-action, the simplest and therefore least expensive; automatic, so named because of a spring-powered retrieve mechanism; and the multiplying kind, with a gear train that effects more than one revolution of the spool with each turn of the crank. We'll elaborate more on this trio later. For now, suffice it to say that the cost of a fly reel depends upon type, size, model and manufacturer. You'll see price differences as you wander through our showroom.

By now we shouldn't have to say it again, but we will anyway: When you shop for a fly reel, concentrate on name brands and buy the best you can afford at the time. Quality is especially important with the automatic and multiplying types. They have more parts to go sour if the reels are inferior. Generally, gradations in prices are a reasonable yardstick for judging differences in quality. And the same goes for fly lines.

## FRESH-WATER GEAR

### RODS

It has been estimated that fully 95 percent of U.S.-produced fly rods today are of tubular fiberglass. Such has been the acceptance of that material, even by discriminating purists. Fiberglass fly rods are light, possess great strength, come with a wide range of actions, and are priced at all levels. Many long-timer fly casters may argue that nothing matches the smoothly flowing power and delicate response of a well-made Tonkin cane rod. We won't debate the point, but say only that fiberglass has made it possible to produce quality fly rods at prices more within reach of most anglers.

### Some Guidelines

It's no more possible to recommend a specific rod to you here than to order a pair of shoes for you. It's a question of "feel" and "fit." However, we can offer some general suggestions that should prove helpful.

You must give consideration to the kinds and size ranges of fishes you'll be seeking, as well as to the types of areas in which you'll be doing much of your angling. For instance, if most of your activity will be on small streams where long casts are not essential, and you'll be rigging small, very light flies, you can look to one of the lighter-caliber rods. Usually recommended for this kind of service is a 7½- or 8-foot model, weighing up to about 3½ ounces, and able to handle a No. 6 sinking line or No. 7 floating line. Its taper and action will be such that it can cast wet and dry flies. A 7½- or 8-footer also is serviceable for panfishes with small flies or cork popping bugs.

On the other hand, if you contemplate working large rivers, where longer casts and bigger artificials are involved, or maybe fishing lakes for bass with the bulkier, more wind-resistant lures, you have to give thought to a longer, more powerful rod—say, one in the 8½- or 9-foot class, perhaps 9½ feet long, handling line weights to Nos. 11 and 12. Same would go if you have your sights set on the larger game, such as muskellunge and river-running tarpon. These rods are proportionately heavier, of course.

Here's another example: If much of your fishing involves small streams with a lot of underbrush to impede casts, you might better go to a 6- or 6½-footer handling No. 4 or No. 5 lines.

For your information, fly rods have their heavier calibers too. There are 9- to 10- and 10½-foot salmon rods ranging up to about 8 ounces, and two-handed salmon-fishing models going from 11 to 14 and 14½ feet, with weights up to 16½, 20 ounces.

If there's a compromise for a novice, it's probably an 8- or 8½-foot rod weighing up to 4½ or 5 ounces. That's about as close as any for "all-purpose" use under average conditions. If you're looking ahead to fishing in a variety of situations you probably will have to think in terms of at least two outfits—eventually, anyway. As with other kinds of gear, no one fly outfit can be all things at all times. With the variety of lines available, and reels with interchangeable spools, two properly selected outfits can cover a surprising variety of assignments.

It has been argued that maybe too much emphasis is placed on fly rod weights and actions for newcomers and less-experienced users, and we're inclined to agree. There's time enough to become discerning in those details as experience dictates. So far as weight is concerned, a simple criterion is how a rod feels to wield. This is an intangible, varying from one individual to another. Length and weight are factors. Hefting different models in a tackle shop can't tell you how they will feel after hours of continuous use, but it will give you a rough idea of whether or not you can handle them comfortably, and so should at least aid in elimination.

We defined the different degrees of rod action, extra-fast to slow, in "Salt-Water Tackle Showroom." The same specifications apply to fly rods. Regulars have their own ways of checking a rod's action before buying. One is to lightly cradle the handle in one hand and let the rod's tip rest on the floor. This is approximate at best, but it gives some indication of the degree of bend. Some fishermen hold a rod vertically and whip it back and forth—ceiling height and electrical fixtures permitting. Another method, not particularly liked by shop owners, is to tie a length of line to the rod's tip and carefully pull against it to exert gradually increasing pressure. And there are also practice casts with a dummy lure. But these are methods for seasoned anglers. Novices can rely on the judgment of tackle shop personnel for recommendation of a suitable type of action for them.

Fly rods are available in two-section and three-section models. A choice between them is personal, some regulars believing that the fewer joints a rod has, the better for continuity of action. In any case, it's a point of debatable importance to beginners. There are also models designed for easier carrying in air travel and on pack-in trips to remote regions, and they disassemble into more than three sections.

### What to Look for in Fly Rods

Speaking about quality now, you can employ the same criteria we outlined for conventional and spinning rods in "Salt-Water Tackle Showroom." The same standards apply to a fly rod's material and hardware—including proper number and alignment of guides, and overall workmanship. And again you can depend upon the integrity of name-brand manufacturers, with prices as a pretty good yardstick for measuring degrees of quality. Unless you have a specific manufacturer in mind, you will do well to talk with other fishermen, ask about their equipment, and look over the rods produced by different builders.

## LINES

Earlier we talked about the importance of balance between rod and line in fly fishing. So the logical step when buying a rod is to get matching line for it at the same time.

Balancing is primarily by line weight. The larger and stronger the rod, the heavier the line it requires. Fly lines are size-graded according to specific diameters and weights, a system simplified by the use of digits—No. 3, No. 8, No. 10 . . . The larger the number, the heavier the line. Most rod builders have facilitated balancing by suggesting a particular weight of line for optimum performance of a given rod, and indicating it on the rod. Look for such a label. If a rod doesn't carry one, be sure to ask the tackle dealer for his recommendation.

Once the proper weight of line is determined, you can go into the type and design of line best suited to your fishing.

Basically there are two types of fly lines: floating and sinking. Those designations tell how they behave in the water. A floating line is buoyant to remain in the surface layer and is designed for dry flies and artificials which float on top, often in imitation of some insect. A sinking line is made to submerge and is used with wet flies, nymphs and similar lures that are fished at lower levels.

Actually there's a third type, a relative newcomer, that combines the two. A floating line is easier to pick off the water than a sinking type, but there are times when it's desirable to present a lure below the surface. Accordingly, Cortland Line Company introduced its Sink-Tip concept in the mid-1960s. The main portion of this line floats for easier picking up, but a ten-foot outermost section (in a contrasting color for identification) sinks, to submerge flies as much as four to five feet.

Originally a floating line was the classic way to fish flies, but it had a drawback in that it more or less limited casters to species feeding at or near the surface. Development of sinking lines added a whole new dimension by taking lures down into deeper places where fishes lurk. Often such targets can't be reached with standard floating lines. The properly equipped flyrodder, therefore, carries lines of both floating and sinking types, utilizing either an interchangeable spool for his favorite reel or a separate reel.

After line weight, you have to consider three basic line *designs:*

**1. Level design:** "Level" means uniform diameter throughout, as opposed to any tapering. Because of this, level lines are easier to produce than tapered types, and it's reflected in cost to consumers. Preference is largely a matter of economy. Level lines are fine for novices learning the rudiments of flycasting, and they serve in situations in which casts are moderate and there are no wind problems. In actual fishing, the tapered designs are superior and therefore favored by experienced anglers.

**2. Double-taper:** Viewed in profile, a double-taper line could be likened to a pencil sharpened at both ends. Its outermost tip sections, one at each end, are small in diameter, which gradually increases toward the line's center until its main body diameter is attained. Since they're finer in diameter, the tapered sections are more flexible, less bulky and, very important, enable fly and leader to be cast onto the water with a minimum of surface disturbance. The lengths of the tapered sections vary from maker to maker, but generally run 8 to 12 feet. In addition to better presentation of flies, double-taper lines permit longer casts into wind than level lines do. They're a versatile component of fly fishing gear. In floating and sinking types they can be employed with a variety of flies, dry and wet.

Double-taper lines are not without an economy factor. Commonly they're made in 90-foot lengths. Since few flyrodders cast more than 50 feet consistently, a good 40-plus feet remain unused on the reel. At season's end this line can be taken off its reel, turned around end for end, and put back on. Now the worn section is on the inside and a fresh length is ready for action, doubling the line's life.

**3. Weight-forward design or "torpedo head":** This too is a tapered line. It consists essentially of a larger-diameter, heavier section out toward its forward or outermost end, followed by a "running line" of somewhat smaller diameter. In operation that heavier section could be likened to a sinker. Its concentration of forward weight makes for longer casts, handles bulky artificials, and is a distinct advantage in breezy situations. Further, manufacturers have added to weight-forward lines' versatility by incorporation of a long, slender front taper, ahead of that heavier section for delicate presentation of small flies.

Manufacturers offer weight-forward fly lines in a variety of combinations of heavier body sections and slender running lines, with total lengths usually 30 to 35 yards.

## About Fly Line Nomenclature

Fly lines have a lingo all their own to designate designs, weights and types. We can start with "L," "DT" and "WF." As if you hadn't guessed, they stand for Level, Double Taper and Weight Forward. Okay, now we add a number—3, 5, 8, and so on—to indicate weight. Then an "S" or "F," for Sinking or Floating, brings up the rear. Putting these designations together, we come up with line labels such as "WF8F" (Weight Forward, No. 8, Floating), "DT5S" (Double Taper, No. 5, Sinking), and "L4F" (Level design, No. 4 weight, Floating type).

This labeling was devised by the American Fishing Tackle Manufacturers Association in 1961 to replace a system that had become obsolete. Under the old arrangement, classification was based on diameters (indicated by letters of the alphabet), which was satisfactory when practically all fly lines were made from silk. But with the advent of nylon and Dacron the system had to be changed because of differences in the specific gravity of materials and the development of new braids and finishes. Diameters became useless as a standard—too many variations. Instead, AFTMA adopted a weight system. Its unit is the grain, smallest unit in the U.S. and English system of weights (437.5 grains = 1 ounce). To represent line weights in grains AFTMA assigned numbers 1 (60 grains) through 12 (380 grains), with manufacturing tolerances for each. The result is a uniform system, regardless of line materials, diameters, finishes or whatever. The segment of a fly line weighted to give it a number is the first 30 feet of its "working section," exclusive of any taper or tip.

Also in the AFTMA system are the designations "ST" for Single Taper (tapered only on one end, as opposed to a double taper) and "I" for Intermediate to indicate a floating-or-sinking line.

Because of the very nature of flycasting, more specialized demands are imposed on its lines than on those in other kinds of fishing. A floating line, for instance, must be light enough for buoyancy yet possess enough weight to bring out a rod's casting action. Tapered lines must be designed correctly in order to "turn over" a fly in proper presentation. And there are other details, such as textures that will pass smoothly and efficiently through rod guides while resisting wear, and line weights that are within close tolerances of those indicated on their packages.

Flycasting is indeed precision fishing, which sweetens the sense of accomplishment considerably.

Much of the credit for the continuous increase in fly fishing participation goes to the development of modern lines. They have made the sport easier to learn, more pleasurable, and more efficient. Moreover, they have broadened flycasters' horizons enormously. By combining weight, design and type with advanced materials, manufacturers offer a wide variety of lines to meet all fly fishing situations. Understandably, we can't specify a particular line for you, but a knowledgeable tackle dealer will, and if you stay with name brands you won't go wrong in the performance department.

**Leaders and Backing**

An essential item in a fly angler's kit is a tapered leader, and this too is specialized.

In a sense a tapered leader is a more delicate extension of the fly line. Its purpose is to provide a gradually decreasing amount of stiffness—or increasing flexibility, if you prefer—to continue the flow of momentum from the line and "turn over" a fly properly for presentation. In profile this leader tapers from a butt section, that which joins the line at its tip and is usually at least two-thirds the diameter of that tip, to a fine diameter at its outermost or tippet end, where the fly is attached.

Do-it-yourselfers create their own tapered leaders by joining lengths of monofilament material in gradually decreasing strengths (diameters) by blood knots. Thus they may start with a length of 25-pound mono, add a length of 20-pound, then 15-pound test, and so on down to 6-pound test or finer for the tippet end until they have the desired total leader length. This is an opportunity to incorporate their own ideas and experiment.

It's much easier, however, to buy knotless tapered leaders already to rig. They come in different lengths, commonly 7½, 9 and 12 feet. An important marking on the package is that referring to the size of the tippet end. Different tippet diameters are indicated by "1X," "2X," "3X," and so on. Selection of tippet sizes is determined by flies' hook sizes. The smaller the hook (or fly), the finer the tippet must be to make a natural presentation.

Cortland Line Company offers this table as a guide to matching tippet sizes and hooks:

| Tippet Size | Diameter (Inches) | Pounds Test | Hook Sizes |
|---|---|---|---|
| 1X | 0.010 | 7 | 4-6 |
| 2X | .009 | 6 | 6-8-10 |
| 3X | .008 | 4.5 | 8-10-12 |
| 4X | .007 | 3.5 | 12-14-16 |
| 5X | .006 | 2 | 14-16-18 |
| 6X | .005 | 1.5 | 16-18-20 |
| 7X | .004 | 1 | 18-20-22 |

**Tapered leader tips for novices:** (*1*) A good attachment to your fly line is via a nail knot. It's easy to tie, isn't bulky, passes readily through rod guides. A coating of Pliobond rubber-base cement will make it even smoother. (*2*) A new leader right out of its package, or one that has been on a reel for a time, often will coil like a spring. These annoying coils are removed easily by drawing the leader through a doubled piece of rubber held between the fingers. If no rubber material is available at the moment, pull through clenched fingers. (*3*) Watch for accidental knots in the leader. A breeze can cause them. They should be removed at once because they can reduce a leader's strength by as much as half.

**Backing** is line that goes on a reel ahead of the regular fly line to fill out the spool properly (to within 1/8- or ¼-inch of its rim) and also provide extra yardage for longer-running opponents. Variously used are braided Dacron, monofilament and braided nylon. Many fishermen favor the first. Strengths of backing also vary, largely according to personal opinion, and range up to 20-pound test. The amount of yardage is influenced by reel spool capacity and the tendency of some fishes to execute long runs in open water. Between fresh-water and marine fly fishing it can range from 25 yards of less up to 100, even more, on the bigger salt-water reels. The stronger the backing, the greater its diameter, and therefore the less yardage that can be accommodated by a given reel.

Backing serves a number of purposes. By helping to fill a reel spool it causes larger coils in the fly line. These, in turn, lessen its chances of kinking and also mean more line retrieved with each turn of the crank. Backing also is a form of economy, being less expensive than fly line. Too, being largely unused, it lasts a long time. At least some backing should be spooled on a fly reel, whatever fish is sought.

Experienced fishermen and tackle shop people can advise you on the strength and amount of backing for your situation. You can determine the backing yardage to fill your reel properly thus: Spool the fly line on *first,* tie the backing to it, and continue spooling until line is within 1/8- to ¼-inch of the rim. Then take both backing and fly line off and spool them back on in the right sequence.

## REELS

You recall the three types of fly reels: Single-action, automatic, and multiplying.

In fly fishing a reel's prime function is to store line. It isn't involved in actual casting, as are a surfcasting reel, spinning reel and the like. Nor is it often used in fighting a fish, except to retrieve line. For these reasons it may be considered secondary to rod and line by some anglers. Nevertheless, it still pays to buy a good one.

**Single-action type:** It's the least complicated, lightest, and easiest kind to use, and adaptable to a full range of angling assignments. Further, because its basic design is simple, it's readily produced in a range of sizes and prices. And there you have the reasons why it's the most popular type in use, recommended to novices, favored by many old hands.

A single-action fly reel is the simplest of the three types because its crank or handle is mounted directly on the reel spool—no gears. One turn of the handle = one revolution of the spool. By the same token, there are fewer parts to develop "bugs," and so it's the easiest to maintain.

Size becomes the first consideration when scouting for a single-action reel. Its size should be that which best balances the rod on which it's to be used, with an eye to spool capacity. Naturally it should be able to accommodate sufficient line for the kinds of fishing at hand. On an average, these reels range from small—with a frame diameter of approximately 2-3/4 inches, for rods in the 6- to 6½-foot bracket—to large models of 4- and 4½-inches diameter for 9- and 9½-foot rods. A practical, all-purpose size for fresh-water service is 3¼ or 3½ inches.

Although not used in as many fresh-water situations as in marine fishing, some kind of drag mechanism is desirable to prevent line from peeling off the spool unnecessarily and, when needed, exert a braking effect to better control a fish. On inexpensive models the drag is supplied by a clicker. Superior and costing more is an adjustable drag. Adjustment comes in handy to keep it within limits of tippet breaking strengths. Like the brake on any reel, it should be smooth and dependable, two details for which you can rely on name-brand builders.

A fly reel is mounted on its rod's underside so as not to interfere with casting. Most anglers develop a definite preference for right-handed or southpaw cranking, and seat the reel accordingly. Many right-handed casters keep the handle on the left so they don't have to change hands when playing a fish. Either way, the drag should be readily accessible in *your* manner of fishing.

**What to look for:** Quality of construction is No. 1, of course. It's usually evident on a well-made reel; lack of it is equally a give-away on an inferior model. General appearance is an opening clue, even to less-experienced eyes. Turn the handle a few times. Note how smoothly the spool turns, without any "slap," wobble or binding. Check to be sure the clearance between spool and frame isn't excessive. That could lead to line headaches with a filled spool. Look carefully for any burrs, sharp edges or rough surfaces. They can ruin fly lines in short order. Last but not least, consider the reel's overall finishes and protection of any exposed metal surfaces.

Personally, we'd insist upon a quick-change spool feature. It's well worth a difference in price. You can carry extra spools loaded with different lines, make changes rapidly as needed.

Among single-action reels are the least expensive of the three types, and you don't have to lay out a sizable chunk of cash to get a good one. But there are such details as grades of quality, models and features, and you'll find expensive single-action models.

**The automatic type:** Some anglers swear by this kind; others swear at it. It boils down to personal opinions shaped by experience. We're not going to take sides. We'll present some pros and cons. You can take it from there.

Biggest thing going for an automatic fly reel is the feature prompting its name. Pressing a lever activates a spring-driven mechanism that quickly retrieves line—no manual cranking. This is very handy for taking in any loose or surplus loops, or slack developing when a fish changes direction. It is an advantage.

Critics counter with debit features. Extra weight is one often mentioned. Of necessity, an automatic must weigh more than a much simpler single-action reel. Tackle lightness is a venerable part of fly fishing's catechism, and some casters find *any* extra weight objectionable, most expecially on the lighter rods. (For them the solution is easy: Just don't buy an automatic.) Another drawback cited, one that could be serious when arguing with sizable, rambunctious battlers that run, is the difficulty in paying out line quickly when a fish demands it. With the likes of salmon and bonefish that spells bad news. It also has been pointed out that some automatics do not have sufficient spool capacity for double-taper and weight-forward lines in the heavier gauges, and that such lines can bind if retrieved rapidly without proper tension for smooth spooling.

In case the foregoing debate sounds lopsided, we should return to the credit side to add that automatic fly reels see widespread use in fresh-water fishing. They have their own fan club, for whose members the automatic feature outweighs shortcomings. Then there are anglers who carry both automatic and single-action types for wider coverage. In trying to be objective, though, we do believe that if there is to be a choice it should favor a single-action model for all-purpose latitude, especially for beginners.

This much is for sure: When you purchase an automatic, be certain you get one of the better ones. The reel's heart is that spring-powered mechanism, and it has to be strong enough to survive countless windings of the spool. It doesn't require an engineer's mind to picture the potential headaches with a junky mechanism. You also want to check on protection of metal parts against rust and corrosion. While you're at it, inquire about a spool-changing feature, as well as a take-apart detail for maintenance and cleaning. There will be no concern about seating an automatic for right- or left-hand operation. The activating lever is in the middle.

**The multiplying fly reel:** In comparison with the single-action type, the multiplier is a Johhny-come-lately. Let it be added hastily, though, that we don't mean to imply that it's so new it's still in the experimental stage. It just hasn't been around as long as the other. But the multiplying fly reel is here to stay and is recruiting increasing numbers of users, among them some of the harder-nosed veterans who previously argued up, down and sideways that a true flyrodder recognizes only one kind of reel—you guessed it: the single-action. Now it's becoming more a case of "true flyrodders" equipping themselves with both kinds (maybe with an automatic tucked away in their kit too).

The key feature of any multiplying reel is that . . . well, it multiplies. Multiplication in this instance means neither arithmetic nor reproduction, but that a gear system effects multiple revolutions of the spool with each single turn of the handle. Gear ratios vary according to models and builders, but among fly reels generally go about 2½:1 or 3:1.

What's the advantage? We thought you'd never ask.

A multiplied-retrieve feature is both a time saver and a situation saver. By winding in line two to three times faster than a single-action reel it saves time between casts and when changing locations. In the course of active days that's a worthwhile economy. A multiplier becomes a situation saver when a running fish abruptly—and invariably unpredictably—changes direction and creates a belly of slack in the line. Several fresh-water and marine species are noted for this tactic, as part of an escape attempt or to lessen pressure on that hook digging in. Slack must be eliminated immediately. It can give a fish an opportunity to throw a hook that is poorly planted or has worked loose. A belly of slack also could cause the line to snag on an underwater obstruction.

Weight added by a multiplying fly wheel's gears is offset to a degree by the use of light, strong aluminum alloys. As with single-action reels, some weight also is saved by the spool's numerous holes, which show how much line is on the spool and let air get to it for drying. Basically the multiplying reel is designed for flyrodders whose fishing often involves fairly long casts and opponents that tend to run. But it has application in all the usual situations. A well-made multiplying fly reel combines some of the desirable features of both an automatic (faster retrieves) and a single-action (lightness, good spool capacity).

In light of encounters with running opponents, this type of fly reel especially should have an adjustable drag, one that operates smoothly and reliably. Quick changing of spools is a desirable feature. Easy take-down aids in maintenance. Like any other multiplying reel, this one requires a certain amount of care to prolong its life. It's simple, but involves keeping sand, grit and other foreign matter out of the gears, occasional lubrication, and periodic checking for badly worn parts. It goes without saying that metal parts should be of non-rusting materials or have protection against rust. As standard maintenance many owners wipe their reels at intervals with a soft cloth containing a lightweight oil.

Among long-timers, choice between a multiplier and a single-action reel comes down mainly to personal ideas, influenced by style of fishing and, it's suspected, by tradition. As we said, single-action reels have been around a long time. Knowing fishermen's fondness for tackle very well, it's our guess that a lot of them eliminate any debate by having both. For novices a choice usually favors a single-action model because of its simplicity and versatility—and economy.

## LURES

Fly fishing is angling with artificial bait; and the sport is so old and so widespread that it was bound to see the creation and development of lures by the score. There are hundreds of patterns, variously designed to imitate insects in adult or immature forms (nymphs) or little minnows or other small forage fishes (streamer flies). Dozens of these patterns are standards, time-tested and proven, universally known. Many others are best known in regions. Countless are home-crafted variations and originals. Thousands of fly fishermen all over the world fashion their own lures. Fly tying is a hobby—and an art—unto itself. Very rewarding too, we might add.

Earlier we said that fly fishing is precision angling. We were talking about placing a lure properly so that a fish will seize it. Selection of flies also has its precision. It's precise because the artificials must match the items of food devoured by trout and other sought species in given areas, and these diets vary from region to region, as well as from season to season, according to local insect life, kinds of forage fishes and times of year. For example, flies that are effective on Western streams are not necessarily producers in, say, New England, and vice versa. So each flyrodder's choice of flies becomes customized, based on types most serviceable in the areas he fishes. Similarly, when he visits a strange region he goes to a local tackle store and buys lures applicable to *that* area. If he's lucky, he may be able to use a couple of them back home.

So there's your first *tip*: Base your selection on the artificials most frequently used in the areas you intend to fish. Avoid the common mistake of concentrating on patterns rather than on types. That's important. You could wind up with too many flies designed to do the same job. Seek the counsel of a tackle shop in the area. Talk with other fishermen. A sound basic collection will cost you a few bucks as it is. Going overboard will cost you a small fortune, and you may not get to use half of them.

Your basic kit should include suitable representatives of dry flies and the wet or submersible type.

There are essentially eight kinds of dry flies fished in U.S. trout streams. In general cataloguing they're called bivisibles, hair-wings, midges, divided-wings, spiders, fan-wings, hair-bodies and down-wings. For maximum coverage a basic inventory would include all eight, but again we must say that a choice should be influenced by local conditions. In any event, figure on at least two or three of each type. Popped leaders and entanglements in trees take their toll. You want to have spares.

Your basic fly inventory should include representatives of four types of submersibles: Wet flies; nymphs; streamers; and bucktails. Here again you must seek local guidance for the proper proportions for the four types. This is not only a matter of practicality, but also of economy. Conditions in your area may call for a preponderance of one or two types over the other. And again, it's advisable to have spares of each.

The sizes of hooks on flies are proportionate, of course, depending upon the type and pattern of lure. In the case of fresh water flies, this means a gradation downward to some very small hooks. When you get down to around Nos. 20 and 22 you're dealing with tiny fellas.

## SALT-WATER FLY TACKLE

Modern marine fly fishing is a young sport, one of angling's youngest variations, in fact. But it may surprise many of today's participants to learn that its roots go back to the early decades of this century, when some hardy souls decided to see what it would be like to do battle with striped bass and other salt-water scrappers on fresh-water fly tackle. Their attempts were in the nature of experiments, and it's doubtful that they realized they were laying the groundwork for an entirely new kind of fishing.

Although it still hadn't achieved an identity, salt-water flyrodding was given impetus along about the 1950s when some of the nation's best known anglers tried their hand—still with fresh-water tackle, but modified—at catching an ever-broadening array of marine game fishes. They were successful, but we can assume that there were numerous tackle casualties along the way.

Those 1950s adventures also were experiments. And the experimenters were not only opening a door on a brand-new kind of action, but also shaping a blueprint for an entirely new breed of fishermen who, in turn, would be the inspiration for a specific kind of tackle. In most instances those early pioneers were highly experienced fresh-water flyrodders seeking greater challenges and keener thrills. In contrast, the majority of today's participants may never have tossed a fly in fresh water. They began as salt-water fishermen. But they're like their predecessors in the search for exciting challenges.

Salt-water flyrodding is probably the fastest growing phase of sport fishing. Recruiting ever-increasing numbers of buffs along all U.S. coasts, its theater of operations now extends beyond estuaries, tidal rivers and oceanfront strands to the offshore arena. The fraternity-sorority has its own organization, Salt Water Fly Rodders of America, International, which also is custodian of world records established with that kind of equipment. Further indication of the sport's expansion is in the lengthening list of SWFRA records. Their opponents' potential sizes do not awe marine fly fishermen in the slightest. On SWFRA books are catches such as a 152½-pound tarpon, 146-pound striped marlin, 115-pound Pacific sailfish, 65¼-pound amberjack, 45-pound dolphin, 40-pound striped bass, and 16½-pound bluefish.

Salt-water fly fishing is not difficult to learn. But proficiency in it, as in its fresh-water counterpart, demands a degree of precision and skill, both of which come with experience. And sometimes those demands are heightened by being on open water, where breezes can be a real casting problem.

Marine fly fishing's skyrocketing popularity inevitably led to development of more suitable weapons. Their components and design are essentially the same as in fresh-water tackle, the major difference being in weight or caliber. Understandably, marine equipment must be heavier and stronger, with protection against salt corrosion. In case you're asking, yes, fresh-water gear can be used, but even with the smaller marine species the wielder had better be adept, expecially when playing a running fish. He also should be prepared to lose lures and line—and some catches. Considering the sizes of salt-water battlers, it's a calculated risk. It also calls for added maintenance if the tackle doesn't have adequate protection against corrosion.

Since the tackle is heavier anyway, rod weight isn't a prime concern in marine fly fishing. Of more importance are (*a*) how an outfit—rod, line and reel—is balanced, (*b*) how comfortable it is for its owner to wield, and (*c*) how suited it is to the size ranges of the species sought. Again because so many variables are involved, a beginner should rely on guidance from a knowledgeable tackle dealer or an experienced marine flyrodder. At the outset a novice can get by with one outfit, provided he realizes its limitations. But if he intends to broaden his operations he might just as well get used to the idea that he will need more than one combination to handle a variety of situations and species. Obviously, fly tackle suited to small bluefish, young striped bass, and other fishes of similar weight and fighting power will be out of its depth in more ways than one when pitted against the likes of tarpon, dolphin or sailfish.

## RODS

In their average range salt-water fly rods measure from 8 and 8½ to 9 and 9½ feet. They come with varying degrees of action, slower to faster, in their tip sections. Here's where it becomes mandatory for beginners to seek guidance in selection to find a model best suited to their purposes. Ideally, any casting rod should have the proper flexibility to cast a fair range of artificials, including the lighter ones, yet also possess enough "spine" for arguing with opponents at hand. With the smaller sportsters there's no problems; but for the larger game it often becomes a matter of deciding which asset to favor over the other. A rod that casts a wide range of lures beautifully may not have sufficient muscle to cope with a deep-diving fish, and a number of marine species do go deep when hooked. Conversely, a rod with the lifting power to handle bigger, more stubborn opponents may not be the best casting instrument. It's all in the way the rods are constructed, and that's why there's no one all-purpose salt water fly rod.

Some general considerations: Flies used in the salt-water version are larger, bulkier and more wind-resistant than those cast in fresh water fishing; and, as we've noted, breezes are apt to be a headache. For these reasons many marine flyrodders favor the casting advantage offered by the longer, somewhat slower-action sticks. At the same time, the action can't be too slow because often there are times when a lure must be placed quickly, before the fish takes off and is out of casting range. Further, a slow-action rod may not have the muscle to cope with a fish that bores deep.

Expert Mark Sosin, who has fly-fished salt water all over the place, strongly accents the "recovery factor" of a rod as a prime consideration in selection. By this he means the tendency of a rod to return to its normal posture after casting power has been applied, with a minimum of vibrations. The recovery factor is important in casting because a rod that continues to vibrate after forward momentum will transmit those vibrations as rippling waves along the line, curtailing casting distance. Any rod has at least some vibrations, but an excess is a drawback. Mark suggests this simple test when selecting a rod: Hold it at waist level and flex it suddenly. Watch the tiptop section and note how much it vibrates before becoming still. This will help betray an excess.

Like their fresh-water counterparts, practically all marine fly rods are made from fiberglass. There are also split-bamboo models for those with the price. Criteria for quality—good hardware, sufficient number of guides, properly aligned, etc.—are the same as for rods in general, as detailed in "Salt-Water Tackle Showroom."

## REELS

Single-action reels are highly favored in marine fly fishing, but the multiplying type is encroaching more and more. Both do a good job and are versatile. Personally, we believe the faster retrieve rate is a distinct advantage in salt water fishing, much more so than in fresh water, for reasons noted in our earlier description of the multiplying reel. But if the budget is tight, be advised that you can enjoy just as much action and success with a single-action reel. Incidentally, an automatic could be used, but its drawbacks could be heightened in salt water, and therefore it's not recommended.

In addition to sturdy construction, two important details of a marine fly reel are spool capacity and a dependable, adjustable drag. Both are required because sooner or later you'll encounter battlers that run. In general, to be prepared for sprinters, a fly reel should be able to accommodate at least 100 yards of backing in addition to the fly line. Even more backing is needed to be ready for distance runners such as bonefish, tarpon and permit. For them 200 to 250 yards are not too much. A dependable, adjustable drag is an asset because it may be necessary to apply braking pressure on a large or hard-driving fish for better control. And it must be a smooth drag, or popped leaders and lines are almost a certainty.

Accent quality when you buy your reel. (See the fresh-water section of this chapter.) If it's well made it will have solid construction you can detect, as well as protection against corrosion by salt. There are expensive marine fly reels, but you don't have to lay out an arm and a leg for a good one. Buy the best you can afford, even if it means stretching the budget a little. After all, this is an investment in pleasure you don't make every day.

## LINES, LEADERS, BACKING

Because of the bulkier lures and frequent breezes, most marine fly fishermen favor weight-forward lines, and for them a special salt-water taper has been developed. Also, because of windy conditions, some anglers employ what is called a shooting head. This is the weighted portion of a fly line, about 30 feet, without the thinner running line. Its purpose is to provide more weight forward, where it's needed in casting. Most often the shooting heads are of the sinking type in salt-water service, but some fishermen favor a floater. A common procedure is to rig a length of monofilament running line of desired strength between the shooting head and the backing.

As in the sport's fresh water phase, line must be balanced to the rod with which it's to be fished, and the weights in general go to Nos. 9, 10 and 11. Also as in the fresh water division, there's a choice between floating and sinking lines. Floaters have been the more widely used, but as the sport develops it's seeing an increase in sinking lines. Considerable activity stars surface-feeding and near-surface species, as well as targets in very shallow water, hence the floating lines. But sometimes it's necessary to sink a lure quickly before a fish takes off, and that's where a submersible type comes into its own. Floating lines usually are suggested for novices because they're somewhat easier to cast and pick up from the water, but seasoned fishermen figure on carrying outfits spooled with both types.

Standard fly line lengths are 30 to 35 yards. Those are ample, since long casts aren't the regular order of the day here. In fact, some veterans spool less than 90 feet to allow for added backing, which becomes more important than fly line with long-running battlers. Too, with more than 50 feet or so of fly line it becomes increasingly tougher to set a hook in a hard-jawed opponent.

Still in its youth, marine fly fishing has lagged behind its fresh water "parent" in development of tapered leaders. It will catch up. Meanwhile, the majority of regulars fashion their own, creating a desired taper by joining lengths of monofilament in gradually decreasing diameters (strengths) from a butt section (thickest) to a tippet (thinnest), where the fly attaches. Every do-it-yourselfer has his own ideas as to how long the leader's sections should be, and in what strengths, according to his style of fishing. When fishes with line-cutting teeth (like bluefish and barracuda) or sharp gill covers (like snook) are involved, a short length of fine wire, 12 inches or so, is added to the leader.

Because of its small, featherweight lures, fresh water fly fishing requires a finer-diameter extension of the line to properly present the artificials. In marine flyrodding this problem is considerably less. But tapered leaders are needed. Presumably more and more of them, already prepared, will be marketed. If you can't find any suitable to your kind of fishing you'll have to make your own, and for this you ask the advice of an experienced angler in your area. Later you'll probably develop ideas of your own.

For backing you can't go wrong with Dacron line. The most popular strengths are 20- and 30-pound test. The former handles most assignments; but give some consideration to the weight ranges of the gamesters you'll be seeking, and if you want a margin of safety go to 30-pound stuff. How much you'll need also depends upon the species sought. As we've indicated, a minimum of 100 yards of backing will handle a variety of assignments, at least with the smaller fishes and those that do not make long runs. With heavier and long-running species you should figure on a reel accommodating at least 200, maybe 250, yards of backing in addition to the fly line. And you should fill your reel spool to the proper level. Do it the way we suggested earlier.

## LURES

Being far younger, marine fly fishing has only a fraction of the flies boasted by its fresh water counterpart—after all, there's a couple of centuries difference in their ages. But the offspring is doing its best to catch up. Many creative minds are at work at the fly-tying benches. A flock of salt water patterns already have been developed; more are appearing all the time.

Salt water flies are divided into two general types, streamers and bucktails, with the so-called top-water poppers in a third division. Anatomically they resemble their fresh-water cousins in one way or another, but the most obvious difference is in their appreciably greater sizes. In comparison with, say, a tiny Black Gnat, a three- or four-inch streamer appears as a giant. The greater sizes in salt water are influenced by the old adage "Bigger bait for bigger fish." Also like their fresh water relatives, marine flies come in a rainbow of colors whose combination are a frequent cause for debate whenever two or more anglers get together for more than five minutes. You'll also hear arguments about the importance of colors, or lack of them. Fact is, more data will have to be collected before that question can be decided conclusively one way or another. As we said, salt-water fly fishing is still young. Meanwhile, a concensus is that white and yellow, maybe orange too, will do nicely for openers.

Hook sizes are a detail of importance. As in general practice, they should be gauged approximately to the fishes' sizes. Accordingly, you'll find a range in salt water. As to be expected, they run bigger than those on fresh-water flies, but there's an upstairs limit. Because of a fly rod's action, it becomes difficult if not impossible to properly set a hook larger than about a 4/0 or 5/0. And you may encounter problems with hooks that size if the fish has a particularly hard jaw or very leathery mouth. Fortunately, the range is such that—everything else being satisfactory—they can handle most of the battlers taken on fly rods.

A basic lure kit should include a few representatives of the major patterns—streamers, bucktails and poppers. These will have a fair amount of versatility in different regions, accounting for a variety of species. But it still is smart to check locally to determine if any specific patterns and sizes are more effective than others.

Opportunities for experimentation, with store-bought lures and home-made versions, are legion in marine fly fishing. Although more and more patterns are appearing, the field is wide open. Chances are, you'll become a fly tier yourself . . . and who knows, maybe anglers in the future will be hooking fish on a pattern you designed and named.

## THE ROD FOREST

### The Orvis Name

Way back in 1856 a Vermonter named Charles F. Orvis built his first bamboo fly rods. Since that remote year the company bearing his name, still in Vermont, has become one of the world's most highly respected producers of superlative fly tackle equipment. It seems safe to say that among fly anglers anywhere, here or abroad, the company needs no further identification beyond the word Orvis. Such is its reputation.

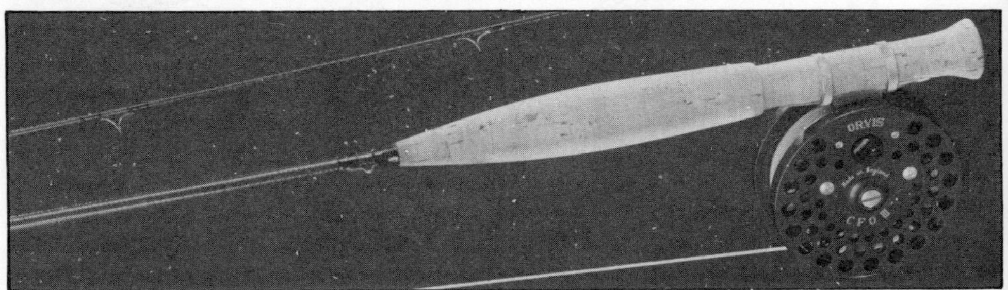

Since its founding more than a century ago Orvis has specialized in split-bamboo fly rods. In recent decades construction has featured Tonkin cane, acknowledged as the finest material from which to build such rods. To give you an idea of the processes involved at Orvis, each section of a Battenkill fly rod consists of six Tonkin cane segments, so that a two-piece model requires twelve, while a three-piece rod with two tips is made from twenty-four separate bamboo segments. These are milled twice, the second time to a tolerance of 1/4 of 1/1000 of an inch, after which they're precision-fitted for exactly the desired taper and action.

Those are among the reasons that Orvis fly rods represent an epitome, considered by many anglers to be the ultimate. They also are among the reasons that Orvis impregnated bamboo fly rods cost as much as they do.

The Orvis inventory of fly rods is awesome. And they're available separately or in balanced rod-reel combinations.

The Wes Jordan series, named for Wesley Jordan, legendary fly fisherman and Orvis rod designer, follows his concept in three models, with an extra tip, each two-piece and coming in its own handsome, saddle-stitched leather case with protective aluminum tube lining and shoulder strap. Metal butt plate is engraved with purchaser's name.

**No. M9750-2,** 7½', 3 7/8 oz., for HDG (6) line, a pure trout rod, $260. With matching CFO III fly reel,line and 50 yds. of backing, leather case, $312.

**No. M9800-2:** 8', 4-3/8 oz., for GBF (8) line, a versatile, all-round fly rod for a variety of conditions, $260. With CFO IV reel, line, 50 yds. of backing, leather case $315.

**No. M9850-2:** 8½', 5-1/8 oz., for GAF (9) line, for salmon, salt water flyrodding, bass bugging, $260. With CFO V reel, line, 200 yds. of backing, leather case, $320.

The Battenkill series: Named for a very famous trout stream and a standard of excellence for generations. There are several models, 6½' to 8½', for 6-, 7-, 8- and 9-weight fly lines, covering a range of sweetwater and marine sport species from trout to salmon, bass to steelhead, bonefish to bluefish and striped bass. Each 1-tip Battenkill comes in a cloth sack and Champion Rod Case. Each 2-tip Battenkill comes in a cloth sack and engraved aluminum rod case. Separately, the rods go from $120 with one tip to $165 with two tips. In combination with Orvis-matched CFO fly reel, appropriate Orvis fly line and 50 to 200 yds. of backing, $221 to $229.

Also available are three-piece Battenkills, with special cushioned transition from ferrules to bamboo so that casting action is indistinguishable from that of a comparable two-piece Battenkill. **M9762-2,** 7½', 4¼ oz., medium action, for 7-weight line, a basic trout rod, with extra tip. **M9808-2,** 8', 4½ oz., medium action for 7-weight line, a versatile rod for handling any fly type, with extra tip. **M9859-2,** 8½', slow action, for 7-weight line, excellent for working wet flies and streamers. All three are priced at $180 each. With CFO fly reel, line, 100 yds. of backing, $240 each.

Other Orvis series, each with rods in a range of lengths and weights, sold separately or as balanced rod-reel outfits: Madison; Orvis Special Function Rods (includes midge, nymph and midge/nymph models) and the Orvis 5/9 Ultralight for 4-weight line, 5'9", 1-7/8 oz.; the Limestone Specials; Orvis Superfine Lightweight; S-S-S Rod (for salt water, salmon, steelheads); and three-piece Rocky Mountain Travel Rods (fly and spinning models, they pack at 26"). All are of impregnated bamboo. Prices start at $105 for a rod alone, at about $131 for rod-reel-line combos.

Orvis also offers its Golden Eagle series of high-density fiberglass (rolled under 2,000 lbs. p.s.i. pressure) fly rods, billed as the "most responsive glass rods ever built," and as close to their bamboo counterparts as modern materials and technology can make them. Among them are ultra-light, all-purpose and heavy-duty models, plus a double spinning rod (two tips, light and medium). Lengths and weights go from 6½' and 1-7/8 oz. to 9' and 5¼ oz., for lines 4-weight to 9-weight. Separately, $75 to $93; in rod-reel outfits, $130 to $169.

You might want to know that Orvis also makes: Impreganted bamboo spinning rods ($120-$130 separately, $145 to $165 with matching spinning reel and line); Fullflex II glass fly rods ($42.50 and $43.50 alone, $63.75 and $64.75 with matching Madison fly reel and fly line); Fullflex glass spinning rods for lure weights to 3/4 oz. fresh and salt water ($33.50-$63 alone, $61.25-$76.25 for rod-reel-line combos).

**Of particular interest** are Orvis's new Graphite Fly Rods, made from graphite fibers originally developed by the aeronautics industry. Features include incredible lightness — 36 percent less than the finest glass; extremely fast recovery power, very important in casting; special Orvis tapers for precise action; new aluminum oxide ceramic stripping guides and tiptop, very light, with much less line wear than carbide guides. They're dark oxford gray with gray windings, engraved butt cap carrying rod specifications and line weight, come in a maroon cloth sack and aluminum rod case. They range from **M9270-2,** 7', 1-5/8 oz., for 5-weight line, to **M9289-2,** an 8'9", 4-oz. powerhouse for 10-weight line or shooting head. Price ranges: Rods alone, $155-$185; with matching fly reel, line and backing, $223 to $269.

**From Scientific Anglers**

Scientific Anglers, now a 3M company, has specialized in fine fly equipment for nearly 30 years, developing what it calls its System (balanced) tackle, which precisely matches rod and line as a unit. Accordingly, they make a different System rod for each weight fly line. Thus there's never a question of which rod for which line. A System **4** rod is for 4-weight line, System **5** rod for 5-weight, and so on.

Their brand name is Peerless. Features include: two-piece hollow construction from premium fiberglass; double-strength twist-off fiberglass ferrules for a continuous action zone from tip to grip; extra-hard chromed stainless steel snake guides and tiptop, Carboloy stripping guide; rich-looking mahogany finish with bronze nylon thread windings. There are 8 models, from System **4** through System **11** for 11-weight line. Among them they cover all fly fishing situations from small streams to sheltered ponds and panfishes to husky tarpon and snook and the open sea for the likes of bluefish, dolphin and billfishes. Approximate price for System **4** through System **11** rods is $75, $80 with extension butt for system **8** through **11** models. Each comes in a tailored cloth bag with leather tabs and snap, plus a lightweight aluminum rod case.

**3M/Phillipson Peerless Fly Rods:** Built from high-quality Tonkin cane, with hand-split, six-strip construction. Each rod has an impregnated finish that is impervious to moisture, never needs refinishing. These Peerless split-bamboo rods are being produced in a limited edition. On request

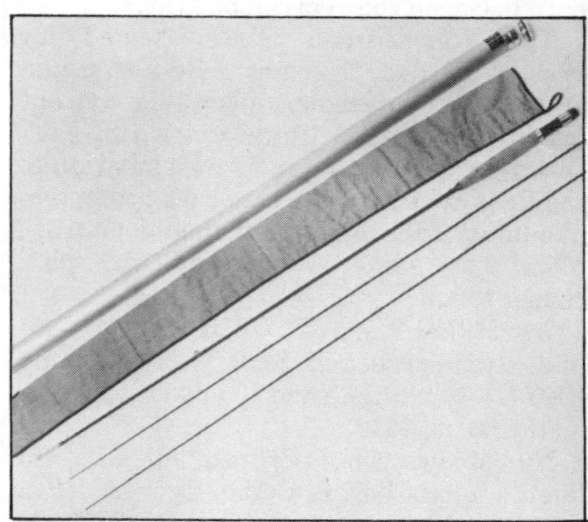

each will be hand-inscribed with its owner's name at no extra charge. There are two models: 7' for No. 5 fly line, 7½' for No. 5 or 6 line. Also a choice of reel seats: Traditional cork with sliding bands for a lighter combination, and a new 424 wood and metal reel seat, combining Indian rosewood and a special aluminum alloy. Reel locking is internally threaded and operates from the rear so there are no exposed threads or reel hoods to rub against the palm. Peerless ferrules are hand-drawn, 18 percent nickel silver, both marked for correct alignment and hand-polished for perfect fitting.

The 7-footer with skeleton cork reel seat weighs about 2-7/8 oz., and 7½-footer weighs approximately 3¼ oz. The approximate price of each is $200. With the slightly heavier wood-metal reel seat, the approximate price is $250. Each comes in a durable cloth bag and aluminum case.

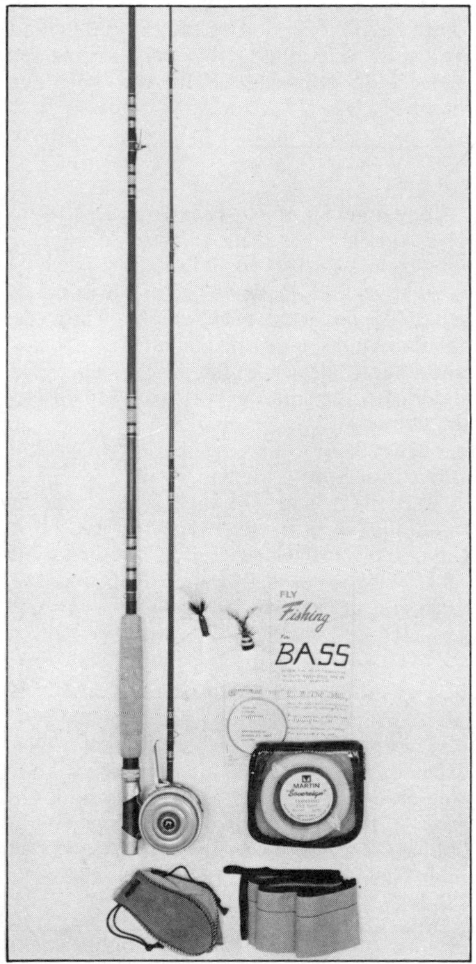


**Martin Reels**

Although it outshops fresh and salt water spinning and spincasting rods and reels, Martin Reel Company calls itself The Fly Tackle People, which gives you a fair clue as to the equipment it likes to accent.

As Martin points out, there's no more exciting way to latch onto a largemouth or smallmouth bass than with a fly rod. When surface-feeding, both species will smack a popping bug or deer hair bug with a leaping crash that gets festivities off to a pulse-pounding start.

Martin offers three balanced Bass Pro Fly Fishing Sets. New to the line for 1975 was the **No. 973/974.** Combination **973** is engineered primarily for largemouths, especially when fishing impoundments and other man-made lakes with submerged brush and trees. It consists of a muscular 7', two-piece Model **73-434** fly rod designed for No. 8 or No. 9 line, Model **83** Blue Chip automatic fly reel, matching 35-yd. WF9F fly line in a fly book for streamers and popping bugs, 9' tapered leader, 2 popping bugs, cloth bag, leather reel pouch, booklet called "Fly Fishing for Bass." Combination **974** is substantially the same, but with 8½', two-piece tubular glass rod **No. 73-437** for traditional bass bugging. Combination **975** is designed for streamer fishing for largemouths, also good for largemouths when not surface-feeding. Includes 8'2", two-piece Model **83-736** tubular glass fly rod with matching WF8S fly line and 7½' tapered leader, Blue Chip **83** automatic fly reel, two streamer flies, otherwise the same as **973.** Approximate prices: $74.95 for **973** and **974**, $76.95 for No. **975.**

**From Trimarc Corporation**

**Trimarc FX8063 Telescopic Fly Rod:** 8' extended, 19¼" telescoped, medium action, with power to deliver long line. Also Models **FQ7553** (7½' and 22"), wet fly action, and **FQ7552** (7½', 22"), dry fly action.

Also from Trimarc, telescoping rods in fly/spin, spinning, spincasting and open-water models, lengths ranging from 5½' to 8½' extended, 15" to 38" closed, in a range of actions from light to heavy. Approximate prices go from about $13.89 to $37.99.

Additionally, Trimarc offers non-telescoping fly, spinning, spincasting and heavy-duty open-water rods. The fly models are tubular glass, with stainless steel wire guides, deluxe double wrappings, glass-to-glass ferrules, double-lock, anodized aluminum reel seat, two-piece construction. From 7' to 9', light to medium

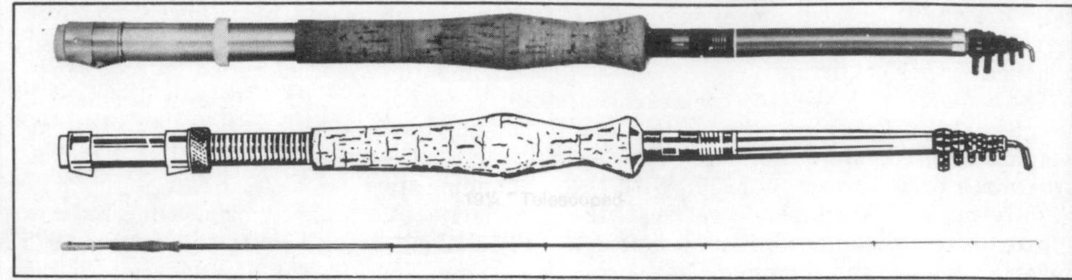

action, from about $13.49 and $13.69. The other types are variously priced from about $12.69 to $25.69.

There are four Trimarc Fishing Rod Sets, spinning, spincasting, fly, and spin/fly combination, complete, with carrying case, about $32.99-$57.69 (two rods, spinning and fly reel). A padded vinyl zipper case for telescoping spinning or fly rod goes for about $7.

**Fenwick**

Fenwick has a Voyageur family of rods, all featuring multi-piece Feralite construction, for anglers who travel light,whether with a back pack, in a canoe, even with airline luggage—any circumstance in which weight and space are factors. The Voyageur family is divided into three groups: fly, spinning, and fly/spin combination.

Voyageur fly rods are 4- and 5-piece, measure 7½ to 8½', pack at 23" to 26", weigh 4¼ to 4-1/8 oz. (13-15 oz., total pack weight). They're designated for No. 6 or No. fly lines, with light to heavy action for arenas ranging from small, bush-lined streams to big trout and bass waters. There are four models, with approximate prices from $40.00 to $60.00.

Voyageur spinning rods are 5'9" to 7' long, handle lures from 1/16 oz. to 5/8 oz., lines from 1-lb. test to 10 lb., multi-piece to pack at 20-23". Rods weigh 2-3/8 to 5-1/8 oz., 12-15 oz. total pack weight. They too handle assignments on small streams to big lakes, and also are for light salt-water action. Approximate prices: $40.00 to $60.00.

Voyageur fly/spin combination rods come in two multi-piece models, 7 and 7½', for 2- to 6-lb. lines and 1/8 to 3/8 oz. lures in spinning, No. 6 fly line. They weigh 4-3/4 and 4-7/8 oz., pack at 21 or 24", with a total pack weight of 14-15 oz. Approximate consumer prices: $40.00 to $60.00.

**Quick Corporation of America**

Under the brand label Finessa, three models from Quick: **No. 6176**, 7½', two-piece, light action, for small streams, lighter weight fly lines. **No. 6180**, 8', two-piece, light to medium action, for dry or wet flies, light tip action for "bamboo feel." **No. 6186**, 8½', two-piece, medium action, for wet or dry flies, also combines a light tip with a power butt to handle bugs and poppers for bass, balanced by Quick fly reels Nos. 45 and 55. Price range: $22.00 to $25.00.

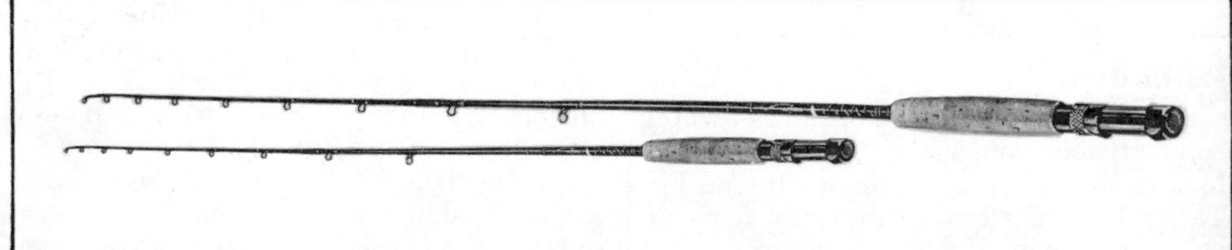

### Shakespeare's Graflite Fly Rod

There are trout fishing purists and longtimers who argue that for fly angling there is nothing, but nothing, like a split-bamboo rod. A lot of substance is on their side. A topflight bamboo fly rod in its way is a thing of beauty, a precision instrument with a personality. However, the gap between bamboo fly rods and those of fiberglass has been narrowed appreciably by improved designing and modern technology, and glass fly rods—the better ones—are no longer as far astern of their Tonkin cane counterparts in "feel" and performance. Too, fiberglass offers definite advantages, not the least of which are less maintenance and care—and a very noticeable difference in price.

Now the gap promises to be widened even further with the advent of graphite carbon fibers in rod manufacture. It has been pointed out that this graphite material is stronger than fiberglass, some three times stiffer, yet 25 percent lighter. As a result, graphite rods can be smaller in diameter than fiberglass sticks of comparable taper, and therefore lighter. Graphite rods are incredibly light. Moreover, the material's stiffness is such that when the rod is at rest it telegraphs nibbles and light hits more sharply, yet it disappears when the rod is in play, and action is continuous from tip to handle. Further, graphite gives a rod remarkable recovery power, a damping effect that minimizes tip vibrations that could be transmitted to a line to lessen casting distance and accuracy. Amazing increases in casting distance have been claimed for graphite rods in field testing.

We said these rods are incredibly light for their strength and power. Shakespeare's Graflite **GF II** is 8 feet long yet weighs only 1 3/4 ounces, and has the muscle to handle a 6-weight line. Other properties, anatomical and esthetic, include: Black-chromed stainless steel guides and tiptop, precisely positioned for perfect line flow; specie cork handle fitted with a lightweight sliding ring reel seat; a gleaming black finish and contrasting white and black winds. Shakespeare's Graflite **GFII** goes for about $135.00 to $150.00.

---

### Fly Rods by James Heddon's Sons

The finest rods under the Heddon banner, top of the line, are those in the Mark V group. Four types comprise the Mark V series: Casting, spinning, spincasting, and fly. Keep the first three in

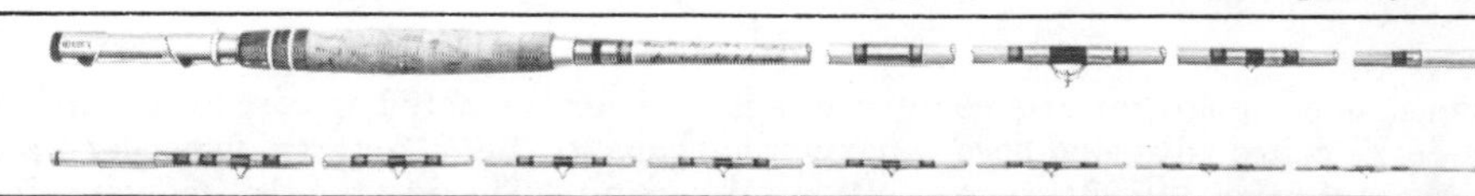

mind for future investigation. Here we'll concentrate on the Mark V fly rods.

In common with other Mark V models, they feature smart styling, genuine walnut inlay on specie cork handle, satin-finish aluminum reel seat (anodized), Sizematic Ferrules and slides handmade from special aluminum alloy and fitted with a neoprene ring for a perfect fit, stainless and Carboloy guides and tiptop, and Heddon's own stainless Wire/Wrap guide windings that can't rot, fray, stretch, slip or corrode, applied over silk base winds. Each Mark V rod—whatever its type—has its own registration number. At the time of purchase a registration card is filled out and returned to Heddon as a permanent record of ownership.

Mark V fly rods are of Heddon's premium fiberglass, handcrafted quality, in two pieces. **No. 8465** is 8'; **No. 8467**, 8½'; **No. 8469**, 9'. All three have Heddon's Controlled-Flex Action for versatility—power in the butt section, tapering rather abruptly into the tip section in about the first third of the rod, with relatively "flat" or slow taper in the tip section and quick recovery. **Nos. 8465, 8467** and **8469** take 7-, 8- and 9-weight fly lines, respectively. Current retail prices of these were not available at press time; but to give you a rough idea, other types in the Mark V series go for about $35.

You might want to know that Heddon also offers fly rods under other series labels. Among them, with a few approximate sample prices: Starcast ($10.15); Lucky 13 (priced for tight budgets); Astro Pal ($13.86); Green Pal ($12.39); Black Pal ($13.86); Brown Pal ($15.40); Mark Special Purpose; Mark I ($18.76); Mark II; Golden Mark (with Heddon's exclusive glass ferrules); Stainless Wire Mark; Pro-Weight Mark; and Mark IV ($30.73).

**Gladding-South Bend**

Gladding-South Bend's Classic I Rod Series includes a two-piece Tuflex tubular fiberglass fly rod in 8' (for 7-weight) and 8½' (for 8-weight) lines. Features: Two-tone anodized brown and gold reel seat; glass ferrule; mono-loop stripper, carbide tiptop; 5 snake guides with durable black

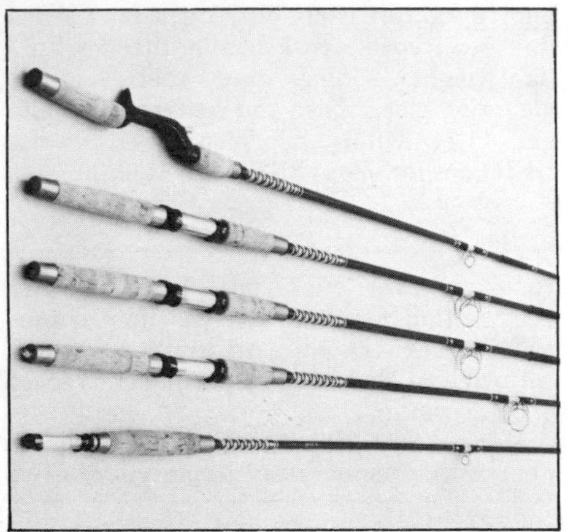

wrappings over gold mylar; contoured specie cork grips; diamond-hard epoxy finish. Average price: $15.95.

Other Gladding-South Bend series with fly fods: Tubular Pack Rods, a 6-section, 6 model in tubualr fiberglass with new Ferrule-Flex design, balanced for No. 7 line, comes in an 18" by 4" padded vinyl case with zipper; and the Outdoorsman Series, a six-piece, 7' fly rod that comes in a 21" zippered leatherette case. There are also fly rods in Gladding-South Bend's Classic IV Series (five versions, 7' to 9'3" for lines Nos. 6 to 10), and in the Classic III Series, an 8-footer balanced for 7-weight fly line.

**From Berkley**

Berkley & Co. markets fly rods as members of six different series: Para/Metric Curt Gowdy Signature; Para/Metric Custom; Tri-Sport; Cherrywood (their color, not their material); Fibre-Flex; and Buccaneer. Among the six groups are nineteen models, 6'3" for No. 4 line to 8½' for No. 8 line. All are two-piece fiberglass, with 4 to 9 chrome-plated steel or chromed stainless steel guides and chromed stainless steel tiptop. Each series has its inventory features, among which are a specie cork grip, double locking rings for the reel, anodized aluminum seat.

Heading the Berkley fly rod parade is the Para/Metric Curt Gowdy Signature series,

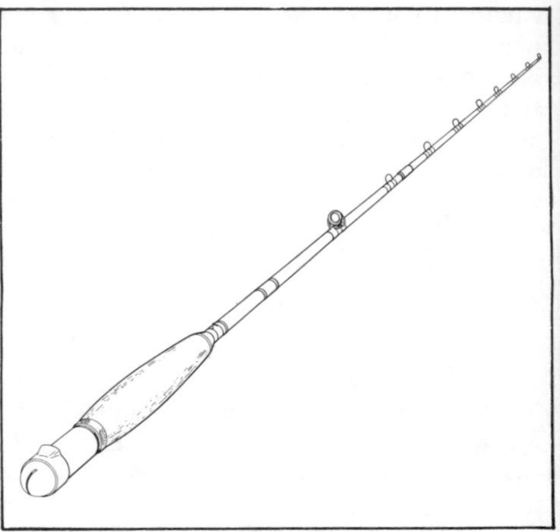

named for the noted sportscaster who also happens to be a veteran flyrooder from Wyoming. There are six models, five designated as **PG40**, but in different lengths: **PG40-6'3"** for No. 4 line to **PG40-8 ½** 'for No. 8 line, each about $73.95. Sixth model in the series is **PG45**, 9'3", No. 9 line recommended, about $84.45.

The budget-priced series is Buccaneer, with two fly rods: **No. B40-8'** for No. 7 line, and **No. B40-8½'** for No. 8 line. Both feature a specie grip, anodized aluminum reel seat, fixed, in brown and gold. Each has an approximate $21.95 price tag.

Other Berkley fly rod prices about $23.95 to $45.95.

**St. Croix Fly Rods**

Imperial XL fly rods from St. Croix in Minneapolis are of the manufacturer's advanced, laminated XL fiberglass fabric (more than three times as many glass filaments for rod length, giving greater strength in lighter weight). Other cited features are controlled elasticity and excellent balance and weight distribution.

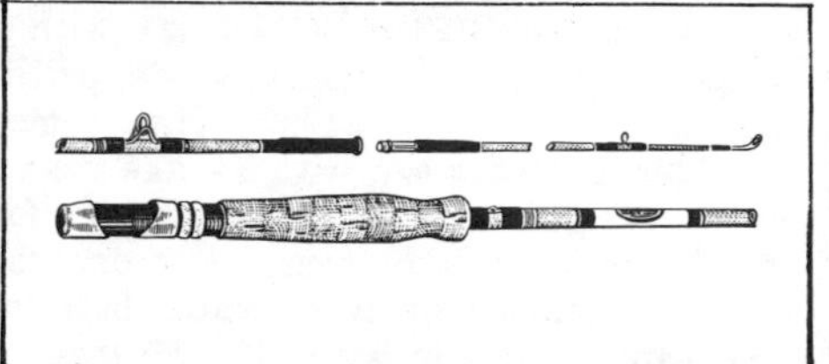

Finishing includes walnut shaft, custom wound in brown and beige, contrasting gold anodized mountings, anodized featherweight ferrule with neoprene ring, contoured handle of specie cork, 6 to 8 stainless steel snake guides, Carboloy stripper guide, hook-keeper. Each comes in a cloth bag and tube. Models: **7090-XL,** 8½', 4 oz., for 8-weight line; **7090-XLM,** 9', 5 oz., No. 9 or 10 line; **7099-XXL,** 6'8", 1-3/4 oz., for No. 6 line. Approximate consumer prices go from $19.99 to $29.99.

If you're interested, you might also ask about St. Croix fly rods with these series labels: Premier; Magna-Taper; Transa-Glas; Criterion; Blue Bandit; and Green Grabber. All are tubular glass in a collective range of lengths and designs for various line loads.

**Fly Rods from Eagle Claw [Wright & McGill]**

Eagle Claw's array of fly rods embraces some twenty-six models in ten different groups, labeled Sweetheart, Deluxe, Champion, Powerlight, Favorite, Denco, Featherlight, Four-Piece Trailmaster, Six-Piece Trailmaster, Heavy Duty Granger. All are tubular glass, fine-fiber or high-density. Except for the pack rods, they're two-piece jobs. Each series has its own list of specifications, among which—according to models—are: Eagle Claw Mini-Ferrules with Uni-Fit construction; specie cork grip; lightweight, anodized aluminum reel seat with single or double locking nut; nickel silver hook-keeper; 4 to 7 stainless steel snake guides and hard-chromed stripper. Their line-balance range is from 6-weight to 10-weight. Pack models come in a Vista Pack carrying case or screw-top aluminum tube. Some of the other models come in an aluminum tube. Lengths go from 6' to 9', and the Six-Piece Trailmaster fits any popular 15" tackle box. Marine anglers might want to note that the 9', two-piece Heavy Duty Granger fly rod is designed specifically for salt-water action and is balanced for No. 10 line.

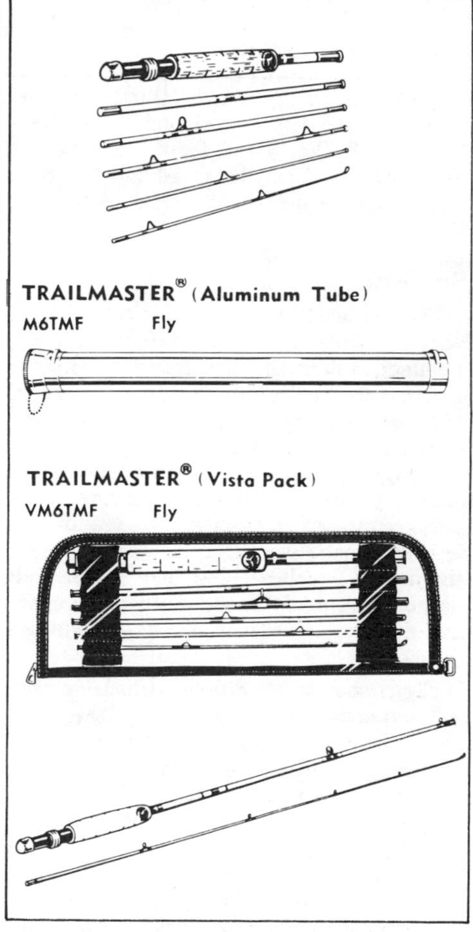


Overall price range of the foregoing rods is from about $15.00 to $36.00.

Eagle Claw also offers budget-priced fly rods in solid glass, separately or in rod-reel combos, complete with line.

## Pflueger Fly Rods

We'll point out one series:

**Powerod 104:** Rich brown finish with contrasting gold trim, light and strong fiberglass construction, Fuji stripper guide,

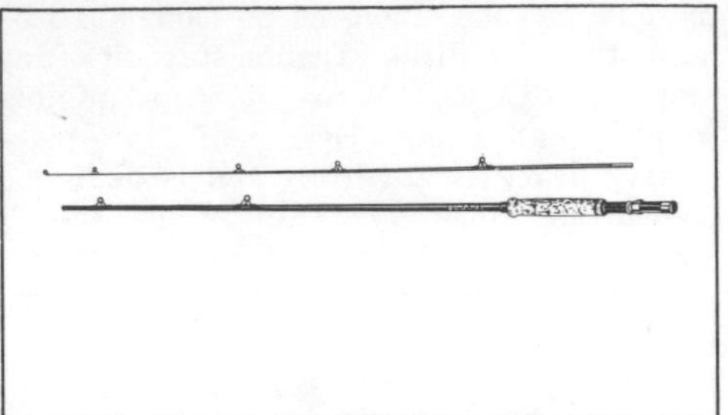

wrapped ferrules, deluxe aluminum reel seat, selected specie cork grip. Two versions: **104F-7½**, 3 oz., for 6- or 7-weight line; **104F-8'**, 4 oz., balanced for No. 8 or No. 9 line. Approximate price: $20.00 to $30.00.

## Browning

The name of this Morgan, Utah, firm is very well known in the outdoor sports field, a collective term that in this instance means equipment for fishing, hunting, archery, camping and bicycling, not to mention sportsmen's clothing and accessories.

Browning's line of fishing rods covers all bases—general casting, spinning, all-purpose spinning/casting, river and surf fishing, boat fishing, rods for popping, jigging and trolling, and blue water rods –all in an equally broad range of lengths and actions. Here we'll accent Browning's fly rods.

Eight models are offered—characterized by extreme good looks, by the way (esthetics are important to pride of ownership). Browning accents its Straight Taper construction for its fly rods, a flexure that sweeps deeply into the butt section, uninterrupted by Browning's precision glass ferrule. Action matching that of fine bamboo rods is claimed for them. Shared features include: Shaped grip of 6X Super Specie cork; ultra-light reel seat with contoured hoods (bronze anodized) and double lock nuts. A tough, smart-looking Cycolac case with screw cap accompanies each rod.

The group begins with an ultra-light 6-footer (**No. 322960**) possessing delicately tuned action for probing small, brush-flanked streams or for rolling a fly beneath overhangs or in other cramped quarters. In two sections, it weighs but 1.9 oz., has 5 snake guides, a stripping guide. Approximate price is $36.95. From there intermediate models range from **No. 322970**, 7', 2.3 oz., with the same number of guides, to **No. 322990**, 9', 4.4 oz., with 6 snake guides and a stripping guide, prices from about $38.95 to $47.95. Then comes **No. 322991**, 9', 5.6 oz., with 6 snake guides and a stripping guide, about $49.95 for steelheads, striped bass, salmon, or whatever marine or fresh water battlers you want to tangle with. Their range of recommended fly lines is from No. 5 for the 6-footer, through 6 to 9, to Nos. 9 and 10 for the big-water **322991**.

## Zebco Fly Rods

After three years of designing, tournament testing and redesigning, Zebco came out in 1975 with an expanded group of rods, its Pro Staff Series. There are seven models in the full group, five for spinning and spincasting, two for fly fishing.

The fly rods are labeled as Pro Staff **PS40** and Pro Staff **PS42**, 8' and 8½', respectively. **PS40** is a trout-action rod. Its running mate, **PS42**, is designed as a bass-action stick. Both are two-piece, featuring Zebco's Transa-Coil tubular glass with hard, durable, flow-coated epoxy finish. They have great good looks, finished in contrasting shades of brown with off-white wrappings and deluxe, double braid, diamond trim. Each ferrule is full-wrapped.

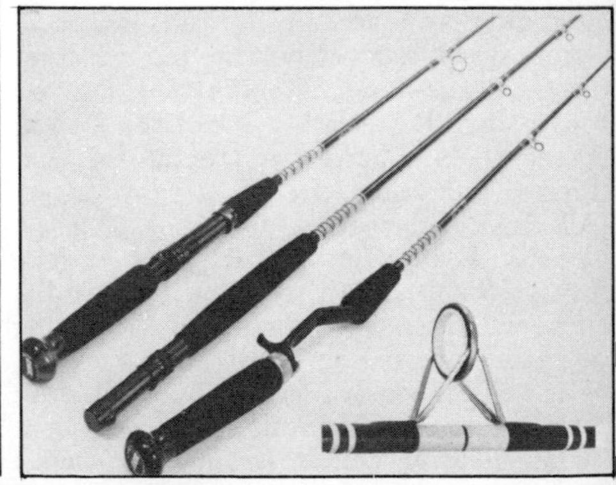

**PS40** carries 5 hard-chromed stainless steel, plus Zebco's Slipstream stripper guide and fly top of aluminum oxide with ABS shock ring inserts. Both have brownish-bronze anodized reel seat, hoods and double locking rings, 8" butt grip of select burnt cork. **PS40** uses No. 7 or No. 8 line. **PS42** takes No. 8 or No. 9 line. Prices for both **PS40** and **PS42** range from $20.00 to $23.00.

**Powerscopic Corporation's Telescoping Fly Rods**

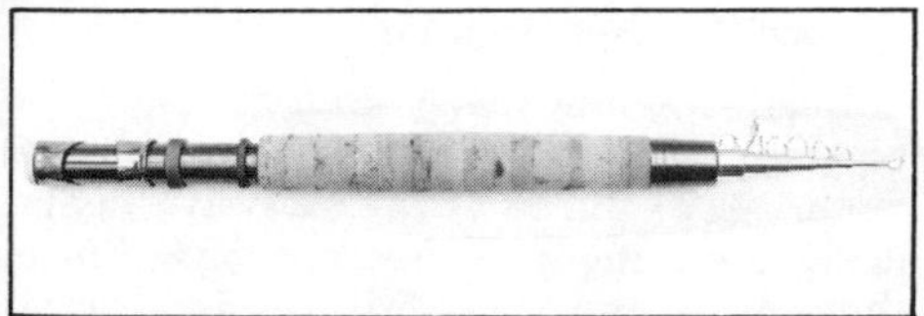

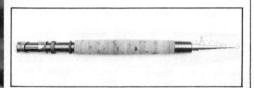

**Powerscopic Fly Rod No. G506:** 4¼ oz., for DT6F and WF7F lines. Telescopes to 16", extends to 8'. Snake guides, genuine specie cork grip. Approximate price, $28.

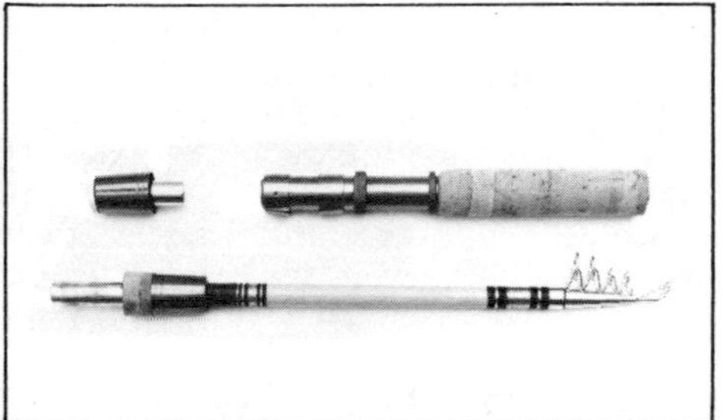

**Powerscopic Spin and Fly Combination [reversible handle] No. G508:** Two rods in one, balanced. Takes lines 6-10. Plug-in grip, specie cork. Closes to 13 5/8", opens to 6'. Approximate price, $28.

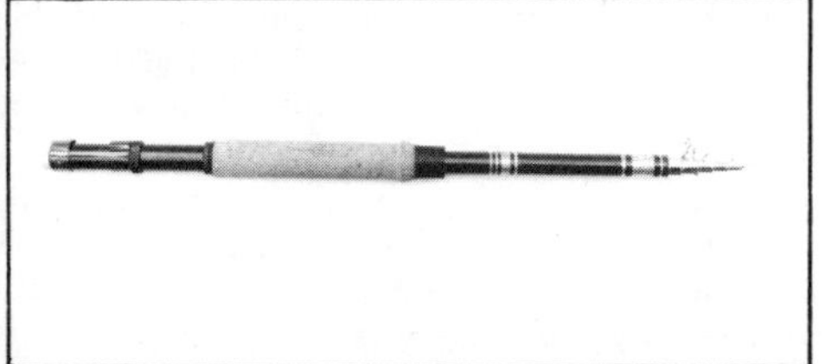

**Powerscopic Fly Rod No. P3000:** Closes to 19", extends to 8'. Composition cork grip. Approximate price $23.85.

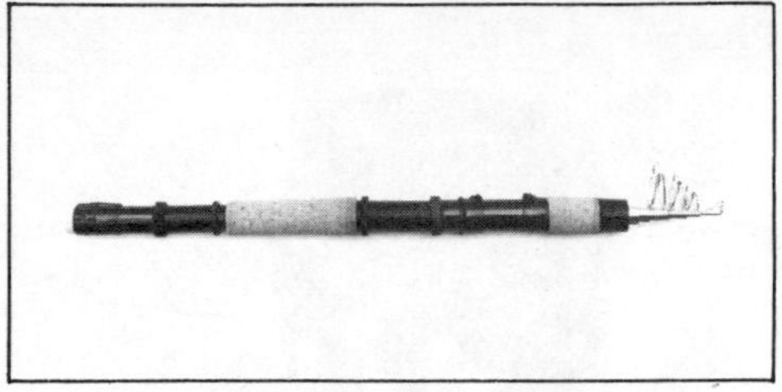

**Powerscopic Spin/Fly Combination No. P4000:** 17" collapsed, 7' extended, about $23.85.

**Daiwa Fly Rods**

Daiwa Maxi Power Fly Rods feature 6 snake guides and stripping guides of stainless steel, chromed tiptop, specie cork grip, anodized aluminum reel seat, fiberglass construction with epoxy finish and polyurethane undercoating. There are four models, all two-piece, each with a price tag of about $16.10; **No. 3044N,** 7½', 4 1/8 oz., for 7-weight line; **3045N,** 8', 4¼ oz., No. 8 line; **3046N,** 8½', 4-3/8 oz., 8-weight line; and **No. 3047N,** 9', 4½ oz., for No. 9 line.

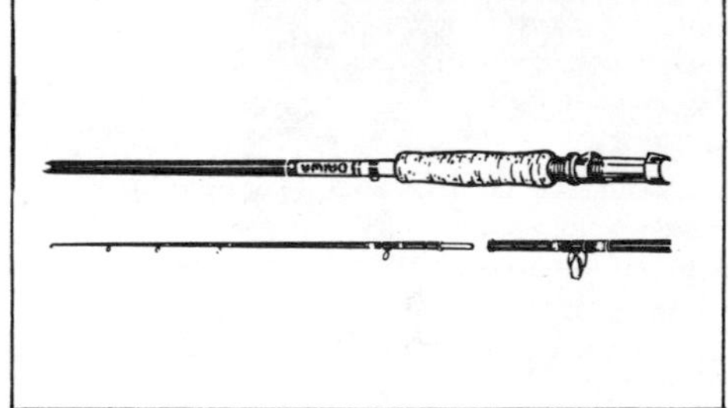

## FLY REELS

**From Aladdin Laboratories Minneapolis**

There are seven models of the horizontally mounted Perrine reels, all free-stripping automatics. All Perrine reels are guaranteed for life, with repairs of replacements by the factory without charge. Available free to purchasers is a removable extension for the line-retrieve lever.

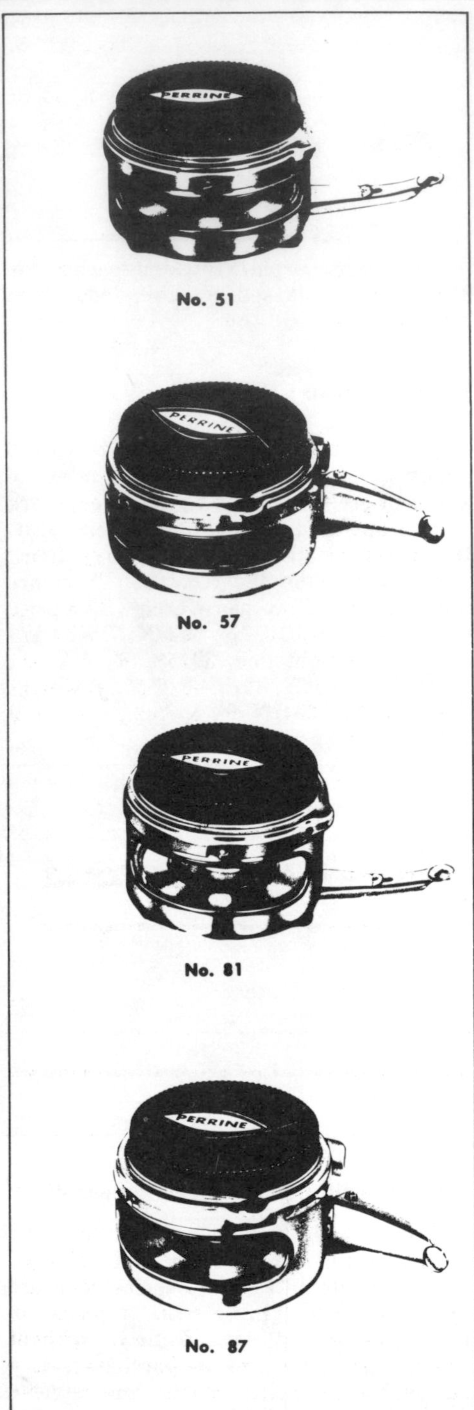

No. 51

No. 57

No. 81

No. 87

(1) **No. 50,** 8 7/8 oz., with snubbing brake, in brown and gold, handles fly line weights up to and including L6F, DT5F, WF9F. (2) **No. 80,** 9 oz., also brown and gold, with snubbing brake, for lines to and including L8F, DT8F, WT10F. (3) **No. 51,** 8 3/4 oz., blue and gold, for lines to and including L6F, DT8F, WF10F. (5) **No. 87,** 9 1/8 oz., green and gold, handles lines up to and including L8F, DT8F, WF10F. (6) **No. 57,** 9 oz., green and gold, for lines to and including L6F, DT5F, WF9F.

Approximate price range: $9 (**No. 51**) to $15.50 (**No. 80**).

**Tycoon/Fin-Nor Beauties**

Headlining the superb craftsmanship and elegant appearance of Tycoon/Fin-Nor reels are three Fin-Nor fly reels, designated simply as Nos. 1, 2 and 3. One of their most important features is a large-diameter brake disc, similar to that in Fin-Nor trolling reels and made from special heat-resistant materials to insure longer life even under constant, heavy drag. Brake adjustment knob has spring-loaded ball detents to maintain sensitive adjustments, feather-touch to steady, heavy drag. Each reel spool and blackplate are precision turned from solid bars of high-density aluminum alloys. Fin-Nor fly reels are available in right- or left-hand models, come with a personally engraved nameplate, and are designed for either fresh or salt water service, or both.

**No. 1, The Trout:** A very versatile, lightweight performer, ideal for trout and salmon. Holds 150 yds. of 12-lb. backing and 30 yds. of No. 6 fly line. Price about $115.

**No. 2, The Salmon:** A middleweight reel for fly fishing combat with just about any marine or fresh-water opponents you feel capable of taking on—snook, salmon, medium-size tarpon, etc. Line capacity, 200 yds. of 15-lb. backing and 40 yds. of 9-weight fly line. Sells for about $125.

**No. 3, The Tarpon:** A big performer, ready to tangle with the heftiest salmon, as well as tarpon, Pacific sailfish, even marlin. Accommodates 250 yds. of 20-lb. backing plus 40 yds. of No. 10 fly line.

**Nos. 2** and **3** are also offered in anti-reverse models, $130 and $140. Extra spools for the 3, $25-$35 each.

And for a purchaser with the price, the Fin-Nor Presentation series: **Nos. 1, 2** and **3** fly reels in a handsome, hand-rubbed, green-lined walnut presentation case, an engraved plate with the recipient's name on each reel and the case's cover. A gift of a lifetime, about $420.

**In the Heddon Family**

**Series 300 Flyweight Reels:** Sturdy single-action reels for people with a modest allotment for tackle. Approximate prices from Heddon, $8.26 to $9.73. Three models, constructed from aluminum alloy, with cast steel spindles and line guards of hard, stainless metal, reversible for right- or left-hand use, standard line capacity. **No. 300,** ultralight, 3½ oz., lines to and including No. 6; Model **310,** 4 oz., for trout and panfishes, lines up to and including 7-weight; **No. 320,** 4½ oz., for medium-heavy rods, lines to and including No. 8.

Heddon Automatic Fly Reels: Exclusive power springs for up to 50 percent more line retrieved without rewinding. Fold-away trigger takes up slack instantly. Stainless line protector, good-looking green anodized finish. Two models: **No. 11,** 9.4 oz., lines up to and including 9-weight, vertical mount; **No. 5,** same as **No. 11** but horizontally mounted, 9.1 oz., for lines up to and including No. 8. **No. 11,** about $20.93, **No. 5,** $16.45.

New in the Heddon line: Mark IV automatic fly reel (vertical mount) and three single-action models—**Nos. 554, 555, 750**—with all-metal construction, brass shaft and click drag. **No. 554,** 4 oz., budget-priced, lines to and including No. 8. Model **555,** 5 oz., lines to and including No. 9. Model **750,** with metal reversible guard, 6 oz., handles lines up to and including 8-weight. All are competitively priced.

**Eagle Claw [Wright & McGill]**

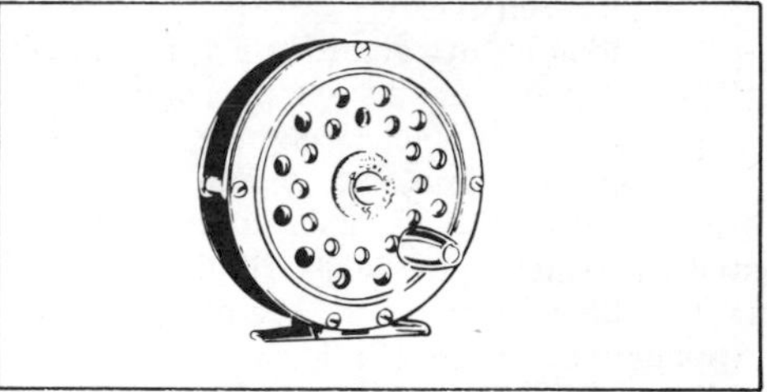

**Model ECD Automatic Fly Reel:** Long-length, zip-fast retrieves—smooth, quiet. Special slip-clutch to protect leaders against breakage. Lever-mounted tension release, adjustable-position release trigger. Three-position spring clamp. Lightweight aluminum construction, finish in a rich shade of brown. Holds 30 yds. of No. 7 line. Sells for about $19.00.

**A. D. McGill Autograph, Model EC3B, single-action:** A new concept in single-action design. It stars Eagle Claw's Slip Spool Drag. Handle remains stationary while spool revolves under drag tenssion until ready to retrieve, then line is retrieved in usual manner, controlling the fish directly from the reel. Other features: Precision built, combining die-cast aluminum for lightness and stainless steel for wear; three-position anti-reverse; audible on/off clicker; long line and backing capacity, with interchangeable spool; for right-hand or southpaw operation; smart-looking, corrosion-proof finish in brown and gold. Approximate price: $27.00.

Also from Eagle Claw: Blue Pacific series single-action fly reels: **EC-10** (3½ oz., 30 yds. of No. 5 line); **EC-11** (4 oz., 30 yds. of No. 7); **EC-12** (4½ oz., 30 yds. of No. 8).

**Fly Reels by Browning**

This company has an excellent designer, whoever he is. Their reels are as good looking as their rods.

Browning Lightweight Fly'r-4, numbered **1230**, is exceptionally eye-pleasing. It's a single-action fly reel, weighing 4 oz. and balancing No. 5 or No. 6 line. Ideal for trout, panfishes, small bass, ponds, streams, small, quiet lakes. Holds 30 yds. of DT6F, 25 yds. of 15-lb. braided backing. Approximate price, $11.95.

Browning Medium Weight Fly'r-5, Model **5230:** Single-action, 5 oz. For bass, trout, pike, pickerel, larger streams, rivers, lakes. Handles Nos. 6 to 8 lines, holds 30 yds. of DT6F, 50 yds. of braided backing. About $12.95.

Aluminum alloys and chrome-plated brass are these two reels' basic materials, with a heat-tempered, color-coordinated brown finish. Both can be set for right- or left-hand operation, have a quick action click mechanism to prevent line over-run. Their gold anodized spools are supported by one-piece aluminum frames, can be changed in seconds (extra spools available for both, about $3.50, $3.95).

**From Garcia**

**Kingfisher GK-44 and GK-42:** Lightweight single-action fly reels designed in the classic tradition, each with adjustable, shoe-type drag, chromed line guard, ventilated alloy spool with instant release, left-/right-hand conversion. **GK-44**, 5 oz., accommodates up to 100 yds. of backing. **GK-42,** 4½ oz., takes 50 yds. of backing and

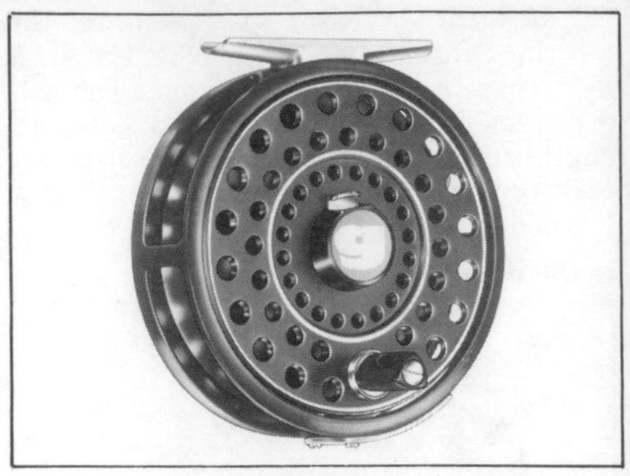

No. 6 fly line. Both are finished in black. Approximate prices: **GK-44**, $11.00; **GK-42**, $11.00.

**Kingfisher GK-50** is an automatic fly reel designed for most trout and panfish assignments, comfortably holds 35 yds. of No. 6 line, is finished in the Kingfisher series, smart-looking black, anodized against corrosion. It has a convenient tension release knob and trigger lock. Costs about $11.00.

Under the Mitchell label Garcia markets:

**Mitchell 754 Single-action Fly Reel:** Strong, smooth drag, with handle and drag on opposite sides to eliminate knuckle-dusting. Other specifications: Light aluminum alloy construction, frame and spool precisely machined to very fine tolerances; adjustable, chromed line guard; positive click—applies more drag when line goes out, less when it comes in; right- or left-hand conversion; good looks. Approximate price: $14.00.

### Fly Reels by Scientific Anglers

This Midland, Michigan, firm (now a 3M company) employs the same System (balanced) tackle procedures for its fly reels as for its fly rods. In essence it means precise matching of reel to line (and rod, of course), with each model designed for a specific weight line. Scientific Anglers has called its models the Rolls-Royce of fly reels—but without Rolls-Royce price tags. It's of interest and importance to note that they're made to Scientific Anglers' specifications by Hardy Brothers, Alnwick, England, world-famed master craftsmen of fly reels since 1872. And they're beautiful pieces of equipment. Each one is precision machined from space era materials by computer techniques, then hand-fitted, hand-assembled and tested by Hardy craftsmen.

There are eight models sharing these specifications: Tough, light, aluminum construction, one-piece frame and one-piece spool; adjustable, uni-directional click-drag; clean, crisp design—nothing to snag on line or clothing; all-metal, instant spring-latch spool release. Each comes with a padded, zippered carrying case. In accordance with its System balancing, the manufacturer designates its fly reels by the model names System **4** (ultra-light, recommended line DT4F), System **5** (light, balances DT5F line), and so on, through System **11** (extra-powerful, for a salt-water taper WF11F). In between are System models **6, 7, 8, 9** and **10,** according to line weights. Prices range from about $47.50 to $58. Extra spools are $20-$22 each.

### St. Croix Fly Reels

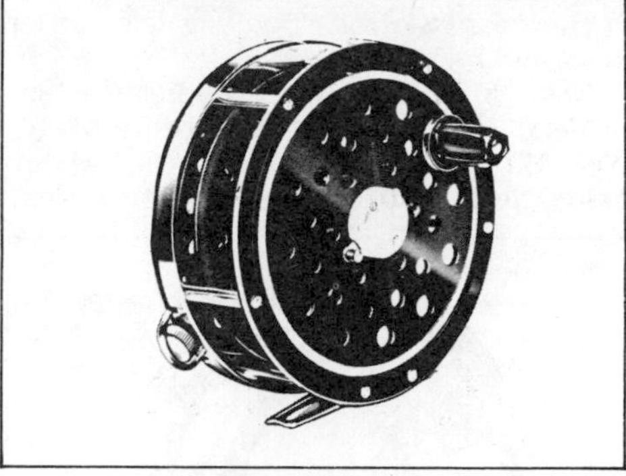

**No. 47 Salmon Fly Reel:** 10 oz., for heavier-duty combat on lines up through No. 11. Features: Adjustable drag; hard-chromed line guard; perforated, easily removed spool; distinctive black enamel, non-glossy finish. Approximate price: $9.99 to $12.99.

**Model No. 25:** Budget-priced (about $4.99 to $7.99), 4½ oz., single-action with off/on click, two-position drag adjustment and free spool, pushbutton take-apart, aerated spool, chromed line guard, black enamel finish. Holds 30 yds. of DT8F or 25 yds. of L8F.

**No. 29 Automatic Fly Reel:** Free-running spool assembly with stainless steel line guard, folding line trigger, free stripping. Weighs 9½ oz., takes 40 yds. of L8F line. Finished in bronze-gold with contrasting burgundy-color drive spring cap. Priced at about $9.99 to $12.99.

**St. Croix 330 Fly Reel:** Single-action, precision built, adjustable drag, chromed line guard, easily removed spool. Gold-tan with brown trim. About $6.99 to $9.99.

**From Pflueger**

**Supreme Series:** Two models given here—both single-action.

**Nos. 577** and **578** are single-action models, 10½ and 12½ oz., respectively. **No. 577** is for heavy-duty fresh-water assignments and light salt-water action,

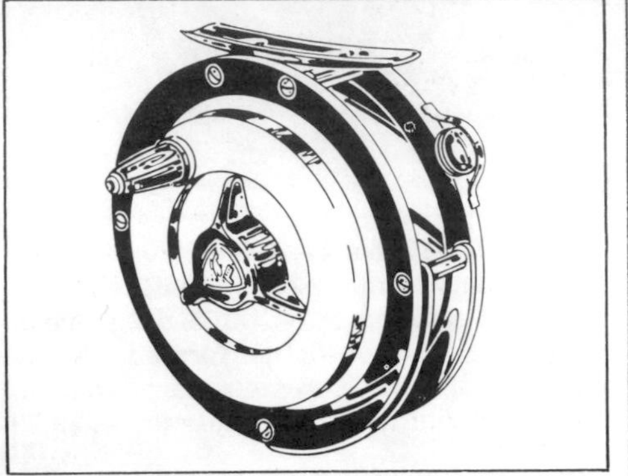

takes any level or tapered fly line and 250 yds. of 15-lb. mono backing or 100 yds. of 15-lb. braided nylon. **No. 578** has larger spool capacity for heavy-duty service, fly line plus 300 yds. of 15-lb. mono or 200 yds. of braided nylon backing. Both models have a solid aluminum spool, nylon bearings, chromed pillars, corrosion-resistant finish, come in a zippered vinyl case with reel wrench, gear grease, reel oil. Another feature of **No. 577** is an adjustable drag with 360-degree circular heat-dissipating disc. Also a line strip control lever permitting line stripping against a set drag. **No. 578** has the same feature, optional. Prices: **No. 577,** about $55.00 to $80.00; **No. 578,** about $55.00 to $80.00.

You might also inquire about these Pflueger fly reels:

Medalist Series: (1) Medalist Automatic, 8.9 oz., for No. 8 or 9 line; (2) six Medalist single-action models, 4 oz. to 6 7/8 oz., (3) the Trump, single-action, 4½ oz.; (4) the Sal-Trout, 5 oz., single-action.

**Berkley and Company**

In its 1975 inventory of reels Berkley presented several fly models:

**Model 570,** an automatic: Winds completely in 8 revolutions. With its spring wound, 570 retrieves 20 yds. of No. 6 fly line. Weighs 9.4 oz. Capacity, 30 yds. of 6-weight line and 50 yds. of 10-lb. backing. Price, $24.95.

Single-action models: (1) **No. 510, $13.50** retail: New adjustable drag, on/off click button, capacity of 30 yds. of Berkley floating line. (2) **No. 530:** With new adjustable drag, 2½" spool, holding 30 yds. of Berkley No. 6 floating fly line, $21.95 retail. (3) **No. 540:** New adjustable drag, spool of 2-7/8" diameter, holds 30 yds. of No. 6 floating line plus 50 yds. of backing; priced at $22.95. (4) **No. 550:** New adjustable drag, big diameter spool (3¼"), capacity of 30 yds. Berkley No. 6 floating line and 100 yds. of backing, $23.95 retail.

**Gladding-South Bend**

Gladding-South Bend offers four automatic fly reels. Three are the traditional vertically mounted type, all in the Oreno-Matic group; the fourth is a flat or horizontal mount.

The Oreno-Matics, with highlights: **No. 1140**—silent winding, effortless free stripping, automatic line brake, fold-away retrieve trigger of chromed brass, gnurled spring tension release, coin-slotted take-down screw, weight of 9½ oz., capacity to 35 yds. of 6-weight line. **No. 1130**—similar to 1140, but 8½ oz. and with less capacity (to 25 yds. of No. 6 line). **No. 1190**—9½ oz., automatic brake, smart anodized finish,

stainless steel line protector, free stripping fold-away trigger, holds up to 35 yds. of No. 6 line. **No. 1180**—flat mounted, 9 oz., tempered steel drive spring, effortless stripping, chromed brass trigger, stainless steel rod clip, rust-resistant anodized finish throughout, up to 35 yds. of No. 6 fly line. Approximate price range: $8.75 to $11.50.

**Single-action and multiplying fly reels by Gladding-South Bend:** The Finalist, **No. 1122**—economically priced, at about $4.95, rugged aluminum construction, quick-change 2½" spool, up to 35 yds. of 5-weight line. **No. 10055,** Kingsize Gear Fly Reel, 2.66:1 retrieve with line-protecting roller (free-turning), two-screw dismantling for cleaning, made in England by Gladding's Morritt Division, capacity up to 125 yds. of WF9F, a heavy-duty model. **No. 1044,** Regular Gladding-South Bend Gear Fly Reel—same fast retrieve and other features of 1055 in a model suited to most fresh-water flyrodding, 100 yds. of DT6F. **No. 1033,** Lightweight Gear Fly Reel—all **1055** and **1044** features in a lightweight model for most stream angling, 75 yds. of DT5F. Approximate price range, $18.90 to $19.60.

**Shakespeare**

Four single-action reels in the Purist series: Light but strong aluminum construction; chromed, rustproof line guide; fast, positive, adjustable drag; changeable spool; easy conversion to left-hand use. The Purists are numbered **7594** through **7597.** Their range of specifications: 4 7/8 oz., spool 2 11/16" by 13/16", up to No. 7 level line (reel **7594**) to 6 3/8 oz., spool 3 1/16" by 1", up to No. 12 level line (model **7597**). Price range goes about $22.50 to $23.50.

Also in the Purist series: **No. 1898** heavy-duty fly reel, engineered for battles with salmon, tarpon, and other huskies. Features Shakespeare's exclusive, fish-saving 6-Drag, on/off non-reverse lever, built-in click on drag. Holds any fly line plus 200 yds. of braided backing. Sells for about $60.00.

Another Shakespeare single-action reel is the budget-priced **1890**, with ultra-light construction of virtually indestructible Cycolac, an ABS material from Borg-Warner. Also has an audible click, release for silent stripping. Costs about $5.50.

Shakespeare's automatic fly reels include three models in the Tru-Art series—two vertical, one horizontal—and two in the OK series, vertical and horizontal. All five feature Shakespeare's new, longer-wearing, positive-grip, ratchet release coil and brake coil of square-section spring wire. All accommodate any level or weight-forward lines, or double-taper lines to No. 6. Other specifications in the group include free stripping, aluminum frame, stainless steel line protector. So you can ask for them, the Tru-Arts are numbered **1826**, **1827**, **1837** (horizontal), and the OKs are **1824** and **1822** (horizontal). Weights go from 8½ oz. (**1822**) to 9.4 oz. (**1826**). Prices are from about $15.00 to $28.00.

**From Quick**

Quick **No. 25:** 4½ oz.; housing, 3½" by 1-3/16" wide; capacity, 30 yds. of DT6S and 50 yds. of 20-lb. backing.

Quick **No. 45:** 6 oz.; quick-change spool; holds 30 yds. of DT6S plus 50 yds. of 20-lb. backing.

Quick **No. 55**, for the more rugged battlers—steelheads, salmon, etc: 6½ oz.; quick-change spool; housing 3½" by 1¼"; capacity, 30 yds. of DT8S and 50 yds. of 30-lb. backing.

Other features of these single-action Quicks are light but strong construction, adjustable silent drag, adjustable on/off ratchet, easy changeover from right to left hand. Approximate prices: **No. 25**, $15.00; **No. 45**, $20.00; **No. 55**, $20.00.

**Martin Reel Company**

A fast nose count reveals that this Mohawk, N.Y., firm fields some twenty-two or so models of single-action, multiplying and automatic fly reels. Here are a couple of representatives:

**Model 72:** A multiplyer with 3:1 retrieve, Martin's own 360-degree, one-way floating disc drag, on/off click, twin hardened, plated line guides, easy change to right or left hand use. Weighs 9¼ oz., holds 35 yds. of WF9F plus 150 yds. of 18-lb. Dacron backing. Approximate price is $30.95.

There's also the Martin **68** multiple-action model, about $19.95.

Under the group name Tuffy are seven single-action reels, model numbers **60** through **66** for a full range of flyrodding assignments, ultra-light and light to medium and heavy.

Models **60** through **63** are for ultra-light and light fishing. Weights are 3½ and 3 3/4 oz., with spool capacities from 30 yds. of DT6F (**No. 60**) to 35 yds. of WF8F (**No. 63**). Features include 2 hardened line guides, on/off click-type drag, non-glare epoxy finish, coin-slotted take-down (**No. 60**), pushbutton spool removal (**Nos. 62, 63**). Retail prices about $5.95 to $8.95.

Other Tuffys are **Nos. 64, 65, 66,** for right- or left-hand operation. They incorporate such features as pushbutton spool removal, positive on/off click drag, twin hardened, plated line guides. Weights are 5 oz. (**No. 65**), 5½ oz. for **66**, 6¼ oz. for **No. 64.** Capacity of **65** and **66** is 35 yds. of WF9F and 130 of 18-lb. braided nylon backing. Model **64** takes 35 yds. of WF9F plus 150 yds. of the same backing. Approximate prices: No. **64, $16.95;** No. **65**, $10.95; No. **66**, $12.95.

**Martin Fly-Wate Model 49 Automatic:** Weighs but 9¼ oz., yet holds 30 yds. of DT8F or 35 of WF8F. Has unique push-button tension release, free stripping, silent winding, adjustable trigger, patented quick-action brake that never needs adjusting, no-tool take-down. In dark maroon and gold, about $19.95 retail.

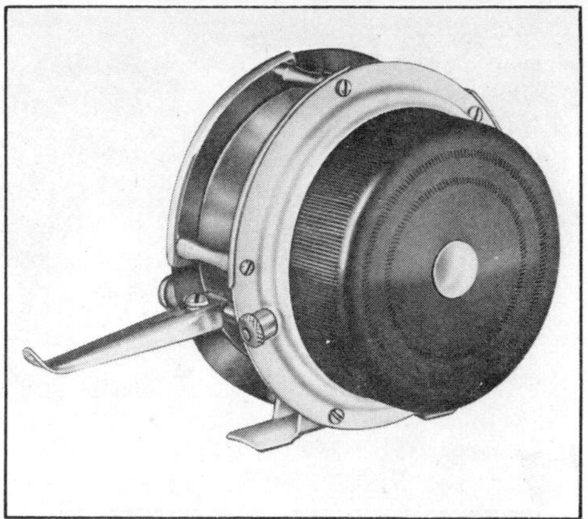

Additionally, Martin offers Tuffy and other Fly-Wate automatics in a range of sizes with attractive prices at the $14 to $16 level. And there's the Blue Chip **83** automatic, with all the desirable Martin features, guaranteed for 5 years against defects—even wear—about $28.95, with soft deerskin pouch. Weighs 9¼oz., takes 30 yds. of DT8T or 35 of WF8F.

**Martin Trol-O-Matic 35A:** Earlier we cited the biggest advantage of automatic fly reels, their being able to take in line quickly, as when a fighting fish changes course abruptly to create slack. Along with that plus, the Trol-O-Matic 35A has a double line guide for use on trolling and baitcasting rods too. Other details: Free stripping; twin spring system retrieves 50 yds. without rewinding; patented quick-acting metal brake; adjustable retrieve trigger; solid-core spool and precision-fitted rim plates for use with mono line. Weighs 15 3/4 oz., holds 35 yds. of WF9F fly line and 150 yds. of 18-lb. braided Dacron backing. Price is about $28.95.

### Fly Reels from Orvis

Charles F. Orvis patented the first ventilated-spool fly reel a hundred years ago. In the ensuing decades the company he founded has done him proud, manufacturing fly reels plainly reflecting the same pride of workmanship that goes into Orvis fly rods. Other companies have referred to theirs as Rolls-Royce reels. Orvis certainly can too, and then some.

C.F.O. Fly Reels were named in honor of the firm's founder and guiding genius. They're designated as the **CFO II, III, IV** and **V.** Each comes in its own fleece-lined, suede leather case. Range of physical details: From CFO **II,** 2 oz., 2-9/16", taking DT3F or WF4F line, to CFO **V,** 4¼ oz., 3-7/16", for lines to WF10F and 150 yds. of backing. Incredibly light, superbly designed and built, CFO single-action reels incorporate a one-side frame for spool removal without line pinch, also a smooth, lever-adjustable drag, instantly reversible for right or left hand. Prices go from about $57.50 to $66.50. Extra spools are available for all four, about $22-$25.

**Orvis Madison Fly Reels:** Popularly priced, good looking. Specifications include: Orvis' patented adjustable drag with finger lever operation for 8 settings, light to heavy (except on the model 4/5); simple lines and strong; quick take-apart by simply pressing a lever. The Madisons are designated by model numbers 4/5, 6/7, 8 and 9, which also give clues to the weights of lines they're designed to handle. Physical aspects go from 4 oz. and 3" (the 4/5) to 6 3/4 oz. and 3-5/8" (Madison 9). The 6/7, 8 and 9 accommodate 100 to 200 yds. of backing in addition to the prescribed fly line. Approximate price range: $16.50-$19.75, with extra spools $6-$6.75.

**Orvis Magnalite Fly Reels:** These are multiplyers, 2:1 retrieve, light enough to mount on 4- to 6-oz. fly rods. They feature: Magnesium construction—very light, strong, rigid, durable; positive, lever-type adjustable drag; overlapping spool rim for sensitive, fingertip "feathering" brake action; simple, trouble-free design. Two models, 5½ oz. and No. 8 line plus 50 yds. of backing, and a wide version, 6 oz., 3½" diameter, taking No. 9 line and 175 yds. of backing. Price about $39.95 each; extra spool, $19.

**Orvis Saltwater Fly Reel:** Field tested from Iceland to British Honduras, a single-action reel with muscle for really tough finned game. Top Orvis quality combined with practical simplicity. Features: Oversized controls for instant access in action; selective anti-reverse—no knuckle rapping; ventilated frame and spool (instantly removable); a big star drag adjusting from a feather-light pull to a dead stop. Diameter is 4", weight is 12¼ oz. In a gunmetal finish, built for marine service with extra corrosion resistance inside and out. (**Note:** It isn't convertible to left-hand wind.) Handles lines from WF8F + 275 yds. of 20-lb. backing to WF11F line + 200 yds. of 20-lb. backing. Price about $59.50.

### Feurer Brothers Fly Reels

The same Swiss watchmaking talent going into their spinning reels continues in the Feurer Brothers fly models.

**The Taurus:** Completely corrosion-proof for salt water as well as fresh. Specifications: Weighs 12 oz., accommodates No. 11 weight-forward fly line and 250 yds. of 20-lb. mono or braided backing; three-way anti-reverse knob can be set for either hand or off; drag control ring at base of grip handle adjusts line tension from a whisper to full on. Taurus is operable with either hand. Model **FB 480**, about $86. Model **FB 480GS**, the Gold Seal Taurus, about $95.

**Feurer Brothers' Gemini I [FB 473] and Gemini II [FB 475]:** Rugged single-action reels for light-tackle buffs. They feature: Stainless steel line guide; double-hardened click pawl; spool and housing of light aluminum; hard, non-corrosive finish; steady clicker—heavy against fish, light on retrieve. Gemini **I,** 5½ oz., 2-7/8" spool, for No. 3 or 4 fly line, 50-yd. capacity, about $13.50. Gemini **II,** 6½ oz., 3½" spool, for No. 5 or 6 line, 50-yd. capacity, about $16.25.

**Daiwa Fly Reels**

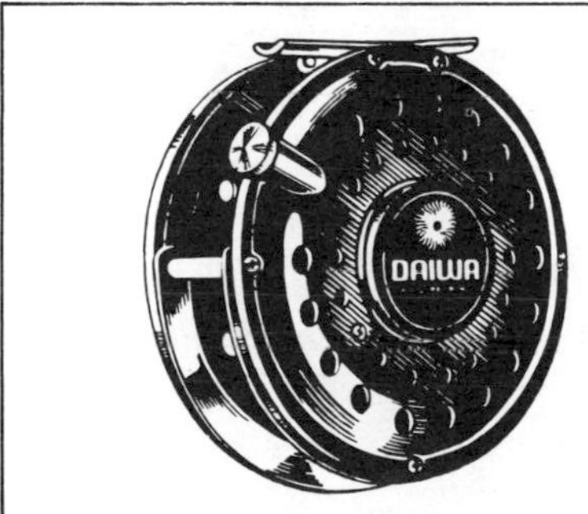


Four single-action models:

**Nos. 254** and **252:** Model **254** is Daiwa's deluxe heavy-duty reel with sealed stainless steel ball bearing. No. **254** also is heavy-duty. Both have: Sensitive shoe-type drag, plus thumb drag control system; 3-7/8" plate, 1" pillars; perforated, quick-take-apart spool. Each weighs 8½ oz. Model **254,** about $19.25; **No. 252,** about $17.50.

**Nos. 710** and **720:** Model **710** is for trout and panfishes, weighs 4 oz., has spool dimensions of 2-7/8" by 5/8", takes up to No. 7 line, sells for about $14.88. **No. 720** handles fly lines up to and including No. 8, weighs 5 oz., has a 3-1/8" by 7/8" spool, goes for about $16.63. Both have one-piece aluminum frame, one-piece, perforated spool, plated line guard, steel click spring and pawls, with guard and pawls reversing for right or left hand.

## SOME LINES ABOUT FLY LINES

As we've said in our discussion of them elsewhere in this volume, fly lines are uniquely different from other fishing lines in design and construction, due to the needs of flycasting. In no other kind of angling do the **lines** supply the weight needed to cast lures.

Naturally, major line companies—Newton, Cortland, Gudebrod, and so on—include fly lines in their inventories. But keep in mind that many major tackle manufacturers also market fly lines, often under their own labels.

Here are some samplings. Generally, inquiries will reveal that a firm markets a full range of fly lines in types and weights. You might also ask about tapered leaders.

**Cortland Line Company**

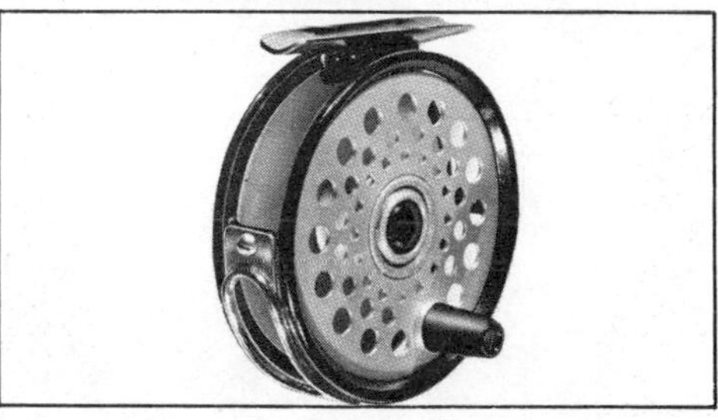

Cortland has been producing quality fishing lines for all kinds of marine and sweetwater fishing for decades, and for at least five of those ten-year spans has been a leader in the manufacture of fly lines. Cortland developments have included oil-impregnated fly lines and introduction of the first synthetic-coated fly line, in 1953. A more recent Cortland creation is the Micro-Foam floating fly lines. In these a unique braided Micron core is surrounded by thousands of tiny globules of air trapped in a foam-like structure that floats **on** instead of **in** the water. A tough, very slick finish completes the Micro-Foam lines.

Micro-Foam Floating Fly Lines are available in all sorts of tapers—durable, rocket, salt-water, etc.—and in weights from 4 to 11.

Other Cortland fly line labels—floating or sinking types, assorted tapers and weights—include: 333 Micro-Sink; 333 Glo-Line; Fairplay. The company also produces Micron Braided Fly Line Backing, 333 Knotless Tapered Leaders, Cobra Flat Monofilament, and fly line cleaner.

**Universal Vise Corp. [22 Main St., Westfield, Mass. 01085]**

Universal Sink Leaders: In 7½' and 9' lengths, green color, tippet sizes from 5X through OX and OOX (OX and OOX in 9' only). Three leaders in reusable bag, 7½' and 9'. Also sinking tippet material, 6X through OOX, 30' spools.

**From U.S. Line Company**

This Westfield, Mass., firm has the following labels, all prefixed by "U.S.":

**Royal Trout:** Floating, green color, for rugged service, with tough, smooth finish. Level, weight-forward or double taper, Nos. 3 to 7, 25-35 yds.

**Queen of Waters:** Floating line with pearl white, slippery smooth finish for frictionless casting and greater shooting distance. Level, weight-forward or double taper, 25 yds. (level) to 35 yds. (torpedo taper), 5- to 9-weight.

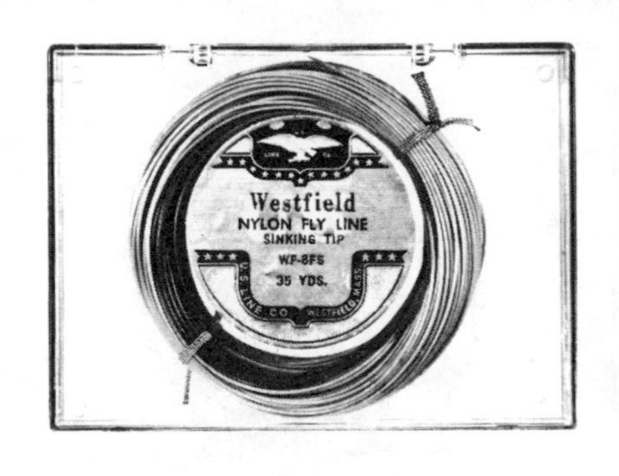


**Westfield Sinking Tip:** Designed especially for wet fly and nymph fishing, where it's desirable for the line's front section to submerge. Steel-green with darker tip.

**Westfield Floating:** Bonded finish, low specific gravity for high floating, balanced, smooth finish, steel-green. In level, double taper and torpedo taper profiles, from L3F, 25 yds., to WF10F, 35 yds.

**Professor:** Extensive streamside research produced this one. Meets all requirements for a sinking or "dredging" fly line. Billed as ideal for nymphs, wet flies and streamer trolling. Dark gray in color. Available in 35-yd. torpedo tapers, 30-yd. double tapers, 25-yd. levels, 3-weight to No. 10.

Also from U.S. Line: Fly line backing, Dacron or braided nylon, 18- through 30-lb. test, tan or black stripe. Fli-Restore, to improve flies' appearance and buoyancy. U.S. Fly Line Cleaner. U.S. Fly Line Eyelets for easy attachment of leader to line, eliminating bulky, "spooky" knots. And U.S. Dry Fly Spray, 2 oz. in aerospray can, coats any dry fly with silicone to make it float high and dry.

Gudebrod G-5 Floater

**Fly Lines from Gudebrod**

**Hi-Spot Floater:** Green, amber, one coil per box. Hi-Spot Floater has durable plastic finish, good floating qualities. Casts smoothly and picks up easily, recommended for young flyrodders.

**Sink-R-Dacron:** Designed for wet flies, nymphs, streamers. Sinks fast for a natural, drag-free presentation. Smooth plastisol finish for good handling, easy pickup. Dark walnut-brown for low visibility in water. A metal eyelet comes with each line for leader attachment. In double tapers, levels, weight forward tapers, 25 and 30 yds., weights from L6S to WF10S.

Gudebrod Sink-R-Dacron

**G-5 Floater:** Of Gudebrod's G-5 nylon, soft, smooth, supple, high- and dry-riding, special weight-controlled core with smooth plastisol finish. Levels are 25yds., tapers are 30 yds.

**Gudebrod's Salt Water and Bug Taper:** Of G-5 nylon, high-floating with special weight-forward taper, white.

**Gudebrod Fly Line Backing:** Ultra-thin, braided Dacron—no stretch, waterproof, constant diameter, wet or dry, no special care needed. In 15-, 20-, 30-lb. tests.

**From Orvis**

As you'd anticipate, if you're at all familiar with this company's production of fly tackle, Orvis's inventory of balanced lines is proportionately large. Name a type—floating, sinking, level, double taper, sinking-tip, or whatever—and Orvis has it, with an equally complete range of weights up through No. 11.

Some of the company's own labels are: Orvis Bass Bug, Salmon, Saltwater Taper; AirCel Supreme Floating Fly Line; WetCel II Sinking Fly Line; AirCel Wet Tip Hi-D Fly Line.

**Orvis Shooting Head Fly Line, No. F1483:** 130', handmade, dark green shooting head (30') and light green running line (100', floating), smoothly united by Orvis's own baked epoxy splice.

Backing for fly lines: **No. F1600,** braided, tan Dacron, 20-lb. test, for trout, bass, most fresh-water fly angling. In 50- to 1,000-yd. spools. **No. F1602**, a new salmon and salt-water backing, in braided, tan Dacron, 30-lb. test, 100- to 200-yd. spools.

Orvis offers a 6-inch front loop splice or 3-foot mono butt splice of baked epoxy. Each is tied with .021 stiff mono to transmit line's turning force to leader, slides through guides and tiptop without a bump.

Also from Orvis, precision-made fly leaders: A wide selection, OX through 7X tippets, for flies from 1/0 to No. 28, in strengths from 1¼-lb. test up, lengths from 7½' to 12'. Included are Hand Tied Knotted Leaders, New Two-Knot Leaders, Compound Taper Wet Fly Leaders with Kwik-Klips (for instant change; micro-light), and Knotted Compound Taper Salmon, Salt-water and Bass Bug Leaders. There's also the Orvis Trout Leader Selection, an assortment of 6, 7½' 2X to 12' 5X, in soft vinyl leader wallet with 6 double pockets, 4¼ by 4".

Also from Orvis: Leader tippet material, 7X to 1X (15 yds., others 25 yds.), special mono, in minimum tests of 1.1 lbs. to 23.7 lbs., in a flat packet. Leader Tie Kit: twenty spools of special imported leader mono, butt size (.021") down to tippet size (.004"), with illustrated instruction booklet showing how to tie properly balanced tapered leaders. A new fly line cleaner-conditioner.

**Fly Lines from Martin Reel Company**

Martin's brand label is Sovereign. Types available include: **Floating**—level, double taper, weight forward, 25-35 yds., weights No. 5 through No. 9; **sinking**—double taper and weight forward, DT6S through WF9S; and **special** salt-water taper—WF8F and WF10F. All Sovereign floating lines are in a white that is highly visible to the angler but not to fishes. Sinking lines are a dark, subtle blue-green. Sovereign DT and WF types are packaged in a see-through, Naugahyde-finished, zippered streamer and wet fly book, 5" by 5" by 1", with durable foam pads to hold flies and streamers securely. All but level lines include the fly book.

Martin's Sovereign Knotless, Tapered Leaders are available in two groups: 7½' lengths for short casts, rough/unclear water, 6X tippet (1 3/4-lb. test) to OX tippet (6-lb. test); and in the same strength range in 9' lengths for longer casts and use in clear water.

**Gladding-South Bend**

Since Gladding is one of America's senior fishing line manufacturers, it would be a jolt to discover that they didn't produce fly lines. But they do indeed, a full range. Groups under the Gladding label include:

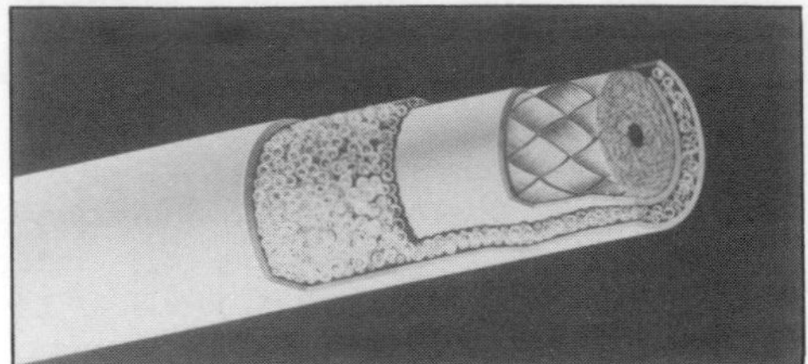

**Super Aerofloat:** Gladding calls it the "floating fly line with MFS," those initials standing for Multiple Flotation Spheres. Another major detail is true diameter, guaranteed to be within .003" tolerance throughout. Each line comes in a 3-in-1 pack with cleaner and a coil of leader. Available as: L3F through L9F, 25-yd. coils; DT5F through DT9F, 30-yd. coils; WF6F through WF10F, 35 yds.; salt-water tapers, WF9F through WF11F, 40 yds.; salt-water tapers, WF9F-WF11F, with 200 yds. of 18-lb. backing; and tapered shooting heads, ST9F and ST10F, 33' coils.

**Super Aqua Sink:** Weighted lead core takes it down fast and deep. Smooth, supple, limp. Also with true diameter guaranteed to within .003", and in 3-in-1 pack. In these types and AFTMA designations: L3S-L10S; DT5S-DT10S; WF5S-WF10S; and tapered shooting heads, ST9S and ST11S.

**Magistrate:** All-purpose fly line. Braided nylon with tough plastic coating, dark green. Available as: L1F-L8F, 25-yd. coils; DT5F-DT8F, 30-yd. coils; WF6F-WF9F, 40-yd. coils.

**Ideal:** A popular fly line, braided nylon with tough plastic coating, dark green. L3F through L7F, 25-yd. coils.

**Gladding Super Fly Line:** Braided nylon with a smooth, tough coating, green color. Available in level and double taper types, sinking, 5- to 8-weight, 25 and 30 yds.

**Lines from Shakespeare**

**Mono-Blend Fly Line:** High-floating, smooth-gliding, clean turnover. Has a flexible, waterproof, ever-float core-coating combination of space age polymers saturated with lighter-than-water air pockets. Off-white color. Mono-Blend 8000 comes as DT4F through DT8F, 30 yds., and as WF5F through WF11F, 35 yds. Mono-Blend 8200 is a slow-sinking version, transluscent mono color, WF5S through WF11S, 35 yds.

**High Floating Purist Fly Line, No. 4300:** A high floater featuring Shakespeare's Wonderfloat construction (millions of minute, plastic-protected air cells for permanent buoyancy), protective plastic coating to prevent moisture absorption, and a smooth, white finish visible under any weather condition. Line comes in a polypropylene container serving as a pocket-size fly and accessory box. L4F through L9F, 25-yds; DT4F through DT9F, 30 yds. WF5F through WF9F, 30 yds., and WF10F and WF11F, 40 yds.

**Presidential 4335 Floating Line:** Shakespeare's most popular floating line, in natural green color to blend with surroundings. LF4F through L9F, 25 yds.; DT4F-DT9F, 30 yds.; WF6F through WF9F, 30 yds., WF10F, 40 yds.

**Presidential 4332 Sinking Fly Line:** Fast-sinking, green color, with small diameter for low wind resistance and easy pickup. L6S through L9S, 25 yds.; DT6S-DT9S, 30 yds. WF6S through WF10S, 30 yds., WF11S and WF12S, 40 yds.

**Sunset Line & Twine Co.**

Stars in Sunset's fly line group are the internationally known Masterlines. These superb fly lines are made in Tewkesbury, England, by Anglers Masterline, Ltd. Jack Martin, British National Champion Fly Caster, aided in their design. And they can be said to represent the end products of five centuries of English fly angling. There's a sizable family of Masterlines in a wide range of types—sinking, floating, sinking-tip, weight forward, shooting taper, etc.—and weights. A few representatives:

**The Chancellor series by Masterline:** Floating (foam white and surface green) and sinking (deep-water gray). The floaters ride high; sinking chancellors go deep quickly. Tapers include: Weight-forward, Nos. 5 through 8, 30 yds., Nos. 9 and 10, 40 yds.; double taper, 4- through 9-weight, 30

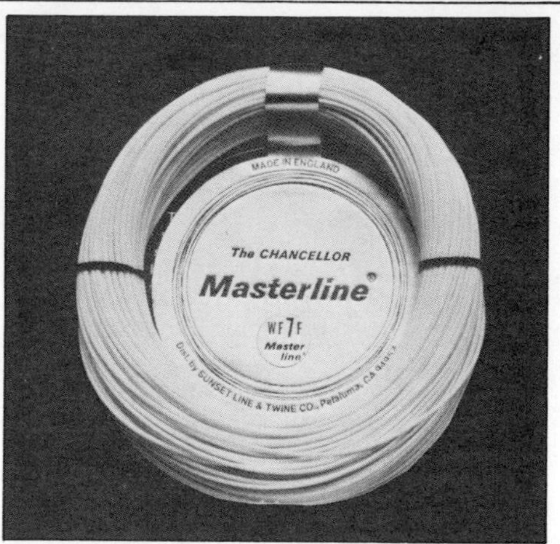


yds.; shooting tapers, weights 5 through 8, 30', 7 through 11, 35'; sink-tip double tapers, dapple gray, Nos. 6 through 9, 30 yds., No. 10, 40 yds. Also in the Chancellor series is the Chalkstream, for the dry fly perfectionist and the clearest waters. Has exceptional flotation, easy pickup. Chalk gray, double taper, weights 4 through 8, 30 yds.

**Masterline Don [VFS]:** The "VFS" is for Very Fast Sinking. For fast water and extra-deep fly fishing, in fresh water or salt, with small diameter for low wind and current (or tide) resistance. In shadow-gray. Double taper, 6- through 9-weight, 30 yds.; weight forward, Nos. 6 through 8, 30 yds., Nos. 9 and 10, 40 yds.; shooting tapers, weights 6 through 8, 30', 9 through 11, 35'.

**Masterline's Oxbridge series:** Floating and sinking lines, blue color, with fortified tips to aid in control and withstand wear. Double taper, 30 yds., weights 6 through 9; weight-forward taper, Nos. 6 through 8, 30 yds., Nos. 9 and 10, 40 yds.

Also from Sunset Line & Twine: Troutmaster Fly Line, light amber, light green, level type, four 25-yd. coils per box in sizes 3, 4, 5; Marabou Weighted Shooting Head, lead-core line with a tough plastic finish, for streamer trolling and extra-long casts, green color, comes with factory spliced loops for joining backing and leader, 18' to 30'; Fan Wing Fly Line, double taper, 30 yds., light green, light amber, Nos. 5 through 8, in individual plastic box.

Sunset also produces Flexon leader material and Flexon tapered leaders. The former comes in tests from 1 lb. (20 yds.) to 40 lbs. (10 yds.), mist color. Flexon tapered leaders are in sizes 1X through 4X, 6' to 9', natural and green.

**Berkley Fly Lines**

**Specialist Fly Lines:** New design, new formulation. Highlights: Exclusive bearing finish—almost invisible microspheres reduce friction and wear, improve shootability; small beads at the surface for a tougher, more durable finish, large beads near the core for greater limpness and better flotation; extensive field proving by professional guides and recognized fly fishing experts. Available in these types and colors to meet all situations: (1) Floating—WF and DT designs, high-visibility yellow, cocoa brown, bright white, also level type in light green, and blunt-tip, weight-forward design for salt water and fresh, sky blue; (2) sinking—in deep brown to blend in with subsurface environment; (3) floating/sinking lines in high-visibility yellow/brown. In 25- and 30-yd. lengths, weights 3 through 11, with Qwik Sink 10' tip. Each Specialist line is unconditionally guaranteed.

Other Berkley fly lines: Perma-Float, in WF, DT, L types, Nos. 4 through 8, in floating density only, ivory color, 25 or 30 yds. Golden Zephyr lines, also in WF, DT and L profiles, Nos. 4 through 10, floating and sinking densities, green color, 25- and 30-yd. lengths.

Dac-Bac is Berkley's premium grade, low-stretch, non-rotting fly line backing, green fleck. In 18-lb. test, two connected 100-yd. spools in see-through plastic box.

**From Scientific Anglers**

This company's System balanced tackle (as described under fly rods and reels) naturally embraces its fly lines as well. All told, Scientific Anglers probably offers one of the most versatile and most sophisticated assortment of fly lines on the market today.

For example, there's the Wet Cel trio: Type I, slow-sinking, for slow retrieves in shallows, for trout, bass, pike, muskies over weed beds 3-5' below a lake's surface, or small to medium streams with a moderate flow; Wet Cel II, fast-sinking, with a wide range of uses when sinking lines are required, an all-purpose sinking line for lakes, also for shad, salmon and steelheads in rivers of moderate depths with moderate to fast currents; and Wet Cel Hi-D Extra Fast Sinking, ideal for salt water, deep fishing in lakes at depths of 15' or more, and for extremely fast or very deep rivers. All three Wet Cel lines are available in a variety of tapers and weights.

Then there's the series of combination floating/sinking lines—their forward section submerges while the balance of the line floats. Three types: Air Cel Wet Tip—floating line with 10' fast-sinking tip—for nymphs, wet flies and streamers just under a stream's surface or over submerged weed beds; Air Cel Wet Tip Hi-D—first 10' section is extra-fast-sinking, for fast river currents or in salt water to sink a fly ahead of a cruising target, handles like a floating line; Air Cel Wet Belly Hi-D—first 20' extra-fast-sinking, same advantages as the Wet Tip, but gets more depth in faster currents. These lines also come in a variety of tapers and weights.

**Garcia Fly Lines**

The Garcia Corporation's seemingly endless procession of tackle items contains fly lines too.

One group bears the Lee Wulff label, named for one of America's most famous fishermen and casters. Lee Wulff Long Belly Fly Line has its namesake's versatility, combining the casting assets of a double taper line with the distance of a weight-forward design. Comes in floating (ivory color), sinking (aqua hue), sinking-tip (gray) types, 5- through 10-weight.

**Garcia's Kingfisher Floating Fly Line:** Has permanent, built-in flotation, won't absorb water. Comes in level, double-taper and weight-forward profiles, Nos. 4, through 9.

**Garcia's Dacron Sinking Fly Line:** Has Dacron's assets, goes deep and stays there until retrieved; can't absorb water, so it lifts readily. In mahogany and aqua. Torpedo taper (Nos. 5 through 8), double taper (4 through 7), 3- through 7- weight.

**Garcia Knotless Tapered Fly Leaders:** Feature a precisely controlled taper, with a long, heavy butt blending into a fine tippet for good turnovers. In a new glint-free finish, 7½' and 9' lengths, 6X (1½-lb. test) to OX (8-lb. test).

**Fly Lines from Newton Line**

**Golden River Nylon:** in amber or green. An economical fly line with a smooth finish and close weave for long, straight casts. Golden River level lines in 3, 5, 6 and 7 weights, 25 yds.; in double tapers, weights 6, 7 and 8, 30 yds.

**Phantom Nylon:** Soft to the touch, long-wearing, with pliable vinyl finish. A floating line in white, green or amber, in level (25 yds.), double taper (30 yds.) and weight forward (35 yds.) types.

**Newton Streamline:** The manufacturer's Superfloat Fly Line—smooth, tough, resilient, with Vinylube finish that never needs dressing, correct weight and balance. In amber, aqua green or white. Levels, 25 yds, double tapers, 30 yds., weights 5 through 8, weight-forward tapers, weights 7 through 11.

## NOTES ON FLY FISHING LURES

There are so many, many fresh and salt water flies that a display of just the classic and popular patterns in color—and they should be in full color—would amount to a miniature spectacular. Unfortunately, it also would drive the price of this book right through the ceiling. The latest edition of **McClane's Standard Fishing Encyclopedia** has an impressive gallery of artificial flies in their rainbow of colors; but then, that monumental tome sells for about forty bucks, and even **it** could not cover all the myriad of patterns.

Anyway, this isn't a book about fly fishing. As a guide to selection of tackle it will serve its objective by spotlighting some of the companies around the United States that fabricate flies; and, for the do-it-yourselfers, the firms that market fly tying materials and tools.

**Buz's Fly and Tackle Shop 805 W. Tulare Ave., Visalia, Cal. 93227**

Buz's has a big assortment of wet and dry flies, special patterns, streamers, nymphs, etc., all custom tied to exacting standards. Prices vary according to patterns and sizes, but the general range is 60c to $1 each. If desired, Buz's will furnish a list of materials involved and a label for each fly at 35c apiece.

This outfit carries a full line of fly tying materials and tools—vises (up to about $22.95), scissors (from about $3.95-$5.95), hooks (by the dozen, all standard fly sizes), Bausch & Lomb Illuminated Magnifier (about $21.95), etc.

**Phillips Fly & Tackle Co.**
**P. O. Box 188, Alexandria, Pa. 16611**

Phillips offerings include the famous Muddler Minnow, trout fly streamers, bucktail streamers (made famous by angling great John Alden Knight), the Multi Wing Streamer and Bonefish Bucktail for salt water, Deer Hair Fly, Woolly Worm, Wulff flies (developed by noted angler Lee Wulff), fly rod poppers, and others. Price range is from about 60c to $1.25 each. Phillips also has fractional-ounce lures for spinning, $1.70-$1.80.

**Universal Vise Corp.**
**22 Main St., Westfield, Mass. 01085**

A full line of fly tying tools and materials. Specialty is fly tying vises. Models include: Universal Streamside Vise, for fly tyers matching hatches on the scene, $5.95; Universal Stationary Vise, $5.95; Universal No. 2 Rotating Vise, $9.95; and the ultimate, Universal No. 1 Rotating Vise, $16.95.

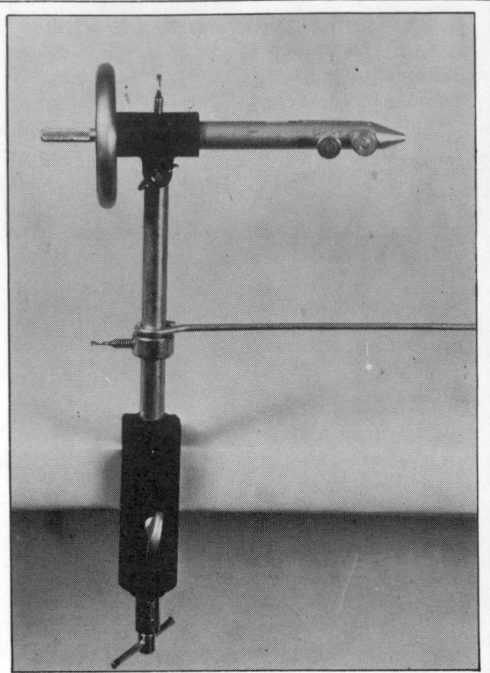

Also from Universal Vise: Fly Tying Kits, complete with materials, hooks and vise, Nos. 4, 6, 8, 10, 12, 12A, $5.95-$23.95, and the Universal Streamside Kit, $13.95. Floating fly boxes, 10¼" by 4½", $2.50; 7¼" by 3½", $1.75.

**Lisk Fly Manufacturing Co.**
**P.O. Box 5126, Greensboro, N.C. 27403**

Ready made flies such as the Tar-Heel Ant for trout and panfishes (three in a package, about $1.25), Ralph the Horse Fly, a small-bodied bug (2 in a pack, about $1.10), Bream Fly (50c), others. Also spinners and jigs.

**Tack-L-Tyers**
**939 Chicago Ave., Evanston, Ill. 60202**

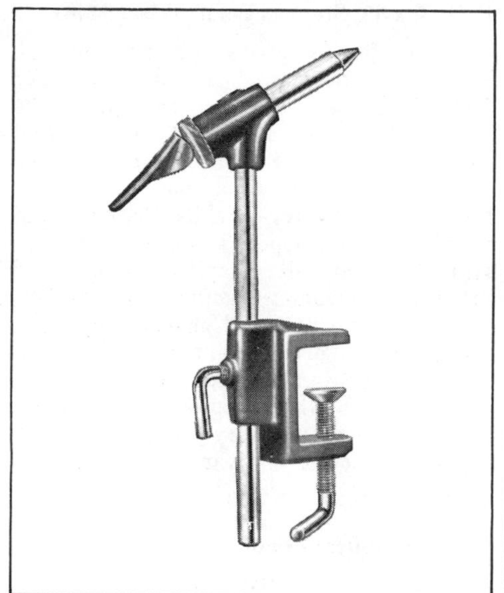

Fly tying materials, kits, vises. Also kits for popping bugs, streamers, jigs, spinning lures.

**The Orvis Company, Inc.**
**Manchester, Vt. 05254**

You really should have the Orvis catalog to learn about their inventory of flies. It shows them in color. Among the offerings, with approximate prices: (1) Dry flies in patterns such as March Brown, Quill Gordon, Lady Beaverkill, etc., 80c to 90c; (2) Orvis wet flies—Parmachene Belle, Brown Woolly Worm, Blue Dun, twenty-two others, 70c-80c each; (3) Orvis "nymphs"—Green Caddis, Leadwing Coachman, Early Black, many others, 80c-85c; (4) streamers—Royal Coachman Bucktail, White Marabou Muddler, Black Nose Dace, etc., $1 each. Also available, terrestrial and "parachute" patterns, salmon flies, hairwing flies, midges, variants, bass bugs, price range, about 80c to $1.50. Orvis salt-water include Honey Blonde, Sailfish Bug, Re and White Tarpon Fly, White Bonefish Bucktail, etc., about $1 each.

Additionally, Orvis offers many selections—Dry Fly, Fluttering Caddis, Nymph, Flymph, Perfect Wet Fly, Bass Fly-Rodding, others, from under $10 to about $40, all in handy carriers. Fly tyers can get materials, hooks and tools from Orvis too.

**Dragon Fly Company, Inc.**
**P.O. Drawer 1349, Sumter, S.C. 29150**

Hand-tied flies in patterns that include bucktails and full-body hackle types, at about 75c-85c each. Also popping bugs in several patterns and a wide range of sizes, at about $1, $1.25.

**E. H. Peckinpaugh Company**
**11982 Comal Dr., Baton Rouge, La. 70815**

This firm's offerings (each preceded by the brand name Peck's) include Tellico Nymphs, Parker Feather Minnow, Streamer Hackle Fly, Carolina Bluegill Popper, Weighted Casting Flies, and of course, Peck's Bad Boy. Approximate prices, 60c to $1.50.

**Earlybird Company**
**P.O.Box 1485, Boise, Idaho 83701**

Some fifty-two dry and wet fly patterns, including numerous classics, are produced by Earlybird, along with a large assortment of nymphs, Woolly Worms, bucktails, streamers, May Flies, specials and patterns for steelheads and bass.

## Fly Fishing Tackle Showroom

**Martin Reel Company ("The Fly Tackle People")**
**30 E. Main St., Mohawk, N.Y. 13407**

Under the brand name Sovereign this company markets a sizable group of dry and wet flies, nymphs and streamers, all expertly tied on Mustad or English hooks. Numerous classic and popular patterns are represented—Royal Wulff, Light Cahill, Brown Bivisible, Royal Coachman, Grizzly King, Mickey Finn, Blue Dun, etc. They're sold individually and in Martin selections of about twelve flies each. Approximate price range of selections is $7.95-$14.95.

**The American Import Company**
**1167 Mission St., San Francisco, Cal. 94103**

Under the L. M. Dickson tackle label this company offers dry and wet flies, streamers and poppers, individually and in sets. For example, there are the Deluxe Dry Fly Assortment (**No. 55282**) and the Deluxe Wet Fly Assortment (**No. 55285**), each with ten different patterns on No. 10 hooks. American Import has district representatives in various parts of the U.S. including a permanent display room in Deal, N.J.

**Gudebrod Fishing Tackle**
**12 S. 12th St., Philadelphia, Pa. 19107**

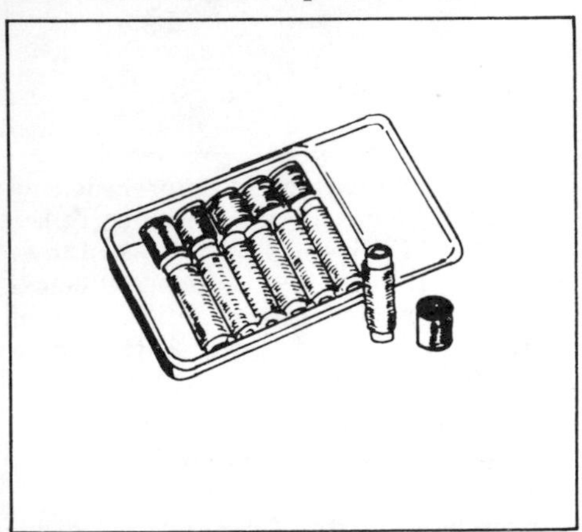

As a part of Gudebrod Bros. Silk Co., it's natural that this division would produce fly tying threads (rod winding threads too). They come in several colors, nylon, silk and rayon floss (silk for wet flies, rayon for dry flies), in stock sizes from 00 through FF, on spools of 20 to 50 yds. and more. Spools are available in lots of 4, 6, 12 and more. Then there's the Champion Fly Tying Kit—seven 10-yd. tubes of silk floss in popular colors and six miniature spools (10 yds. each) of silk fly tying threads.

**The Worth Company**
**P.O. Box 88, Stevens Point, Wisc. 54481**

Known for its spoons, spinners and jigs, Worth also markets lure-making kits for fashioning flies, poppers and jigs. The Worth Fly Tying Kit, **No FT1**, contains all the basic materials and hooks for dry and wet flies, as well as a vise, and is for beginners and veterans alike. Price is about $6.50. Worth Popper Tying Kit, **PT1**, is similarly complete with hooks and materials, including genuine cork bodies, for thirty-five assorted shapes and sizes, plus a vise. Worth recommends this kit as ideal for beginners. Approximate price, $9.75. Worth Jig Tying Kit, **JT1**, about $8.50, comes with twenty-four painted lead-head jig hooks in various styles and weights.

**Other Significant Companies**

Many other outfits around the U.S. produce flies and/or fly tying materials and tools. Since you might have difficulty locating certain of these, we'll list some. You can write to them to learn the full scope of their products; some will have other supplies than are listed for them.

Cascade Tackle Co. (**materials**)
874 W. 14th St., Medford, Ore. 97501

Dan Bailey's Fly Shop (**completed flies and materials**)
209 W. Park St., Livingston, Mont. 59047

D. H. Thompson Co. (**fly tying vises, tools**)
335 Walnut Ave., Elgin, Ill. 60120

Fireside Angler (**materials, tools**)
P.O. Box 823, Melville, N.Y. 11746

Fly Fisherman's Bookcase (**books about fly tying**)
P.O. Box 282, Croton-on-Hudson, N.Y. 10520

Gapen Tackle Co. (**finished flies**)
Highway 10, Big Lake, Minn. 55309

Glen L. Evans, Inc. (**flies, popping bugs**)
P.O. Box 850, Caldwell, Ida. 83605

Harrington & Richardson, Inc. (**imported flies**)
320 Park Ave., Worcester, Mass. 01610

Keel Fly Co. (completed flies)
1969 S. Airport Rd., Traverse City, Mich. 49684

O. Mustad & Son (U.S.A.) Inc. (**hooks for files**)
42 Washington St., Auburn, N.Y. 13021

Reed Tackle (**materials, tools**)
Box 390, Caldwell, N.J. 07006

Syl-Mark Enterprises (**tools**)
8946 Winnetka Ave., Northridge, Cal. 91324

Weber Tackle Co. (**fresh water and salt water flies**)
1039 Ellis St., Stevens Point, Wisc. 54481

Wright & McGill Co. (**hooks for flies**)
P. O. Box 16011, Denver, Colo. 80216

# Hooks 7

## HOOKS: THE STARTING POINT

Fishhooks are believed to have had their genesis sometime prior to the New Stone Age, which dawned on Western Europe approximately 20,000 years ago. That is, they were probably the first fishing devices with a recurving, hook-like form. Earlier, ancient anglers employed a straight gadget known as a gorge. Once on the scene, fishhooks became one of mankind's most important tools for survival. It's conceivable that many isolated island peoples might have vanished from the earth without them.

Prior to the advent of the Neolithic or New Stone Age primitive fishermen were rigging very crude hooks carved from bone. With the Neolithic period came experiments with metals. Man had discovered iron and copper. Somewhere around 5000 B.C., it's recorded, some of his initial copper creations included fishhooks. Copper by itself is inherently soft, and we can believe that lots of fish escaped tables when those hooks straightened out under pressure. A thousand years were to pass before some unsung metalsmith with an experimental bent discovered superior material. He learned that by mixing tin with copper he could produce a harder, stronger, more durable substance. And so, along about 4000 B.C., began the Bronze Age, which spread throughout Europe. Naturally it came to pass that fishhooks would be fashioned from this material. It's interesting to note that such refinements as a barbed point, to prevent it from working free, and a hole in the hook shaft (shank) for attachment to a line were in evidence in Greece and neighboring countries more than 3,000 years B.C.

Man's next advances in metallurgy — and fishhooks — came with the Iron Age, thought to have dawned in Egypt circa 2000 B.C. By ten centuries later this new age had come to Europe. Along the way came the development of steel, at a place and time never pinpointed accurately. Thus did steel fishhooks make their debut hundreds of years before Christ.

What might be called the earliest seeds of modern fishhook production are believed to have been planted somewhere in Europe toward the end of the 1300s, after which they apparently underwent slow but gradual development during the ensuing 200 years. But fishhook manufacture, as an industry, seems to have had its origin in England during the 17th century. At that time London was the center of manufacture of steel needles, and fishhooks were a logical offshoot.

Also around this time, in the 1600s, we begin to encounter names of men associated specifically with the design and manufacture of hooks. One of the earliest and most prominent was Charles Kirby, who in the mid-1600s was producing hooks by methods similar to those still employed. His contributions were major. He devised better procedures for tempering and hardening hook metal. He also invented the Kirby pattern, still widely used in sport fishing. And from his name came the term kirbing for a certain type of hook bend.

For more than 200 years after Charley Kirby's era fishhooks were made entirely by hand, eye to point. Special attention was given to the point and barb: the former painstakingly shaped with a file, the latter fashioned with the aid of a chisel, and both literally sculpted for maximum penetration and holding. Other steps, such as fashioning the eye and bend, also were accomplished by hand. To all intents and purposes, each hook was custom made.

Going into the 1800s, much if not most of the world's fishhook manufacture centered in the English town of Redditch, where needle makers had conceived advanced machinery adaptable to hook production. In time the industry spread to other nations, including Norway, France, the United States and Japan. In the maritime country of Norway it achieved particular eminence with the founding of the company called O. Mustad & Son in Oslo in 1832. Today that firm is a world leader in hook production, turning out every known pattern, plus designs of its own, in every conceivable size. Mustad's inventory embraces some 60,000 hook items.

### Anatomy of a Fishhook

To better understand the development of hooks, how they function, and how they now are made it's necessary to consider their basic parts. These are common to all modern hooks, whatever their design:

**Shank:** We could call this its shaft. Among most hooks it's the longest section, or at least the longest straight section. There are, however, curved shanks among some patterns, notably certain types employed in commercial fishing.

**Bend:** This is its curved section, of course, formed by recurving the shank back on itself. The bend is what makes a hook a hook.

The maximum distance across this bend, between point and shank, is called the *gap*.

The distance between the deepest part of the bend and an imaginary line indicating the gap is designated as a hook's *throat*, and the distance is also called the hook's *bite*. The bite is an important factor in how well a hook digs in.

**Point:** No explanation needed here.

**Barb:** Actually part of the point, with which it forms a kind of spearhead shape. It too is a point, but aimed in the opposite direction from the hook point. Its function is to dig in and so prevent the hook from pulling free. In some release fishing tournaments — *i.e.,* those in which all catches are turned loose unharmed — the barbs are purposely filed off hooks.

**Eye:** A hook's means of attachment to a line (or leader). There are two main kinds, ring eye and needle eye. The former is fashioned by bending the upper end of the shank to create a small, round ring. As its name indicates, a needle eye is like that in a sewing needle, drilled through the shank's uppermost end. Commonly the shank is flattened in the eye region.

There are also eyeless hooks. These are the so-called snelled type. A snell, sometimes also called a snood, is a short length of "gut," tarred line or synthetic leader-like material, permanently attached to the shank's uppermost end, with a loop for connection to the line. Flounder hooks usually are snelled. Old-type codfish hooks carry a snell of tarred linen line.

### Modern Manufacturing Methods

The material most commonly used is a form of carbon steel, although many hooks are fabricated from stainless steel or rustproof alloys for use in waters where corrosion is a big headache. Oversimplified, the manufacturing process can go like this: All hooks begin creation as long lengths of wire, of predetermined diameters, according to sizes desired. The wire then is cut into workable lengths. In one type of procedure, a workable length is enough for two hooks. This goes into a machine which grinds points at both ends and cuts it into halves to produce two shafts of the proper lengths. Other machines take over the chores of forming a ring eye or flattening the shank's end for a needle eye, cutting the barb, putting finishing touches on the point according to type desired, and forming the bend according to that particular pattern of hook (Sproat, O'Shaughnessy, or whatever). Variations in patterns — bending the eye portion forward or backward, curving shanks, slicing shanks (that is, adding tiny barbs to the shank to better hold a bait), etc. — also are effected by machines. Some heavier-duty salt-water hooks of certain designs undergo a forging process to flatten the sides of their shanks and bends for added strength.

Hooks also must be tempered and hardened for a satisfactory combination of strength and resiliency. Heat treatments satisfy this objective, after which they are cleaned of a scale formed during the tempering-hardening step and are then ready for any of the different finishes. There are several kinds of finishes, all intended to prevent, or at least slow, rust or corrosion. They include plating with tin or cadmium, nickel, blueing, laquering, the so-called japan finish, even gold.

Among name-brand salt-water hooks, such as those produced by Mustad, a serviceable finish is a heavy plating of some rust-resistant metal such as cadmium. This, combined with tempered steel, completes a hook designed for long, hard use. Perhaps the best rust- and corrosion-fighter of all is stainless steel, and hooks of this material are available. When first employed for hooks it had a drawback in being softer than other steel, so the non-rusting advantage was accompanied by a flaw. In recent years improved processing has done away with much of that "softness." Even when present to a degree, many marine anglers prefer any possible risks to being concerned constantly with rust.

**Tips:** Only a little care is needed to keep hooks reasonably free from rust and corrosion. One of the biggest invitations to the two villains comes with storing hooks in a damp place during long periods of disuse. In any event, they should be checked periodically, especially during humid weather, and immediately cleaned of any signs of rust. Always give attention to hooks on little-used artificials. Keeping badly rusted hooks is false economy. Hooks are too important — and inexpensive — to gamble with.

### Patterns by the Gross

Hooks for fresh water and marine angling are marketed in hundreds of designs and their variations. Many are performance-proven patterns that continue to march through generations of fishermen. That Kirby design we mentioned is a case in point. It has persisted for 300 years after its invention. Others, not quite as old but just as persistent, include such standards as the Sobey, Limerick, O'Shaughnessy, Chestertown, Eagle Claw (Wright & McGill), Carlisle, Siwash, Pflueger, Mustad patterns, Virginia, and Pacific salmon, and their numerous progeny in the forms of variations and modifications. And there are many, many others. As we said, Mustad turns out some 60,000 combinations of kinds and sizes, employed in either angling or commercial fishing.

All patterns base their distinction upon one or more details of hook anatomy — shank length, type of bend, point design, etc. Literally an astronomical number of combinations is possible. The subject of hook design, therefore, rates a book in itself. Going into it here in such detail serves no practical purpose and would only confuse you, especially since you'll use only a fraction of the available types in your sport fishing career. So we'll content ourselves with pertinent highlights and examples.

**Hook Characteristics**

The cardinal attributes of any hook are its penetration and its holding ability once the point has sunk home. It goes without saying that a hook that doesn't penetrate properly will catch only frustration for its owner. Good penetration becomes all the more important in cases of fish with tough, leathery mouths or hard, bony jaws. Even so, good penetration loses much of its value if a hook has poor holding power, which is a combined function of barb, point and general design. Ideally, a barb should be long to provide a sharp point for digging in, but not so slender as to bend in contact with bone. Further, it should not be able to cut or otherwise work itself free during the antics of an especially lively fish.

A hook's ease and speed of entry naturally center about its point. It should come as no surprise now to learn that several kinds of points, with variations, have been developed. Among them are (*1*) Needle type, ground on all sides and designed for quick, sure penetration; (*2*) hollow-ground, or hollow, with a hollowing or a kind of groove between the tip of the point and the tip of the barb, also designed for fast penetration; (*3*) spear type, a common design; it doesn't penetrate as fast as the first two, but is easier to fashion. There are other types, but they're not commonly in use today.

A point's position relative to the shank also affects penetrating ability. On many hooks the point is "straight" — that is, more or less parallel to the shank. Others have their point "rolled in" toward the shank. Among others it's the opposite, or curved away from the shank. Still other patterns are characterized by a bent-in point. This differs from a rolled-in design in that its entire spearhead, including the barb, is curved toward the shank. Each of these variations has its own penetrating characteristics, which may be more suitable than the others for certain kinds of fishing. The point variations also influence holding power. For example, a rolled-in point is credited with superior holding power, although it doesn't bite in as readily as the others.

Action begins when a hook's point digs in . . . or ends if it doesn't. A hook, therefore, functions with maximum effectiveness only if its point is kept needle-sharp. That may sound like an obvious fact of life, but too many fishermen neglect this crucial part of their hooks. As already noted, rust and corrosion are persistent, sneaky saboteurs. Use dulls points, especially after repeated contacts with jaws and tough mouths. Careless storage also is a culprit. Every angler's kit should include a small hone made expressly for sharpening hooks. Those with badly bent or otherwise damaged points should be discarded. As we said earlier, replacements are inexpensive. Hook points must be examined at intervals for point sharpness. The more a hook is used, of course, the greater the frequency of checking.

The shorter a barb, the faster it digs in, but the greater the chance of its being unseated by an active fish. Conversely, the longer the barb, the less easily it can be planted, but the more likely it is to hold. In any case, barb sharpness should be checked periodically and improved when necessary.

*Note:* Hone only its *point*. Putting a sharp *edge* on a barb will cause it to cut free.

A hook's entry also is affected by a factor termed *line of penetration*. This isn't something you'll have to brood about, but it's good to know. Simplified, the line of penetration is the angle at which a hook enters a fish's mouth or jaw under pull from the line. Actual planting of the hook is by force exerted on it by the line (you), and the direction that force takes is called *line of pull*. That and the line of penetration are not necessarily the same. In fact, there's likely to be a difference. Apart from any peculiarities a species may have in seizing a bait, a hook may enter a fish's mouth at one angle, then assume another angle when the line is tightened. From a standpoint of theoretical physics it would be ideal if the lines of penetration and pull were the same to better utilize the fishing line's force. But they usually are different, due to such hook details as shank length, type of bend and its gap, and nature and positioning of the eye. Appreciable differences could cut down on penetrating ability. A hook's overall balance — the proportions of its various parts to each other — also is a factor in penetration.

The aforementioned "ideal" arrangement between lines of penetration and pull isn't always optimum. With certain variables — the way in which a species seizes a bait, the toughness or softness of a fish's mouth parts, etc. — a difference between the two lines can actually be an advantage.

So it is that a number of details, alone or in combination, influence a hook's penetrating and holding talents. They also are details separating the various patterns and contribute to the superiority of some over others in various kinds of fishing.

Shanks are an anatomical detail subject to great variation among hooks, not only in length and diameter (according to strength), but also in profile and cross-sectional shape. A shank can act as a lever, both favorably and adversely: favorably in driving a point home under force from the line; adversely in tending to pry the hook loose during battle. Length is a factor in lever action.

Shank lengths depend upon hook patterns — and, of course, hook sizes within those patterns. They range from extra-long to extra-short, based upon uses and functional reasons. For example, a hook with a short shank is better concealed in a small natural bait, such as a little shrimp or even a salmon egg, a subterfuge that is helpful with species that easily become suspicious. Short-shank hooks also are used in tying small artificial flies to achieve maximum flotation without adding weight. Too, a short-shank hook has good penetration in fishes with soft mouth parts. Long to extra-long shanks, in contrast, are protection against the teeth of species that otherwise would bite through a leader or line. A long shank also is an advantage with species that tend to take a hook deep inside the mouth or in the gullet. It facilitates removal. Long- to extra-long-shank hooks also are designed for fishermen who cast their own metal squids (molds are sold for this purpose) and by fly fishermen who tie their own streamers.

Viewed from the side, shank profiles vary and include these: (*1*) Straight, from eye to bend. This is the most familiar form. (*2*) Bent-down. Here a short, uppermost portion of the shank is slanted inward somewhat, toward the point. Its intent is to minimize the difference between line of penetration and line of pull. (*3*) Central draught. Essentially this is the reverse of No. 2, with the shank's upper section bent in the opposite direction, away from the hook. Quick entry is cited as its advantage. (*4*) Hump shank. Here the shaft carries a single small hump or little S-curve in its midsection. Fresh water anglers sometimes use a little piece of cork or other flotation material to help keep the hook at a desired level. The hump or curve prevents the cork from shifting.

There's also what we call a sliced shank, commonly seen in both fresh water and marine angling. During manufacture a machine "slices" or nicks the shank just above the bend to create tiny spikes. Their purpose is to keep a soft bait, such as a worm or strip of fish, moored and extended in realistic fashion, instead of "bunching up" on the bend.

Hook bends also vary in profile, seen when viewed from the side. Most common is a U-shape. Some, with rolled-in or bent-in points, look like the letter "C." Still others are more like a partially flattened "J." And there are variations. Their gaps vary accordingly, and many also exhibit marked differences in the depths of their throats.

Remember that term "kirbing" we mentioned previously? It enters the picture in connection with the bend and point. You'll have to think in three dimensions to visualize kirbing. If you hold an unkirbed hook with its bend uppermost and point aimed at you, you'll see that those sections are in direct line with the shank. A kirbed hook held the same way will have its point and adjacent section of the bend slanted somewhat to your left. In a variation, called reverse kirbing, the bending is in the opposite direction. The advantage cited for kirbing is that it heightens chances of its point digging in — snagging, if you will — somewhere if the hook slides out of a fish's mouth. It's kind of desperation grabbing, so to speak. Only trouble is, you never really know when kirbing did its job. Further, a kirbed hook is a bit harder to set than an unkirbed one.

Another hook-profile detail is encountered among many fresh water types, notably in shallow-water pond and lake fishing. This is a weed guard device, and hooks carrying it are designated as "weedless." Weed guard designs vary somewhat from manufacturer to manufacturer, but all function on basically the same principle. A typical weed guard consists simply of a short length of flexible wire that is attached in the vicinity of the hook's eye, then arches outward slightly to barely meet the point or overlap it slightly. There's no attachment at the point, of course. Its function is to prevent aquatic vegetation from tangling with the hook, perhaps even cluttering it so that it becomes obscured, and it does by literally shoving weeds and the like aside as the hook moves through the water. At the same time, a guard's design should be such that it doesn't interfere seriously with setting the hook. In really weedy areas no guard can be a hundred percent effective, but it will cut down appreciably on annoyances.

There isn't much to be said about hooks' cross-sectional anatomy. Hooks start as wire, and wire is usually round. *Ergo*, hooks are round in cross-section. Notable exceptions are a flattening of the upper shank on needle-eye patterns and the flattening of the sides of the shanks and bends of heavier-duty marine hooks for added strength.

More than cross-sectional shape, hook-wire diameter is of importance to fishermen, for it is this detail that gives hooks their strength and flexibility, characteristics that assume varying degrees of value according to the kinds of angling done.

Hook diameters are broadly graded from fine to stout, to which could be added extra-fine and extra-stout to cover extremes. Progressive grades are indicated by the letter "X," preceded by a figure.

Varying degrees of diameter have practical applications. Examples: *Fine-wire hooks* are particularly suitable to small, live bait, such as minnows. The finer wire is less apt to injure the bait and also, because of its lightness, permits the bait more freedom, which is the name of the game in live-bait angling. Finer-wire hooks also are more practical for soft or fragile bait, which would be torn by heavier hooks. Further, because of their lightness, they lend themselves to dry flies, whose flotation is important. Fine hooks penetrate more readily than those of heavier gauge, but they also can be bent or sprung out of shape more easily. Fine hooks also are more readily damaged by fishes' teeth. *Heavier-wire* and *stout hooks* are the opposite, so to speak, of all the foregoing. Their greater strength and decreased flexibility are their biggest assets. Therefore, they have their greatest application in marine angling, although they also have application among the larger fresh water artificials, such as streamers and bucktails.

### About Hook Sizes

Hooks are graded for size by a simple system. The scale has two parts, one for the larger hooks, one for the smaller. For that half covering the larger hooks, sizes are indicated by a figure, a slash and a zero, thus: 1/0,, 2/0, 3/0, etc., up through 20/0, which is about the largest sport fishing hook used. On this side of the scale, the larger the figure preceding the zero, the *larger* the hook. In the lower half the scale goes the other way. Sizes of these smaller hooks are indicated by "No." and a figure, thus: No. 1, No. 2, No. 3, and so on, through No. 20, which is a little hook indeed. On this side of the scale, the larger the number, the *smaller* the hook.

This arrangement is only for comparative purposes. It tells us nothing about such specifications as shank length, type of bend, gauge of wire, etc. But then, a grading system encompassing all those details would be difficult to devise, because of myriad variations, and might be so complex that no fishermen would bother with it. Overall length, top of shank to bottom of bend, might seem like a logical standard with which to measure and indicate sizes; but again other specifications upset the equation. For instance, two hooks might have the same overall length, yet the gap — bend — of one will be significantly larger because of its pattern. As it works out in use, the size-grading system is largely based on the sizes of the bends. Broadly speaking, the larger the hook, the larger its bend, with other specifications more or less in proportion.

For reasons still unfathomed, there is no standardization among hook sizes. Thus a 1/0, we'll say, in one pattern will be a bit smaller or larger than a 1/0 in another style. Fortunately, such differences are for the most part minor and not of great consequence. In fact, there's usually latitude in hook sizes for a given species. Only when fishes have very small mouths do sizes become a matter of any precision; and even there the only thing to worry about is going too large.

The persistent size-grading system has served generations of anglers and is good enough in its way. When writers are willing to stick their necks out, you'll encounter recommendations of specific sizes for various species. These are an adequate guide. As fishermen gain experience, however, they become visually familiar with sizes among patterns they favor. Gauging them to the weights, mouths and combat characteristics of species sought becomes almost automatic, with assurance that there's some latitude in either direction. As a group, hooks are divided into three kinds: Single; double; and treble.

All told, the single is the most common and familiar, with universal applications in salt and fresh water. It's standard for natural bait, whatever the angling method. Many lures — artificial flies, metal squids, bucktails, feather jigs, etc. — incorporate a single hook. According to lure model, these may be fixed or swinging.

Less frequently seen is the double. A double hook is fashioned from one piece of wire to form two shanks, two bends and two points. The result looks like two hooks back to back, bends curving in opposite directions. Its two shanks, a continuous piece of wire, are parallel to each other. Attachment is via a common loop or ring-type eye at their top. The principal application of double hooks has been on certain artificials, such as plugs.

As its name implies, a treble hook — called a gang hook sometimes also — is three hooks in one and looks like a miniature three-pronged anchor. The three shanks are attached to each other, with a common eye at their top, and the bends are equally spaced (120° of arc between them). Trebles are most frequently seen on artificials, notably plugs and on some metal jigs. They are always swinging. According to size and model, a plug will carry one or two trebles; and there are some long jobs with three. Some metal jigs carry a swinging treble on their trailing end. Trebles seldom are rigged by themselves in bait fishing. But they do see service in a freshwater method known as snagging, usually employed for species that do not readily take a hook in the usual manner. In snagging, two, three or more unbaited gang hooks are secured to a line and continuously jigged — moved up and down — in an effort to snag or foul-hook any passing fish.

### In the Final Analysis . . .

. . . there can be no one all-purpose hook, which is why so many styles continue to thrive. But this is good because the variety provides opportunities to select hooks better suited to specific angling assignments. Every pattern has something going for it. It remains for fishermen to try different styles, then narrow them down to those best suited to their needs.

## Hooks

Hooks are sold in packages, with sizes indicated thereon. Hooks also are available singly, to be rigged according to their owners' ideas, or to replace defective armament on lures, or for incorporation in artificials of the anglers' own making. Store-bought lures come already equipped, of course. As theories and ideas dictate, fishermen often change the hook arrangements on their artificials — adding or removing a treble, or modifying hook position, substituting a swinging hook for a fixed one, etc. There's lots of room for interesting experimentation.

Same thing goes for sizes. There are patterns that are versatile in that they can be rigged for any number of different species, the only variations being in sizes.

**O. Mustad & Son (U.S.A.) Inc.**

These are fishhooks from the Stone Age, at least 5,000 years old. They were found in Skipshelleren Cave, Norway, site of fishermen's and hunters' settlements lasting into the Viking Age, 800-1300 A.D. Actual lengths among these and others found, approximately 0.72 to 1.72 inches.

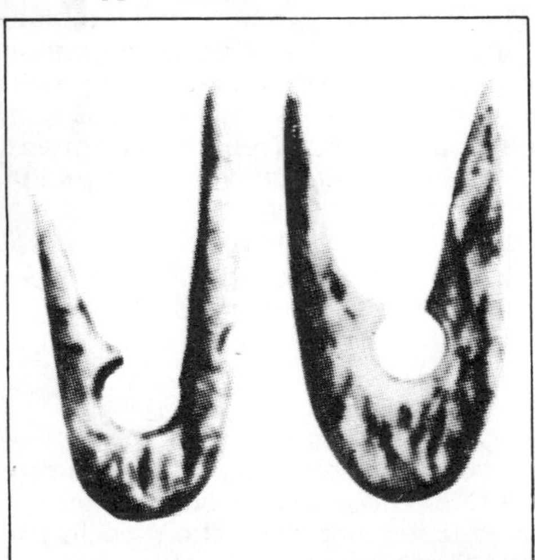

**O. Mustad & Son (U.S.A.) Inc.**

Samples of bone fishhooks fashioned by Lapps at Kjelmoy, on Varanger Fjord, northern Norway, some 1,500 years back. Lacking contact with Iron Age people living farther south in Norway, they made hooks and tools from bones and antlers instead of iron and bronze. Actual length, from just under 3 inches to about 4 inches.

**O. Mustad & Son (U.S.A.) Inc.**

Among the hundreds of types of hooks produced by Mustad today:

1. Superior Mustad Treble, Sproat bend, short shank, ring-type eye

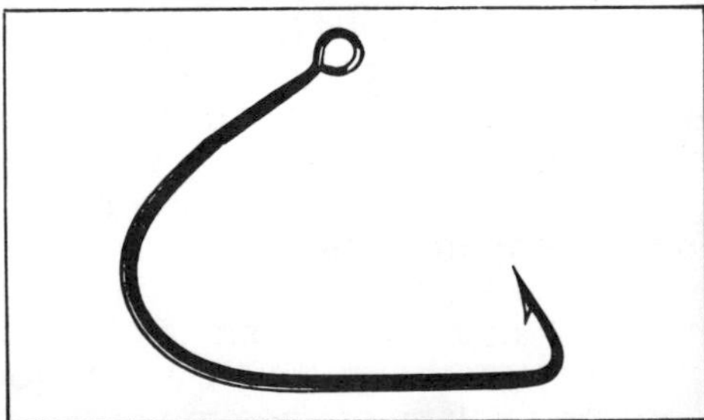

2. Mustad Pike Hook with forged, tapered eye

**Wright & McGill Co.**

Under the brand banner Eagle Claw, Wright & McGill produces many hook patterns and styles for marine and fresh water fishing. Shown are but a few.

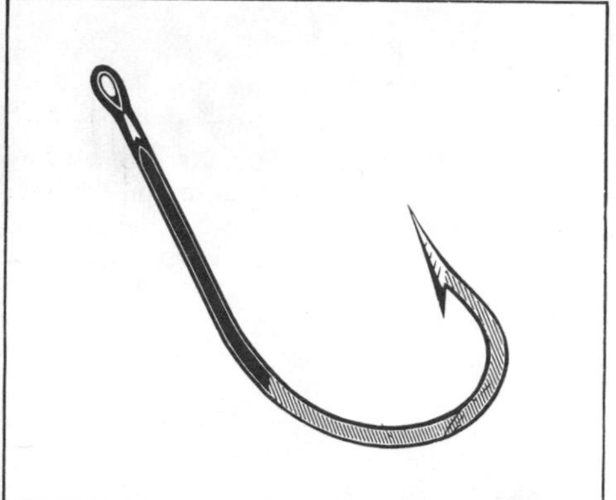

3. Knife Edge Point Mustad-Sea Demon Hook, with flattened shank (for strength) and forged needle eye, in sizes up to 16/0 for marine big game

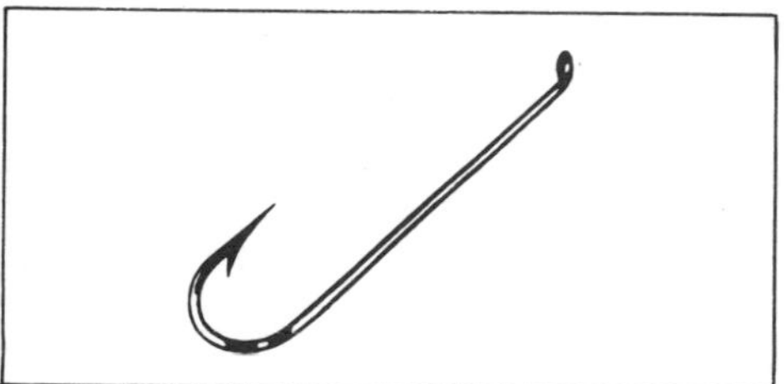

4. Fly Hook—note turned down eye, long shank for tying fly

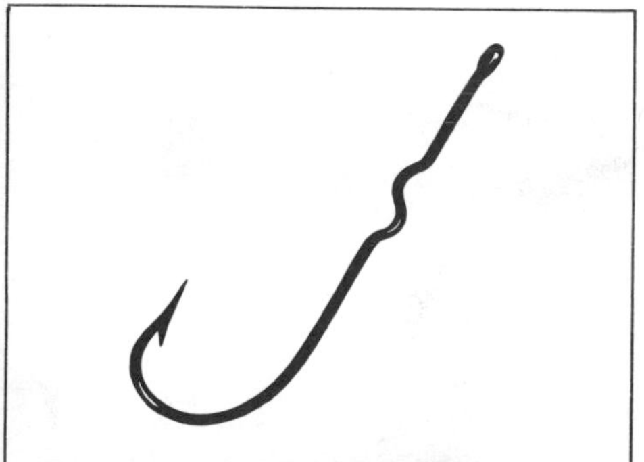

5. Mustad Kink Shank Hook (also known as hump shank), with a kink to hold a piece of cork in place or help keep a bait extended

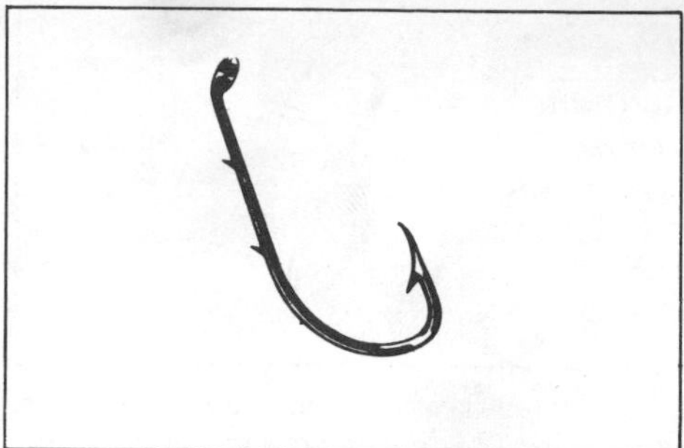

1. Sliced Shank Eagle Claw Hook, with slices or tiny spikes on its shank to keep a bait in place

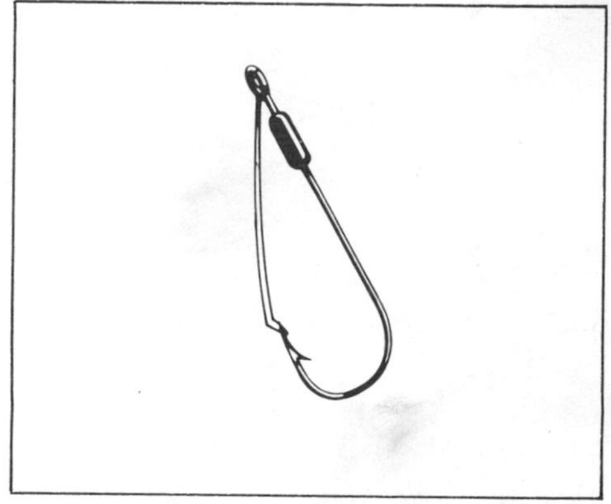

2. Eagle Claw Weedless Hook, Aberdeen pattern—note wire guard to prevent point from fouling in underwater vegetation

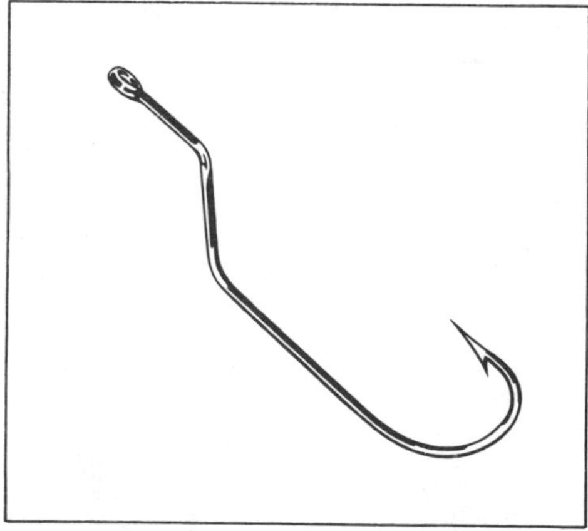

3. Eagle Claw Keel Hook, long shank for flies, designed to ride with its point upright within a fly's wings

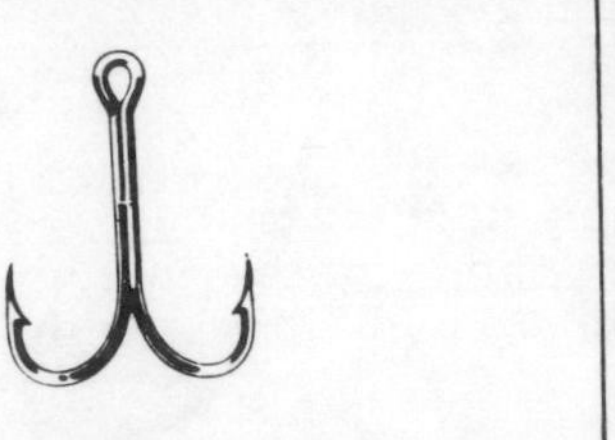

4. Eagle Claw Double Hook, ring eye type, with 120-degree spread between the two hooks

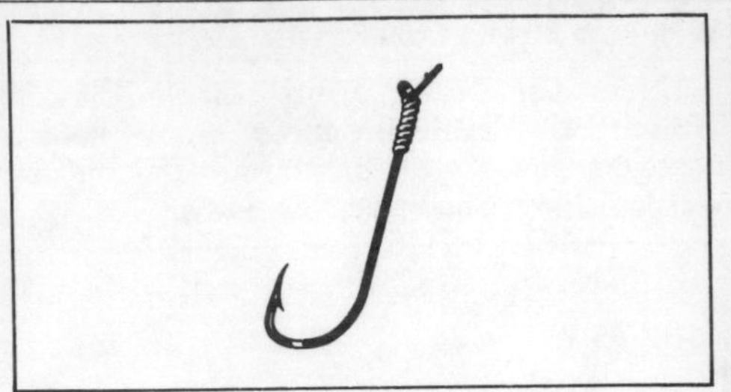

5. Nylawire Snelled Hook, for fishes with sharp teeth, comes with a nylon-coated wire snell attached

# Terminal Tackle and Lures 8

Components of terminal tackle differ according to method, kinds of fishes sought and conditions. In addition to hooks and lures, the list takes in leaders, sinkers, deep-trolling devices such as drails and planers, extra attractors like flashing spinner blades, and assorted "hardware," such as swivels, snap-swivels and the so-called fish-finder employed in surf-casting.

## First, The Hardware Store

Commonly called "hardware" by fishermen, swivels and other connectors are links holding terminal tackle together as a unit. They serve to join leader to line, lure and leader, and snelled hooks to line, as well as in multiple-hook rigs. (Incidentally, some lures have a built-in swivel, eliminating a need for any other at that connection.) All these links come in assorted forms, sizes and strengths:

**Barrel swivel:** This is one of the most common, especially in marine fishing, and has widespread application in just about all techniques short of flycasting. A barrel swivel consists of two small eyes or loops connected by a metal pin in such a way that they can turn freely and independently. The pin is covered by a tiny housing whose shape reminded someone of a barrel, hence the name. Occasionally this type also is referred to as a "two-way" or "two-loop" swivel. In addition to its function as a connector, a barrel swivel minimizes twisting of leader and line by lures that spin or rotate in action. In this respect they're particularly useful in trolling, but perform the same service in other methods.

**Three-way swivel**, occasionally called a "three-loop" swivel: A first cousin to the barrel type, this is a Y-shaped connector consisting of three ring-like, swiveling eyes around a central collar. They too can turn independently. The most common application of a three-way swivel is in salt-water fishing, notably in bottom rigs. The line is tied to one eye; a sinker is attached to another; and the third receives a leader or snelled hook. Its prime advantage is that it helps to minimize tangling of those three components. A variation that serves the same purpose is the so-called crossline swivel. This also has three loops, but the swivel has a T-shape and the swiveling eyes are connected by a barrel-like housing instead of a collar. A crossline swivel's major use is in salt water bottom fishing; and it's handy for tying in a higher, second hook somewhere above the first.

**Snap-swivels**: There are variations, but basically a snap-swivel consists of two parts: A swivel section; and a connector which opens and closes on exactly the same principle as a safety pin. In one variation the former is a barrel swivel; in another it's a small housing containing a ball bearing. In both the connector section or "snap" is kept closed by a metal sleeve. You can buy snap-swivels as units; or, if variations in sizes of their components is desired, purchase barrel swivels and snap sections separately and fashion your own — in seconds. For big-game fishing there's a heavy-duty type whose snap section is of stiff wire, bent on one end for closing on itself. Here the snap is permanently attached to the swivel.

Except in flycasting, snap-swivels are very useful terminal tackle items. Every angler's kit should contain a few in different sizes. Like other swivels, they lessen twisting of leaders and lines by bait and artificials that tend to spin. More importantly, they facilitate changing of rigs with minimum loss of fishing time. You might want to switch to another lure, for example; or perhaps you're trolling and your bait has been badly mutilated by a hit and needs replacement. If you have other rigs made up beforehand — and you should have — you can make the change 1-2-3. With ordinary swivels you would have to re-rig. A good arrangement is to tie a snap-swivel to the end of your line, where it can receive a loop in the leader's free end. It also can be attached to the leader's end, but this is an inferior setup because it (*a*) can impair the action of a bait or artificial, (*b*) may not be as effective in minimizing leader and line twist as it would be between line and leader, and (*c*) could, conceivably, make a fish suspicious, being so close to the attractor.

**Simple connectors:** Fashioned from wire, these have a loop or eye on both ends and are kept closed by a sliding sleeve in the middle. They serve the same purposes as barrel swivels, but, since they do not actually swivel, are not as effective in lessening line and leader twist. These are more suited to connecting terminal tackle components when twisting isn't a problem.

Here's a useful gimmick involving a simple connector. It's the improvisation of the so-called fish-finder rig in bottom fishing the surf. Just a couple of steps are required: (*1*) Tie a barrel swivel to the end of your line; (*2*) to the swivel's remaining loop attach your leader with its hook; (*3*) select a simple connector with one eye small enough so that it can't pass beyond the swivel; to the connector's other eye attach a pyramidal surf sinker. Step No. 3 is the actual "fish-finder" portion of the rig, and it should be free to slide up and down the line as far as the barrel swivel. This is how it works: The impelling force of a cast shoots that pyramidal sinker like a bullet, and it fetches up against the barrel swivel to add momentum. There it stays as the rig finds bottom. The sinker holds bottom, but the line is free to pass through its connector; and this, in turn, gives freedom to leader and baited hook. Further, any fish hooked also has freedom and can fight to the fullest, unhampered by the weight of the sinker. While we're at it we also should mention a refinement. Crabs can be a bait-stealing nuisance when fishing close to the bottom. A couple of small pieces of cork on the fish-finner rig's leader will buoy the bait up out of their reach.

Barrel swivels and other connectors are made variously from brass, plain or plated, stainless steel, and steel, with or without nickel plating. Also available are dull black and brown finishes to decrease visibility when a connector is near a lure or bait. And most of them are surprisingly strong for their size. One of the smallest barrel swivels, its wire diameter only 0.021 of an inch, is rated at 20-pound test. One of the largest, with a wire diameter of 0.08 of an inch, is graded at 250-pound test. There are snap-swivels, same diameter of wire, rated at 350 pounds.

Its probably because of this great strength in smallness and the latitude it affords, coupled with the items' lightness, that you seldom will hear or see specific sizes of swivels and similar connectors mentioned in recommendations of terminal tackle. In fact, we're not sure that all fishermen are even aware that this hardware has its own size-grading. Nevertheless, it does. And it's very similar to that used for hooks. The scale has two parts, an upper for the larger sizes, a lower for the smaller ones, and the same designations are employed as for hooks. In the scale's upper half, sizes are indicated by 1/0, 2/0, 3/0, etc. The larger the number preceding the slash, the larger the item. In the range's lower half, sizes begin with 1 and continue as 2, 3, 4, 5, etc. The larger the number, the *smaller* the item. Strength per size varies among manufacturers. Samples: A No. 1 snap-swivel, 100- to 150-pound test; a 4/0, 195- to 350-pound test.

Theoretically, swivels and other connectors should be matched approximately for strength to sizes of fishes sought. Practically, there's a lot of latitude. That 20-pound-test barrel sinker we mentioned a minute ago is a little No. 12. That's strong enough for many kinds of battlers. Add a couple of sizes up to 1 and 1/0 and you have strengths to about 100- and 120-pound test, respectively. That would provide coverage for most of the opponents an average angler encounters in a lifetime. If you're going in for big game, choose connectors rated up to 350-pound test and more. Actually, such strengths as those aren't necessary, since the heaviest line you'll ever use probably will be 130-pound stuff. All other things being within reason, your line will break before a properly made swivel or snap-swivel will let go. In years of fishing this writer has never seen one come apart under normal use.

## Leaders

We've already discussed these — their purposes, materials, etc. — in the section headed "Personal Aspects of Tackle." We'll just add a few general notes here.

1. If you're fishing with braided line it may be desirable to incorporate a leader of monofilament because of its somewhat lesser visibility per diameter, in which case it can be in approximately the same strength as the line. If you're fishing with braided line in areas where there are chances of it being frayed by coral, barnacle-encrusted rocks or other underwater obstructions, you can gain a measure of protection by rigging a leader of the more abrasion-resistant monofilament. Here it's customary to add a little more protection by using mono in a somewhat heavier strength than the line.

On the other hand, if you're fishing with monofilament line and single rig you won't have to interpose a length of mono between line and terminal tackle, unless you want that greater abrasion-resistance we just mentioned. If your terminal tackle involves more than one hook and requires leaders, you can fashion those from some of your mono line.

2. Monofilament is good all-round leader material for both marine and fresh water angling. It's not a bad idea to carry a couple of small, separate coils of it, in the strengths you commonly use, for this purpose.

Leaders of one material or another are available already made up; some may include swivels or other connectors. Similarly, there are packaged rigs that come with leaders incorporated. But most seasoned fishermen have their own ideas about leader lengths, and keep a coil or two of material in the tackle box for tailoring to desired lengths.

3. Different situations call for leaders of varying lengths. In big-game angling they go up to 15, 20, 25, even 30 feet. For most fresh and salt water purposes shorter lengths up to about 6 feet, possibly 8 to 10 at the outside for the larger gamesters, do nicely. Some, notably among those rigged with artificials, are as short as 6 or 8 inches to 12 and 18. Regular leaders are rigged mainly to get a lure away from the potentially distracting effect — scary or suspicion-provoking — of the line, or to provide decreased visibility between line and attractor, or to give more freedom and generally better action of the offering, which can be very important with live bait. Sometimes leaders have specialized uses. Surf fishermen using heavy rigs or large bait, such as eels, sometimes rig a monofilament leader of heavier caliber than the line as a kind of shock absorber in casting. Some big-game anglers rig heavier than usual leaders as a safety margin in handling rambunctious fish alongside the boat. Wire leaders are employed solely for protection against sharp teeth (on bluefish and others), rough hide (sharks), tough scales (tarpon), sharp gill covers (snook) or abrasive bills (marlin).

For the most part, the shorter the leader you can get away with while satisfying requirements, the better. Except in trolling, this applies especially to artificials. Overly long leaders — wire in particular — can impair lures' action. In rigging a wire leader for a toothy rascal, for instance, either with an artificial or a natural bait, you really need only enough wire to keep the line beyond their fangs when they strike.

Many species are anything but shy when it comes to grabbing a bait or lure. For them, if there's nothing about them or their surroundings that could fray a line, no leaders are required.

Except in such situations as mentioned above, leader strengths are matched approximately to those of their lines. There's leeway in either direction. Sizes of opponents permitting, it might even be desirable on occasion to go to a leader lighter than the line for decreased visibility or better working of a lure. In any case, just remember that the maximum strength of a line-leader combination is that of its weaker component. In other words, you could rig a 200-pound-test monofilament leader with 80-pound line, and the ensemble's maximum strength still would be 80 pounds.

**Memo:** Along with other gear involved, leaders for fly fishing are discussed in the section devoted to that sport's equipment.

### Sinkers

People in remote ages were not exactly bright, measured by our standards, but their fishermen weren't dummies. There's evidence indicating that even those of prehistoric times were aware that a weight was required if they were to get their rigs down to fishes hanging around at lower levels. And so the first sinkers were stones — what else? Representing a later but still ancient era are the stone weights unearthed among artifacts of South

America's Inca civilization. It's said that many of these bear a surprising resemblance to some used today.

Modern sinkers are made in a host of shapes and sizes, from a fractional-ounce split-shot, that looks as though it would be more at home in a shotgun shell than in fishing, to a hefty bank type weighing upwards of half a pound. All are designed for various situations, yet all have two things in common: They're cast in lead because of its weight; and their sole function is to take a rig, leader or line down to a desired depth, and, in the case of bottom fishing, moor it there. These are, among the types rigged in marine and fresh water fishing:

1. Bank sinker: This kind is universally used in salt water bottom fishing at anchor. In profile it bears a passing resemblance to an elongated tear-drop, widest near the bottom, narrowest at the top, where's there's a built-in eye for attachment. Bank-type sinkers have been standard in bottom fishing for generations, and apparently very little change in their shape has been necessary, because among the Inca sinkers were some that are very similar. In the proper weights, bank sinkers effectively moor rigs against the vagaries of passing currents. They come in sizes from 1 ounce to 8 and more, and the weight is shown as a raised figure on the sinker.

2. Pyramid type: Its name tells you its shape. Actually it's an upside down pyramid, since its apex is lowermost and attachment is made via a wire ring in its base. Available in graduated weights, pyramid sinkers are part of every surfcaster's standard gear because (with their pointy corners) they're designed for good holding in sand when fishing the bottom. This is the kind of sinker most often used with a fish-finder rig, described earlier. Although seldom seen much anymore, there are also double and triple pyramids, with more corners for greater bottom-holding ability.

3. The dipsey: It could be described either as a fat teardrop or a lopsided egg, narrowest at the top, wider below, with a rounded bottom. Attachment is by a swiveling eye at the top. Its smooth, rounded shape and swiveling eye make a dipsey better suited than a bank sinker to situations in which a rig should be in motion along the bottom for added attraction, as when drifting or in casting-retrieving along a bay, lake or ocean floor. A dipsey is less likely than the bank type to catch on some obstruction along the way.

4. Split-shot and clinch-on sinkers: Among these are the very smallest sinkers, and they're very handy when only fractional-ounce weights are required. Such situations occur in near-surface and upper-level angling, except in trolling. Sometimes a current or a boat's drift is such that the bait is thrust higher than desired. A regular sinker would be too much weight, but a split shot or two, or a clinch-on sinker, provides just enough. As its name implies, a split shot looks like a fugitive from a shotgun shell, except that there's a deep, narrow slot on one side. The line goes into this, after which the shot is pinched in position by fisherman's pliers (you'll meet these when we get to accessories). A clinch-on (sometimes also called pinch-on) sinker is a little more elaborate. Shaped like a skinny spindle, it has a tab on either end and a lengthwise slit. The line goes into the slit, whereupon the two tabs are bent over it to keep the weight in position.

5. Egg and ball sinkers: Here again their names describe their shapes. They differ from other sinkers in having a little hole completely through them in the center. Instead of being tied to a line, like a bank type of

pyramid, the line is fed through them, so that it can pass back and forth freely. This is part of the idea of using an egg or ball sinker. Once it finds bottom, the sinker's roundness allows it to roll readily hither and yon, giving both freedom and motion to a bait. Further freedom is afforded by passage of the line through the hole. This can be doubly important when bottom fishing with live bait. For maximum efficiency, live bait always must be given as much liberty as possible. Further, when a bait is seized, free passage of the line through the sinker gives a fish more freedom to fight, unencumbered by a sinker's weight. In this respect an egg or ball sinker functions like a fish-finder rig, and in similar fashion adds momentum to a cast. Fact is, an egg or ball sinker could be substituted for a fish-finder.

6. Trolling sinkers: They comprise a little family unto themselves, and all are designed to take rigs deep when necessary.

(a) Most common are the so-called drails. They vary a bit in form but are substantially alike. A typical drail in profile suggests an aeroplane with its wings removed and only the vertical portion of the tail remaining. Its "fuselage," of solid lead, is roughly cigar-shaped. A drail is interposed between line and leader, the former attaching to an eye in the nose, the leader being secured to a similar wire ring atop the vertical tail. The tail is an oversized fin that helps stabilize the lure and prevent its spinning. It's rigged with or without swivels, according to preference. Drails come in a weight range from less than a pound to 2, 3 or more pounds. They can be rigged with regular line or, if even greater depth is desired, with wire line. They do their job, but with two drawbacks: Extra strain on tackle; and a fish has to battle their weight too, detracting from the fight.

(b) Keeled sinker: Essentially the same as a drail, its body is a streamlined cigar or torpedo shape. The major difference is its triangular keel underneath. Simple models have a wire eye at each end for attachment. Others are outfitted with a bead chain and eye in front, a bead chain and swivel or snap-swivel in the rear. Like a drail, it's interposed between line and leader. These sinkers also come in assorted weights, with the same drawbacks as for drails.

(c) Trolling planer: It suggests a small airplane with short, stubby wings, and has a torpedo-shaped body. It performs the same function as a drail or keeled trolling sinker, taking a rig deep, but has an advantage in being adjustable. Depths can be regulated by adjusting its wings. Some models have a release mechanism whereby the planer holds the line until a strike, then lets it go so the fish can fight unhampered by the device's weight. In this arrangement the planer is like an underwater "outrigger" and is towed on its own line. In other words, it isn't an integral part of the terminal tackle.

7. Miscellaneous types and gimmicks:

(a) Diamond sinker: This has an elongated, skinny diamond shape, with an eye at each end. Used in bottom fishing, it's designed for incorporation in a rig — in the line itself or between line and leader — at a point higher than usual for a bank sinker or a dipsey. Thus it provides weight but is away from the bait.

(b) Break-away sinkers: There are various forms. One resembles a bank type and is made from lead in weights to 8 ounces and heavier. Another, appropriately called a cannonball, is cast iron and weighs up to 3 pounds and more. These break-aways are expendable, rigged so they can be jettisoned when a fish strikes. A fishing guide once told this writer that the the floor or Boca Grande Pass on Florida's west coast "is paved with sinkers" dropped by tarpon hunters.

(c) Hidden sinkers and bait-weighting: Sometimes it's advantageous to weight the bait itself, instead of, or to supplement, a sinker rigged in customary fashion. With a whole-fish bait, a sinker of suitable weight, any type, is sewn inside the body cavity. Or an egg or ball sinker can be fed onto the leader and slid down inside the fish, next to the hook and out of sight, or simply allowed to ride against the bait's snout. Clinch-on sinkers are employed in similar fashion with small bait.

(Hidden sinkers have been used for quite another purpose. More than one unscrupulous participant has attempted to cop a prize in a fishing contest by secreting a sinker inside his entry. Fact is, it has been tried so many times that most contest judges are wise to it. Needless to add, a dim view is taken of the practice.)

(d) Improvisations: Lacking something better for the situation, anglers have been known to weight bait and artificials by bending a short, thin strip of lead, or even a couple of coils of heavy wire or solder, around a leader. And if the truth were known, nuts, bolts and odd pieces of metal have served as sinkers in bottom fishing emergencies, as when a fisherman's regular sinkers weren't heavy enough. But a properly outfitted rod-'n'-reeler usually doesn't have to improvise.

*Tip:* Don't rig excessively heavy sinkers — any kind, in any angling method. Use only enough weight to satisfy the situation's requirements. Every extra ounce of dead weight tires a fish just that much quicker and so detracts from the action. For larger or more muscular battlers a little extra sinker weight may not be critical, but among smaller and less active species it becomes increasingly more important.

## Floats

A float is a kind of miniature buoy, and it's employed in still-fishing — *i.e.*, from an anchored boat or from shore. Its use is determined primarily by the species sought and its feeding habits. A float performs two major services. In one it suspends a baited hook at a desired depth, usually fairly shallow for surface- and near-surface feeding targets. Since it's adjustable on a line or leader, so can the depths of the dangling hook be regulated. In its second major service a float is particularly useful with small, live bait. In addition to suspending it at a desired level, it allows a live bait more freedom by absorbing the weight of the line. In both services a float also acts as a signal, its bobbing action and being pulled under announce a fish nibbling at the offering. For this reason floats sometimes are called bobbers.

Floats in many different shapes have been devised over the years. Here are some samples: (*1*) Egg shape, widest toward the top, with a slender wooden post running lengthwise through its center for attachment to the line, and usually painted red and white. For many years this was one of the most common types, especially in salt water. (*2*) Round: Identical to No. 1 except for shape. (*3*) Casting floats: These are variously torpedo- or spindle-shaped, streamlined to minimize wind resistance. A center post or similar arrangement provides for attachment. (*4*) Plastic bubble: Round and transparent, this type can be filled with water to varying degrees to alter its buoyancy, instead of adjusting it on a line or leader. (*5*) Pencil floats: These are long, skinny spindles designed for light fishing. Along the same lines, and even skinnier, are the so-called porcupine quills and quill floats.

In past years, float bodies were made from cork or wood, often cedar. Today, plastics have taken over. The familiar red and white, egg-shaped cork float has been largely replaced by round models in red, white or yellow. But their uses remain the same. *Tip:* In a pinch, a float for light fishing can be fashioned from an ordinary cork. It can be secured by wrapping the line or leader around it a few turns, but then it won't be adjustable. A better arrangement for attachment is to thrust a lollypop stick or short, small piece of wood through it.

Special floats:

In shark fishing blocks of cork are put on the leader to suspend a baited hook at a desired level. Attachment is made simply by cutting a slit part way through the cork and inserting the leader. This arrangement allows the cork to be flipped off if a shark shows more interest in it than in the bait. Blocks of styrofoam also can be used, but are less satisfactory because their whiteness can prove to be a distraction.

Toy balloons also are used in the same fashion as floats, attached by thread that snaps when a shark or other opponent takes the bait. Balloon floats are not recommended for shark fishing, for the same reason as styrofoam, in which case they can't be jettisoned.

There are similar drawbacks to using plastic jugs, such as those that household bleach comes in. However, if you can find one with a cork instead of a screw cap, it at least can be rigged so that it comes free when a fish hits. Simply jam the line or leader inside the jug's mouth with a moderately tight cork.

Plastic and glass jugs have an interesting application in the South in angling for big catfish. A baited rig is suspended from a stoppered jug and turned loose on the river, the angler following it in a boat. When that jug is pulled under he has a "cat" on, whereupon he can handline the fish or, in a refined arrangement, detach the jug and hastily snap on a line from his rod and reel. Followers call this method of fishing "jugging."

Still another adaptation of plastic bottles is practiced by members of New Orleans Big Game Fishing Club when fishing the Gulf of Mexico. Sharks are a problem there, and — the writer learned this from his own experience — chances are fairly high that a blue marlin, tuna or other hooked gamester will be demolished before it can be brought to the boat. The NOBGFC lads tried assorted stunts, including firearms. Nothing worked. Packets of shark repellant tossed overboard were eaten like peanuts. Finally someone conceived this idea: In a Y-shaped rig two baited hooks are tied to a plastic bottle and tossed overboard when sharks appear on the scene. Hopefully, one will seize each hook, which results in a tug-o'-

war that keeps at least two marauders out of mischief. It doesn't always work, but it seems to be better than firearms and shark repellant.

### Lures

Lures are artificial or human-made bait. There are many kinds — and we're talking about types, not models. But whatever their types of models, they all have one thing in common: They're designed to attract fishes through general appearance or shape, movement in the water, color — especially when combined with shape, size, special antics in addition to motion — fluttering etc. — or a combination of any or all of those. Many add a sonic feature for added attraction, gurgling, rattling, popping or loud swishing sounds as they move through the water. Often this sonic feature is helpful in murky water or at night, when a lure might otherwise escape notice. Sounds also arouse the curiosity of fishes sometimes. Another feature, with an obvious advantage, is a natural bait scent incorporated in lures. Plastics technology has aided this immeasurably.

Lures are designed mostly to simulate items of natural food. Thus dry flies are tied to imitate various insects that fall into the water and are devoured by trout and bass. There are plastic eels, very lifelike looking, that wiggle through the water to attract striped bass, billfishes, sharks and other gamesters. Then there are small fake fish made to simulate various kinds of minnows on which many fresh water species dine. And plastic worms, used effectively in both fresh water and salt water. And so on. Name an item of natural food, salt water or fresh, and chances are someone has come out with a phony to imitate it. The range is from tiny insects to plastic squid. Sometimes it requires stretching the imagination to see any similarity between an artificial and a counterpart in nature. There have even been outlandish models that bore no resemblance whatsoever to anything in life. Yet such creations can work because of their action or other feature that either looks appealing to some dunce of a fish or at least arouses his inquisitiveness, which may or may not prove fatal. For instance, this writer has caught young bluefin tuna on a shiny beer can opener to which a hook had been soldered. It seems safe to say that few fishes see beer can openers in the sea (beer cans, yes, but not openers), and even fewer eat them. Years ago there was novelty luro made in thr form of a mermaid, with a treble hook dangling from her tail. It nailed a fish hore and there, but was designed more to catch fishermen.

Practically all artificials depend upon some kind of action in the water to be effective. In this respect they can be divided into two camps. A fine line separates the two, but there's a technical difference. In one camp are lures with a built-in action that comes to life automatically when they're retrieved or trolled. Darting plugs and lures with erratic movements are examples. In the other camp are those without any special built-in action of their own, whose motions and antics are generated by manipulations with the rod. Metal squids and certain jigs are among those in this division.

As we hinted earlier, you couldn't even begin to keep apprised of all the artificials trooping through the fresh water and marine arenas. Already numbering in the thousands, their ranks swell virtually by the day. At the most recent edition of the American Fishing Tackle Manufacturers

Association Trade Show in Chicago there must have been dozens of new models introduced, not to mention the uncountable others being turned out by small firms and one-man operations across the nation.

Fortunately, you don't have to try to keep apprised of all these attractors. Fact is, it would serve only to confuse you or, what's worse, discourage you.

However, what you should do is familiarize yourself with the *basic types* and some of their purposes, wether you use them or not. Only then can you be in position to best select those suited to your situations. Having made that selection, you can keep eyes and ears open for new models among them.

Cataloging artificials according to basic types can become involved. We'll try to keep it simple.

1. Plugs: Essentially these are casting lures ("plugging"), although they're trolled too. Once made from wood exclusively, sometimes hand-crafted, most of them today are mass-produced from plastic. There's nothing wrong with wooden plugs, performance-wise, by the way. It's just that the plastic jobs offer such advantages and permanent colors and finishes (wooden plugs are enameled, vulnerable to fishes' teeth) and generally greater durability. Also, a greater variety of shapes and finishes is possible with plastics.

Many plugs are the shape of minnows or other small fishes. Others are suggestive of mice, small birds and other creatures that find their way into fish stomachs. Plugs are workhorses, one of our most versatile and valuable items of terminal tackle in both fresh and salt water fishing. There are literally thousands of them. Their colors run the spectrum of the rainbow and beyond. In lengths and weights they range from mini-plugs as light as 1/16 ounce to impressive models 8 to 12 inches long weighing up to 4 and 5 ounces.

Numerous refinements have been incorporated to heighten their attraction. For instance: Lifelike finishes resembling skin or scales; a metal lip at the head end that can be bent upward or downward to make the plug travel at different levels; "eyes" in the head for realism; bright colors that are almost fluorescent in their visibility; sound-producing designs; jointing of the longer models, intended to imitate eels, for a more enticing action; and tiny propellers, fore and aft, to generate a bubbly wash that arouses fishes' interest.

Hook armament also varies, according to plug sizes and models. Plugs usually carry treble hooks, and the most common arrangement is two, one trailing astern, the other dangling from the underside at about the middle. Very small plugs may be outfitted with only one treble, trailing. Longer models have three sets of gang hooks, fore, amidship and aft. Veteran pluggers frequently add little embellishments of their own, like garnishing the tail hook with a skirt of bucktail (animal hairs) or bright bits of feather. Or they may alter a plug's hook arrangement — removing one set of trebles, going to larger or smaller sizes, etc.

Incidentally, treble hooks are both a blessing and headache: a blessing because there are three points to dig in, helpful when a fish makes a sideways or halfhearted pass at the lure; a headache because they can be a job to remove when a customer takes a plug deep in the maw.

The plug family is subdivided into clans, according to their respective kinds of action, thus:

(a) Popping plugs or poppers: These possess a concavity or bevel on their front end. At rest, they float. Activated by movements of a rod tip, they duck just under the surface to utter popping sounds and leave a bubbly wake. Poppers are primarily for shoal-water casting, where the customary procedure is to let them rest until the splash of their landing has subsided, after which they're retrieved in a series of lifts of the rod tip. Their sonic effects may be the extra that attracts a quarry from a deeper level or out from under cover. (In this particular instance slow retrieves are indicated because a fish must be given a chance to tune in on the popping or gurgling, then find its source.) For the same reason, poppers have application at night, or in cloudy water, or in areas where there's a lot of vegetation cover in which fish can be lurking. They also can be effective in fresh and salt water when game fishes are clobbering schools of bait at the surface. When in a feeding frenzy predators often will strike at anything, but attention-getting sounds of popping plugs give them something with which to compete with the real thing.

As you can see, poppers are for surface and near surface operations. Until you become familiar with the characteristics of specific models, try fishing them slowly in a series of alternate jerks and pauses.

(b) Surface-disturbers: Their name gives you a clue to their action and attraction. Variously outfitted with tiny propellers fore and aft, a flapping tail, or appendages that flutter, these plugs' magnetism is based on their creating a little ruckus as they move through the water. Like poppers, they float when at rest. Unlike poppers, they can be worked in different ways and so have a potentially greater versatility. Some are allowed to stay in one spot and simply twitched with the rod. Others can be retrieved at speeds ranging from slow to fast, or in combinations of different speeds. Some models have a regular swimming action; others are erratic. Frogs, little birds and mice are among the creatures they're designed to simulate. Surface-disturbers are standard equipment in fresh-water bass anglers' tackle boxes.

(c) Darting plugs: These also are are surface and near-surface lures and are essentially for shallow water service, where they combine some of the features of surface-disturbers and floating-diving plugs (coming up next). They float when not activated. In retrieves they submerge anywhere from a few inches to a couple of feet, according to model and retrieve speed. "Darting" isn't really a good description of their action. Actually it's more of a slow, teasing wobble or weaving motion. They come in a wide range of shapes, finishes and sizes, including fractional-ounce models. They can be worked at varying speeds, with or without pauses, and have proved themselves with an assortment of gamesters that include largemouth and smallmouth basses, tarpon, northerns (northern "pike"), snook and striped bass.

(d) Floating-diving plugs: As you've guessed, they float when at rest, dive when you turn the reel crank. Diving is effected by front-end designs that include a metal or plastic lip, a grooving, a bevel, etc. They plane deeper than darting types, submerging to perhaps three to six feet; and they behave more erratically, with a more pronounced side-to-side weaving. Floating-diving plugs have a versatility all their own. By varying retrieve or trolling speed they can be made to ride high in very shallow areas, then go deeper in channels and along drop-offs. Or they can be retrieved at varying speeds, interspersed with pauses and twitches. Muskellunge and largemouth bass are among their victims.

(e) Sinking models: Once they hit the water they begin to submerge immediately. Sinking speeds vary among different models; but since the submersion rate is consistent for a given plug, the user learns to judge how long it takes to reach different levels. Sinking plugs offer two big advantages: They can be fished in both shallow and deep water; and they can be worked in various ways at different levels as they sink. How shallow or deep you want them to go can be regulated by the length of the delay before starting the retrieve. Similarly, they can be retrieved at a slow, moderate or fast rate, or a mixture of all three. Because of their submersibility they are particularly suited to probing strange waters. Here a procedure is to start at an upper level, pausing a few seconds to let the plug sink before beginning the retrieve . . . then a few seconds' pause to let it drop to another level, retrieve again . . . another pause and retrieve . . . and so on all the way down to cover different planes. Most sinking plugs have an elongated, slender form, but some are in the shape of a small fish. They're rigged in both marine and fresh water action and have accounted for largemouth and smallmouth bass, bluefish, pike, snook, speckled or spotted sea trout, and other species.

(f) Deep-diving plugs: These are designed to reach quarry hanging around at a lower level, like fresh water species escaping summer heat. Although some deep-divers float when at rest, most of them submerge as soon as they hit the water. They're characterized by a broad, prominent metal lip extending forward from the head end. This lip could be likened to a submarine's diving plane, since it is what makes the lure proceed to lower levels. Bending it up or down influences the depths at which it rides. The amount of line out also is a factor. The more the line, in casting or trolling, the deeper it will dive. In the effect of the lip you see a major difference between deep-divers and sinking plugs, whose depths are governed by their specific gravity and retrieve speeds. Although deep-divers go about the farthest down of any plugs, they do have limits. They're rigged in both fresh water and salt.

Because there is such a gigantic collection from which to select, and because some often are better suited to specific areas, kinds of fishes, methods, seasons, water conditions (i.e., deep or shallow, clear or murky, rough or calm, etc.), it becomes most important that fishermen make local inquiries as a guide to choice, getting opinions on sizes, colors, techniques for working, etc. How a plug is fished can be as important as its anatomical details. Sometimes manufacturers enclose recommendations. Tackle dealers also can advise.

Keep in mind that many plugs can be used interchangeably in fresh and salt water angling. Too, a given model can be effective for several species.

Another huge family of versatile and valuable lures is gathered under the banner SPOONS. Old Julio T. Buel, credited with the first commercial development of spoons in the U.S., would sit up and smile in his grave if he could see the vast assortment that has evolved.

Today spoons are among the most widely rigged artificials in fresh-water and marine fishing, for casting and trolling. Collectively they account for a long list of species. Among their victims are striped bass (salt and fresh water), largemouth bass, bluefish, lake trout, dolphin, salmon, bonito, northerns ("northern pike"), smallmouth bass, barracuda, pickerel and channel bass. Spoons are extremely versatile lures that can be fished interchangeably in salt water and fresh. Fact is, you can rig a spoon of suitable size for almost any sport fish.

Size is a major guide to selection. Spoons are marketed in sizes ranging from mini-models for flyrodding to the giants of the tribe, the big 'bunker spoons up to 12 inches long and about 4 wide. In between are small, medium and large models of 3 to 6 and 8 inches. The idea is to gauge, at least approximately, the size of the spoon to the size of the quarry, with some consideration of the fish's mouth size. Nothing complicated here, just common sense. A fish with a small mouth can't very well engulf a spoon that is too large. Sizes of their hooks should be in proportion too, for the same reason and for suitable strength. A big-mouth striped bass might very well be attracted to a small spoon as readily as to a larger one, but the former's hooks may be too small (weak) to hold the fish.

Hook arrangements differ. Many models are armed with a swinging treble at their trailing end. A few carry a swinging single hook. Others, such as that monstrous 'bunker spoon, are outfitted with a single fixed hook. Sizes are in proportion to the spoons, going from smaller than a No. 1 up to huskies of 8/0 to 12/0 (these larger ones in single hooks). As with plugs, owners alter hooksizes on their favorite spoons, according to personal ideas. Too, hooks may be left nude, decorated with bits of feather or bucktail, or garnished with a piece of pork rind or perhaps a juicy worm. There's plenty of room for interesting experimentation.

Traditionally, spoons are oval in shape, frequently "dished out" to form convex and concave sides. There are also models bent in an *S*-curve, or in the front or rear. Others are suggestive of little bait fishes. Then there's that big 'bunker spoon, whose shape (roughly teardrop and dished out) is intended to simulate a mossbunker or menhaden, a herring-like forage fish appealing to striped bass, bluefish and other finned predators. By and large, spoons' appeal lies in a swaying, wobbling, fluttering or sashaying action when retrieved or trolled. The illusion of a bait fish, either trying to escape or crippled, can be heightened by erratic crank-and-pause retrieves.

Spoons are stamped out of metal, often brass, stainless steel or copper, and are variously polished, left with a natural stainless steel finish, chrome-plated or enameled in bright colors. There are also silver and gold finishes. The idea is to give them flash and glitter for added attraction. According to their weights and trolling or retrieve speeds, they can be tried at varying depths.

Names prominently mentioned in spoon production include Eppinger (famous for Dardeveles), Johnson (Sprites and others), and Hopkins (No = Eql models).

Second cousins to spoons, in a way, are spinners. These too depend upon flash as well as movement for their attraction, and through their spinning action add vibrations that can arouse intended victims' curiosity. Essentially a spoon consists of a small metal blade mounted on a wire shaft or a swivel so that it can revolve or spin. Arrangements vary. Among models popular in fresh water bass fishing are some on which the spinner blade is mounted on a short arm extending at right angles to the lure's hook portion. According to models, the blades may be oval or teardrop in shape, or like an elongated leaf (one is called a Willow Leaf). Some are kidney-shaped; others, like the Colorado pattern, are nearly round. Like the blades of spoons, they're stamped from metal and are available in different finishes, natural to chromed to enameled.

Spinners are complete terminal rigs unto themselves, with armament about equally divided between single hooks and trebles. In different sizes and weights they're fished in both fresh water (notably for black bass) and salt water (where they can be lethal to the younger striped bass). They can be cast or trolled. Those employed in casting generally have somewhat heavier blades and/or a metal head or body to add weight. For trolling there are multiple-blade spinners, with anywhere from two to six or more blades in tandem to heighten attraction. There are also fractional-ounce models for use with fly rods. Variations include small glass beads, mounted near the blade, and skirts of brightly colored plastic or of bucktail for the hook. Similarly, they can be fished as is, or with the hook decorated with a whole live worm, piece of pork rind, or a live or dead minnow. Finding great favor among fresh-water bass fishermen is a spinner on whose hook is impaled a plastic worm.

As in the case of all artificials, including flies, it will pay to inquire locally concerning specific models. There are so many kinds of spinners that this becomes practically a must, although you can have interesting experiences trying them experimentally.

*Tip:* The spinners we have been talking about are the units complete with hooks. But the blades alone — one, two, three or more — can be incorporated in the rig just ahead of a natural bait or an artificial other than a spinner for added attraction — effective in trolling, drifting, retrieves. They're sold separately for this purpose. Here again you can perform interesting experiments.

## Jigs

Long popular among marine anglers, jigs also have come into widespread service among their fresh water brethren. A typical jig is characterized by a stubby, chunky appearance and is weighty for its length. Its main feature is a heavy head, molded from lead, often with a single hook imbedded and trailing astern. Hook variations include attachment by a short wire and a dangling treble. The hook is dressed — or disguised, if you prefer — by a skirt of little feathers, bucktail or other animal hairs, or brightly colored rubber, nylon or plastic strands. Attachment to a line is usually via an eye atop the head, and the lure travels with its hook up. Jigs can be cast or trolled. They're especially suited to casting because they're heavy for their size and their compactness offers little wind resistance. Moreover, they sink quickly. Because they ride with their nose down a bit and their hook up, they also are suited to bottom bouncing in areas with rocks and other obstructions, where lures such as plugs and spoons might snag easily.

Jigs are made with heads of various shapes: bullet; oval or egg; round; keeled; etc. Also called leadheads, these lures come in a rainbow of colors that include all white, red, yellow, black or brown, or combinations of those. They also are available in a span of weights, from less than 1/4 ounce for spinning tackle and other light gear on up to 3 and 4 ounces and heavier. One deviation in shape is the diamond jig. It has a body shaped like an elongated skinny diamond, molded from lead around a single hook. Many are chrome plated. Standard equipment among salt-water fishermen for generations, diamond jigs can be jigged, cast or trolled effectively for Atlantic mackerel, sea bass, and other species. Their hooks are in a range of sizes, and some anglers add a piece of pork rind or a worm as an extra come-on. Jigs depend mainly upon motion and color for effect.

*Tip:* Because of their design, how they sink and behave in the water, and the way fishes often hit them, it's most important that jigs' hooks be kept at maximum sharpness. A jig with a dull hook can spell lost fish.

### Plastic Imitations

Plastics technology has spawned an amazing array of artificial bait. Dozens of items of natural food of fresh-water and marine fishes now have phony but startlingly lifelike counterparts in plastics (and, among some, in rubber). For flyrodders and other light-tackle casters there are insect simulations that include crickets, hellgrammites, spiders, nymphs and grasshoppers. Small and feather-light, these sometimes are cast with a very small sinker weight just ahead of them. Also for fresh water fishermen are imitation worms, frogs, minnows, crayfish, eels and other yum-yums. Salt water anglers have their plastic squid, bloodworms, sandworms and eels. In recent years, notably among black bass hunters, plastic worms have become a popular artificial. Although they can be used alone, they're particularly deadly in conjunction with a spinner. They're produced in a variety of lengths, weights and colors. There are natural colors to better simulate nighcrawlers, but you'll also see them in purple, blue, "strawberry," red, exotic green, yellow, flourescents, etc.

Collectively, these plastic lures can be fished in any of the standard methods, according to species sought. Their attraction is due mainly to their lifelike appearance, supplemented among some by a built-in natural scent. But it's up to the angler to impart realistic action to them in a series of jerks, twitches or erratic retrieves.

### Miscellaneous Artificials

1. Surgical tubes: Relative newcomers to the salt water scene, these unique lures have achieved fast-growing popularity on the U.S. East Coast, notably in the New England-New York-New Jersey region, where they have proved deadly to striped bass and bluefish. They're in a class by them-

selves, not readily catalogued with other types of artificials, and are still new enough that their full potential is not yet known. Unless we miss our guess, they will see ever-widening service in salt water and will invade the fresh water arena too.

They derive their incongruous name — usually mentioned as "tube lures" or, among those in the know, simply as "tubes" — from the plastic tubing employed in medicine for transfusions and the like. Their origin is obscure. No one seems able to say for sure when, where and by whom the idea was conceived. But we do know that it caught on, largely through the efforts of striped bass fishermen.

We can't say for sure why surgical tubes are effective. The theory is that they suggest small bait fishes and eels. No one knows what they look like to their prey, and the fish as usual aren't talking. However, most anglers are content to know only that they *do* work, and not worry about why. These tubes are designed as trolling lures, the water rushing through them combining with their flexibility to create an enticing wiggling-fluttering action.

A pioneering firm in mass production of surgical tube lures is Sportsmen's Creative Manufacturing Company in Brooklyn, New York. "Bingle" is their market name, prefixing such model designations as "Lancer," "Boa," and "Banana." They come ready to do their work, armed — in standard fashion for all tubes — with a single hook of appropriate size.

For do-it-yourselfers plastic tubing designed for adaptation as artificials comes in different diameters and colors, including red (a favorite), amber, white, green, brown and black. The tubing is cut to desired lengths, which may be 2-1/2 or 3 inches for the smaller ones up to 12 inches or more if the intent is to simulate an eel. In a special arrangement, up to 9 or more small tubes are strung out with short lengths of wire from a spreader in a sizable rig that has been given such nicknames as "Christmas tree," "coat hanger," and, by its detractors, "an abortion." When trolled, this multiple-tube rig suggests a school of small bait fish streaking through the water. It has been known to account for two, even three, striped bass at once when a school is worked, and for that reason is frowned upon by conservation-minded bass buffs. Some fishermen attach a tube to the metal head of a feather lure. Others add a few red beads just ahead of a tube for extra appeal. Data on this particular use are still sparse, but it would seem that surgical tubes should be effective in casting to a surface-feeding school.

2. Metal squids: Made from lead, so-called block tin and other metals, these lures have been in use for decades among surfcasters and salt water trollers. Many are chrome or nickel plated, since lead loses its luster quickly and must be sandpapered or polished with steel wool to restore an attractive brightness. Glitter is part of the squids' stock in trade. So is shape, and accordingly they're made in a variety of forms to suggest forage species such as sand eels (a misnomer, by the way; they are not eels), spearing, silversides, marine minnows, small mullet, etc. They most commonly are outfitted with a single hook, imbedded in the body, although a dangling single or treble can be used too. They can be fished plain, but many users decorate the hook with a piece of pork rind, or a bit of bucktail or small, bright feathers.

Metal squids started out as primarily a casting lure, along an oceanfront beach or from boats, but they also are trolled with equal effectiveness for a variety of marine gamesters that include striped bass, bluefish, northern weakfish and channel bass. They range from midgets of less than an ounce to models weighing 4 and 5 ounces. Each model generally has its own brand of action and depths at which it is most effective. Unless there are specific recommendations, different reeling and trolling speeds should be tried to determine which bring out optimum action.

3. Chicken-bone and turkey-bone lures: You don't hear much about these anymore, but old-timers used to salvage the leg bones of chickens and turkeys demolished by their families, bleach them white, and string them on a short length of wire with a hook. Some years ago it was said these bones were being reproduced in rubber, or perhaps plastic, but this writer never encountered them. In any case, they were primarily trolling lures and, 'tis said, effective for striped bass and bluefish.

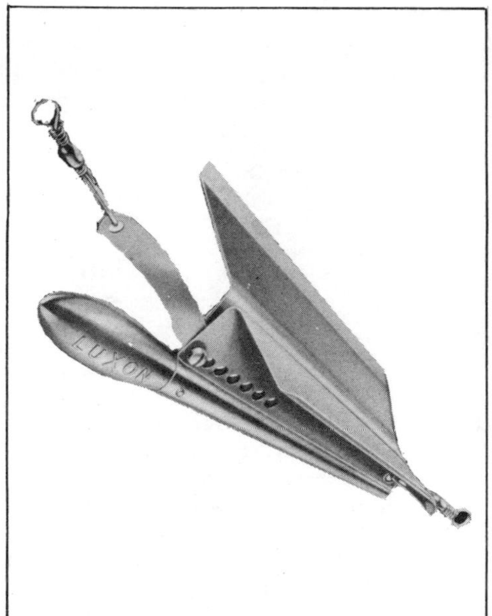


**Trolling Planers**

Trolling planers such as this stainless steel Luxon Magill model from Gladding-South Bend are rigged for deep trolling. They have an advantage over drails and similar trolling sinkers in being adjustable for depths. The Luxon Magill is credited with catches as deep as 72 fathoms (432 feet). When a fish is hooked, the planer automatically assumes a surfacing position. There are 2½- to 5½-inch Luxon Magill planers for lake and deep sea trolling.

**Sinkers**

Here's an inkling of the variety of sinkers employed in marine and fresh water fishing. Each is best suited to a certain use—the pyramid for surf bottom fishing, the bass swivel for moving a rig along the bottom, etc. The most common sinker in salt water angling, universal in bottom fishing, is the bank type. All come in a range of ounce-weights, sometimes indicated by a raised figure on the sinkers. These are from Maxwell Manufacturing Co. (Grizzly Fishing Tackle).

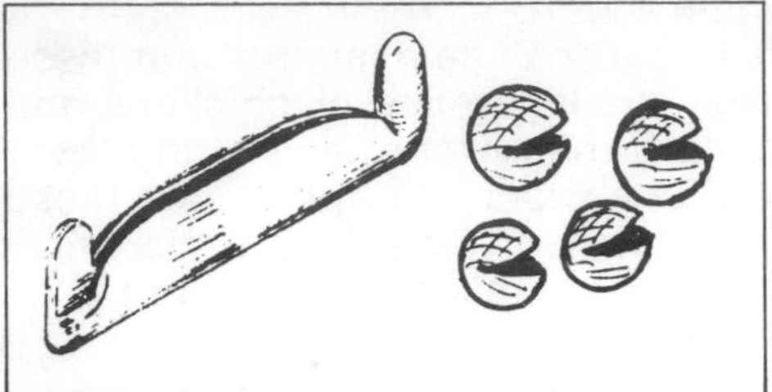

**Fractional-Ounce Sinkers**

Sometimes only fractional-ounce sinkers are needed. Example: In still-fishing near the surface, just a little weight is required to counteract the upward thrust of a current or moving tide. Split shot and clamp-on or pinch-on sinkers fill the bill. Many tackle firms market them. The samples here are products of Maxwell Manufacturing Co., Vancouver, Wash.

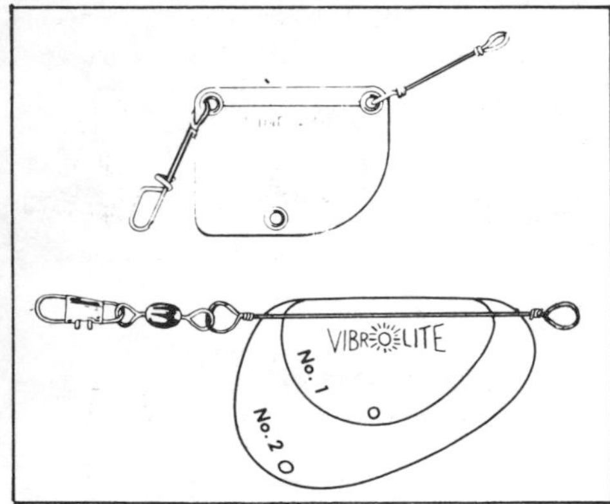


**Trolling Rudders and Keels**

Some natural baits and artificials tend to spin when towed, giving them an unnatural appearance and twisting leaders and lines excessively. Trolling rudders and keels, such as these Linesaver and Vibr-o-Lite models from Maxwell Manufacturing Co., eliminate or minimize those undersirable effects.

**Barrel Swivels**

Among the major items of terminal hardware, notably in marine angling, are barrel swivels, employed variously to connect lines and leaders, snelled hooks to lines, etc. They're surprisingly strong for their sizes. (The American Import Co., San Francisco)

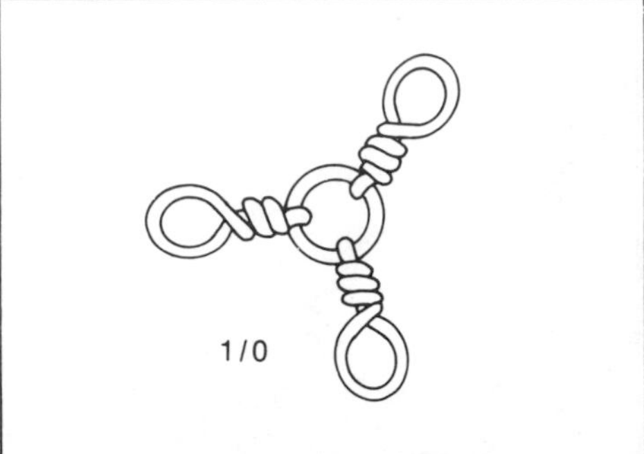


**Three-Way Swivels**

Performing the same functions as barrel swivels, but where three connections are involved (e.g., sinker, line and leader), thus as three-way swivels. They too are marketed in graduated sizes and are very strong. Example here is from St. Croix Corp., Minneapolis.

**Bead-Chain Tackle**

Terminal tackle connectors from Bead Chain Tackle Co., Bridgeport, Conn. From the top: (1) New 3-way Swivel developed by Bead Chain, strong, rustproof, serves as a kind of spreader for 2-hook rigs as well. (2) Plain bead chain connector. In all these connectors each bead is a swivel unto itself, an added advantage against twisting. (3) A single-snap type, also available with a snap at both ends. (4) Lock-type snap. Snaps facilitate changing of lures.

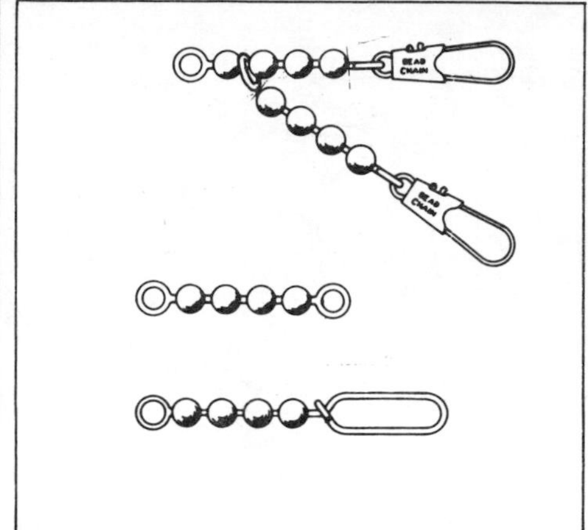

Bead Chain Tackle Co. shows a couple of the supplemental items that can be rigged in combination with a lure or a natural bait for added attraction. The flash and movement of a spinner blade are an eye-catcher. Sometimes two or more are rigged. The little propellers on the Dual Prop K Spinner (this model also incorporates a keel) serve a similar purpose.

**Ready-Made Rigs**

Many fishermen fashion their own rigs, usually to get desired variations or try out personal ideas. Others prefer to buy theirs ready made by professionals. There are all kinds of prepared marine and fresh water rigs on the market. A few examples (top to bottom): (1) Flounder spreader rig from Dragon Fly Co., Sumter, S.C. Its nine-inch spread prevents two hooks from tangling. Sinker goes on the bottom, middle loop. (2) Also from Dragon Fly, a coastal bluefishing feather rig. This one is 48 inches overall, carries white-red-yellow feathers and is armed with 3/0 Mustad Pacific bass hooks. (3) A panfish rig from Lindy/Little Joe, Brainerd, Minn. (4) Worth River Rig from Worth Fishing Tackle, Stevens Point, Wis. Designed to take a bait deep, for pike, basses, other sport species.

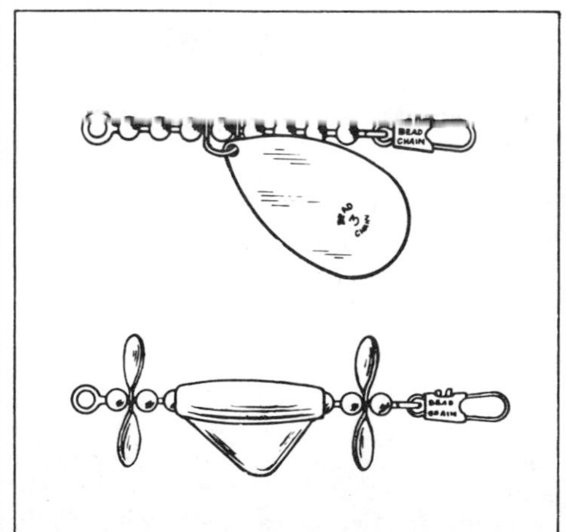

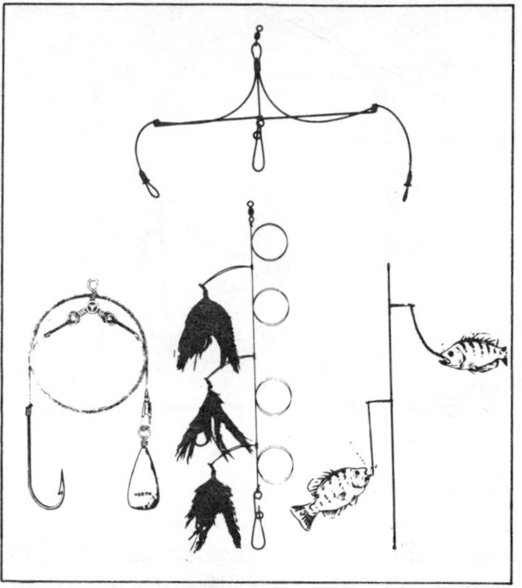

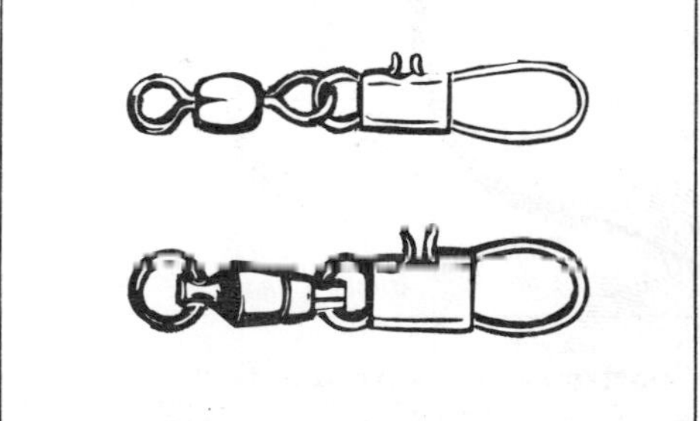

**Snap-Swivels**

These Eagle Claw snap-swivels from Wright & McGill Co. typify still other kinds of terminal tackle connectors. On the left is a nickel-plated brass crane swivel with a stainless steel interlock or safety snap. On the right is a ball bearing snap-swivel, stainless steel. The snaps make it possible to change rigs, lures and baits in a hurry.

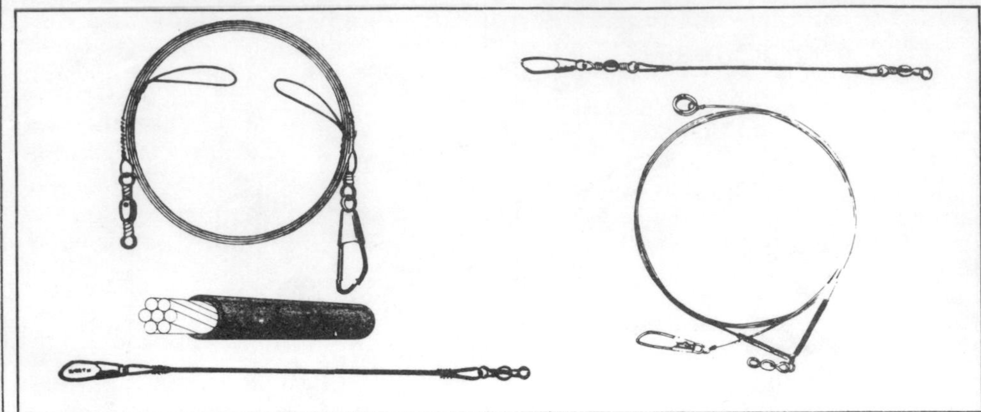

## Ready-Made Leaders

You'll find ready-made leaders for a very wide range of fresh water and marine assignments, streamside flycasting to blue water big-game combat. They come in a variety of materials, including monofilament, wire and cable, in lengths of only inches to several feet. Here are a few examples:

A) A surf leader with barrel swivel and snap-swivel, made from nylon in strengths from 10- to 50-pound test by St. Croix Corp.

B) Nylon leader from Worth Fishing tackle—stainless steel wire covered with nylon, with swivel and safety snap. Comes in lengths from 6 to 18 inches, 10- to 30-pound test.

C) Also from Worth, a Nyflex trolling and casting leader, soft nylon, with swivel and snap connector.

D) Combination wire leader with spreader incorporated, from Maxwell Manufacturing Co. (Grizzly Fishing Tackle).

## The Lure Shop

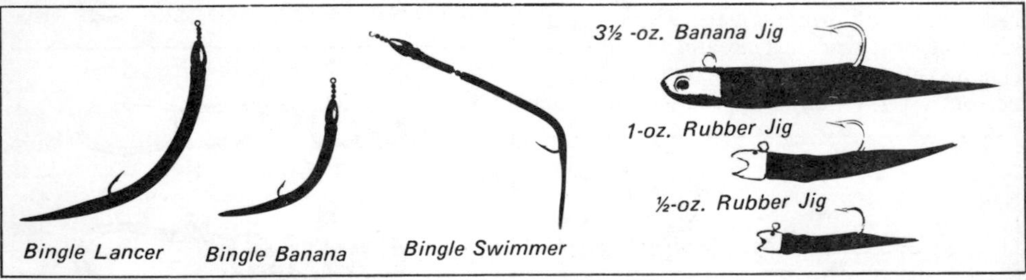


**Sportsmen's Creative Mfg. Corp.**
**439 Ave. U, Brooklyn, N.Y. 11223**

Proven grabbers of striped bass, bluefish and other marine battlers are the so-called surgical tubes. Sportsmen's Creative has delivered an even higher degree of effectiveness with its latex rubber Bingles, made to simulate eels and small forage fishes.

**Bingle Lancer:** A new concept. This imitation sand eel will not twist line. Head tracks true while the tail revolves. For trolling, casting. Four sizes, ½ oz. to 2 3/4 oz., 7" to 12", approximately $1.50 to $3. Shown is 1¼ oz. Lancer with 85 lb. test stainless steel chain, 8/0 Mustad hook.

**Bingle Banana:** For all game fishes, casting or trolling, effective in chumming too. Proven on Northeastern party boats and a favorite among their mates. Easily worked. In two sizes, both with 85-lb. stainless steel bead chain, Mustad forged hooks: 2¼ oz., 10½", 9/0; 1¼ oz., 7½", 6/0. About $2.25 and $1.75.

**Bingle Swimmer:** Realistic imitation of an eel, 1¼ oz., 11" long, 85-lb. stainless steel bead chain, 9/0 Mustad forged hook. About $2.

**Three more Bingles, all latex rubber:** For jigging, trolling; can be used with pork rind. Very durable. For weakfish, striped bass, bluefish, other species. Top, 3½-oz. Banana Jig, 8/0 forged Mustad, about $1.75. Middle, 1-oz. Rubber Jig, 7/0 forged Mustad, about $1. Bottom, ½-oz. Rubber Jig, 3/0 forged Mustad, about $.75.

**Six-Arm Umbrella Rig:** Made to simulate a moving group of sand eels or worms. Incorporates twelve Bingle lures, $10.50. Also available, and functioning on same principle, is a Four-Arm Umbrella Rig with eight lures, about $7.

**Bingle Coathanger:** A smaller version of the Umbrella, same principle, five lures. About $6.

**Lou J. Eppinger Mfg. Co.**
**6340 Schaefer Hwy., Dearborn, Mich. 48126**

Since the turn of the century the name Lou Eppinger has been synonymous with spoons, and vice versa. But in a sense his company is much older than that, for it has reproduced the Sagamore pattern, a spoon that revolutionized angling when it was created by Julio T. Buel nearly 150 years ago.

And unquestionably the most famous name among Eppinger artificials is Dardevle, a fixture on the U.S. angling scene for generations. The Dardevles and their close cousins—Dardevlets, Seadevle Imp, King and Junior Flutter Devles, etc. —comprise a huge family. Among them is a wide range of weights, from fractional-ounce models for spinning to 3 and 3-1/8 oz. They also come in a variety of inside and outside finishes that include copper, nickel, brass, hammered finishes, and a rainbow of color combinations. Among them they can handle an equally large assortment of fresh water and marine fishing assignments.

**The Dardevles:** Senior members of the family, 1 oz., 3 5/8" by 1¼". Available in some fifty one finishes—colors, plain and hammered nickel, brass, copper. About $2.40.

**Dardevle Imp:** 2/5 oz., 2¼" by 7/8", in many finishes, about $2.10 each.

**Mousiedevle Imp:** For light tackle and spinning. Mouse shape, sparkling silver eyes, squirrel tail streamer. Nickel inside; gray and brown outside; 2/5 oz. about $2.35.

**Eppinger's Notangle Spinner:** Newly designed with a unique bend that prevents line twist. In three sizes—1/8, ¼, ½ oz.—many finishes, with and without squirrel tail, about $1.40 to $2.30.

**Generic Systems Inc.**
**P.O. Box 256, Rockaway, N.J. 07866**

Although young in the lure business, Generic Systems' products are receiving increasing acclaim in the fresh water and marine angling arenas. They also have received plaudits from fishing writers in some of the leading outdoor magazines.

**SOSY Baitfish and Eels:** These are amazingly realistic soft-plastic lures—they even feel like flesh to the touch—that become animated when worked in the water. SOSY Baitfish look and move like small forage fishes. The SOSY Eel has the serpentine motion of the real thing. Among the species these artificials have racked up are muskellunge, striped bass, brown

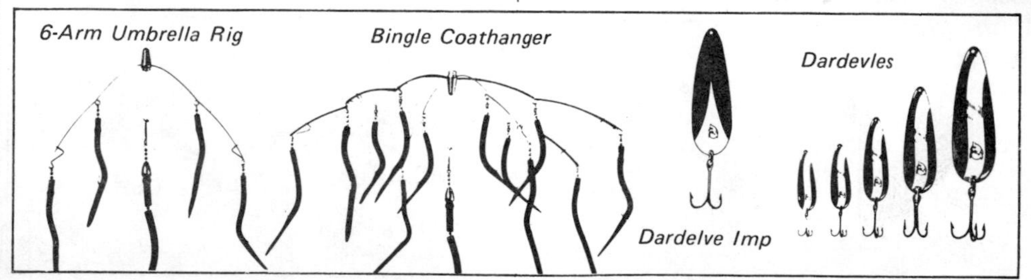
*6-Arm Umbrella Rig* *Bingle Coathanger* *Dardevles* *Dardelve Imp*

trout, weakfish, largemouth and smallmouth black basses, northerns, and channel bass. Sizes go from 1/8 oz. and 1¼" to 2 3/4 oz. and 6½", with corrosion-resistant hardware from 25- to 100-lb. test. Colors include perch, blue, gold. Other features include: Keel-weighting so they ride with dorsal fin up; stainless steel body wire; tough body; removable hook and wire snap to permit re-rigging without tools. Incidentally, SOSY lures reportedly established quite a reputation for themselves from Europe to Mozambique and South Africa before being introduced to the United States and Canada. Prices range from about $2.25 to $6 each, according to size and model.

**Padre Island Co., Inc.**
**2617 N. Zarzamora, San Antonio, Tex. 78201**

In business for more than forty years, this firm is perhaps best known for its Pico lures, but its line also includes metal and soft-plastic artificials.

**Pico Side Shad, Series SS:** ½ oz., 2½". Floats on its side like a crippled shad. Unusual body shape and large propeller generate additional attraction. A top-water lure in nine different color schemes. Approximate price: $2.30.

**Hot Pants, Series HP:** ½ oz. Large double spinners on a long wire makes this lure virtually weedless. Also features large, plastic, reverse skirt. In white, chartreuse, black, and other colors and combinations. Can be fished with a plastic worm. Approximate price: $1.60.

**Pico Bull Worm, Series BW:** Its unique design and colors make it equally effective in fresh water or salt, where it's cast, allowed to sink, then retrieved with a hopping motion by means of the rod tip. Can be used with jigs, sliding weights or spinner lures. Its victims include redfish, walleyes, speckled trout, northerns, coho salmon, large-mouth and small-mouth basses. Approximate price: $.78.

**Atom Manufacturing Co., Inc.**
**880 Washington St., South Attleboro, Mass. 02703**

It seems safe to say that any U.S. coastal angler who has fished intently for striped bass, casting or trolling, probably has rigged an Atom plug at one time or another. Incidentally, that doesn't restrict Atoms to one species, because the family has swimmers, poppers and divers, in weights from ¼ oz. to 4 oz., including a group of fractional-ounce versions for spinning.

**Talking Striper Swiper:** One of Atom's best known models, with a concave head for "sonic effects" battlers find attractive. Five sizes, 7/8 oz. to 4 oz., with two sets of treble hooks, the trailing set dressed. According to sizes, colors are blue silver, red yellow, silver white, white, pink, orange, mackerel. Approximate prices: $3.35 to $4.05.

**Spit'n Striper Swiper:** Similar in body design and hook armament to the Talking Striper Swiper, but with a somewhat different head end to create an eye-catching ruckus. In the same colors. From 3/8 oz. to 2 oz., about $2.60 to $3.55.

**Atom Swimmer:** A big plug—3¼ oz.—for battlers who go for big morsels. And they get a mouthful with this one—note three treble hooks. Metal lip is for depth control. One size, in squid, white and blue colors, about $5.25.

**Atoms for spinning:** Six sizes, ½ oz. to 7/8 oz., in blue silver, red yellow or silver white, about $2.30 to $3.50.

*Mousiedevle Imp* *Eppinger's Notangle Spinner*

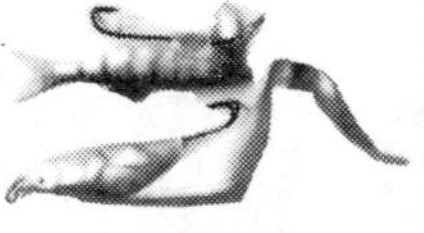

*SOSY Baitfish and Eels*

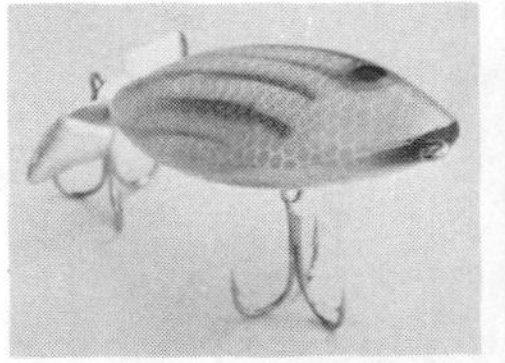

*Pico Side Shad*

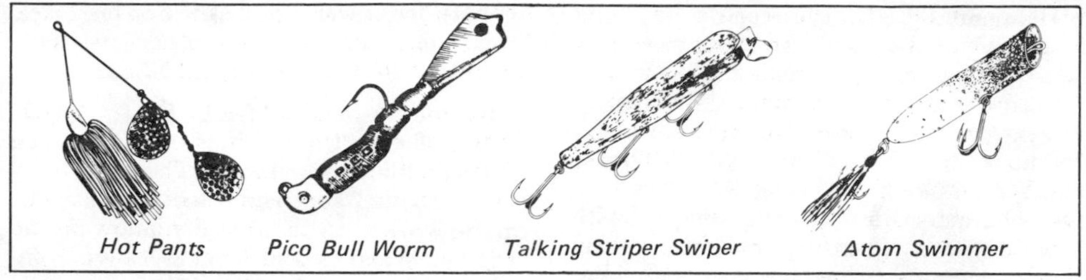
Hot Pants Pico Bull Worm Talking Striper Swiper Atom Swimmer

**Wig-Wag Worms:** Featuring a scorpion-like tail that wiggles and swims at the slightest movement for lifelike action. Currently they come in 2- to 9-inch lengths, ten colors. They're available ready-rigged on fresh and salt water jigs, as well as in bulk packs for do-it-yourself rigging with spinner lures, jigs, etc. Approximate retail prices: **No. 220,** 2" Wig-Wag jig with four spare bodies, 1/8 oz., $1, spare pack of six, $0.80; **No. 240,** 4" Wig-Wag jig with two spare bodies, ¼ oz., $1, spare pack of four, $0.90; 7" Wig-Wag, bag of twelve, $2.50; 9" Wig-Wag, three for $1 or $3.50 per bag of twelve.

**Burke Fishing Lures**
**1969 S. Airport Rd., Traverse City, Mich. 49684**

This company specializes in soft-plastic artificials, and with its know-how and imagination has come up with amazing imitations that include frogs, crayfish, several kinds of insects, minnows, worms, eels, even snakes. Burke also makes spinner lures and a revolutionary new **plastic** pork rind called Hawgahide.

**Burke's Dedly Dudly:** A new black bass lure that features a patented, free-wheeling spinner that rotates at the slightest tug, flashing brightly. Whirling blade also sets up a hum to lure bass out of hiding. Can be fished on top as a "buzzin' " bait or sent down deep among the stumps, where the spinner design acts as a weedless device. In white, yellow, solid black.

**Bead Chain Tackle Co.**
**110 Mountain Grove St., and**
**Bridgeport Silverware Mfg. Co.**
**65 Holland Ave. Both in Bridgetport, Conn. 06605**

These two firms are subsidiaries of Bead Chain Manufacturing Co., very well known producer of terminal tackle items.

**Bead Chain Stainless Steel Spoons:** For marine and fresh water fishing, trolling and casting. Offered in eight shapes and sizes, including a 1/16 oz., fish-shaped model (**No. SS 8**) for fly fishing. Other sizes, ¼ oz. to 1 oz. All are stainless steel, with a trailing treble hook, and proven fish-catchers. Their attraction is an unusual shimmering motion that simulates a crippled bait fish. Approximate prices each: 88c for the 1/16-oz. **SS 8** to $1.80 for the 1-oz. **SS 1.** Bead Chain Tackle also makes spinners and casting and trolling leads—and, of course, bead chain.

**VI-KE Lures by Bridgeport Silverware:** In 10 sizes, ¼ oz. to 16 oz., for all kinds of salt and fresh water fishing—casting, trolling, spinning, jigging. Proven effective features are the VI-KE action and high-luster nickel finish. All are armed with a swinging treble hook. Approximate prices: 94c for the ¼-oz. size to $4.25 for the 16 ouncer.

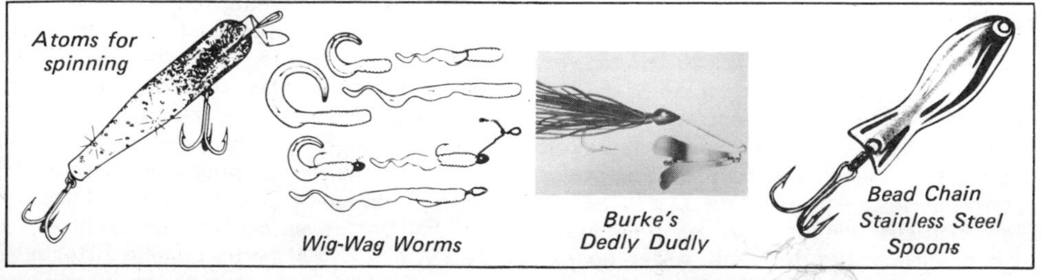
Atoms for spinning Wig-Wag Worms Burke's Dedly Dudly Bead Chain Stainless Steel Spoons

**Diamond Jigs:** On the scene a long time and proven killers, in fresh water as well as salt—jigging, casting, trolling. They're also effective in ice fishing. Bridgeport Silverware offers three: **No. W1,** ¼ oz., 1", 1/0 hook; **No. W2,** 1/3 oz., 1½", 2/0 hook; **No. W3,** ½ oz., 2", 3/0 hook. All three have the characteristic diamond shape, with separate eye, dazzling polished nickel finish, single O'Shaughnessy hook, imbedded in body. Approximate prices: 48c, 52c, 58c.

Bridgeport Silverware also produces: Diamond jigs, 1 to 16 oz., with swinging treble hooks; diamond jigs without hooks, 1 to 16 oz.; diamond squids with a single fixed hook and clog-proof swivel, 1 to 8 oz.; stainless steel Silver King, Silver Queen and Silver Knight, ½ oz. to 1 oz., for spinning, casting, trolling; surf spinning lures; mackerel jigs; drails and trolling sinkers in graduated weights to 4 lb.

**Norman Mfg. Co., Inc.**
**P.O. Box H, Hwy. 96 East, Greenwood, Ark. 72936**

Owner Bill Norman has built himself quite a reputation as both a fisherman and a creator of lures. He's a member of the Fishing Hall of Fame and recipient of the Silver Dolphin and Gold Medal Awards, and his artificials are known all over the country. Those shown here are just a couple of representatives of Lures by Bill Norman. All are fully guaranteed against defects in materials or workmanship.

**The Deep Runners: No. 2000-DR** weighs ½ oz., is 4½" long. For trolling. It gets down 15 feet on a medium retrieve. Can be fished in fresh water or salt, has taken cohos, large black bass, striped bass, many other species. Approximate price: $2.50. **No. 3000-DR** weighs 1 oz., is 5½" long, armed with heavy-duty salt water hooks, for both fresh water and salt. For big black bass, coho salmon, and other battlers. Travels at 20 foot level. About $2.50.

**Jointed Minnows Nos. 500J, 1000J, 2000J, 3000J:** "Old faithfuls" with a record of production consistency. They normally run at about 2 feet and 3 feet depths, but can be worked as an injured minnow on the surface. Weights and lengths range from 1/8 oz. and 2½" (**No. 500J**) to 5/8 oz. and 5½" (**No. 3000J**). **No. 2000J** carries three trebles; the others have two. About $2.25, $2.50.

**Chugger-Flash No. 120:** A top-water artificial with a new cup-like nose that generates enticing gurgles, popping, chugging sounds. It weighs 3/8 oz., is 3½" long. Comes recommended for black bass, but also is reported effective on near-surface marine species. Approximate price, $2.25.

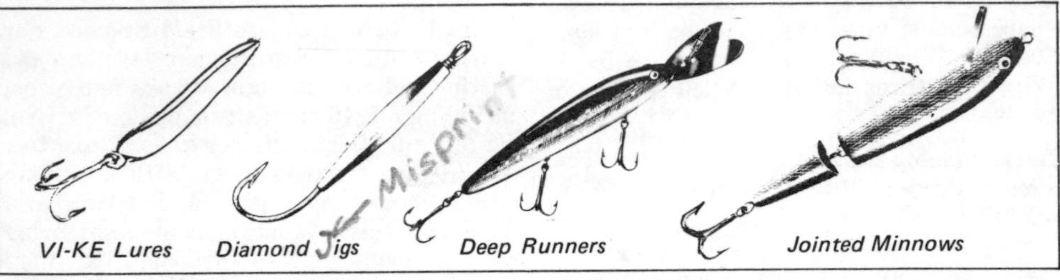
VI-KE Lures — Diamond Jigs — Deep Runners — Jointed Minnows

**Fred Abrogast Co., Inc.**
**313 West North St., Akron, Ohio 44303**

Arbogast is another old, familiar name in the U.S. angling scene, notably among inland fishermen. The company markets a very large family of artificials to collectively cover assignments in baitcasting, spinning and spincasting, fly fishing and marine angling.

**Jitterbugs:** Among Arbogast's best known lures, designed to attract largemouth and smallmouth basses, and other surface-feeding species. Especially helpful in night fishing, their double-lobe lip creates a loud paddling sound. There are several models in a range of sizes and many color patterns for spinning, spincasting, fly fishing, baitcasting. Size range: 1/8 oz., 1¼" **680 Series,** with a No. 6 treble hook, to the 1¼ oz., 5" **700 Series** muskie Jitterbug, with three heavy-duty 2/0 trebles. Included is the ¼-oz. **630 Series**. Spinning Jitterbug. Approximately $1.70 (**680 Series**) to $2.90. (**700 Series**).

**Scudder:** A salt water popper with strong 3X hooks and through-wire construction, weighted for long casts. Deep mouth generates loud popping sounds. Large eye attachment sheds weeds, floating debris. **Series 2450** weighs 1 oz., is 4½" long. **Series 2430** is 1½ oz., 4½". Both have two No. 1 trebles, come in several color patterns, at about $2.80. Also available, at about $2.95: **2400 Series** Scudder, 2¼ oz. 5", with two 3X, 3/0 trebles.

Other Arbogast salt-water artificals are: Dasher; Scooter; Saint; and the Hammerheads.

**Hustler:** A mid-depth bait. Sinks slowly, swims with hopping action, maintains its level once retrieve is started. In many color schemes. **Series 890** is ¼ oz., 2½", No. 5 trebles. **Series 870** is ½ oz., 4½", No. 2 trebles. Both about $2 each.

**Hula Popper:** Another famous Arbogast lure. The "Hula" comes from its skirt, which gives it added action in the water. It can be popped, twitched, jerked or plunked to create attractive commotion and noise at the surface. It comes in several models 3/16 to 5/8 oz., prices about $1.70-$2. Also available are three Hula Poppers, 1/32 to 1/16 oz., and three Luminous Hula Poppers, 1/32 to 1/16 oz., all for flyrodding. Approximate price range, 65c to $1.

For information about still other artificials, including spinner rigs and panfishing attractors, write to these Fred Arbogast subsidiaries: Prescott Spinner Co., 1000 Fairview Ave., Hamilton, Ohio 45015; and Arndt & Sons Inc., same address. Ask for catalogs.

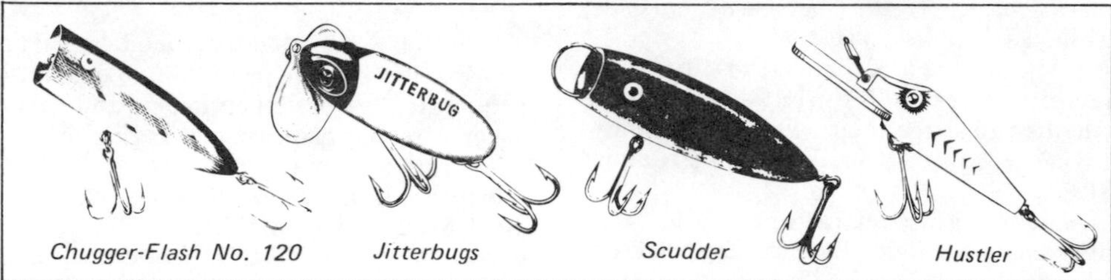

Chugger-Flash No. 120 Jitterbugs Scudder Hustler

**My Fair Lady Products**
**2031 Yosemite Blvd., Modesto, Cal. 95351**

Mike, the Fisherman's Lure, is made from plastic, weighs 1/3 oz., and is unique. Its manufacturer calls Mike "six lures in one." The illustration shows why. Choice of two hook-ups, one for shallow or surface action, one for trolling and deep diving. It can be worked to imitate natural or crippled swimming action, and it leaves a trail of attractive bubbles. Most unusual of all, Mike has a little compartment that can be opened for loading with BB shot for sound effects and extra weighting, or bait (worms, salmon eggs, etc.) for scent, or tiny sinkers for extra-deep running. Among battlers for which it's said to be effective are trout and black bass. About $2.98. Comes with instructions.

**Uncle Josh Pok Rind Baits**
**For Atkinson, Wisc. 53538**

This firm's products are probably the best known pork rind baits. They should be because they're an Uncle Josh specialty, and have been for years. Cut from high grade skins, they have the fluid movements of live creatures; and, being natural flesh, soft but resilient, they also resemble closely the body texture of many forms of forage food in appearance and feel. In one or another of their many Uncle Josh forms, pork rind baits can be used by themselves or in conjunction with artificials. They come in jars for toting in tackle boxes, ready to go as needed.

**Uncle Josh Striper and Muskie Strip, No. 70:** Designed in shape and size for husky fresh water and marine scrappers, it "dances" through the water. Also can be rigged for pike, bonito, salmon, cod, pollack, tarpon, school (bluefin) tuna, amberjack, others. Each strip is 5¼" by 5/8", available in white, green, red, yellow, black, blue. Five in a jar, price about $1.30.

**Uncle Josh Striper Hook Strip, No. 180:** These pork rind baits also come with hook incorporated. **No. 180** happens to be a tough bait designed specifically for salt-water service for stripers, tarpon, bonito, weakfish. It carries a 3/0 forged Nikkel hook that won't corrode, peel or discolor the rind. The strip is 5¼" long by 5/8" wide. Comes in white, red or yellow, four to a jar about $1.50.

**Uncle Josh Original Pork Frog:** In four

oz.) to a fly frog (**No. 21**, 1¼" by ½", ¼ oz.). Three to six per jar, according to sizes. All four are $1.30 per jar. Again according to sizes, pork frogs will take panfishes, black bass, trout, northerns, muskies, walleyes, bonefish, sea trout.

Uncle Josh Pork Chunk, **No 40:** An old favorite: stock can be whittled by anglers who like to shape their own. In white only, 1 3/4" to 1 1/8", ¼ oz. Four in a jar, about $1.30.

Among other attractors Uncle Josh offers: Blood Bait; Salmon Eggs; Trout Cheese Bait; Catfish Cheese Bait; Carp Fruit Bait; Uncle Josh Weedless Hooks. The firm's Pedigo Division (same address) produces spinner lures.

**Hopkins Fishing Lures, Inc.**
**1130 Boissevain Ave., Norfolk, Va. 23507**

Under the brand name No=Eql, Hopkins stainless steel lures have long been known to East Coast fishermen. In their smaller versions, the Hopkins Shorty, they have achieved recognition among inland anglers across the nation. (A Shorty broke the Arizona state record for striped bass with a 47½-pounder caught in the Colorado River.) The No=Eql lures resemble mullet and herring-type bait fishes. The Shortys are more compact and designed to simulate butterfish and shad-type forage fishes. All can be used in salt water or fresh for casting, jigging, trolling, ice fishing, and as a terminal lure in multiple rigs. Construction features: Indestructible stainless steel, can't rust—ditto their rings; high-gleam hammered finish, augmented by polished concave reflective surfaces at each end. Further, they have a natural swimming action that entices gamesters attracted by minnows and other live bait. They're available with plain or dressed hooks. Dressings include yellow feathers, white or yellow bucktail, red marabou feathers, squirrel tail, lime green fluorescent Dynel fibers. Their victims range from amberjacks to yellowtails in salt water, arctic char to yellow perch in fresh water.

**No—Eql and Shorty models:** The No=Eql lures range from the 1/3 oz. **No. 1** to **No. 4H,** 3¼ oz. (plain hook), and carry either a treble hook or a swinging single. Prices range from about $1.90 to $3.70. The Shortys go from 1/8 oz. to 2¼ oz., run from about $1.10 (plain hooks) to $3.55 (dressed hooks). They too come in single-hook and treble models.

**Hopkins Hammered Spoons:** Same rugged stainless steel construction as the No=Eql and Shorty, ported in the "gill" region" (an opening near front end) to permit passage of water for lifelike action and to reduce trolling drag. Available in polished stainless, all-white, and red-and-white finishes (colors are hard, baked-on-enamel), with a single fixed hook or swinging treble, plain or dressed hooks, ¼ oz. to 1 3/4 oz. Can be jigged or trolled (they don't twist lines). Price range, according to size and whether with plain or dressed hook, $1.50-$3.30. Also available in

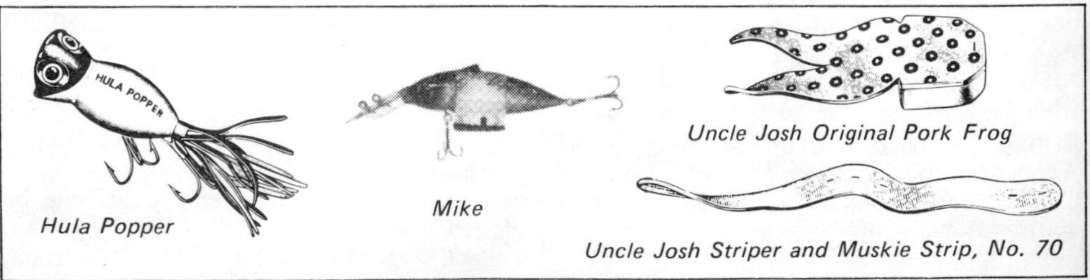


*Hula Popper*

*Mike*

*Uncle Josh Original Pork Frog*

*Uncle Josh Striper and Muskie Strip, No. 70*

some size range with a weed guard, about $2.00-$3.45.

Additionally, Hopkins offers the HammerTail series, with a highly reflective hammered finish, chrome-plated head molded on a stainless steel hook, dressed with bucktail. From 3/8 oz. and 2/0 hook to 1¼ oz. and 7/0 hook, choice of bucktail colors, about $1.30-$1.80.

**Earlybird Company**
**P.O. Box 1485, Boise, Ida. 83701**

Earlybird markets salmon eggs—red, cheese-color and natural—in jars under four Shoshoni labels—Renegade, Fireball, Rustler, and Clusters (Indian style), plus the Arctic label. They also offer jumbo salmon eggs in packets, same colors, as well as Shoshoni marshmallows, choice of three colors, in 1-lb., 8-oz. containers. Approximate price: $.95.

Also under the Shoshoni banner are spinner rigs that include the Propeller (shown), Renegade, Colorado, and Bear Valley designs. Among them are several finishes—nickel, copper, hammered brass, etc.—and treble hooks that are either plain or dressed (feathers, squirrel tail). Sizes range from 0 to 3/0, according to models. Approximate price: $3.75 a dozen.

**Creek Chub Bait Co.**
**Garrett, Ind. 46738**

Creek Chub produces a sizable family of plugs, including jointed models, in a variety of shapes and many color patterns (mackerel, frog, silver shiner, mullet, fluorescent green, etc.) for fresh-water and marine angling. Sizes range from 1/8 oz. and 1 5/8" to 4 oz. and 14" (Giant Jointed Pikie). Among them are top-water lures, medium runners, poppers, deep-runners. Some models have a metal lip for "depth control"; others feature a concave or beveled head, or propellers fore and aft for attractive commotion and sound effects. Armament varies between two and three treble hooks, according to models and sizes.

**Creek Chub Streeker:** For fresh or salt water, rust-resistant, 3/8 oz. or 1 oz., 3" or 4½", in half a dozen color schemes. An underwater rider with twin sonic propellers. Approximate prices: **No. S,** the 3/8 oz. size for spinning. **$2.65; No. LS, 1** oz., $3.90.

**Creek Chub Jointed Darter:** A top-water lure that darts, dives, wiggles. This **No. 4900-W** weighs ½-oz., comes in 7 color patterns. About $3.75.

Other Creek Chub lures include: 1½ oz., deep-running Wiggle Diver for salt water; the famous Straight Pikie, ½ oz. to 3½ oz., in use for fifty years for husky fresh water and marine species; Jointed Pikie, ½ oz. to 4 oz., for fresh and salt water—a world record 69-lb. 15-oz. muskie was taken on this one; Cray-Z-Fish, ¼ oz., a deep-running imitation of a crayfish for walleyes, bass, pike, others; and the ½ oz. Tiny Tim, a bottom-bumper for deep feeders.

**John J. Hildenbrandt Corp.**
**Box 50, Logansport, Ind. 46947**

Spinner lures carrying the brand name Hilde's are the specialty of this house. The firm also manufactures spoons, weighted bass flies, spinners for rigging separately, and spinner-fly combinations.

**Hilde's Wee Willie:** "Small but very deadly." For trout, white bass, crappies, bream. Weighs ¼ oz. Tough vinyl skirt comes in six color schemes, including yellow and red/white, is replaceable. **WW-1N** has a bright nickel finish; **WW-1G** is gold. Hook size, **No. 4.** Price about 90c.

**Hilde's Jigolo:** For panfishes, white bass, trout, black bass. A deep-runner with vibrating action and lots of flash. Lure body

*No=Eql and Shorty*

*Hopkins Hammered Spoons*

*Renegade*

*Propeller*

*Creek Chub Jointed Darter*

Hilde's Skitter Spoon
Hilde's Jerk-Jigger
Lazy Ike Tail Shark
Lazy Ike Wigly Crawler
Johnson's Sprite

comes in six colors—nickel, shad flash, perch flash, spotted, tiger stripe, gold. From 1/4 oz. with No. 8 hook to 5/8 oz. with No. 6 hook. All cost about $1.25 each.

**Hilde's Skitter Spoon:** A bass-nailing weedless spoon in 1/4- and 3/8-oz. sizes. Solid brass, plated overall. Can be retrieved on top (its rear is weighted, or underwater. In nickel or gold, sharp No. 5 hook. Also available as a skirted model (choice of colors), about $2.05 and $2.15.

**Hilde's Jerk-Jigger:** For salt water—mackerel, bluefish, sea trout, redfish, others. Two models, 3/4 and 7/8 oz., with green, blue, or red head, bare hooks, about $1.65 each. Also in three skirted models, 3/4 oz. and 1 oz., same head colors, with fluorescent skirt of red, green or red/green, about $1.95. With nickel body, 7/8 oz., about $1.80.

**Lazy Ike Corp.**
**P.O. Box 1177, Fort Dodge, Iowa**

The name Lazy Ike needs no introduction to bass hunters and other fresh-water fishermen. Lazy Ike lures have been on the scene since 1939.

**Lazy Ike Wigly Crawler:** A sinking, soft-plastic lure with a spoonbill that makes the lure wiggle and wag its tail. For further action, the tail floats up off bottom. It wiggles enticingly even on slow retrieve, also can be fished on a straight, medium retrieve, or twitched along the bottom. Semi-weedless and semi-snagless, with two hooks, one in the rear for short-strikers. In 1/4- 3/8-, 1/2-, 3/4-oz. sizes and five—blue, red, black, natural, purple. Approximate price: $1.50.

**Lazy Ike Tail Shark:** Designed for heavy-duty fresh water assignments, salt-water service too—cohos, striped bass, offshore battlers. Has extra-strong 4X hooks, oversize screweyes, good balance. It's 2 1/2" long, weighs 1/2 oz., comes in twelve colors and combinations. Approximate price: $2.50.

Also from Lazy Ike, several other models that include Chug Ike (floating/diving), Flex Ike (jointed, floating/diving), Eliminator (plastic nightcrawler), Wigly Squid (soft plastic lure for casting, fresh-water and salt), Hippy Spinner, and others.

**Louis Johnson Company**
**1547 Old Deerfield Rd., Highland Park, Ill. 60035**

Johnson spoons have taken their place in nearly every phase of sport fishing, from spinning and spincasting fractional-ounce models to surfcasting along U.S. seaboards to chinook fishing in Alaska, not to mention waters in between.

**Johnson's Sprite:** "Granddaddy" of the line, for marine and fresh water action. Precision forged and cast like a bullet, Sprites come in two basic designs, weedless with bucktail and non-weedless. The former type is available in ten finishes, including chrome, gold, red/white, copper, blue mullet, green/white. **Nos. 1, 2** and **3** weigh 1/4, 1/2, 3/4 oz., respectively. 1 3/8 oz., with single or treble hooks. Finishes are chrome, brass, black nickel and 4 scale colors -- white, green, blue, yellow. Lucky Lujons have racked up an assortment of fresh-water and salt-water species, from pan-fishes and chinook salmon to mackerel and yellowtails.

Among other Johnson spoons are the Silver Minnow (weedless, can be fished with plastic worm), Silver Salmon Sprite (new, for chinooks, cohos, steelheads, others), and Bucktail Spoon (convertible between weedless and non-weedless).

**Rebel Lures**
**P.O. Box 1587, Fort Smith, Ark. 72901**

The red and blue word REBEL is the market banner of artificials made by this

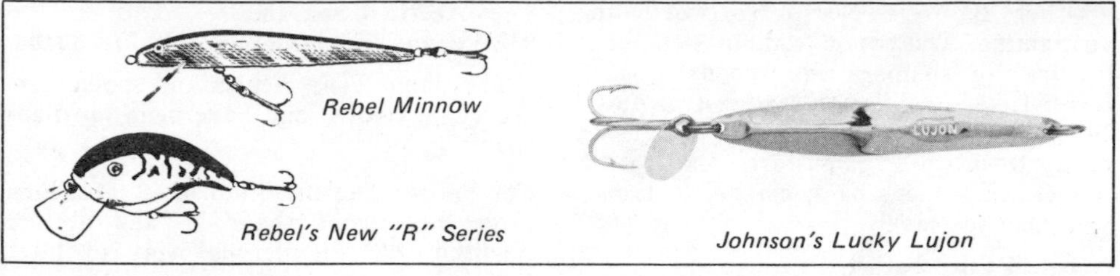

Rebel Minnow

Rebel's New "R" Series

Johnson's Lucky Lujon

division of Plastics Research and Development Corp. A cursory glance at the manufacturer's current list reveals some seventy-seven or so models in a price range from 85c to $3.50. Here are random representatives:

**REBEL Minnow:** This is probably the manufacturer's most famous lure: and, from the standpoint of number of users, its most popular too. There are several versions for fresh, and salt water, including at least a dozen floating, sinking, shallow- and medium-running types. Shown is the largest of the Minnow series, a versatile fresh and salt water model, 7" long, armed with two 3/0 tinned, extra-strong trebles, available in several color patterns. It comes in 1 oz. (**No. F400**, a floater) and 2-oz. (**S1400**, a sinker) weights, $3.50 each. Others in the Minnow series range from 1½" and 1/16 oz. (**No. F49**, a floater/shallow runner) to 5½" and 1 oz. (**No. SB1300**, a bucktail sinker/medium runner). According to models, they carry two or three short-shank bronze trebles, No. 10 to No. 2, with some available with salt-water hooks.

Added to those are four jointed "Broken Back" Minnows in the "J" series, floaters /shallow-runners, 1/8 oz. and 2½" to ½ oz. and 5½", and two models available with marine hooks: about $2.35 to $3. Also the Super Minnow, extra-weighted for casting, with two swinging trebles, for fresh water or salt water (tinned hooks). Two versions: **No. WX8000,** 1¼ oz., 5½", 1/0 short-shank hooks: **No. WX8900,** 2 oz., 7", 3/0 long-shank hooks. Prices about $3 and $3.50.

**REBEL Destroyer:** In two versions, both with a ball bearing swivel, available in a choice of several colors. The only difference is that Destroyer II, shown, has two spinner blades, whereas the nearly weedless Destroyer I carries just the larger of the two. Prices about $1.95 and $1.85. Both also are available as a Destroyer Witch version, with long rubberband "legs" for additional attraction.

**REBEL'S New "R" Series:** Designated as the Wee-R, Mini-R and Maxi-R. Six models, three floaters, three deep-runners, all with the manufacturer's exclusive tuned sound chamber noise-maker. According to models, they travel from 0'-6' and as deep as 20-plus feet. Sizes range from 3/8 oz. and 2" to 7/8 oz. and 3". All carry two triple-strength bronze trebles. Hooks go from No. 6 to No. 3. Price range, about $2.35 to $3.

Also under the Rebel banner: Bonehead Poppers; Skippers; top-water lures; Rocket and Racket Shads.

**Bay De Noc Lure Co.**
**P.O. Box 71, Gladstone, Mich. 49837**

**Swedish Pimple:** Used in Sweden for more than fifty years, fresh water and salt, summer and winter. An excellent jigging lure, proven effective for trout, salmon, walleyes, black bass, northerns, panfishes, many marine species. Forged from solid copper or brass, available in five lustrous metallic finishes (anglers' preference runs to nickel) and now in color tones, from 1/10 oz. at 98c to 2 oz. at $3.20. There's also a **No. 1** series, 1/7 oz. to 1/3 oz., about $1.15 to $1.45. These are fluted for a special wiggle, whether cast, trolled or jigged.

**Do-Jigger:** Proven effective as an ice fishing jig, equally productive as a spin-casting spoon in summer. Generally preferred for perch, walleyes, northerns, trout. Its action is a lazy but flashing flutter. Comes in nickel or gold finish, with highlight stripe of fluorescent orange or yellow, gold-plated, extra-strong hooks, **No. 8** or **No. 6**, 1/16 oz. and 1/5 oz., about 85c to $1.20.

Other Bay De Noc lures worth investigating: The Svede (combines the best features of spinners and spoons); Coho-Laker Taker (trolling or casting); Swedish Ol' Wive (an old Swedish spoon design for husky fresh water gamesters); the Noblur (for casting—black bass, northerns, trout, and other species).

**Normark Corporation**
**1710 E. 78th St., Minneapolis, Minn. 55423**

Normark markets a sizable fleet of artifical baits under the brand name Rapal. Coming from Finland, they're earning an ever-widening reputation in U.S. freshwater and marine fishing theatres. You might want to note that Normark also produces ice angling gear, fishing knives, other accessories.

**Original Floating Rapalas:** Crafted in Finland by Lauri Rapala & Sons. They feature: Stainless steel wire encircling select basal wood; rugged, transparent outer sheath; lifelike, reflective scales; needle-sharp hooks secure to the wire reinforcement; careful balancing. Each is hand-tested in a tank at the factory for proper action. Original Floating Rapalas have taken muskellunge, trout, big black bass, walleyes, many kinds of marine scrappers. Overall specifications: Lengths, 2" to 7"; hook arrangements, two No. 10 trebles to three No. 1 trebles; gold, silver, blue, fluorescent red, some in combination. Model shown is nicknamed "the $2 lure."

**Jointed Rapalas:** Two models, **Nos. 9** ana **11**, are new in the line. Finnish-made, they float at rest, slink just under the surface when retrieved. Varying retrieve speeds can work them effectively in several ways. **No. 9** is 3½" long, has twin **No. 5** trebles. **No. 11,** is 4 3/8", carries two **No. 3** trebles. Both come in silver, gold, blue or fluorescent red.

**Tony Acetta & Son, Inc.**
**932 Avenue "E", Riviera Beach, Fla. 33404**

The name Tony Acetta and spoon lures are synonymous, and have been for many years.

**Pet Spoon:** The most famous Acetta lure, used throughout the U.S. and abroad, credited with numerous wins in local, national, international contests. The secret of its success is a unique design imparting a wounded-minnow action. Features are very rugged construction, extra-strong, needle-sharp hooks. In four versions: Standard—for trolling or casting, can be used with pork stripe; F model—hand-matched feathers conceal the single fixed hook; Double Thick T Model—same body as the standard, but with a swinging treble; GF Model—addition of a weedguard makes this a weedless, snagless, feather-dressed lure with a single fixed hook. Overall specifications-range of the four versions: From the **No. 12** Standard, 1/24 oz., 1¼", No. 4 hook, to the **No. 23 F** Model, 6½ oz., 10½", 14/0 hook. Available colors, according to models, are chrome, 24-k. gold, glow red/green, glow green/white, all white, red, black, fluorescent green, yellow. Overall range of prices among the versions, $1.25 to $7.90.

**Tony's Spoon:** A versatile lure in two models. The weedless-snagless version (shown) has a weed guard and a single fixed hook hidden among feathers (white, red, fluorescent green, black, yellow), comes in chrome or gold finish. Sizes, 1/8 oz. and 1¼" to 5/8 oz. and 2 3/4", hooks 1/6 to 5/0, prices about $1.50 to $2. The other version of Tony's spoon incorporates these details: Weights, 1/8 oz. to 1 1/8 oz.; blade lengths, 1¼ to 2 3/4"; swinging treble hook, **No. 5** to **No. 1**; chrome or gold finish; trailing streamer in red/white, yellow or black/white. Prices, about $1.40 to $2.35.

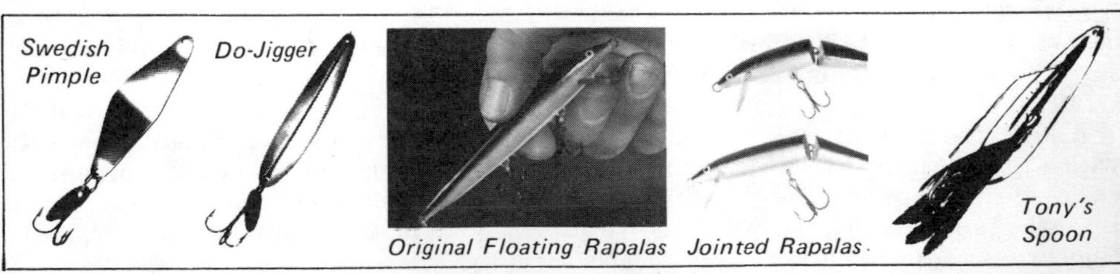
*Swedish Pimple* · *Do-Jigger* · *Original Floating Rapalas* · *Jointed Rapalas* · *Tony's Spoon*

**Sheldons', Inc.**
**P.O. Box 508, Antigo, Wis. 54409**

Under the brand name Mepps, Sheldons' produces a large array of spinners that have become tackle box standard lures among uncountable fresh-water anglers from coast to coast.

Also from Tony Acetta & Son: The Jigits and Jigaroos, each in seven sizes, jigs for salt and fresh water; Spin Dodger, a weedless plastic worm; Bonefish Special; and the famous Jigit Eel, up to 12" long, for bluefish, striped bass, kingfish, other marine species.

**Maxwell Mfg. Co.**
**801 W. 8th St., P.O. Box 649, Vancouver, Wash. 98660**

You may know this company better by its products brand name, Grizzly Fishing Tackle.

**Original Andy Reekers Trolling Spoons:** In service for years along the Pacific seaboard, U.S. and Canada, these spoons have spread throughout the Midwest and Canadian lakes eastward to New York and Florida. That provides a clue to their versatility. They're reported highly effective for lake trout, as well as other fresh-water targets and marine game fishes. Ten sizes: **No. 0,** 1" blade, to **No. 8,** 4 3/8" blade. Standard finishes are brass, flame and chartreuse. Special finishes are chrome, copper, neon green, neon blue, neon red. Approximate prices, 80c to $1.95.

**Grizzly Trout Teaser:** Not only for trout, but also for panfishes, shad and kokanees. Available in plain or hammered pattern. Standard finishes are brass, copper, flame, chrome, chartreuse. Special fishes are 50/50 brass, 50/50 copper, sunrise, redhead, flame outside/pearl inside. Approximate prices, 80c and 90c.

Also from Maxwell: A wide assortment of spinners (Colorado, Apollo Weighted, Indiana, Doc Shelton Vibr-o-Lite, others), trolling rigs, terminal tackle items, accessories such as landing nets and gaffs.

**Mepps Aglia, the original French spinner:** Its range of sizes, 0 through 5, 1/12 oz. to 1/2 oz., make this a lure that can be handled by fly rods, ultra-light spinning rods, spincasting rods—sizes 0 and 1 for the first two, 3 through 5 for the third. There are blade colors for bright days/clear water, dark days/murky water, night angling: Gold, silver, copper, red/white, black, fluorescent red, black/white, chartreuse. Prices, about $1.20 to $1.60. Also available with a dressed hook (white, gray, brown or black), or with a streamer (white, purple or yellow), both types in the same sizes as the first Aglia, about $1.75-$2.30 each.

**Mepps Giant Killer:** For casting or trolling, fresh water or salt, and husky opponents. Lure has a 3" blade, weighs 1 oz., carries double-strength 4/0 Lion D'Or treble hook. Blade colors are plain gold, plain silver, gold with red dots, silver with red dots, fluorescent red, blue or black. Price, $2.55. Also available with dressed hook double-tied, permanently dyed white, red, brown, yellow, black or yellow), weighs 1 oz., $3.75.

Other notable Mepps spinners: Comet, Black Fury, Aglia Long, Kriss, Musky Killer, Aglia Tandem Mino-Spin, Aglia Mino Jig.

**Lure Corporation**
**20800 Chesley Dr., Farmington, Mich. 48024**

Happy Hooker (not the two-legged kind): Two sizes, **No. GX-370,** 3 3/4" with 1/0 treble, and **No. GX-280,** 2 3/4", 3/0 treble. Color patterns include: Plain silver, plain brass, two solid colors (red/white, green/yellow, etc.)—shown; and two colors, background and dots (silver/red

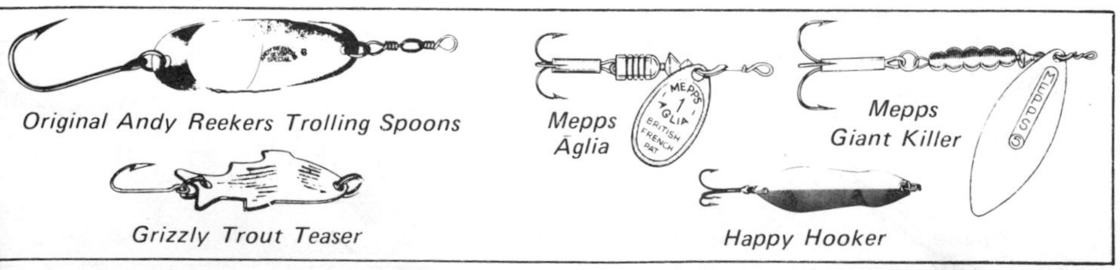

Original Andy Reekers Trolling Spoons
Grizzly Trout Teaser
Mepps Aglia
Mepps Giant Killer
Happy Hooker

dots, fire red/black dots, etc.). Approximate prices: **GX-370**, $2, **GX-280**, $1.60.

Kush Spoons in 6 sizes, all with swinging trebles: **No. 100**, 1/16-oz., No. 8 hook; **No. 200**, 3/16-oz., No. 4 hook; **No. 300**, 3/8-oz., No. 2 treble; **No. 400**, 3/4 oz., No. 2 hook; **No. 450**, 1¼ oz., 5/0 hook; **No. 500**, 2½ oz., 7/0 hook. Approximate prices, $1 to $3.40 each.

**Capt. Jim Strader's Recreational Development, Inc.**
**P.O. Box 4029, Tallahassee, Fla. 32303**

**Diamond Rattler:** In two sizes: 5/8 oz. for casting, 3/8 oz. for spinning, Each offered in six solid colors, plus frog and coach dog combinations. Each, $2.50. Also from Captain Jim Strader, the streamlined, fish-shaped Diamond Rattlesub (not shown), 3/8 oz. and ½-oz., both with two swinging trebles; in blue, silver, gold or bronze, about $2.50 each.

**Rattleworm Head:** A weedless sound chamber with a slip sinker inside for better casting. Not only activates worms, but also saves them. (One of these nailed a 13 3/4 bass in Florida's Lake Jackson.) Price about $1.75

**Carolina Miss:** A popping bug for bass, stream and lake panfishes. Tail is white rubber; hackle is black/white or black/yellow; body is yellow, white or radiant yellow. Price about $1.

**Salty Shrimper:** Rated as a popular artificial bait for seatrout, flounders, weakfish. In three sizes: ¼ oz., 2/0 hook, red head, choice of six body colors, tail is shrimp color, about 75c; 1 oz. size, 5/0 hook, red head, six body colors, shrimp-color tail, about 90c; 2½-in. size, six body colors, shrimp-color tail, about 90c. Tails are replaceable and available separately.

**No. 8NS High-Low Bottom Rig:** 15" overall, 40-lb. nylo-steel, two twisted metal arms, No. 5 nickel barrel swivel at one end, nickel interlock snap at the other, red fluorescent beads, about 45c. This is one of many ready-made rigs by Dragon Fly for marine species—bluefish, cod, pompano, flounders, mackerel, weakfish, etc.

**National Expert, Inc. (Nebco Lures)**
**2928 Stevens Ave. So., Minneapolis, Minn. 55408**

**Nebco Vibro-tail Swimming Spin & Minnow:** "A plastic lure that swims" with a lifelike tantalizing action of its tail, simulating a minnow. Made from plastisol, soft sturdy body. Vibro-tail is a patented Nebco feature. Body colors include brown, pearl shad, chartreuse, fluorescent yellow, black, also combinations. Blade colors include chartreuse, nickel, copper. Series designation is **VTS**. From ¼ oz. with single spinner to 3/4 oz. with tandem. Blades are Colorado pattern. Hooks range from No. 2 Aberdeen to 4/0 O'Shaughnessy. Price range: $1.55-$2.40, with extra minnow.

**Nebco Vibra-tail Swimming Jig & Minnow:** Same realistic Vibra-tail minnow in a different type of lure. Essentially the colors, plus purple and shrimp pink, for body and jighead. In 5 sizes: Mini, small, medium, large, medium salt-water, large-salt-water, 1½" and 1/16-oz. to 4¼" and 1 oz. Packaged as 1 or 2 jigs with 1 or 2 extra minnows, according to models, about $1.45 and $1.50.

**Nebco Ok Doke:** A senior member of the line that has accounted for a long list of fresh water and marine gamesters, black bass and northerns to striped bass and redfish. Body of tough Tenite plastic, won't crack, break, chip or peel. Color is molded-in, lasts the life of the lure. Ten colors, including metallic silver and gold, green scale; combinations with red or black spots.

*Diamond Rattler*

*Rattleworm Head*

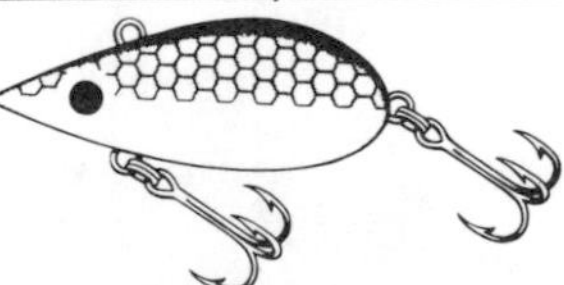

*Nebco Vibro-Tail Swimming Spin & Minnow*

*Nebco Vibra-tail Swimming Jig & Minnow*

*Nebco Ok Doke*

Sizes: **No. 20**, 1½", 1/16 oz., for flyrod, other ultra-light tackle; **No. 21**, 2¼", 1/8 oz., for spinning; **No. 22**, 3", ¼ oz., casting or trolling. Prices about $1.80 and $1.90.

Also from Nebco: Dixie Spoons—hammered nickel, copper or brass, with color inserts (seven colors), 1 7/16", 1/8 oz., to 2½", 7/8 oz., for trout, walleyes, northerns, redfish, cohos, others. Nebco Spoon Flies—combinations of spoons and flies in a choice of finishes and colors, all 1¼", 1/16 oz.

**Fish-IT, Division of IT Inc.**
**P.O. Box 1033, Torrington, Conn. 06790**

This company spawns unusual, innovative and interesting ideas for fishing lures. For instance:

**ReDo-IT Decal Tape:** A permanent, plastic, stick-on, water/abrasion-resistant tape in some seventeen colors and patterns—silver, gold, white, green, red, etc., in solid colors, multi-stripe, checks, fluorescents, etc. Apply it to refinish old lures and change new ones, in the field or at home. Single tape, about 15c.

**Catch-IT Change-A-Plug:** For salt water or fresh. Comes as twin plug units that can be fished separately or joined, rigged for four different actions—diving, popping, etc. Transparent cylinders come with changeable colored plastic liners, or they can be filled with water or sand for ballast. Or the twins can be covered with ReDo-IT for many color pattern variations. All kinds of opportunities for experimentation. Change-A-Plug comes with twin components, three of Fish-It's Snap-On Hooks, two multi-colored ReDo-IT tapes, colored plastic liners. In three sizes—½-, 5/8- and 3/4-inch diameters, about $2-$2.50. Hooks are cadmium-tin-plated on steel for salt water.

**Catch-IT Change-A-Lure:** Four designs to cover all the major fish-getting motions of lures: **Mark I**, specialized for high-speed trolling; **Mark II**, customized for longer-range casting; **Mark III**, jerking, fluttering actions; **Mark IV**, weaving and wobbling. Each of the four comes in nine weights, ¼ oz. to 3 oz. All are made from heavy brass, with choice of bright, silver-like plating, gold finish, or clear white plastic coating. They come packaged as two similar forms, three Snap-On Hooks, two multicolored ReDo-IT decal tapes, about $2.35-$2.95. Also available singly, with one Snap-On Hook, one decal tape.

Also from Fish-IT: Gleam-N-Glo Activated Colors (thirty-two patterns); Aqua*Star*Plure colors ("color that starts under water"), 5 hues; Fish-Rite Lures (nine irridescent patterns in gold and silver, embossed on mylar); and Snap-On hooks for replacements on lures, cadmium-tin-plated on steel, in singles and doubles, sizes No. 0, No. 2, 1/0.

**Zebco Division, Brunswick Corp.**
**P.O. Box 270, Tulsa, Okla. 74101**

Zebco adds lures to its big family of rods and reels. Here are some samplings:

**Zebco Doll-E-Pop:** New in the line. A top-water/sinking plug designed primarily for salt water action, notably with surface-feeding species. Reported deadly to bluefish and stripers. Its scoop mouth makes it rise and break the surface like a jittery bait fish when retrieved. An internal rattler adds attractive sound effects. In six color patterns and four sizes, with bucktail-dressed treble: ½, 3/4, 1, 1½ oz. The ½ and 3/4 ouncers come recommended for schooling black bass, fresh water stripers. Price range: $1.85 to $2.25.

**Zebco Super Secret:** Also new to the line, Zebco's contender in the "pregnant plug" craze, with hardened aluminum diving lip. A floater/diver that can be twitched on the surface or retrieved seductively around

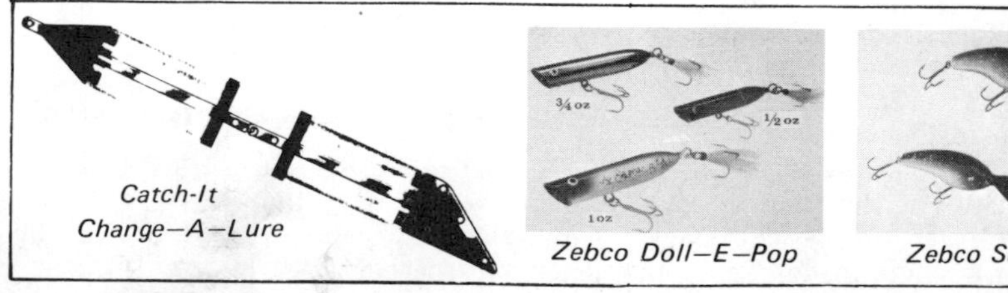


Catch-It Change–A–Lure

Zebco Doll–E–Pop

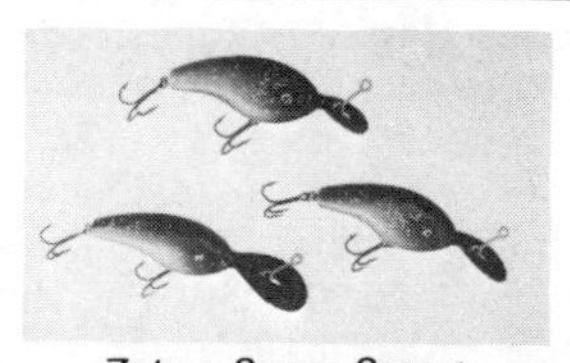

Zebco Super Secret

weed beds, along rocky outcroppings and other hiding places. Weighs 1/2 oz., with No. 5 hook, comes in twelve color patterns. Choice of three lip sizes: S (shallow), causes lure to go down to about 3 or 4 feet; M (medium), to approximately 6-8 feet; D (deep), to about 12-14 feet; all depths according to retrieve speeds. Price range: $1.85 to $2.25.

These lures also come from Zebco, variously for fresh and salt water angling: Top Secret (floating/diving), with or without skirt; Doll Fish (shallow- to medium-runner, with internal clicker); Shal-A-Minner (floating/shallow-running); Droop Snoop (floating/diving); Ditch Digger (floating/deep-diving); Zebco Z-Spin (spinner), plus other spinners; Ya-hoo (plastic worm body and hackle feather collor); and others.

**Storm Manufacturing Co.**
**P.O. Box 265, Norman, Okla. 73069**

ThinFin is this manufacturer's brand name. Among lures carrying it are Storm's Chug Bug, Silver Shad, Fatso (with two-tone rattle), Shiner Minnow, Hot's Tot, ranging in sizes from 1/4 to 5/8 oz., 2 1/2" to 3 1/2". Also in the line:

**Whiz Bang:** Capitalizes on the attraction of game fishes to sounds. It has Storm's exclusive VibraSonic action—motion plus sound. Twin rattles inside the lure's body generate both sound and a vibrating swimming movement for double attraction. Whiz Bang's measurements, 1/3 oz., 2 1/4". In sixteen color patterns—solid, dotted, metallic, two-tone. Price about $2.40.

**Bass Hog:** A spinner rig rated as nearly weedless and snagless because of design. Lead head comes in several chip-resistant colors (encased in resilient plastic against chipping). Skirt and blade also come in several colors. Shown is the tandem spin model. Also made in short-wire and long-wire models with a single blade. Tandem spin model runs at about $2.40. Other two models, about $2.30.

**Whopper Stopper Inc.**
**P.O. Box 1111, Sherman, Tex. 75090**

**Hellbender:** New in the line. Four sizes: **800 Series**, Magnum Hellbender, 7/8 oz., 5 1/8", running depth to 35 feet, for heavy casting, deep trolling; **900 Series**, Hellbender, 5/8 oz., 4 1/2", running depth to 25 feet, for casting, trolling; **1100 Series**, Midget Hellbender, 1/2 oz., 3 3/4", running depth down to 15 feet, for casting, trolling, light tackle; **Series 1000**, Baby Hellbender, 1/4 oz., 3", running depth to 8 feet, for spinning, general light tackle fishing, trolling. In thirty four color schemes. All sizes at about $2.25 each.

**Salty Boogie:** 3 oz., 4 1/2", a compact plug with minimum wind resistance for long casts, plus a natural swimming motion and continuously vibrating action. For marine battlers—tarpon, striped bass, bluefish, snook, channel bass, kingfish, etc. Body of

Bass Hog — Hellbender — Salty Boogie — DeLong Night Crawler — DeLong Frogs

**DeLong Frogs:** No matter how they land in the water, they flip right side up by themselves. Floating, weedless. Dark tough Tenite plastic with permanent finish, rugged hardware, 3/0 hooks in 3X strength. In ten colors, including menhaden, mullet, shad, butterfish. Approximate price, $3.

Also from Whopper Stopper: Hellcat (for all game species); Hellraiser (spinning, casting); Dirtybird (surface and sub-surface); plastic worms and eels; Stinger (jig and worm rig); Whirlybird Weedless Jig-Spinner lures; Bayou Boogie (fractional-ounce plugs for spinning, casting, trolling).

**DeLong Lures, Inc.**
**85 Compark Rd., Centerville, Ohio 45459**

DeLong calls its lures "naturalized," which is to say that they're lifelike simulations. Some samples, with approximate prices:

green with black spots or brown with black spots. Large frog (**No. 508**) 2½", 1/0 hook, $1.75. Medium size (**No. 504**), 2", No.1 hook, $1.10. Tiny frog, 1 3/8", No. 6 hook, $1.10 (two in package).

**DeLong Crawfish:** Three sizes. Large crawdad (**No. 208**), perfectly detailed, olive green or olive brown, designed to "crawl" belly down, No. 1 double hook rides up, 3½", ½ oz., $1.50. Medium size (**No. 217**), 2½", 1/6 oz., brown or olive green, No. 2 double hook, $1.10 (two in package). Small crawfish (**No. 207**), 1 5/8", 1/8 oz., light brown only, one No. 6 hook, $1 (three in package). There are also tadpole sizes.

**DeLong Night Crawler [No. 110]:** 4½", red or black, on long-shank hook (choice of 1/0 or No. 1), 65c (two in package).

Also from DeLong: Act-Alive and Specialty Worms; Kilr Worms (rigged); Kilr Eel and Spring Lizard (salamander), both rigged; Flash Minnows, with spinner; assorted insects; Action-ized Jigs and Spinners; simulated Perch Eyes. Also, the Bluegill Assortment ($1.20) for bream and sunfishes. Contains: 4" worm, 2" tiny eel, cricket, roach and sand ant, all with hooks.

**Lindy/Little Joe Fishing Tackle**
**Route 8, Box 488, Brainerd, Minn. 56401**

With this firm the accent is on lures, a large squadron of them in numerous types.

**Lindy Fuzz-E-Grub Spin:** Combines the magnetism of both jig and spinner. Body carries a marabou tease tail, comes in eight colors and combinations—spinner blades in different colors too. Sizes, 1/6 oz. to 3/8 oz. Rated as a versatile artificial, fresh water and salt, nailing panfishes, crappies, bass, walleyes, northerns, sea trout, redfish, weakfish. Approximate prices, 85-96c.

**Lindy Dingo Jig:** Always lands upright, "sits like a live critter," hook and pulsating tail always up. Unique collar has gill-like action for added attraction. Practically rock-proof, can be tipped with live bait. In eight bright, eye-catching color combos, including perch and hot yellow/tiger: ¼, 3/8, ½ oz. Approximate price, all sizes, 96c.

**Lindy Worms:** Plastic worms are a must in black bass anglers' tackle boxes, fishes alone or in combination with spinners, and other artificials. Lindy's are in 6-, 7¼- and 9-in. lengths, nine colors that include purple, chameleon, red, blue. Nine-inchers come four per pack; 7¼" size, six per package; 6" length, eight. Suggested list price per packet, $1.05. Also offered in rig packs, same numbers of worms, plus two hooks and two sinkers (colored to match the worms), at about $1.35 per package. Lindy worms have realistic segments, like the real thing, and feature the manufacturer's unusual Swipe Tail. In the spring of 1974 Ferret, fractional-ounce Spinning Dodger, and 1/16 oz. Worth Fly Rod Spoon.

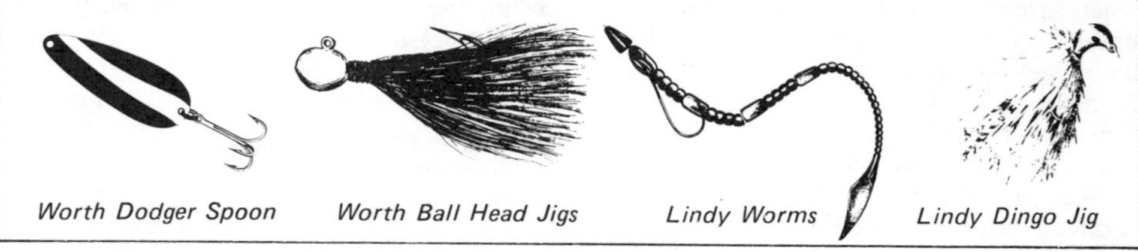

*Worth Dodger Spoon* · *Worth Ball Head Jigs* · *Lindy Worms* · *Lindy Dingo Jig*

**The Worth Company**
**P.O. Box 88, Stevens Point, Wis. 54481**

It can be said that spoons and spinners are Worth specialties, and in their catalogue you'll see page after page of them, along with numerous other items that include ready-made leaders, rigged worms, weedless hooks and fly leaders.

**Worth Dodger Spoon:** A famous casting spoon in six sizes, from 1/8 oz., 1 3/16", with No. 10 hook, to 3/4 oz., 3½", with 1/0 hook. Some twenty-two finishes and colors, including plain plated (also in a hammered finish), green/white stripe, yellow/black spots, fluorescent orange/white strip, etc. Approximate prices, 40c to 65c. The same general design is available as the 1/32-oz.

**Worth Ball Head Jigs:** You can get them in: six sizes—1/64 oz., No. 8 hook, to ½ oz., 3/0 hook; twelve colors; three streamer styles—bucktail, feather, marabou. Approximate prices, 45-65c.

Lindy Fuzz-E—Grub Spin

Heddon's Sonic Series

Lindy worms helped contender Al Lindner out-fish a field of 191 angling pros to win the Tennessee Invitational Tournament conducted by Bass Anglers Sportsman Society (BASS).

**Lures by Heddon**

In a way, lures were the original name of the game at Heddon, for the company's founder, James Heddon, was a U.S. pioneer in development of artificials. Listed here are random representatives of the present Heddon family. Construction is tough plastic, colors molded in.

**Heddon's Sonic Series:** Five lures, for all fresh water game fishes. They feature a unique resonator fin generating a high-frequency sound "heard" and felt by fishes. A mirror-like flash is another attraction. For example: **No. 325,** the Ultra Sonic, 1 1/8", 1/8 oz., two No. 8 trebles. Color choices are black, perch, shad, yellow, redhead, coach dog. Price, about $1.61.

**River Runt Spooks:** Based on Heddon's famous River Runts. They sink slowly, have a fast wiggling action on retrieve. For bass, crappies, steelheads, walleyes, pickerel, trout, other fresh-water gamesters. **No. 9010,** Midget River Runt Spook, is $2\frac{1}{4}$", weighs 3/8 oz., carries two No. 2 trebles, with a choice of six color patterns, $1.61. Also in three other sizes, $\frac{1}{4}$ to $\frac{1}{2}$ oz.

**From Cotton Cordell**

A good guess is that anglers in the South, Midwest and Southwest contributed the most toward Cotton Cordell lures becoming known. In any case, the firm sires a very large family of tough-plastic and realistic soft-plastic artificials for fresh-water and marine fishing.

**Big O, Series 8300:** This is the salt-water version of a fresh-water lure that literally became a legend in its time, the Big O. The marine edition also has its patented Sling Shot feature—a weight that shifts aft to add casting momentum, then settles into a retrieve position for a lively swimming action. The **8300** Big O weighs about 2 oz., has a blue back and white body, sells for about $3.50.

Other Cotton Cordell lures for salt water include: Blue Striper, **5400 Series,** 1 oz., about $2.95, for bluefish and other marine battlers, as well as striped bass; a surf lure called Plopper, **6900 series,** $1\frac{1}{2}$ oz., with "fish-caller rattle," about $3.25; Sea Hag, **Series 9100,** a long-casting wiggler suggested for bluefish, striped bass, and other toughies, about $3.50; Pencil Popper, **6700 Series,** for surf and inlet casting, with the Cordell brass hook anchor, about $3.50.

Cotton Cordell soft-plastic baits include a big fleet of worms in a variety of types, lengths and colors, as well as simulated lizards, spinner combinations, etc. Prices are competitive and start at about $1.

**Tiny Pigtail Spinner, Series TGS18:** 1/8 oz., a small, lively spinner teamed with a 2" Pigtail teaser (choice of colors), $1, packed with two extra tails.

**Tattletail Worms:** In 6" and 8" lengths, fifteen different colors. Both lengths, about $1 per pack of 6.

**Gladding-South Bend Lures**

The Doodly Bob from Gladding's Glen L. Evans Lure Div.: Combines the time-proven cherry bobber with a prismatic Electolite flashing helix for a flashing, twisting, squirming action that begins

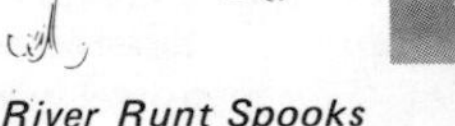

River Runt Spooks

Big O, Series 8300

Gladding-South Bend Wood Lures
Oreno label

instantly on retrieve. In nickel and gold/brass patterns.

**Gladding-South Bend wood lures:** There are fleets of these carrying the long-known Oreno label—Bass Oreno series, Spin-Oreno series, etc. These, along with the Midge-Orenos and Babe-Orenos, all are in Gladding's Magnum Bass Tackle classification because of their effectiveness with black bass, but they take other fresh water species and marine scrappers too. Lengths go 2-2 3/4", weights from about 1/4 oz. to 1/2 oz. All carry two treble hooks, from No. 6 to about No. 1, and are available in several color patterns.

Also among the Gladding-South Bend wood lures are the Spin-I-Diddee and Nip-I-Diddee series. Lures in both groups are armed with treble hooks, carry little flashing propellers fore and aft for added attraction, are offered in several color patterns. They also are classified as Magnum Bass Tackle (for lunker-size black bass). Spin-I-Diddee is 3 3/8" long, weighs 1/4 oz., has two No. 4 trebles, and is designed for bass, pickerel, channel bass, pike, weakfish, many other fresh and salt water species. Nip-I-Diddee is 3" long, weighs 5/8 oz., carries three No. 4 trebles, and will take the fishes listed for the Spin-I-Diddee.

**Glen L. Evans Squirm-Worm:** A unique attractor combining the proven effectiveness of a lifelike plastic with the rotating flash of a metallic helix.

**Lures by Gudebrod**

Gudebrod's fame has been based solidly on its fishing lines, but the old firm also produces artificials.

**Gudebrod Goodie:** An underwater swimmer with an unusual open-mouth design, minnow-like irridescent finish, fast fibrating action. For fresh and salt waters, 2 7/8", 1/4 oz., about $1.95.

**Gudespoons:** Spoons are all-purpose lures, among the oldest artificials in fresh water and marine fishing. Gudespoons are of solid brass with a highly polished nickel-chrome finish, extra-strong O'Shaughnessy hooks. In sizes for trout to tuna, 3/16 oz. and 2 1/2" to 1 1/2 oz. and 6" (overall), about $1.20 to $2.20.

**Gudebrod Trouble Maker:** A surface plug for fresh and salt water. Floats at rest. On retrieves the cupped head can generate a delicate popping sound on quiet fresh water or stir up an attractive ruckus for stripers and bluefish in the surf. Its transluscent scale finish looks like the real thing. Available in fourteen colors, with or without skirts, 1 1/2" and 1/8 oz. to 5 1/4" and 1 3/4 oz., about $1.65-$2.95 each.

**Lures from Garcia Corp.**

After browsing through other showrooms in this book you'd be surpirsed if Garcia **didn't** market lures too. But they do. A few samples follow. We have to add that Garcia prefers not to suggest consumer prices on **any** of its tackle items, so you'll just have to ask at the stores.

**Alou Eel:** One of the most famous Garcia salt water lures in the Northeastern U.S. A classic—and deadly—for striped bass. Shorter lengths take bluefish and virtually all fresh water and marine gamesters. A very lifelike imitation, for trolling and casting. In 8" (3/4 oz.), 10" (1 1/2 oz.), 12 1/2" (3 oz.) sizes, in eel skin blue, red, amber, natural gray, black. The Tube Alou is a tough, rubber, surgical tube version, a killer for bluefish, striped bass, king mackerel, barracuda, and other salt-water scrappers. Comes in red or black, 1 1/2, 3 and 6 oz.

**Garcia Silver Jigging Rig:** You can jig it, troll it, cast it. Designed for gamesters feeding just below the surface, its dancing silver tubes look like a small, isolated school

Glen L. Evans Squirm-Worm — Gudebrod Goodie — Gudespoons — Gudebrod Trouble Maker

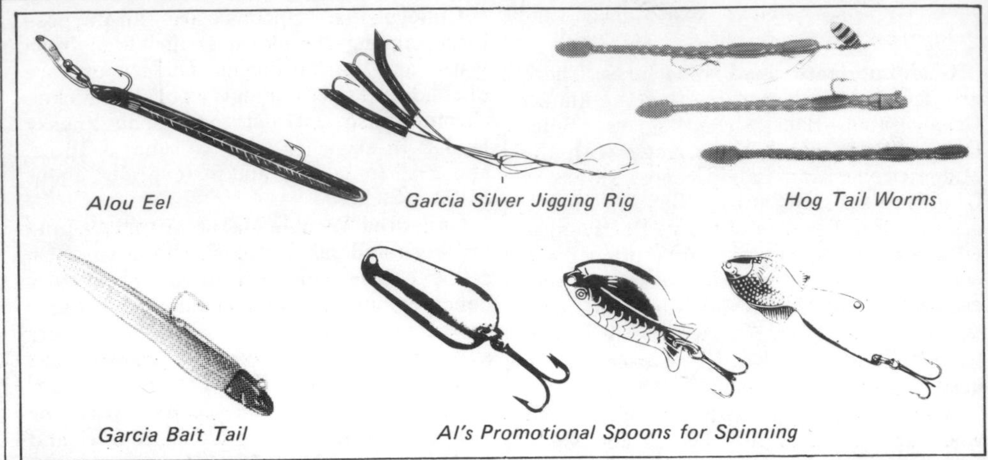

Alou Eel — Garcia Silver Jigging Rig — Hog Tail Worms

Garcia Bait Tail — Al's Promotional Spoons for Spinning

of bait fish—silversides, sand eels, etc. Will take sea trout, mackerel, yellowtails, shad, bluefish, fluke, etc. In silver color only, with No. 4, No. 1 or 5/0 hooks.

**Garcia Bait Tail:** Virtually a universal attractor. Except for billfishes, there probably isn't a popular sport species it hasn't nailed. It's so effective that the late Al Reinfelder devoted an entire book to bait tail fishing. In five sizes, 1/8 oz. to 2 oz., in a wide range of colors. Comes with extra tail. Also available as the 3/8 oz. Shrimp Bait Tail, for bridge fishing, casting, trolling and jigging wherever shrimp are found.

**Hog Tail Worms:** Soft-plastic, wiggly, for bass, with flavor and scent molded in. Lengths are 5½", 7", 9¼", in red, purple, black, yellow, blue or plum. Available unrigged and rigged.

**Also from Garcia:** Spinners, including the Abu-Reflex; Flash Buck (bucktail); Sierra Spoon; Alta Minnow (spinner and soft-plastic minnow); Veltic Spinner (fresh water); Eelet (for trout, bass, northerns); Muddler (soft-plastic minnow); and others.

**Al's Goldfish Lure Co.**
**516 Main St., Indian Orchard, Mass. 01051**

Al's Promotional Spoons for Spinning: twenty shapes, in nickel or 24-karat gold finish, each with a swinging treble; about 55c.

Al's Goldfish Lure Co. has a sizable collection of fractional-ounce top-water, swimming, popping, deep-running, minnow-type and floating/sinking lures, 1 5/8" to 4½" long, ¼ to 3/4 oz., in various effective color patterns, for fresh and salt waters, all in durable plastic, from about $1.05 to $1.60 each.

# Fishing Accessories and Boat Gear 9

## ACCESSORIES AND BOAT GEAR

Any angling accessory, to be worthwhile, must make fishing either more effective or more enjoyable—or, better yet, both. You'll encounter numerous items that satisfy those cardinal requirements to one degree or another, and as you do you'll have to decide how well they fit into your *modus operandi*. An item that is indispensable to one angler may be secondary to another, useless to a third. If you keep utility and enjoyment in mind you will save yourself some money along the way. And when you decide that an item fills the bill in one way or another, buy it. Chances are it will pay for itself many times over.

There are accessories whose use and value are shared generally, whatever the kind of fishing done. Then there are accessories that are placed in the essential category in relation to types of fishing. We'll concentrate on those two groups.

### Community Inventory

A detail that may be overlooked, for a while anyway, by inexperienced fishermen is one we'll call a utility kit. It's not a piece of baggage to be toted separately, but a small collection of items for which some room should be reserved in a tackle box. It can be useful in the field, notably for making emergency tackle repairs.

The kit's components vary according to kinds of fishing, but here are some general suggestions: (*1*) A roll of electrician's tape for temporary securing of loosened rod guides or defective reel seats; (*2*) a bottle of clear nail polish for finishing touches to knots and splices, as well as for emergency repair of guide wrappings that have started to unwind; (*3*) whatever lubricant and small tools are needed for servicing of reels (see section on the care of tackle); (*4*) a couple of corks in which to imbed loose hooks before they stick into fingers; (*5*) some rubber bands in different sizes for various uses; (*6*) two or three pieces of clean cloth for the equipment, plus a few paper towels for the hands; (*7*) a couple of small plastic bags for little, extra odds and ends; and (*8*) a bottle of colored nail polish for marking lines—other than fly lines—at intervals to show how much yardage is out; this is mainly a salt water gimmick for trolling and jigging. It goes without saying that if you do any night fishing you should carry a flashlight—and check its batteries regularly. Some fishermen also include an insect repellent as part of their utility kit.

Every boat should carry a first aid kit. Shoreside and inland fishermen will have to be guided by common sense and conscience. In our opinion they should have one if any fishing is done at night or in lonely areas or beyond access to a telephone or the police. The need may never arise in a lifetime of angling; but a first aid kit is like insurance, mighty good to have if it is needed. And it's cheap insurance at that.

As you probably know, there are compact first aid kits that fit readily in a tool box or even a large jacket pocket. Or you can assemble your own in a plastic box or waterproof bag. Basic items include: 1- or 1½-inch roller bandage; gauze pads in different sizes; adhesive tape; ready-made dressings like Band Aids; mercurochrome or tincture of iodine; burn ointment; smelling salts; motion sickness preventive; rubberbands; salt tablets; clean scissors or packaged razor blades for cutting gauze and tape; and maybe fine-tipped tweezers for splinters. Sundry other items are added as regions or possibilities dictate. These include a snake bite kit, water-purification tablets, and any special medication required by the owner. The important thing to remember about such a first aid kit is that it's *just* for first aid and for relatively *minor* injuries. Also, make sure you have sunburn cream or lotion.

## About Tackle Carriers

Nowadays a small book—well, a fat pamphlet, anyway—could be written about tackle boxes alone, so numerous are the different models. There's no debating the need for one. It's essential. The problem, if any, will come with choosing from among a large array produced by topflight manufacturers.

At the other extreme is an undersized tackle box. If there's to be an error in judgment, it might better favor a carrier that's a bit too big over one that could turn out to be a runt. If you have to walk around with pockets bulging with spools of line and other essentials you're defeating the purpose of a tackle box. Don't let economy sway you in the wrong direction. Considering the length of time you'll have that carrier, differences in prices for sizes are minor.

Equipment needs naturally vary among individuals and situations. How, then, can an individual decide on required size beforehand? An experienced fisherman knows his needs. For a beginner the judgment may be a little more difficult. As a guideline we generally suggest considering what gear will be needed for a single day's fishing of the kind ordinarily done. Accordingly, we further suggest considering these items in addition to the rod-reel-line outfit slated for use: (*1*) A spare reel loaded with line of a different strength than that already on the rod, or (*2*) an extra spool or two, preferably interchangeable on the reel currently in service, containing line in a different strength; (*3*) a reasonable selection of lures—plugs, spoons or whatever—judged to be best suited to that day's program, including a spare for each of the more frequently used artificials; (*4*) the required components of terminal tackle, including spares; (*5*) a couple of the useful tools which we'll list for you in a few minutes; and (*6*) that utility kit mentioned earlier, should you decide to assemble one.

Here are some details to consider when making your selection:

*Size:* We've already covered this one generally. Now we want to add a couple of specifics. Be sure there's enough storage space under the tray for the gear you'll be carrying. Pay attention to the clearance between trays and bottom to be sure it's sufficient for your extra reels. You want to be able to close the carrier. This should be no problem, except possibly with some of the smaller models.

*Construction:* There are carriers of aluminum and of steel. You may see an occasional one still made from wood. Such a model examined by this writer was really handsome, varnished to a faretheewell, with shiny brass corners and green felt lining, for fly fishermen who can afford a split-bamboo rod. But the majority of tackle boxes today are constructed from high-impact plastic. It's an excellent, extremely practical material. It can't rust or corrode (like steel), can't dent or crust (like aluminum), doesn't scratch or gouge easily (like wood), and will withstand a lot of rugged use. Moreover, colors are impregnated in it, so the boxes retain their neat appearance. Additionally, these modern materials are resistant to gasoline and motor oil, a detail of importance to outboard anglers.

The latch keeping the lid closed is more important than any lock. It must be sturdily constructed and dependable. You can imagine what it would be like to have a tackle box come open in transit and spew its contents all over the place. Don't worry about a lock. If a tackle box has one, fine, but don't veto it if it doesn't. About the best a lock can do is keep out kids at home and maybe discourage chronic borrowers. As for preventing theft, forget it. No one is going to steal anything if the box is beside you; and if you leave it unattended a thief will grab the whole works, in which case you deserve it.

While scouting around take note of any bonus features offered by the different manufacturers. These may be in design, construction of special items. For example, a battery-operated light for night use; of a carrier for shoreside fishermen that is styled like a cabinet, with vertical door and drawers, and that doubles as a seat. Special features are not necessarily a criterion for a good tackle box, and they usually add to the cost. You have to decide if they're worth it to you.

## Useful Tools, a Check List

1. Fisherman's pliers: Here's an accessory that has universal application in just about all kinds of angling, marine and fresh water. It incorporates two very good features, jaws for gripping and a cutter. The jaws have several uses—seizing a deeply imbedded hook to work it free of a fish, twisting wire, opening and closing a hook's eye when bridling it on another hook in tandem, and so on. The cutter is for working with lines and leaders of wire, and for cutting regular lines and leader material too. If you intend to fish with wire in any form, this tool is a must. It usually comes in a little holster that goes on the belt for easy access. Get a good one, and check it periodically for rust or corrosion.

2. Clipper: This is standard equipment for fly fishermen and fresh-water anglers in general. It's for trimming leader when changing lures, cutting lengths of leader material, and similar severing chores. It can perform similar services in marine fishing too, but you won't see it as often there. The simplest, cheapest form is one of those little pocket-size fingernail trimmers. Superior and more versatile is a clipper called Angler's Pal. In addition to cutting jaws it has an awl for clearing out clogged fly eyes and a little disgorger to aid in removing hooks.

3. A hone: Every fisherman's tackle kit should contain one for sharpening hooks. Small hones are made expressly for this purpose, and they come in mighty handy out in the field. They also can be used to touch up the edges on knives.

4. Knife: This implement offers such broad service in fishing that it could be considered a must. Anglers use knives for everything from

opening beer bottles (and cans) to filleting catches. There are dozens of suitable knives on the market in a variety of lengths, designs and prices. The type we advise against is a folding pocket knife. True, it takes up less space, but sooner or later it is going to be all boloxed up with fish slime and scales, sand, pocket debris, and rust or corrosion. Besides, the blades really aren't a practical size for all-round fishing use.

5. Fishing thermometer: Most anglers are aware that water temperatures play a vital roie in fishes' habits and movements. More and more are using that lore to their advantage. The knowledge is valueless without a means of measuring temperatures, of course, and fishermen's thermometers have been developed for this purpose, readily carried in a tackle box. These instruments are not yet in the category of a must, except among the more intent fresh-water rod-'n'-reelers, but we predict that someday a fishing thermometer will become a standard item of equipment. There are different prices, but it's not a costly item, and it could be worth its weight in gold to a fisherman who knows how to use it.

## Other Items

In this section we'll discuss accessories whose value ranges from helpful to essential, according to kinds of fishing.

1. Hand gaffs: Essentially a hand gaff is a large, sharpened hook secured in a handle of suitable length, and its purpose is to make certain the capture of a fish when brought close enough to plant its head or hook. In design these are what we call "straight" or fixed-head" gaffs (to separate them from the big flying gaffs we'll discuss elsewhere, whose head pulls free when planted). These gaffs come with handles of various lengths. There are short-handled models for attachment to the belt. These find favor among surfcasters and beach fishermen. There are also folding models for easier (and safer) toting. To those you can add straight gaffs with handles of varying lengths for boat or jetty service. Jetty jockies often require a gaff with a fairly long handle. There are also extra-long-handled models for bridge fishermen. Usually the heads or hooks are of stainless steel, and in any case must be kept needle-sharp. Handles may be of wood or appreciably lighter aluminum. Price tags naturally vary according to models and makers.

*Tip:* When buying straight gaffs for boat use be sure they have handles long enough to comfortably reach from cockpit to water.

Generally speaking, straight gaffs are more widely employed in marine fishing because of the greater number of larger gamesters, but they also see service in capturing the fresh water arena's big contenders. They're often needed for husky or ornery species. In jetty fishing, where an angler may not be able to get to the water's edge to seize his catch, a gaff can be a must. In other situations many veterans disdain the use of a gaff, either because they can't be bothered with one or just don't like it. Too, it's no easy matter to contain a struggling fish with the rod in one hand and swing a gaff with the other, especially in a lively surf. And it's a fact that ineptly swung gaffs have knocked more than one catch off the hook.

2. Landing net: This accessory performs the same function as a gaff, supplying a *coup de grace* to end a battle, but does it in more genteel

fashion. It's slipped under a fish *before* the catch is lifted from the water, to prevent escape by flipping off the hook—several species are adept at that. Basically there are two types of nets. One is a short-handled kind for easy carrying, popular among fresh-water fishermen. The other is a longer-handled model for boat use in salt or fresh water. And there are some with telescoping handles for different lengths. A good landing net is light (aluminum handles save weight), has a sturdy frame and netting material—usually a synthetic—that resists rot. Check to see if the bag is sufficiently deep to accommodate long-bodied catches.

3. Deboner: This is a specialized item for marine use. We include it here because it's a helpful tool with whole-fish bait. It consists of a hollow metal tube with a cutting edge at one end and a handle at the other. Its sole function is to remove the backbone of a whole-fish bait to give it a more lifelike flexibility when trolled. Deboners come in graduated diameters.

4. Catch carriers: You'll need some means of transporting your catch, and there are several options.

Simplest is what fresh-water anglers call a stringer, which is merely a length of stout twine or some clothesline swiped at home, or something similar but fancier bought in a tackle store. The fish are carried on it by feeding it through the mouth and out under a gill cover. For trout fishermen and other inland anglers catching small game there's the traditonal creel, which is merely a light wicker basket with an open hatch in its lid to accept fish. Also for these anglers is an accessory mentioned earlier, a canvas shoulder bag that totes both tackle items and a catch.

The most common carrier among coastal fishermen is a large, strong plastic bag. This is especially good because it allows icing-down a catch for trips home in warm weather. These bags are sold in many sport fishing ports, but if you're wise you'll keep a couple in your car, just in case. *Tip:* When there's a fairly long trip home in warm weather a good icing-down arrangement calls for two plastic bags. You fit one inside the other. In the innermost bag you place your fish, then fill the space between the two bags with ice. In this way water from melting ice doesn't get to the fish. *Another tip:* Always guard against spoilage in warm weather. Some species, particularly those with oil or soft flesh, can "go bad" practically as you look at them. And never place a catch, even with ice, in a car trunk in hot weather. Temperatures there can hit 130 degrees or higher. Keep the catch in the vehicle's back seat section, with windows open for circulation of air.

5. Live-bait carriers: Considerable fresh water and marine angling is done with live bait. Although other creatures—worms, crabs, eels, etc.—are utilized, much of this activity involves little forage fishes such as minnows and killies of mummichogs. The problem is to keep them alive until needed.

Simple and inexpensive, long in use by coastal fishermen but adaptable to fresh water as well, is the killy car, so named for the marine bait fish known as killies. This is just a small, simple, floating cage of wood, with a hatch on top for access to its contents. It's kept in the water, tied alongside the boat. A killy car is so inexpensive that it's hardly worthwhile building one at home.

## Some Optionals

Among accessories in this category you have to decide which are desirable in your kind of fishing. They're not essentials, but they can be helpful.

1. Hook disgorger or remover: The writer has never owned one, can't even recall the last time he saw one used. Nevertheless, it's a time-saving device when a fish takes a hook deep in the gullet. It also can prevent your being bitten by the likes of bluefish, pike and barracuda when trying to dislodge a hook or lure. Simplest is a metal tool about six inches long that is slid down the line to the hook to force it free. You can get bitten using the disgorger if you're not careful. Better is a device with extended jaws and a pistol grip. That will keep your fingers out of the critter's mouth.

2. Head lamp: The idea was borrowed from miners, who wear a light strapped to the head to leave their hands free. Same arrangement here, with power supplied by batteries. In our opinion this is a very worthwhile accessory for anyone doing appreciable night fishing. It leaves the hands free for changing lures, re-rigging, untangling backlashes, etc. But carry a flashlight too, as a spare, if nothing else.

3. Aid to fish-cleaning: Slippery fish can be a pain in the neck to dress for the table. Sure, you can use a piece of cloth for gripping, but there's a better arrangement. On the market is a cutting board with a strong clip to hold a fish firmly by the tail for surgery. You'd be surprised how much easier this makes cleaning and filleting. One thing is, it's for the smaller fishes. If you dress a tuna or steak a muskellunge you'll have to make other arrangements.

## Boat Gear

There's a fairly lengthy inventory of equipment, embracing items involved directly or obliquely in fishing. It isn't within this book's scope to delve into them in detail, but we'd be remiss if we didn't at least cite some of the major ones. Overall, their price range is from comparatively inexpensive to quite costly. It remains for prospective purchasers to decide if usage in their cases justifies the investment.

1. Rod holders: Among the more modestly priced items, these are a necessity aboard boat. Their function is to keep rod and reel outfits out of the way yet instantly available. They serve during stretches of inactivity and when trolling. A rod holder is essentially a long sleeve. Chrome-plated metal models cost more, but those of high-impact plastic serve well too. Ideally, they should have some kind of cushion lining to protect rods. They're available in two styles: One type, usually factory installed, is mounted flush with the deck alongside the cockpit. The other style, which purchasers can install themselves, is screw-mounted on a gunnel or coaming.

2. Fishing chairs, fighting chairs: Here you can invest modestly or go for a nice slice of cash.

Most expensive—they run to $1,000 and more—are the rugged models for cruiser installation. Features include heavy chrome plating, adjustable back and foot rest, a gimbal to support the rod, built-in rod holder, cushions and waterproof covers. They have a stout base that fits into a flush-mounted receptacle in the cockpit floor, and can be removed when desired. They rotate 360 degrees, but also have a locking mechanism to prevent swinging when not in use.

Smaller, lighter, much simpler—and therefore more within reach of budget-tied fishermen—are the portable fishing chairs. These resemble the tubular aluminum chairs seen on patios and beaches, except that they're equipped with a gimbal. They do not have the bigger chairs' refinements—adjustable back, foot and leg support, etc. But then, they don't cost as much either, and their portability is an advantage. They also are suited to small craft on which one of the larger chairs would be impractical or impossible. Too, with their mobility they double as cockpit furniture. It should be added, though, that their lightness and mobility are drawbacks when arguing with larger game fishes.

3. Any boat destined to engage battlers of respectable size or noted for their stiff opposition should carry at least a couple of straight gaffs in graduated sizes. Boats looking to heavyweights—big tunas, sharks, marlins, *et al.*—must carry at least one flying gaff. Two are even better: one is a spare, or, if the boat has a wide cockpit, one for each side. A flying gaff is distinguished from a straight or fixed-head gaff by its much larger size—the hook or head goes to 6 inches and more across the bend—by a barb to hold the hook in a fish, and by a head that pulls free when planted (a length of rope secures it to the boat). *Tip:* As with hooks, keep a flying gaff's point sharp, but don't sharpen its barb or it will cut its way free.

4. Outriggers: Solely for surface and shallow-depth trolling, these are two skinny arms that reach nearly horizontally to starboard and port when at work, swing back vertically when not in service. They make it possible to tow multiple rigs and keep them separated. They also troll lures and bait clear of the craft for boat-shy species. Each 'rigger has a halyard and clip. The fishing line goes into the clip for trolling, pulls free when a fish strikes. Outriggers come in different lengths and designs for boats in a range of lengths, outboards to large sport fishing cruisers. Chrome-plated hardware, aluminum poles and secure locking in the vertical position are features of good outriggers.

5. Downriggers: Relatively new in the scene, at least in their present refined marketed form, these are solely for deep to extra-deep trolling. You could call them underwater outriggers. Their purpose is to take bait or lures deeper than otherwise would be possible, and they come in handy for species such as lake trout, for which trolling may be 100 feet down or deeper. The basic downrigger consists of a heavy weight, resembling a cannonball, to take rigs down, a clip arrangement to hold a fishing line in trolling and release it when a fish hits (so the fish won't be encumbered by the weight), a spool on which the weight's line is stored, and a crank with which to lower and raise the "cannonball" to desired levels. The unit is mounted alongside the cockpit in the stern.

6. Gin pole: Essentially a vertical boom going to 7 to 8 feet or so above the cockpit floor, a gin pole's function is to hoist large fish from the sea after gaffing. Actual lifting is done by a block and fall or pulley system at the top. Gin poles are square or round in cross-section and constructed from either wood or aluminum. Because of the great strain on it during hoisting, at which time it's like a big lever exerting pressure at its base,

good installation is extremely important and should be done by professionals. Usually a gin pole stands in a forward corner of the cockpit, where it can be secured to the deckhouse bulkhead and gunnel. In a good mounting it extends below and is moored to the hull's frame at its base. Depending upon anatomical details and installation, gin pole lifting capacities go to 500 pounds and more, but there is a limit. Gin poles are standard gear aboard offshore big-game boats.

7. Binoculars: They're mighty handy to have aboard a boat. In navigation they spot buoys, landmarks and other aids. In fishing they're used to look for surfaced game fish in the distance, to distinguish between wind riffles and disturbances caused by feeding fishes, and to see how other boats are faring. Along similar lines they can be useful to beach fishermen too.

8. Gimbal belt and fighting chair harness: The former is a wide belt with a gimbal or reinforced socket to receive the butt end of a rod. It's worn in stand-up combat with opponents of fair size. For such action a boat should carry at least two. The fighting chair harness is a rig that goes across the back and has straps that secure to a reel. The large reels have places for attachment on their end plates. The harness is a big-game angling accessory that helps distribute the tackle's weight and strain by bringing its wearer's back and shoulders into the act.

9. Fish boxes: They're to hold catches, of course, and are variously built-in, home-made and store-bought. Some fishing cruisers have a box built in at the transom, but the trend now is more toward a container that can be removed for more cockpit space when the craft isn't engaged in angling. Many skippers use portable ice chests. Whatever its construction, a fish box should be able to hold water from melting ice and be easy to clean, preferably with a drain for thorough hosing down.

10. Bait carriers: You'll see various types, built-in and portable. Many boats, including outboards, designed specifically for fishing have a live-bait well with an arrangement for continuously circulating water. Usually it's under the cockpit floor, where it can be covered. Then there are those other carriers we mentioned earlier. For cruisers doing a lot of fishing there are freezers to maintain a supply of bait aboard. Also used, but on a day-to-day basis, are portable ice chests.

There now, we told you that the inventory is quite extensive—right? But be of good cheer. You won't need all those items as a boat fisherman, and those you do require you can pick up as finances allow.

---

**Woodstream Corp., Lititz, Pa. 17543**

Woodstream fields a huge array of tackle boxes in every conceivable style, meeting all requirements and with price tags to fit all wallets. Construction features this long-time manufacturer's specially selected plastics.

**PF 1400:** Developed for all soft-plastic baits, unaffected by them, as well as by oil and most chemicals. In lively yellow. Strong drawbolt latch, luggage-style handle, 12 7/8" by 7 3/8" by 5", one cantilevered tray with seven compartments, one lift-out tray with three. About $8.80.

**PF1636:** Green. Lift-out rack holds 100 spinners and 50 lures. Also three worm-proof cantilevered trays with eleven compartments. Strong drawbolt, lockable latch. 15¼" by 9 1/8" by 7¼". $17.30.

**TS9050:** Old Pal Tackle Seat. Combines a tote seat, tackle carrier (two removable trays), insulated lower section to keep beverages cool or hot for hours. Built for years of use, with convenient grab-and-go handles and latched top. 1975 model is in good looking two-tone brown. About $28.10.

**TS500:** Old Pal Tackle Satchel, a deluxe carrier that holds a lot of gear compactly. Measures 12½" by 15½" by 10¼", with key lock, two sliding shelves, eight slide-out, compartmented plastic boxes, in tan and brown, gold hardware, cream-colored trays, can be personalized with gold initials on handle. About $58.83.

**Pocket Lure Box, No. 380:** Yellow plastic body has nine compartments on one side, seven on the other, with see-through lids. Rounded edges for easy, snag-free slipping in and out of pocket. 9" by 4" by 2", about $6.90.

**Woodstream's Air Feeder Bait Buckets:** Molded from wax-impregnated fibers with tight-fitting lid, light. They keep bait alive and lively for extended periods. Four sizes, 2 to 10 qts., from about 90¢ to $1.70.

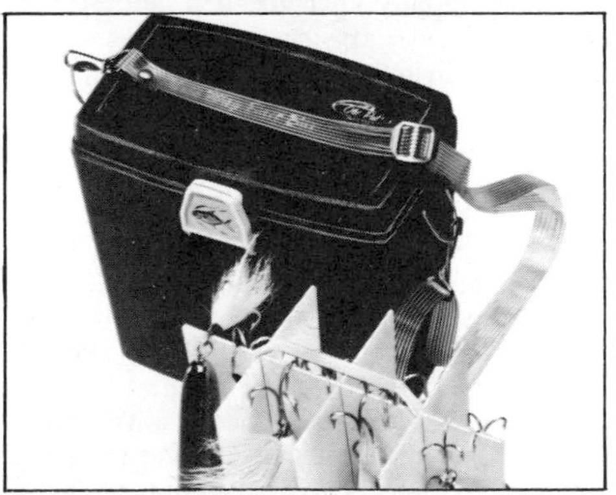

**Wader Lure Box (P31) and Three-way Bait Box (P30):** Both of rugged polypropylene. **P31** stores large lures, other items, when wading, has removable rack for hanging lures, worn around waist or from shoulder, about $1.30. The three-way bait carrier, **P30**, can be used as a wading minnow can, has lift-out tray to lift bait for selection. Worn from the shoulder or around waist. About $5.40.

**Old Pal Sport Crabber:** New, unique design, of tough plastic, dark green to blend in with underwater environment, won't rust or corrode. Features: Molded-in lead weights for fast sinking; plastic float in draw cord signals when crabs are at the bait. **No. 666,** 15" by 16" by 10" closed, easily stored. About $10.

**Plano Molding Co., Plano, Ill. 60545**

Long a name in tackle boxes, Plano sailed into 1975 with an eye-opening new carrier designated as the **777.** Closed, it's a smart-looking case in leather-brown and beige. Open, a front panel is hinged to slide under the bottom drawer. Six drawers pull out to make their contents readily available: five drawers are 1¼" deep, one is 3¼", together they have fifty-seven compartments. Overall measurements, 19" long, 9½" wide, 13 5/8" high—occupies only 14 3/4" when fully open. Other features: Rugged ABS plastic construction; easy-grip handle; bail-type latch; a unique lock bar preventing accidental removal of drawers (the tackle box's, that is). Weighs 12 lbs. Approximate price, $59.95.

That's the king of the Plano line, and it leads a lengthy parade of other models, all very handsomely styled, all built from high-impact plastic materials for lightness, durability, long service.

**Cutter Laboratories, Inc.**
**Fourth and Parker Sts., Los Angeles, Cal. 94710**

**Cutter Trail Pack: No. 550-20.** Contents include adhesive bandages in different sizes, ammonia inhalant, sterile pad, antiseptic pads, burn ointment, alcohol prep pads, surgical blade. In compact, unbreakable case that keeps out dirt, dust, moisture, about $4.98.

**John Chatillon & Sons, Inc.**
**83-30 Kew Gardens Rd.**
**Kew Gardens, N.Y. 11415**

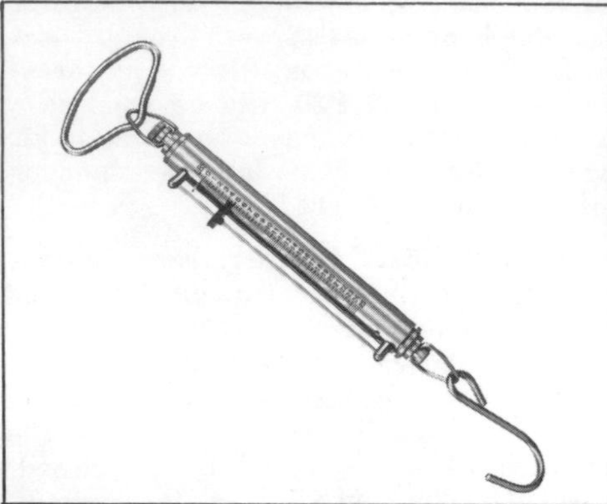

Chatillon has manufactured scales, force-measuring instruments and precision springs since 1835, which is a few years. Stretching the truth a mite when it comes to talking about weights of catches is a time-honored part of fishing, but there are times when more accurate measurements are required. And Chatillon has the answer in a group of dependable instrument scales whose capacities range from 2 lbs. to 60 lbs. Their model designation is the letters IN, followed by a number indicating their pounds capacity (2, 4, 6, 10, 12, etc.) Prices go from about $14.50 for **IN-2** to $40 for **IN-60.**

**Ed. Cumings, Inc., 2305 Branch Rd., Flint, Mich. 48508**

Landing nets are this firm's specialty, and it produces a large variety of designs and sizes.

**Catch-O-Matic Stream Net:** Truly collapsible, but instantly ready at a flick of the wrist. One-hand action collapses it for easy carrying storage. Light—of fine quality, corrosion-resistant aluminum, strong enough to handle huskies. Length open, 2½', bow diameter 14", bag length 20". With handy belt clip, about $5.45.

Cumings offers trout and bass landing nets variously with the standard shape or the new scoop shape, aluminum frames, polyethylene or nylon netting, with fingerfit grip or aluminum floating handle. Wide range of economical prices, $2.35-$6.

**Tempo Products Co., 6200 Cochran Rd., Cleveland, Ohio 44139**

**New Tempo rod holder:** Of durable, lightweight aluminum alloy, with very durable coating against corrosion. Features an exclusive "drop-back" ring to leave both hands free. When not in the fishing position, ring functions as a rod retainer. Adjustable in three positions. Easily mounted with four screws or bolts. About $12.95.

**Ranging, Inc., 90 Lincoln Rd. No., East Rochester, N.Y. 11445**

**Rangematic Mark V:** How far is it to that next buoy, or how far along the surf front to that jetty? Rangematic V answers such questions for distances from 50 yds. to 2 miles with an accuracy level of 90% at 1,000 yds., 99% at 100 yds. Measures 10½" by 1½" by 1¼", weighs 22 oz., comes in a trim looking, zippered case, about $42.95.

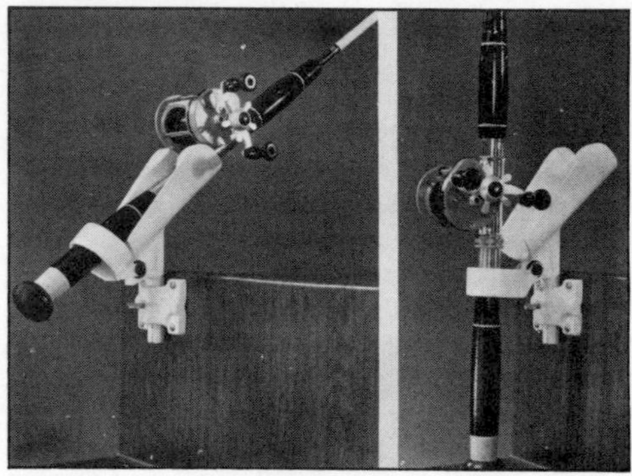

**IPCO Inc., 331 Lake Hazeltine Dr., Chaska, Minn. 55318**

This company specializes in landing nets of all kinds, streamside and boat, as well as minnow, shrimp, crab and shad nets and crab traps.

Even the most ardent anglers aren't crazy about the chore of cleaning their catches. Anything that makes the task easier is a boon. The Clean-A-Fish Fillet Board does just that. Board is either a hardwood or styrene (according to models), with 12" sharp-tipped grooves, to prevent side-slip. Strong clamp has spring guaranteed for life of device. Built-in hone, 6" by 1", on side of board. Rubber legs—six on lighter styrene models, four on hardwood boards—prevent device from sliding. Nine models. Standard size is 24" by 6"; Standard model (molded woodgrain), about $5.95; deluxe model, northern hardwood, about $10.95.

Clean-A-Fish Boards and Fillet-A-Fish Knives are sold in sets, from about $11.50-$17.75. There's also the Lunker Board for cleaning and filleting, fully 36" long by 6" wide, deluxe hardwood, super-size jaws, around $17.95 (without knife). And the Filleting Clamp is available alone as a portable gadget for quick attachment and detachment on boards, tables, etc., about $4.95.

**Franklin Trout Net:** All aluminum, embossed hoop for extra strength, colorful non-slip plastic grip, long elastic cord, 4½" handle. **No. AT1,** 11½" by 14", 18" poly netting, about $2.55; **No. AT2,** 13½" by 16", 24" waxed cotton net, about $2.89.

**Franklin Bass Net:** All aluminum, embossed 14" by 19" hoop and 12" handle, 24" net, long elastic cord. Model **AB3P,** about $3.11.

For boat service Franklin produces aluminum floating models that feature embossed hoops and handles for extra strength. In a wide range of hoop sizes, to 22", and handle lengths, to 48", from about $3.11-$5.33. Also telescoping models of these floating nets, with handles telescoping to 29-42", extending to 47-72" from around $5.55-$6.99.

**Stratton & Terstegge Co., Inc., P.O. Box 1859, Louisville, Ky. 40201**

**My Buddy Aluminum Tacklemaster Tackle Boxes:** In four models, pebble-grained embossed aluminum, trays with Royalite liners. No. 1416 RL is 16" by 8 3/4" by 9 3/4", only 4 lbs. Four large trays, a full 4" wide, solid brass hardware, heavy luggage-type handle, 6¼" deep under trays. About $24.

**Vlchek Plastics Co., Middlefield, Ohio 44062**

Vlchek sires a large family of fine equipment carriers ranging from see-through worm boxes and a **No. 1099** tackle box of crushproof copolymer with a six-compartment tray for about $4 to a No. 1986, an exclusively designed biggie with six Select-O-Matic trays, forty compartments, at around $43.95. In between are all kinds of tackle boxes with a variety of tray arrangements from about $5 to $34.50.

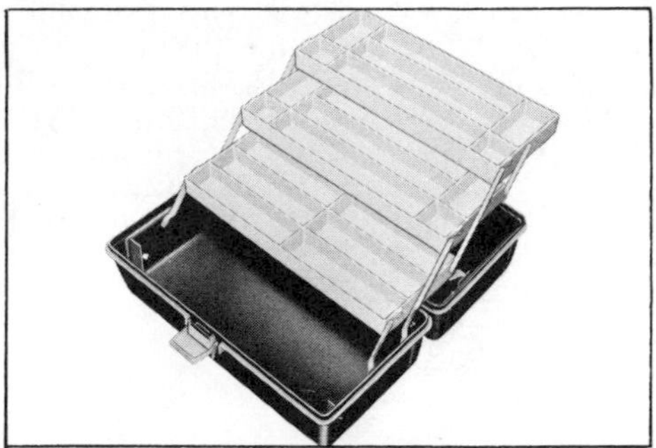

**Vlchek Model 1743,** one of the manufacturer's most popular: One reason is its price, about $14.95. Other attractions: Neat lines; three wormproof cantilevered trays with built-in supports making the carrier tip-proof; safety latch; recessed handle; construction—continuous tongue and groove, in crushproof, textured, green copolymer; size—16½" by 8 3/4" by 7½".

**Umco Corporation, P.O. Box 608, Watertown, Minn. 55388**

Umco itself The Strong Box Company. They're talking about tackle carriers, not safes.

**Umco No. 1283:** Here's an all-purpose fresh/salt water box in Umco's new styling. Features include: Injection-molded plastic case in two-tone honey color and brown, 14 3/4" by 8½" by 8 5/8", 3 3/8 lbs., wormproof; three white ABS trays, twenty-three compartments, immune to soft plastic baits; deep storage in bottom for reels. About $12.75

**Umco No.1273:** New in the line. Same construction features and colors as No. 1283—three cantilevered trays with twenty-three compartments, etc., but with the addition of a spinner caddy with twenty-two slots. Size is 17¼" by 8¼" by 8 5/8", 3 3/4 lbs. About $17.75

**Maxwell Mfg. Co. (Grizzly Fishing Tackle), 801 W. 8th St., Vancouver, Wash. 98660**

**Sand spikes from Maxwell:** For streamside, shore and surf fishing. Three types: **No. 136,** Atlantic design, 18" long, for sandy shores, \$2.60. **No. 20,** Pacific design, heavy-duty, V-shape for maximum strength, heavy-gauge steel, arc-welded, cadmium-plated, in two pieces, easily disassembled for carrying by loosening thumb nut. Two sizes for this one, 19" closed and 28" open, about \$5.16, and 34" closed and 44" open, about \$6.39. **No. 134,** E-Z Pal Sand Spike, of rust-proof

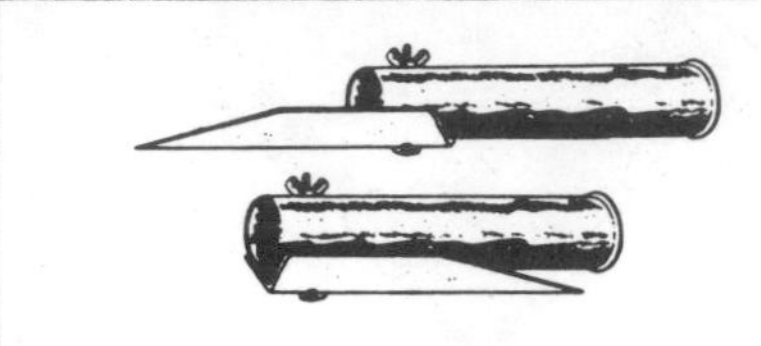

aluminum, opens and closes in seconds. Four sizes, spikes 6" to 36" long, tubes 1½" by 6" to 2" by 12", from about \$2.90 to \$6.02.

**Lindy/Little Joe, Route 8, Box 488, Brainerd, Minn. 56401**

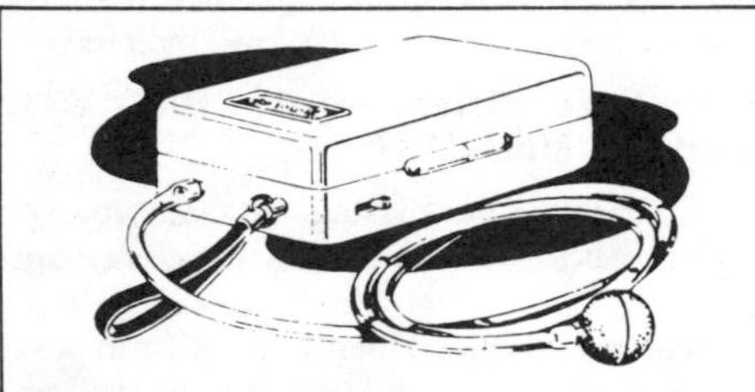

**Little Joe Air Pump:** It will pay for itself in the minnows and other live bait it saves through aeration. Has a 1.5-volt miniature motor that is powered by one "D" flashlight battery. Its case stores an extra battery, comes with a plastic loop and a clip for attaching to a minnow bucket. Approximate price: \$5.25.

**The Orvis Co., Inc., Manchester, Vt. 05254**

Miscellaneous Accessories:

1. **Stream Thermometer:** 6½" long, clips to fishing vest pocket. Light metal casing—part of instrument—protects against breakage. Favored by fisheries, biologists. About \$5.75.
2. **Flex-Light:** A handy flashlight clipping on pocket or belt. Light swivels on flexible gooseneck, giving a bright beam for changing lures, etc. while leaving hands free. In bright metal finish, 9½" with 3 3/4" neck, about \$5.95, less batteries.
3. **Fly Threader:** No bigger than a ballpoint pen, clips on pocket, puts any size fly on a leader instantly, a great time-saver at dusk, about \$3.95.
4. **North Fork Pocket Net:** Folding landing net of stainless steel, anodized aluminum, with nylon net, 9" long when folded, locks open to 8" by 13" loop with 24" deep bag, opens with one hand, carries out of the way, only 11 oz. about \$19.50.

**Aladdin Laboratories, Inc., 620 S. 8th St., Minneapolis, Minn. 5504**

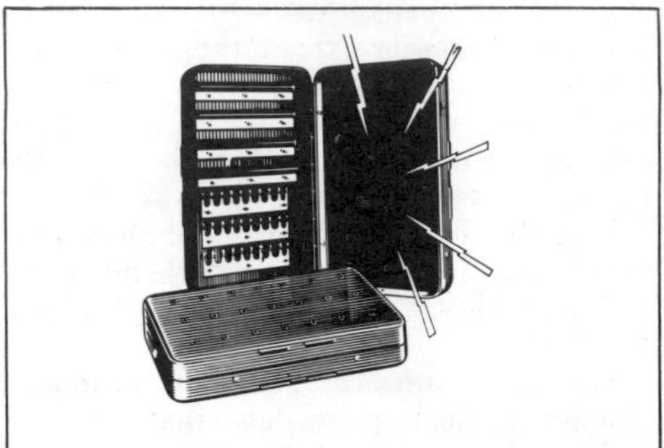

**Fly and Spinning Boxes:** Anodized aluminum, strong, light and self-locking, in several sizes and interior arrangements, with capacities of up to 200 eyed flies. New in the line are two magnetic boxes, **No. 69**—2 3/4" wide by 3 3/4" deep by 1 1/8" thick—and **No. 101**—3 3/4" by 6" by 1¼". Approximate prices, \$2-\$4.75. Also new, Aladdin's **No. 95** Salmon Fly Box, 3 3/4" wide by 6" deep by 1 ¼" thick, with sixteen large five-point clips, holding eighty large salmon and trout flies, about \$3.25.

**Martin Reel Co., 30 Main St., Mohawk, N.Y. 13407**

**Model 660 Fly Box:** Martin's exclusive design, 3 3/4" by 4¼" by 1¼", with six compartments, weighs 4 oz. With it you can label flies, see the box's contents at a glance without opening it. For small dry and wet flies, midges, nymphs, etc.Of durable ABS plastic, impervious to lacquers, dopes, etc. It floats, even full of water. Retail, \$2.95.

**Model 641 Fly Safe Fly Box:** Anodized, non-glare aluminum, ventilated (flies can be steamed right in box). For wet or dry flies, bass bugs, streamers, jigs. Stainless steel clips hold lures safely and securely, does not touch hook points or barbs to dull them. Measures 6¼" by 4" by 11/", for hooks No. 16 to 1/0, around $9.95.

**The Coleman Company, Inc., P.O. Box 1762, Wichita, Kan. 67201**

It seems safe to say that there isn't a camper in the U.S. who hasn't heard of Coleman and who hasn't either owned or come in contact with their propane lanterns and stoves, tents, sleeping bags, or other items of camping gear.

King of Coleman's high-impact plastic models is the Colossal Cooler, **No. 5256C,** of interest to boat fishermen. Its capacity is 80 qts. Its ice tub is designed to hold a 25-lb. block of ice, and it comes with a one-gal., polyethylene water bottle. Recessed handles and a cam-action safety latch are other features. It sells for about $43.00.

**Burke Fishing Lures, 1969 S. Airport Rd., Traverse City, Mich. 49684**

**Heat-'N-Fix:** Here's a handy pocket repair kit for fishermen's boots and waders and campers' items. Can be used for wood, plastic, metal, other materials too. Comes in stick form, functions when heated with a match or lighter. About $1.95. And for hard-to-get-at places are Heat-'N-Fix Stix, cigarette size. They effect the same repairs as the kit, but are designed for smaller jobs in awkward places. Package of 7, around $2.25.

**Anglers Mfg. Corp., 7729 N. Eastlake Terrace, Chicago, Ill. 60626**

**Anglers 3 in 1 Fishing Tool:** Combines a hook disgorger, hook sharpener and cutting blade for lines, has a clip for pocket wear. Price, about 59c. You'll have to look for it in tackle shops. Manufacturer says minimum mail order is a gross.

**Generic Systems, Inc., Rockaway, N.J. 07866**

**Saturn Bobber:** A bobber of unique design, specifically for monofilament lines of 2- through 10-lb. test. In addition to standard use as a bobber or float to suspend a rig at intermediate levels, Saturn can be rigged in bottom fishing, is aerodynamically balanced for casting, even serves as a lure on retrieves. Has been cited by writers in **Sports Afield** and **Outdoor Life.** In a 6-pack, about $2.25.

**Allan Tackle Mfg. Co., Inc., 325 Duffy Ave., Hicksville, N.Y. 11801**

Allan has been manufacturing fishing tackle hardware since 1946. From them you can get all types of guides, in sets and assortments, other items such as reel seats, ferrules, fresh and salt water rod handle assemblies, double-slotted gimbal nocks, rubber butt caps, and rod and pole holders.

**Allan Portable Spotlight**—for boat or car: 35,000 c.p., 12-volt sealed beam unit plugs into boat or car cigarette lighter, stainless steel construction, contoured hand grip of vinyl, on/off switch, with wire and socket plug, about $16.95. A useful accessory for small craft fishing at night.

**The American Import Co., 1167 Mission St., San Francisco, Cal. 94103**

**Cartop rod carrier with padlock:** Clamps on car's rain gutters, with suction cups to hold it in place, unichrome steel clamps with sponge rubber lining. Accommodates five rods of average size.

**Fisherman's Glove:** Heavy vinyl, with metal grippers, washable, good for landing and cleaning fish. Comes with belt clip.

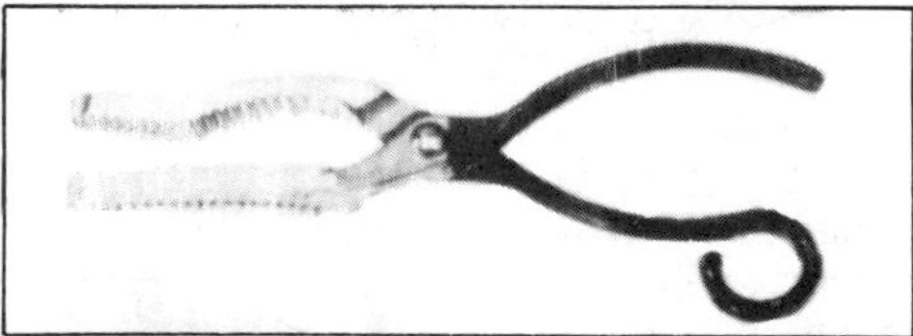

**Fish Gripper:** Aluminum, with red painted handles, 8" long, bottom edge is a scaler.

**Fish Tector:** A handy device with two gauges, one for depth, one for water temperature.

**Bait Aerator:** Operates on standard D battery, plastic case holds spare. Comes with metal clip, plastic bucket hose.

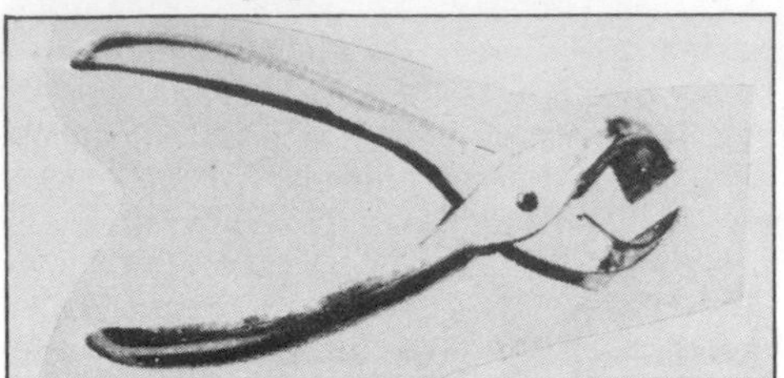

**Handy Fisherman's Tool:** Combines line and leader clipper, small-hook disgorger, hook eye cleaner, tempered steel knife. A good accessory for fly anglers.

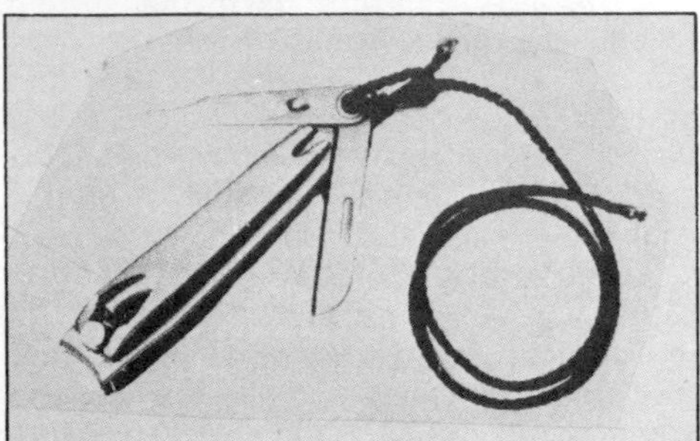

**Fish Skinner:** Really grabs the skin. Nickel-plated steel, 5¼".

**Creels:** American Import offers 7 models—three in traditional rattan, one in plastic, one in waterproofed nylon, one in rubberized rayon, one large size, 19" by 12" in rubberized rayon canvas. Examples: No. 56870, in rattan, vinyl pouch in front, 15" to 20" widths; No. 55374, rubberized rayon, olive drab color, 10" by 16½".

## BOAT FISHING GEAR

**Rock-Away, Yale and Myrtle Aves., Morton, Pa. 19070**

**Rock-Away Bimini Chair:** The ultimate in fighting chairs. Among its details: Extra-heavy-duty castings throughout, with special under-seat housing, cast as a solid X-frame unit; 4" diameter stanchion; double ball bearing assembly—easy rotation without binding, even when standing on footboard; exclusive seven-position drop gimbal, adjustable in seconds without a wrench; twenty-four position footrest with curved, laminated hardwood footboard with non-slip, wearproof surface; deck mounting with Rock-Away flush deck mount, complete with flat deck plate and all necessary hardware; removable cushions—white, waterproof vinyl, upholstered; two deluxe rod holders, a beverage glass holder; fitted waterproof cover. Model **BCB-1** is aluminum, painted white, weighs 100 lbs., sells for about $1,250. Model **BCB-1** is chrome-plated bronze, weighs 200 lbs. There's also Model **BCB-ITM,** same as BCB-1 but with through-deck mount.

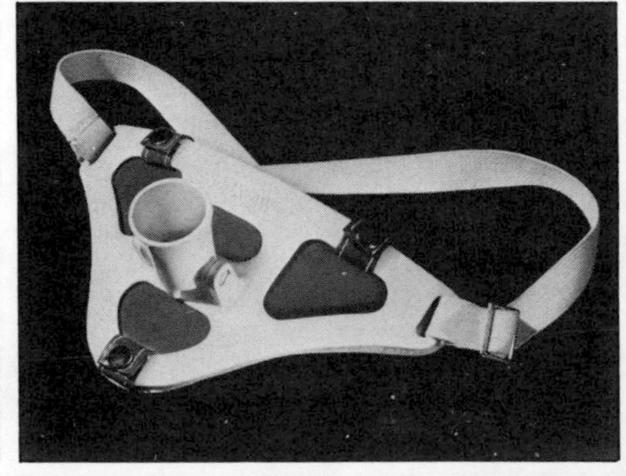

**Rock-Away Belly Harness or gimbal belt:** A must if you-re contemplating stand-up arguments aboard boat with battlers of any size. This **No. BH-2** is very light—cast aluminum (painted white), but strong, very comfortable to wear. Freely moving gimbal is stopped at 90 degrees. A deluxe harness, with adjustable belt, snap for easy removal, heavy padding, around $28.

**Mac-Jac Mfg. Co., 1590 Creston, P.O. Box 821, Muskegon, Mich. 49443**

The downrigger, a kind of underwater "outrigger' for deep to extra-deep trolling, has really come into its own for lake trout and other far-down fresh water and marine species. Once improvised by fishermen, often crudely, downriggers now are manufactured in refined, sophisticated versions.

**Mac-Jac's Salty Mac Downrigger, Model 201:** Primarily for salt water, but equally serviceable in fresh. Among its features: Anodized, machined aluminum frame and base, easily disassembled for cleaning; stainless moving parts; deep-walled, sun-shielded ABS plastic spool; stainless drag-lock system; 20" rod, ½" in diameter. Comes with 150' of 7-strand cable, with clip, about $62.95.

**Waller Corp., Box 340, Crystal Lake, Ill. 60014**

Wise anglers know that water temperatures constitute a major influence on habits and movements of fishes—and make it pay off. That's why a suitable thermometer, whether of the tackle box type or one of the more sophisticated instruments, is an excellent investment.

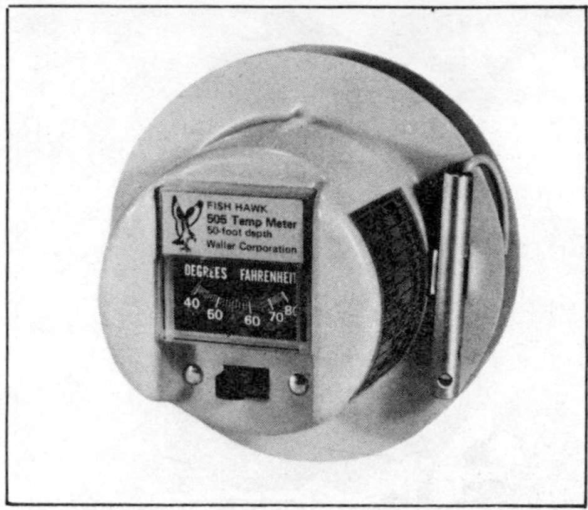


**Fish Hawk 505:** Inexpensively priced at about $34.95. Compact and easily held, instantly and accurately measures temperatures down to 50'.

**Fish Hawk 530:** Here's a truly sophisticated instrument. In addition to accurate temperature measurements a digital read-out of depths to 100', it also has a light intensity gauge and a lure color analyzer to aid you in selection of the proper lure colors (best seen by fishes under those conditions). With extra-heavy probe, protected but open sensor, big reel for fast lowering and retrieve, around $69.95.

**Fish Hawk 550:** Even more sophisticated than Model **530**, the **550** incorporates all 530's features and adds oxygen-content measurement, another factor of importance to anglers, especially at the greater depths. Oxygenation also influences habits and movements of fishes. Capability of Fish Hawk **550** is 100'. Price is $209.95.

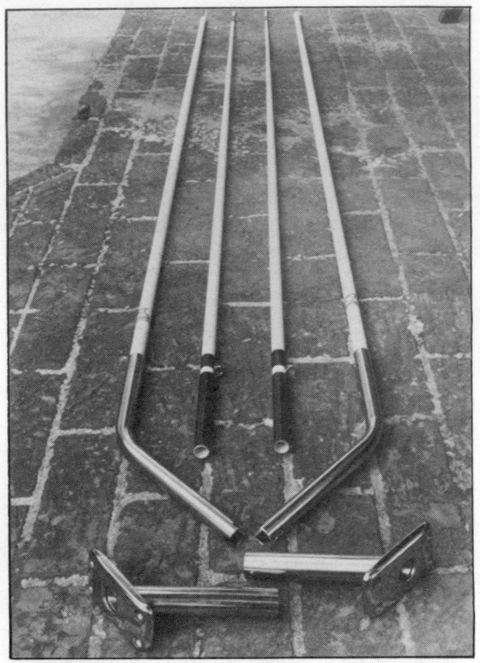

**Fish Hawk 600:** Here's an innovative portable depth sounder, complete in itself, including transducer. Nothing to hook up. Simply hold it over the side of the boat, even at trolling speeds, and press the organ button for readings down to 80'. With strong construction, solid state electronics, sealed from rain and spray moisture it folds to 12 3/4" long by 2¼" deep by 6½" high—can even be carried in some tackle boxes. Price, about $59.95.

**Pompanette, Inc., P.O. Box 276, Dania, Fla. 33004**

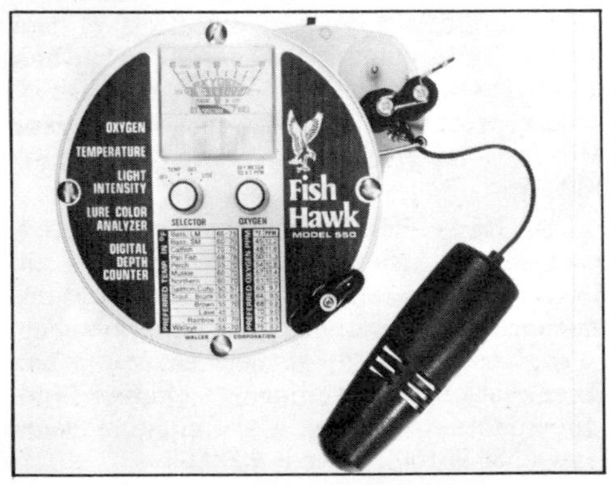


**Pompanette Skiff Outriggers:** Designed for boats 26' and under. All stainless steel fittings. Gunnel-mounted outrigger pole holder is rugged 316-L stainless, top grade. Pole fitting also is stainless, with 1" outside diameter. Outrigger poles are fiberglass, each in two sections, first 7½' solid fiberglass, second section in tubular glass. They adjust to three positions. Price per pair about $139.00.

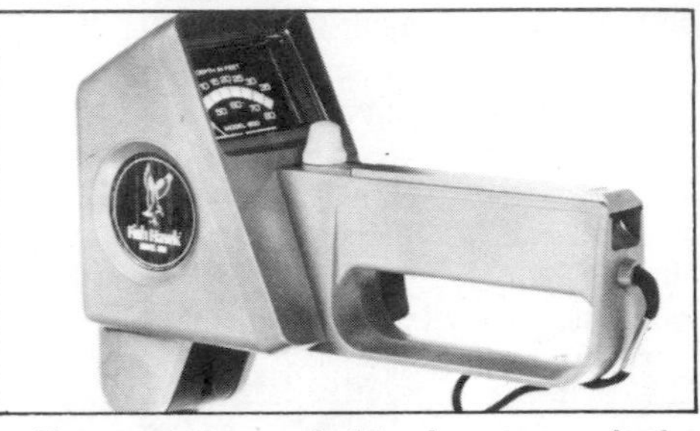

Pompanette probably has one of the largest selection of gaffs. They range from a 9-inch spin gaff and a barbless hand gaff for release of catches to a mighty 8-foot fly gaff with a 6-inch hook for the heavyweights. Features include aluminum poles that float, stainless steel hooks, securely fastened in the fixed-head types, unbreakable fiberglass handles, non-slip grips. Examples with approximate prices: 9-inch Spin Gaff, $8; Release Gaff with 2" or 3" hook, $8.10, $12; **No. 24** Gaff, fixed head, 4' handle, 2" hook, $12.25; **No. 44** Gaff, fixed head, 4' handle, 4" hook, $19.30; 4" Flying Gaff, $44.75; 8" Flying Gaff, $71.45.

Pompanette also has a new series of fiberglass fixed-head or straight type. Details: Tough, reinforced fiberglass handles; stainless steel hooks, epoxied, secured with stainless steel pins; non-skid grips, like golf club handles. Those with 2" hooks have 2-, 3- and 4-foot handles; those with 3" hooks, 4' and 6' handles. Other combinations are 4" and 4', and 6', 5" and 8', 6" and 8'. Approximate price range, $20.85 to $44.90.

**Bob Lewis Fishing Kite:** As an aerial outrigger in offshore fishing, or in surf fishing to get a rig out beyond casting range. Complete kit includes kite and rod, reel and line for kite, about $85. Kite alone, about $20. Kite rod and reel, about $65. Outrigger pins for kite, about $1.

**Byrd Industries Inc., 201 Rock Industrial Park Dr., Bridgeton, Mo. 63044**

Electric trolling motors now are standard equipment on fresh-water bass boats, and they're seeing widespread use in angling when quiet is desired, as well as on small lakes where gasoline outboard motors are banned. Their No. 1 asset, of course, is virtually silent running. Lightness and easy transportation are other pluses.

All Byrd Lazi-trol outboard motors feature all-aluminum construction, permanent magnet motors with low amperage draw, salt-water corrosion-proof paint, and are backed by a full one-year warranty.

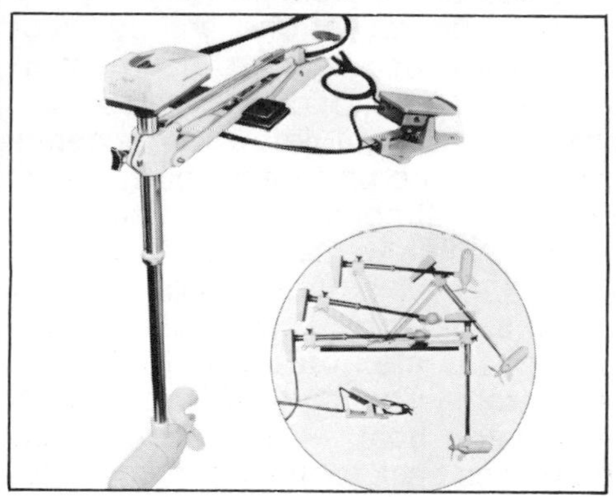

Byrd's most popular model is the Lazi-trol Eagle, with remote control, available as a permanent mount (**S-2250**) or portable version (**S-2275**) for rented boats. In addition to the above Byrd features, the Eagles have a new three-speed control, battery-saving motor operating on 6- or 12-volt batteries, ball bearing steering, 30" or 36" shaft (purchaser's choice).

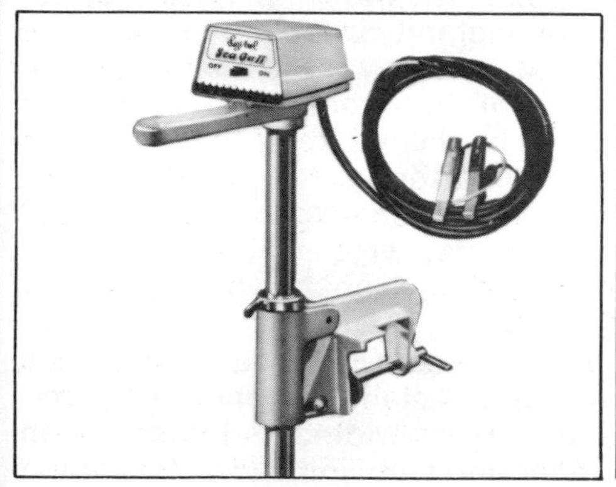

Other Lazi-trol electric outboard motors, all with Byrd's quality features: (1) Sea Gull **S-500**, single speed, $6\frac{1}{2}$-lb. thrust, 9 amps, 6- or 12-volt operation, 27" shaft, weighs 9 lbs., budget priced at about $65; (2) Lazi-trol **S-1000**, portable, six speeds, 2 to 7 lbs. of thrust, 6-10 amps, 6- or 12-volt operation, 30" shaft, quick-change adjustment mount, shipping weight of 14 lbs., about $115, (3) Lazi-trol **S-2000**, portable power—4 to $12\frac{1}{2}$ lbs. of thrust, three forward and three reverse speeds, 9-17 amps, 6- or 12-volt operation, 30" or 36" shaft, Tru-Course Steering (steady, without constant attention), handy built-in night light and cigarette lighter, plug for spotlight or electric razor, about $135.

**Riviera Model 300:** For total deep trolling, with gear-driven depth meter to accurately indicate rig depth, raising and lowering, plus safety drag for close-to-bottom trolling. Unit includes 7-lb. trolling weight, 200' of stainless steel line with release, leader, troller mount, mounting hardware, guarantee, instructions. Price about $105.00.

**Models 200 and 600:** For smaller boats, they feature a one-piece extra-heavy-duty transom or gunnel mount, with toggle-type clamp for alignment on irregular mounting surfaces. They come with same items listed for Model 300. Approximate prices: Model 200, $75.00; Model 600, $111.00.

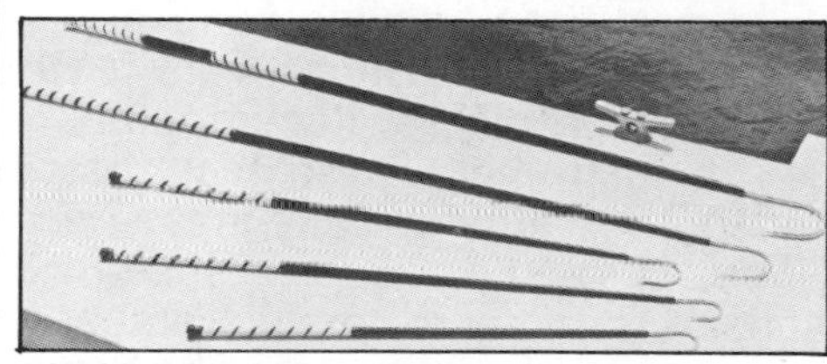

**Riviera Manufacturing, Inc., 3859 Roger Chaffee Blvd., S.E. Grand Rapids, Mich. 49509**

Riviera bills its products as "the finest in controlled-depth trolling," and there's support in their appearance and construction specifications—like heavy gearing, pre-balanced spools, exclusive center-drive crank for easy reeling from any depth. There are several models, from which these representatives have been culled.

# Electronic Aids to Fishing 10

## The Depth Sounder, Your Underwater "Eyes"

For fishermen, the benefit of World War II came with the development of sonar (an Americanese shortening of "sound, navigation and ranging"). As you know if you've seen any of Hollywood's numerous versions of that conflict's naval engagements, sonar is a device for detection by submarines of enemy vessels and otherwise unseen underwater obstructions. Actually, nature gave man the idea for sonar. Long before the first human was even clever enough to invent shoes, bats were breezing around in pitch dark caves without bashing their brains out on walls by virtue of a form of sonar in which they emit ultrasonic squeaks which bounce off obstructions in their path and return for reception by the animals as warnings — all in less time than it took to write this sentence. Sonar works on exactly the same principle, except that transmissions and receptions are by electronics. Incidentally, whales also have a form of sonar to aid them in navigation and apprise them of the presence of danger of other whales.

From sonar came the more peaceable instrument know as a depth sound, and it functions on the same principle, the unit being both transmitter and receiver, what we call a transceiver. Simplified, it operates like this: The device transmits ultrasonic pulses, which we can liken to sounds for our purposes, except that their frequency (cycles per second) is much too high to be heard — perhaps 50,000 c.p.s. or more. These pulses leave via a kind of antenna, called a transducer, mounted on the outside of a boat's hull, which beams toward the bottom. The bottom, along with anything of any substance between it and the boat — a school of fish perhaps — acts like a wall to bounce the pulses back to the depth sounder. Now the transmitter becomes a receiver. In this round-trip process the transceiver is like someone shouting at a mountain and hearing his echo bounce back.

Transmitting and receiving signals are only two of a depth sounder's functions. Without the others it would be useless. The instrument is, in effect, a lightning-swift computer.

The instrument is so fast that its procedures are paractically simultaneous. It automatically measures the the time of the signals' round trip. Then, since it knows the speed of its pulses in water — 4,800 feet per second is an approximate average — it can instantly calculate the distance between boat and bottom, or between boat and any intervening objects, and communicate this intelligence to its dial. In a fraction of a second it has measured the depth. With equal speed, by the nature of the responses on its dial the user is apprised of the type of bottom (sandy, muddy, rocky etc.) in that area, holes, channels, drop-offs, submerged boulders and trees, and other such fish hangouts as reefs, wrecks and gardens of vegetation on the floor. Additionally, if any fishes happen to glide by under the boat, the depth sounder indicates them too.

Depth sounders are marketed in two basic types. One is designated as a "flasher" because it indicates depths and other details by bands or "blips" of light, usually red or reddish orange, of varying widths and intensity on its dial. The other kind of sounder is a recording type. Instead of indicating depths, etc., by blips, it records them in a ziggly, shaded line on a continuously moving strip of graph paper. Therein lies its principal advantage over the flasher type, a permanent record for later study and filing. Because of this, charter and party boat skippers invariably favor the recording type. They save sections of its graph for use with navigation charts to pinpoint payoff grounds. You pay for this advantage. A recording sounder is appreciably more expensive than a flasher model.

**Should You Buy a Depth Sounder? Which Kind Is for You?**

We're talking about a sounder specifically as a fishing aid, its uses in navigation aside.

The answer to the first question above is yes — if you're a serious fisherman and will make fullest use of the device.

Which type is for you, a flasher or recorder?

Both types are dependable, accurate, do their job well and are valuable angling aids. However, because of money and space economy, most outboard and other other small-craft fishermen buy a flasher type, with which they do every bit as well as with a more expensive recording unit. For most of their action, particularly on inland waters and bays, the latter type really isn't necessary. Owners of cruisers, especially those engaged in offshore fishing, generally purchase recording sounders, often because of their greater range needed in very deep water. So a choice really boils down to state of health of the wallet, available space, water depths in some instances, and how much an angler wants or needs a permanent record.

Both types provide a continuous stream of useful information, so an instrument's value is in proportion to how well its user learns to interpret the messages. And its value can be heightened further by teaming it with navigation charts and a water temperature thermometer.

What should you look for when buying a sounder?

First thing is quality. You want the best you can afford. A sounder isn't a nickels-and-dimes investment, but it will pay to stretch a financial point if necessary to be assured of quality. Go with established names in the boat electronics field — Columbian Hydrosonics, Raytheon, Lowrance Electronics, Ray Jefferson, Vexilar, and the like. In addition to the performance, dependability and service life that comes with quality, you want a manufacturer that stands behind his product and maintains a service network, preferably with a representative near you. If possible, query owners about specific makes and models beforehand.

We've already mentioned availability of space. Along the same lines you also want to consider the durability of finishes and the protection of internal parts against weather, both details are especially important in saltwater use. If you're in the market for a flasher, give some thought as to whether you want it to be battery-powered or operate off the boat's electrical system. Battery power means greater portability, but it also means periodic renewal of the power source. Worry about failing batteries is eliminated in the other setup, but with the power supply on an outboard you may have to take into consideration lights and accessories already being fed by it. A good-looking appearance is nice, and many models have what passes for good looks among depth sounders, but it's minor in comparison with other, far more important details.

You also have to keep in mind the average water depths — or let's say the average range, with an accent on the maximum — in the areas in which you'll be doing most of your fishing. The "reach" of depth sounders varies considerably, from 60 feet among shallow-water flashers to 300 and more among offshore recorders, according to models. Generally speaking, flashers have less range than recorders, but let it hastily be added that the former are designed with plenty of reach for the boats on which they're used. There are models with single dial scale calibrated to 100 feet. Others have two scales, one for shoaler operations, the other for deeper water. For example, there are dual-scale flashers reading from 0 to 60 feet and from 0 to 120 and others with calibrations of 0-120 and 120-240. With the exceptions of some offshore operations and extra-deep trolling, as for lake trout, far and away most angling is done in water 150 feet deep at the most, and often appreciably less.

Readability of a dial is worth checking too, and here we're talking about flashers. They do not keep a record, remember; glances tell the story. And since they're being viewed in daylight most of the time, glare from the sun on the dial can be a nuisance. Most flashers have a swiveling, tiltable dial that can be adjusted to eliminate a lot of glare. Some units lessen it further by the nature of their dial face and by a recessed glass. Intensity of the flashes also is a factor in readability. Recent refinements have created brighter flashes than on earlier units. It should be noted, however, that the blips' intensity will vary on any flasher according to the nature and distance of objects. Sometimes a weaker signal, coupled with its other characteristics, is a help in identifying an object.

Too, a sounder's response naturally varies with water depths. Flashes differ in intensity as a boat shifts between shallows and deeper areas, since more power is required in the latter to bounce signals off the bottom. Accordingly, units have a gain control adjustment — "gain" in this instance being roughly comparable with volume in a radio or television set. As a boat moves into deeper water, it becomes necessary to turn up the gain control so the instrument can send and receive suitably strong pulses. On most models the gain control is manual, but Columbian Hydrosonics has units with automatic gain control that enables boats to shuttle back and forth between shallows and deeper areas with a minimum of adjustment.

Earlier sounders, notably the flasher type, had a problem with engine interference, which can raise hob with dial signals. This headache has been largely removed on advanced models by improved circuitry — chiefly solid-state — and by a built-in interference-eliminator which discriminates between desirable signals and undesirable ones and literally filters out the latter. This is a refinement to ask about when shopping.

In most installations the mounting of the transducer is of the through-hull type. But some flasher owners, averse to anything that smacks of drilling holes in their hulls, use a portable-type mount that is outside. There are various kinds of through-hull transducers. There's one that should be considered if a boat will be doing a lot of fishing in very shallow water. A transducer beams its pulses toward the bottom in a cone-shaped pattern that becomes increasingly wider the deeper it goes. Therefore, the deeper the water, the wider the cone's circle and the greater its coverage. By the same reasoning, the cone is narrower when it hits bottom in very shallow water, and so its scope is more limited. Accordingly, there's a wide-cone transducer for such situations.

Another type of transducer is designed for operation at higher speeds. Depending upon hull design, how a boat is operated and her speed, bubbles from water passing under the hull or from the craft's cavitation sometimes can impair a transducer's function when she is underway. There's no way of predicting the extent of this for a given sounder and hull combination. Too many variables. But buyers who will be using their sounders under way at fair speeds much of the time should look into the transducers designed for this service.

With the obvious exception of portable flashers, all sounders are best installed by professionals. And since hull design, boat uses, speed ranges and handling are variables involved, it will be worthwhile to consult with the installer about those details beforehand so that the transducer can be given optimum positioning.

## Navigation Aids in Fishing

Today's angling skipper is fortunate in having available sophisticated electronic and electrical equipment to aid him in getting to and from fishing areas accurately and safely. For some of the items, however, he also has to be fortunate in the finances department. They can come high. In the interest of completeness we'll consider some of this gear; but since the items are not sport fishing tools in the sense of the term, we'll review them briefly.

1. Radio direction finder (RDF): Along U.S. coasts at strategic locations and intervals are radio beacons that continuously broadcast simple signals like dots and dashes. Each beacon has its own signal-characteristics identifying it. Therefore, if you can recognize a given signal you know where on the coast it's coming from. (Lists of radio beacons and their identifying signals are made available by U.S. Government agencies.)

Purpose of an RDF is to zero in on a radio beacon signal. This is easily accomplished by its antenna, which turns throughout 360°; and since there is a compass rose for use with the antenna, the instrument then points a course to that beacon — very handy if it happens to be near an inlet or other point toward which you want to head. It's also possible to pinpoint your position with an RDF in a process called triangulation, whereby the instrument zeros in on two beacons. First a course to one is determined, and indicated by a line on a navigation chart. Then the RDF "takes a fix" on the second radio beacon, and that course also is laid out on the chart. Where the two lines intersect is where the boat is at present. In the same way it also is possible to note the location of an offshore fishing ground on a chart for return at another time.

2. Radar: Like sonar, another bit of good from World War II, you might say. Radar's operational principle is essentially the same as that of a depth

sounder, except that transmissions and receptions are in air, its ultrasonic pulses bouncing off buoys, other vessels, landmarks and other masses at varying distances ahead of the boats according to an individual instrument's range and beam characteristics. Its "eyes" peer through darkness and fog, registering any sizable objects in its path as blips on its scope. Its greatest value is as a safety device at night and in fog, especially in unfamiliar waters. A charter skipper friend claimed that it's possible to occasionally detect a large billfish, such as a swordfish or marlin, with radar when at the surface.

Radar is expensive. You can figure on a price tag in four figures. This places it financially off-limits for many private boat owners. Its space needs, not the least of which is for a motorized revolving antenna, rule it out for many others. Power supply also can be a factor. For small craft such as outboards it just isn't feasible. Besides, the average outboard skipper isn't inclined to buy an item of equipment, however useful, that is likely to cost as much as or more than his hull and motor. But many cruiser owners outfit their boats with radar, and the device has become standard gear on fleets of party and charter boats as a safety feature.

3. Loran ("long-range aid to navigation"): This is a highly sophisticated and accurate instrument for guidance on large bodies of water. Its operational principle is complex. Suffice it to say that loran makes possible precision pinpointing of a boat's position, and by the same token enables professional fishing skippers to record the locations of reefs, wrecks and other productive spots for return at later dates. It's also expensive; and that, coupled with space and power requirements, rule it out for many skippers. It should be added hastily that they do not suffer because of the lack.

4. Automatic pilot: Its name tells you its service. Like "George," the automatic pilot on aircraft, it steers a boat on a predetermined course. It's a luxury item, you might say, and very handy on long trips or when trolling, but hardly an essential. Again price is a factor; and space and power requirements rule it out for the smaller boats.

### Communication Instruments

We're talking about radiotelephones. Appraisal of their value ranges from convenience to necessity, or both. Assuming that the wallet is in satisfactory condition, consideration of a radiotelephone is based upon a boat's uses and, more importantly, where she operates. The kinds of areas in which she spends most of her time also spell the difference between convenience and necessity. A lake as opposed to the ocean offshore, for example.

Radiotelephones are marketed in a good assortment of models, sizes, and transmitting-receiving ranges to satisfy all requirements, with advanced engineering features that include transistorized and solid-state circuitry, minimizing of interference, and improved weatherproofing. Price tags escalate according to such details as transmitting power and number of channels via which the instrument can send and receive. These so-called channels are specific frequencies and include those for ship-to-ship calling, ship-to-shore telephone, the U.S. Coast Guard, and one designated as International Calling and Distress. Each has a crystal precisely pretuned to that particular frequency. Channels can be selected at the time of purchase, often with an option of adding others later. A unit may have three or more. Turning a control knob shifts the instrument from one channel to another. Additionally, many models have a standard broadcast band for receiving shoreside programs. Reception of weather advisories is still another important radiotelephone service.

Cost naturally is a prime factor in selecting a radiotelephone, but when safety is involved it must not be a factor ruling out purchase. If you can afford to buy and operate a boat, you can find a radio within your means. How far you want to be able to transmit is another consideration, and this is something you'll have to match to your particular situation. Government regulations control transmission distances, but there are units with enough reach to cover all necessary situations. Available space may be another influence in selecting a unit.

The nature and capacity of a boat's power supply also is a consideration: that is, whether the radiotelephone will draw from the engine's battery or a separate battery just for accessories, or from a generator or alternator. In the case of batteries, factors are their ampere-hours capacity and how well they're kept charged. Every power source aboard boats, whatever it may be, has a certain capacity, so consideration must be given to lights and accessories already fed by it. The more powerful a radiotelephone, the more "juice" it requires. Boats with a relatively limited power supply might better consider a lower-powered, transistorized unit with low drain.

Because of economy in cost, space and power drain, many small craft today go to the CB — Citizen's Band — walkie-talkie type or radiotelephone. These generally are powered by 6- or 12-volt batteries, although many also operate on household AC current, making it possible to have units both at home and aboard boat for communication. Several channels already are available to CB transceivers, and in some areas local skippers set up their own little informal networks for communication among themselves.

Their transmission power is limited by the Federal Communications Commission, and they are essentially short-range instruments. For many boats, however, their range is sufficient. CB operation is what they call a "line of sight" type. Accordingly, its range depends upon antenna height and any intervening structures. On open water it can reach up to 15 or 20 miles, perhaps more. Where buildings, hills, etc., get in the way, transmission distance is reduced proportionately. Some CB models operate on a single channel (crystal); others can function on more. It's important to inquire about the most practical channels in your area.

### Thermometers

Although non-electronic, so to speak, water temperature thermometers are included here because some of them are electrical.

More and more fishermen, fresh-water and marine, are recognizing the value of a water temperature thermometer as an accessory. Water temperatures are among the leading factors affecting the presence (or absence), movements and habits — including feeding (and acceptance or rejection of your bait or lure) — of fishes. Some species cease feeding when temperatures drop. Many fishes seek deeper, cooler levels in the heat of summer. Rising or falling water temperatures can drive schools out of one area and into another temporarily, or for the rest of that season, and cause wholesale migrations. Some species just won't appear in a region until water temperatures are to their liking. Very important in some instances, temperatures trigger the spawning migrations on which anglers depend for action. Learning about such temperature reactions of species and employing a thermometer accordingly can make appreciable differences in anglers' catch records.

There are water temperature thermometers for permanent installation aboard boats, including outboards, with a dial conveniently mounted on the craft's control panel. Costing appreciably less are those which resemble an ordinary thermometer and are lowered on a length of twine. A sinker will help take these down in currents, and a wise procedure is to mark the twine at intervals to indicate depths. These simple thermometers have two advantages over the permanent type: They can be used at varying levels, top to bottom; and they're easily carried in tackle boxes.

**Allied Sports Co., P.O. Box 251, Eufaula, Ala. 36027**

Full name of their flasher-type depth sounders is Tom Mann Humminbird Super Speed. They offer 6 trim looking versions, boasting such major details as: High-speed operation—functioning at any boat speed without loss of even small targets; super-bright light, a Humminbird exclusive, readable even in bright sunlight without a shade; slim-line flashes for readings as shallow as 1'; large transducer with crystal 2" in diameter to concentrate power in a narrow beam for pinpointing the smallest targets; transistorized noise rejection circuit with positive exclusion of ignition and other electrical interference; waterproof connections and internal seals to keep moisture out; electrical system monitor indicating if power source is sufficient for operation. Humminbirds operate at a frequency of 200 KHz., have an accuracy within 2 percent of depth indicated.

**Humminbird Standard, Model HB1:** Power source, 12-volt dry or wet cell external battery; sound beam, 20-degree cone; scale graduated from 0 to 100' in 1' calibration, guaranteed readings to 200'. Controls are off-sensitivity, for on/off and gain control, and noise rejection for variable elimination of interference. In black or beige case with black front panel, $179.95.

**Vexilar, Inc., 9345 Penn Ave. S., Minneapolis, Minn. 55431**

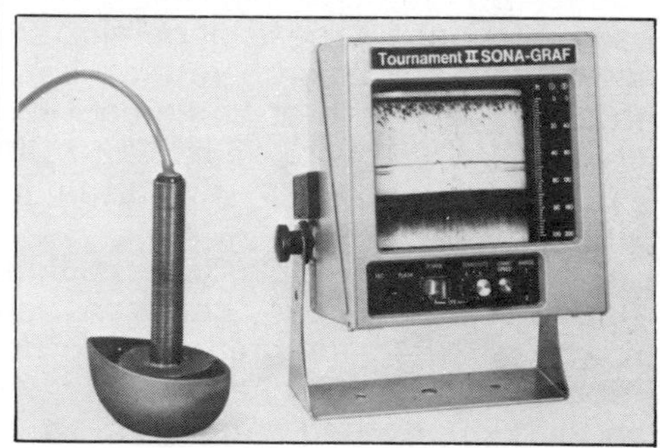


**Tournament II Sona/Graf, Model 510:** Developed jointly by Vexilar and Japan Radio Co., one of the world's largest producers of commercial marine electronic devices. New in the Vexilar line, Model **510** combines printed chart and flasher readout capabilities, with a straight-line readout for both. Its flasher readout has a solid state, light-emitting diode, with light-shielding cover to eliminate glare for easy visual reading. The chart readout plots information on a 4" by 30' roll of sensitized paper, with variable roll speed from about 1/2" to 1 1/2" per minute to make a roll last eight to fifteen hrs. Its depth detection capability can be used to track descending lures, monitor downriggers and, under certain conditions, record fish striking a lure. For salt or fresh water use, approximate price, $529.

**Vega Automatic Direction Finder by Vexilar:** Features include: three frequency bands—radiobeacon (175-420 kHz.), standard broadcast (535-1290 kHz.), marine (1250-3000 kHz.), with accuracy of plus or minus 5 degrees at 35 dB, plus or minus 2 degrees at 50 dB; full 360-degree

rotation, with immediate, automatic bearings and rotating azimuth ring for true or relative bearing. No possibility of 180-degree error because feathered indicator always points to station. Comes with vinyl carrying case, 16' grounding cord, about $399.

**Vexilar Deptherm II, Model 116:** A sophisticated fishing thermometer. Find the preferred temperature zone of the species you seek on a table on the instrument's handle, dial that temperature, lower the probe in the water until the needle indicates that you've found the temperature you want. Probe wire is marked in feet, down to 80', to give exact depth of temperature zone. Measures temperatures of 35-95 degrees F., runs all season on one C-type battery. Price, less battery, about $29.95.

**Lowrance Electronics, 12000 E. Skelly Dr., Tulsa, Okla. 74128**

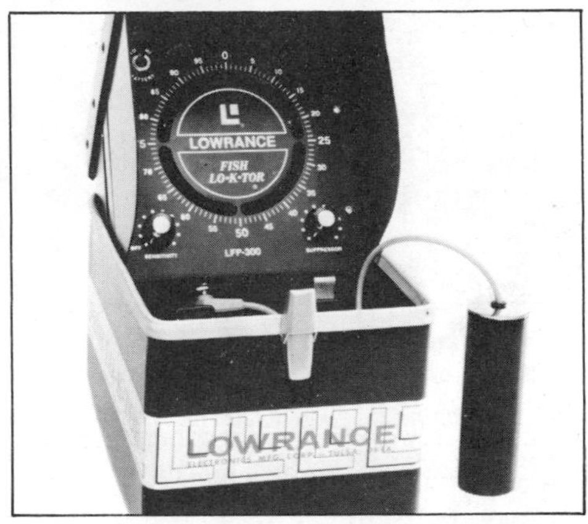


Top of the Bluewater Pro flasher line, at about $269.95, is the **LFG 660,** a powerful, high-performance instrument for offshore fishermen or for navigation. Its dual depth range has a 0-60' scale for shallow water, 0-360' for deeper areas. Its high-sensitivity electronics registers depths and fish even at high speeds. Built to withstand rugged salt or fresh water service, with a filter and suppressor system to counteract electrical and cavitational interference. Power drain is approximately 130 hrs. of continuous operation from a standard 12-volt (wet cell, 60 amp/hr.) battery. Dimensions, 7 7/8" high, 5 5/8" deep, 9 3/4" wide, shipping weight of 9 1/2 lbs.

This firm pioneered in development of electronic fishing/boating devices. And the one that probably has done more to make the Lowrance name widely recognized, especially in fresh-water bass angling circles, is its original portable "green box" sonar unit, the refined version of which is better known as the Fish Lo-K-Tor, Model **LFP 300.** It's an enormously popular unit, selling for about $214.95. Reasons for its popularity: Complete portability; interference suppressor; non-glare face plate; elimination of interference from air bubbles passing over the transducer and electrical interference from ignition and electrical motors aboard; compactness—6" wide by 9" deep, weight of 8 lbs.; an easily read dial calibrated at 1' intervals for 0-100', plus a capability down to 300'.

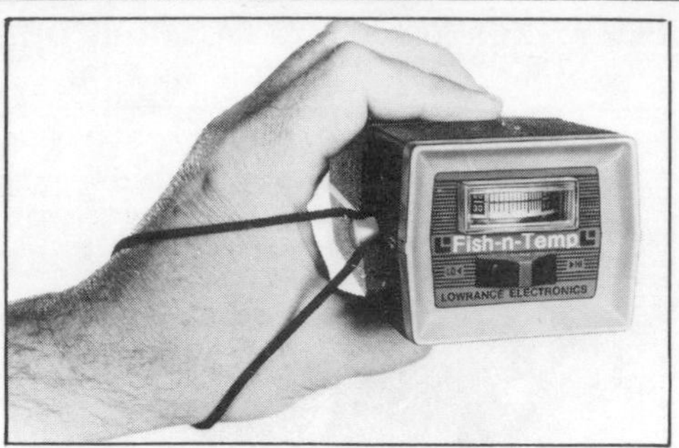


**Fish-n-Temp, Model LTP 100:** Here's a portable, hand-held temperature/depth indicator, for fresh or salt water. Gives accurate temperature readings, 30-90 degrees F., depths to 100'. Stores easily in a tackle box. Complete with battery, 100' of cable and temperature sensor element, around $39.95.

**Apelco Marine Electronics, 676 Island Pond Rd., Manchester, N.H. 03103**

Apelco Radiotelephone, Model **AF34M:** An economical, FCC-approved, solid state communicator designed for small boats or supplementary use, for limited coastal station service. In addition to a 10-watt output and 12-channel performance, it features two weather frequencies plus factory installed crystals for Channels 6, 16 and one weather channel. Approximate price, $339.95. Additional crystals are available, $15 per channel separately, $10 each when ordered with instrument.

**Fishmaster Products, Inc., P.O. Box 9635, Tulsa, Okla. 74107**

**Fishmaster DF-7 Fishfinder** has these cited features: Range, 0-100' in 1' increments, range to 200'; extra-bright signals, fine-line readout; no-glare, watertight dial with extended shade for brilliant sunshine; clear readings even at top speed; solid state circuitry; interference eliminators; light but rugged construction; brass-encased transducer with double-shield transducer case. Operates on 12-volt battery power supply, internal or external. Complete with transducer and bracket, it's permanent mounting, about $169.50.

An interesting detail of the **DF-7** Fishfinder is a plug-in for the optional DMS Satellite for readings in two locations aboard boat. Very handy for a craft with a flying bridge. Satellite, complete with suction cup mount, about $44.50; with gimbal bracket, around $49.50.

Without the Satellite plug-in, **DF-7** sells for about $149.50, permanent mounting.

**Fishmaster Depth-o-Lite:** The depth and degree to which light penetrates water are important factors in lure visibility, and therefore in selection of lure colors too. The Depth-o-Lite measures both factors and can be a valuable supplement to a water temperature thermometer. Its meter is calibrated in percentage of light, with a convenient lure-color code table right under it, and the probe cable is marked every 5 feet for depth reference. Depth-o-Lite comes in two versions: Model **DL-30** is complete with 30' coded cable and carrying bag, about $34.95; Model **DL-60** is the same but with a 60' cable, about $49.95.

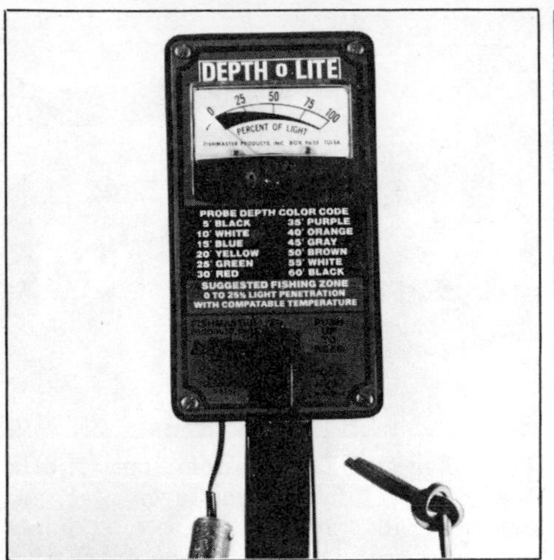

**Ray Jefferson [Div. of Jetronic Industries, Inc.], Main & Cotton Sts., Philadelphia, Pa. 19127**

This outfit has been in boating/fishing electronics a long time, upwards of thirty years. The author remembers when Ray Jefferson, its founder, had his shop in Freeport, N.Y.

**Ray Jefferson Model 170 Fish Flasher:** A lower-cost flashing-type sounder featuring the most advanced transistorized circuitry for a highly dependeable, very sensitive device. Because of its compactness—less than 5" square—it fits aboard the smallest fishing boat, drawing minimum current from her 12-volt supply or equal external source. Model **170** reads down to 70'—deeper in favorable conditions—registering bright neon signals on a matte-finish dial with large white numbers. Other details: New flush-type transducer to eliminate "rooster tail" interference; 20' of twisted, two-conductor shielded transducer cable, molded connector, transducer transom-mount bracket. Approximate price, $119.95.

**Raytheon Marine Co., 676 Island Pond Rd., Manchester, N.H. 03103**

An old name in radio and electronics, Raytheon provides the widest possible variety of electronic aids to fishing and boating. Here are but a few samples:

**Raytheon Model DE-728A Fathometer:** A flasher-type sounder designed specifically for small craft and ideal for bays, lakes, rivers. Signals show depths and bottom contours in 12-volt operation. Its range is 50'. About the size of a 4½" cube; only 3½ lbs. With through-hull transducer and transom mount, attractively priced at around $125.95.

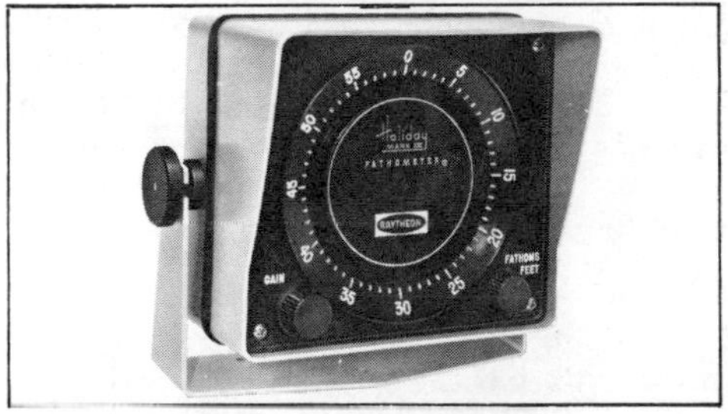


**Holiday Mark IV Fathometer:** Instant readout from almost any distance in the boat, thanks to a big display. Front panel switch provides quick selection of 0-60' or 0-360' on same display. Super-bright signals, all solid state circuitry and tiltable U-bracket mount are other features. Size, 8¼" high by 10" wide by 6" deep, 5 1/8 lbs. Through-hull transducer normally supplied, other types available as options. Price, about $299.95. A "junior version," the Holiday Sport, Model **DE-738L**, embodies basically the same features, including the dual range, but is a little smaller. With through-hull transducer, about $229.95.

**Pflueger Sporting Goods Div., P.O. Box 1308, Hallandale, Fla. 33009**

Pflueger, a well known name in fishing tackle ("Pfish with Pflueger"), also is on a line of electric outboard motors. Their brand name is Electric Sneakers, which we think is pretty clever. There's a wide range of models.

**Ray-1205:** An SSB model for long distance communications on far-offshore fishing trips and cruises. Has 65 watts output for the high "talk power" and clarity of single sideband transmission, with automatic gain control. Has eight crystal-controlled channels covering 2-3 mHz. intership service, plus 4 and 8 mHz. long distance, high seas frequencies, and compatible AM. Unit is 5" high by 11" wide by 15" deep, weighs 6 lbs., costs about $795. Crystals installed, $40 per channel.

**Pflueger Model M-4:** A small, sporty, economically priced unit. Motor is a permanent magnet type, single speed—swivels a full 360 degrees for reverse, in a special Lexan housing, with Cycolac prop. Six-volt battery operation. Has 27" shaft, heavy-duty aluminum mounting bracket with adjustment for mounting variations. Delivers 8 lbs. of thrust normally, 5½ lbs. after 30 or more minutes of continuous running. Priced at about $35.00 to $45.00.

**Gladding-South Bend Tackle Co., Inc., South Otselic, N.Y. 13155**

**Gladding Aqua-Troll Electric Fishing Motor, Mark II:** Two speeds—850 and 1,350 r.p.m.—for 2.2 to 5½ lbs. of thrust. It operates on 12 or 6 volts, drawing 4 to 7 amps—a full day's fishing on one battery charge. Has forward/reverse control, full 360-degree steering, sealed Cycolac lower unit to increase motor life. Weighs only 4½ lbs., ideal for transom or gunnel mounting on smaller boats, inflatables, canoes. Approximate price: $39.95.

**G R Industries, Inc., Purdy, Mo. 65734**

Silvertrol Total Electric (T.E.) System, battery charger: With so many fishing aids running on batteries these days, an angler might do well to consider a battery charger as a worthwhile, pay-for-itself accessory.

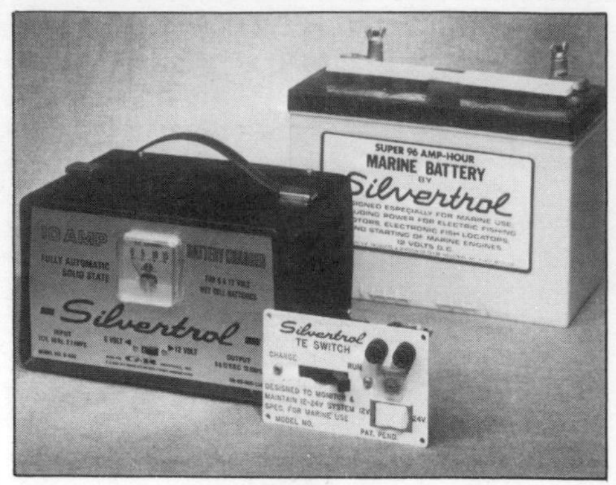


This Silvertrol T.E. System consists of a heavy-duty, fully automatic charger, industrial-grade plugs, receptacle, stainless steel terminals and bolts; and innovative T.E. Switch, double-fused for protection, with monitor meter to indicate both 12- and 24-volt energy reserves.

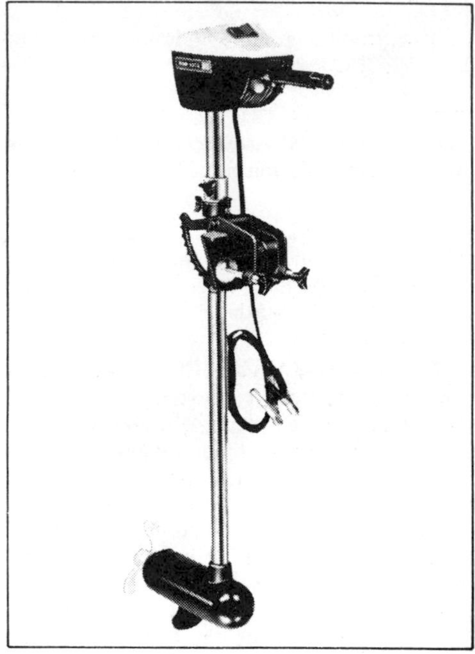

**Minn Kota 65:** New in the family. Weighs only 17 lbs., yet its 12-volt, 3¼-inch-diameter motor (a Minn-Kota exclusive) delivers 18 lbs. of thrust, drawing but 23 amps. Other specs: four speeds, regulated by twist grip control; forward/reverse rocker switch in head; strong ten-position bracket; 30" stainless steel shaft; night light. Four to 18 lbs. of thrust at 1,280 to 2,610 r.p.m., 8-23 amps. Approximate price, $115.00.

Four bow-mounting, remote control motors, designated as the Minn Kota **535, 555, 565, 575.** Shared features: Now with more power per amp because of the new, stronger, 3¼-inch-diameter motor; patented gear and roller chain steering; integrated food control console; indicator showing direction of thrust at a glance; one-piece stainless steel shaft, 36"; flexible housing enclosing 54" steering and electric control cables (72" or 96" cables optional). $170.00 to $230.00.

**Jetco. Inc., 1133 Barranca, El Paso, Tex. 79935**

Jetco offers you eight electric outboard motors under the brand banner Electra Pal. Among them are models to cover all electric outboard assignments—inflatables, bass fishing trolling, auxiliary power—as for sailboats, etc. Here are a couple of representatives with their "vital statistics" (prices to nearest dollar).

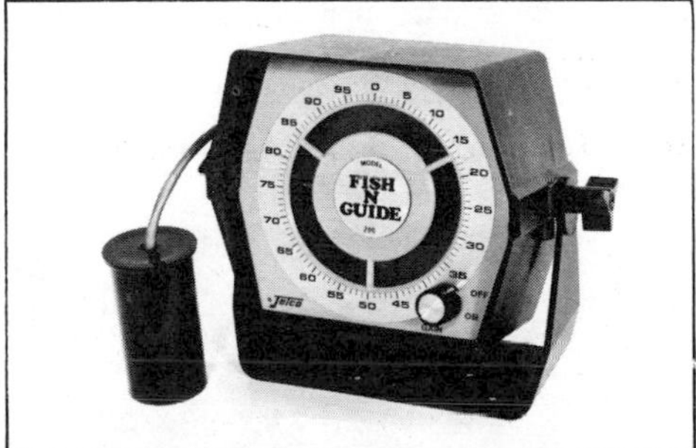


**Muskie 0040:** 9 lbs.; 31" shaft; two speeds; maximum thrust, 6 lbs.; 6/12-volt operation, 9 amps maximum at 6 volts. About $55.

**Shark 0024:** 14 lbs., 31½" shaft; variable speed; maximum thrust, 7½ lbs.; 6/12 volts, 12½ amps maximum at 6 volts. About $83.

**Ranger II 0016:** 30 lbs.; 37" shaft; variable speed; maximum thrust, 12 lbs.; 6/12-volt operation, 17 amps maximum at 6 volts; remote control. About $180.

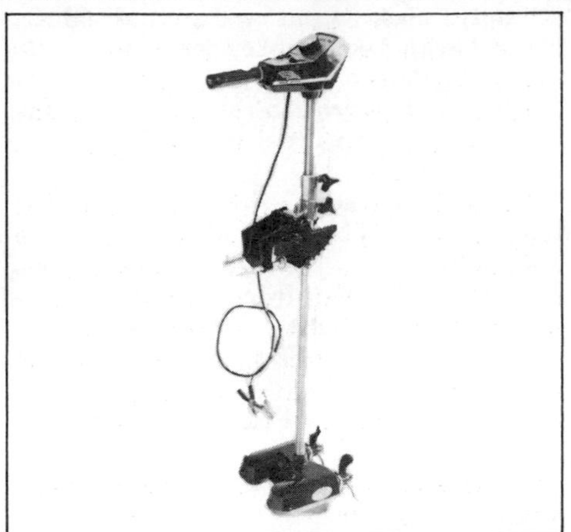

**Electra Pal Side-By-Side 0060** (note twin props): For heavier-duty service. Weighs 25 lbs.; 37" shaft; variable speed; maximum thrust, 24 lbs.; 6/12/24-volt operation, 17 amps maximum at 6 volts. About $180.

Under the brand name Fish'N Guide, Jetco offers five depth sounders. Again, a couple of representatives, with some major details:

**Fish 'N Guide 200:** 100' range; flasher, 12 volt d.c.; dimensions (to nearest inch), 8 wide by 7 high by 4 deep, weighing 3 lbs., non-portable type. About $85.

Not shown are Fish 'N Guide portable models **239** and **269,** both a 12-volt flasher with 200' range. **No. 269** has an alarm too. Model **239,** 9" by 10" by 13", 7 lbs., about $105. Model **269,** same dimensions and weight, about $125.

**Tycoon Fin-Nor Corp., 7447 N.W. 12th St., Miami, Fla. 33126**

Tycoon Fin-Nor big-game fishing accessories:

**Leather gimbal rod belt for stand-up action:** Top-grain leather with adjustable metal socket, around $20. Deluxe version, about $27.50, is of Monel plate, handsomely covered with white-piped blue sail cloth, backed with a foam rubber pad, adjustable, anodized aluminum socket with pin to fit any slotted rod butt, strongly woven waist belt with corrosion-resistant buckle.

Deluxe kidney harness: For extra support in a fighting chair. Wide part of harness goes across the small of the back, is strongly made from waterproof fabric, padded with foam rubber for comfort. Its heavy web strap easily adjusts to size. Its hardware is corrosion-resistant, and the snaps securing on a reel are heavily plated. Price, about $75.

**Fighting harness with seat,** for the toughest kind of combat and heavy tackle in a fighting chair. It's like a bucket seat, strongly fashioned from five-ply waterproof fabric, contoured to the human body and padded with thick foam for comfort of same, with double woven straps adjustable to wearer and tackle. Price, about $150.

**The Garcia Corp., 329 Alfred Ave., Teaneck, N.J. 07666**

It should come as no surprise to anyone at all familiar with Garcia to learn that the firm also markets electronic aids to fishing—all embodying advanced electronics, of course, including solid state circuitry, etc. Electro-Sonic is the brand name of Garcia's depth sounders.

**Electro-Sonic 9400 Flasher/Chart Recorder:** Designed specifically for small boats and priced within reach of their owners. It flashes to 240', chart-records to 60', with flip-open window for direct notations on chart paper (three-speed chart motor). All materials are corrosion-resistant. Instrument is readily removed for safe keeping. Choice of no-hole, through-hull or transom mounting of transducer. Comes with 20' of transducer cable, about $225.00.

Electro-Sonic 9500 Flasher/Chart Recorder is essentially the same as Model 9400 in all details except range and price. It flashes **and** records to 240' in 60' close-up increments. Price is about $260.00.

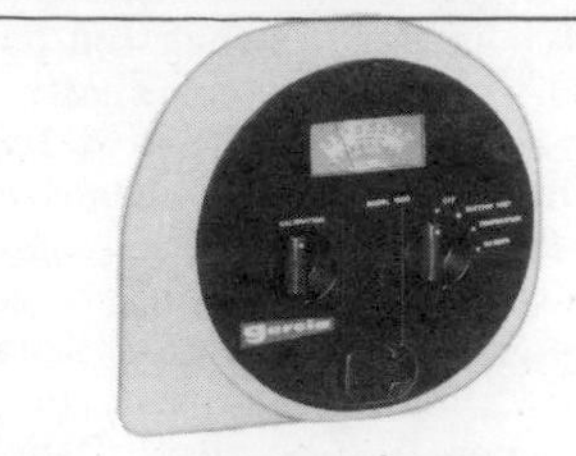


**Garcia 8500 Oxygen-Temperature Probe:** One of the most modern devices for serious fishermen. It measures two of the most vital factors in fishes' lives, oxygen for survival and temperature preference for their comfort. It tells you not only where fishes want to be, but also where they **don't** want to be. OTP **8500** is simple to use. Just let its probe sink to the desired depth and get direct readouts of water temperature and oxygen content. The instrument is only 7½" high, completely self-contained, including batteries, probe and cable, storage, and built-in-reel. Batteries can be changed instantly. Comes with an extra supply of electrolytic gel and osmotic membrane, so it doesn't have to be returned for recharging like some other units. OTP **8500** is highly accurate—plus or minus 2 degrees F., plus or minus ½ part per million of oxygen. Complete with carrying case, about $140.00.

**Big Jon, Inc., 14393 Peninsula Dr., Traverse City, Mich. 49684**

The Big Jon Siderigger **400** is a downrigger with a special advantage. Because of its reach it functions like an outrigger too. Thus it can be transom-mounted to clear any obstructions like a stern boarding platform, I/O drive unit, etc. Or, if one or two downriggers already are installed on the transom, a Big Jon **400** can be gunwale-mounted on either side to supplement them—meaning more lines out—and keep rigs separated.

# Clothing for Fishing 11

Anglers living in semitropical climes or places with mild winters are fortunate. Their chief clothing concern has to be only protection against rain and sun. Elsewhere, cold and wind are additional headaches. On or around the water, wind can be synonymous with cold, even when the thermometer isn't especially low. As you know, it's wind that increases the chill factor. Keep a breeze out and you're well on your way toward staying warm. And remember that wind in one degree or another is almost a certainty sometime during the day on open water, whether it be a lake, bay or whatever. It depends upon the locality and season, of course, but often a lightweight waterproof jacket is sufficient for comfort, simply because it shuts out wind.

Development of synthetic materials for outdoor clothing has been a big plus. Fishermen, boating buffs, campers and hunters can choose from an excellent variety of garments that afford protection against the elements without being heavy or bulky. Even insulated items weigh a fraction of what they used to, and freedom of movement is particularly important to casters.

The available outdoor wardrobe lists garments for all occasions. There are feather-light jackets — some with a hood that stores compactly in the collar — that keep rain and wind out and can be folded for easy carrying in a tackle box. Fresh-water anglers should look into fishing vests. Not only do they provide warmth, but also pockets of different sizes and loops at the waist for toting accessories such as a landing net. They're marketed in various materials and weights, with and without insulation. Some also incorporate a flotation material to double as an emergency life preserver. That could be vital to a non-swimmer who happens to stumble into a deep hole while wading. There are also parkas in assorted lengths, weights and materials, with and without insulation, all with a handy hood (on some it unzippers to form a collar when not in use). In rain gear you can select from among jackets, very light parkas, or complete "suits" consisting of a jacket with hood and pants, designed to be worn over other clothing for warmth as well as protection. These outfits are so light and non-bulky that they can be stored readily in a tackle box.

As we've said, "fashion" shouldn't be a major criterion in selecting outdoor wear, but in most instances nowadays you get styling anyway, along with attractive colors. Prices vary, naturally, according to items, any special features, material, quality and manufacturers. Good outdoor wear isn't cheap. You can pay up to $25 and more just for a jacket. But again, as in the case of tackle, there is quality gear within financial reach of everyone; and it pays to buy good stuff because it will last for a long, long time.

Every fisherman's equipment should include rain gear, at least a water-repellant jacket, preferably with a hood. It comes in mighty handy in an open boat, doubling as a windbreaker, or beside a stream when showers threaten, or on a remote stretch of oceanfront strand. As for the likes of insulated clothing for colder climes, you'll have to be the judge of what to select. The writer does an appreciable amount of offshore fishing in weather that ranges from chilly to downright polar, and for it he favors a beat-up football parka of wool, with a hood. That's warm. Only trouble is, it isn't waterproof. The tightness of its weave sheds some rain, but in a downpour it gets soaked. It would be perfect if it had rubberizing or some other water-repellent exterior. A parka of that type is a bit bulky, but since casting usually isn't involved, it does fine.

### Footwear

Again, anglers in warmer climes are more fortunate than their northern brethren. For fishing a surf or wading a stream they can go barefoot, or at most wear sneakers to cushion against stones and shells. Northern anglers have to look to boots or waders.

Boots come in half- and hip-lengths. The former reach near the knees and are suitable for wading inches-deep water in very shallow streams, marshy areas and along shores of bays, as well as aboard boat with a rain suit for complete protection. Because of their length they are not practical for deeper streams or a surf. Hip boots are indicated for those situations. Even better are chest-high waders, which look like overalls. Water has been known to come inside hip boots in a lively surf or when a river angler becomes so intent upon casting that he moves into deeper water. Many fishermen own both waders and hip boots, switching as conditions dictate. If there is to be a choice between the two it might better favor waders to cover more possibilities. While you're at it, get some warm woolen socks for inside.

*Tip:* After they have seen appreciable use, boots and waders should be checked periodically for leaks. Chances are, you'll learn about leaks of any size in short order; but sometimes pinpoints and subtle cracks develop. Checking can be done simply by taking them into a dark room and shining a flashlight inside. Follow manufacturer's instructions for repairs of leaks. You can add to the life of any rubber or rubberized-fabric item by reasonable care in storing during long periods of disuse. Make sure they're thoroughly dry before putting away. Avoid folding as much as possible. When you have to, make sure the folds aren't sharp. Avoid exposure to direct sunlight, heat extremes and dampness.

For ice fishermen and winter anglers tramping around in snow it's important that the feet be kept dry. Wet paws become very cold. High, waterproof shoes are a solution: and if they're lined or insulated, so much the better. For ice fishing they also should have non-skid soles.

*Note:* You may hear talk about heavy shoes, boots and waders being potentially dangerous aboard small craft (some anglers fish from canoes). That is, they're not dangerous *in* the boat; but should he suddenly find himself overboard they could be like wearing an anchor. It's not our intent to overdramatize such possibilities, but merely to point out that they do exist. And if the prospect of being pulled under by such gear seems far-fetched, be advised that not too many months before this book was written a very well known Eastern U.S. angler inexplicably wore waders in a small boat while navigating springtime white water on the Delaware River, and lost his life when the craft suffered a mishap. Similarly, a fisherman —

especially a non-swimmer — could be in trouble if knocked down by a strong current or if he suddenly stepped into a deep hole while wearing waders.

Heavy shoes should have an unlacing arrangement whereby they can be shed quickly if it's necessary to swim. Boots usually can be jettisoned without too much difficulty. Waders can be released at their shoulder straps, but often there's a belt to reckon with. Sometimes closed jackets can trap water too, creating a topheavy effect, but they can be shed quickly enough if the zipper or other fasteners are working properly. Air can be trapped in waders worn with a belt on the outside, ditto a jacket with a drawstring at the waist, to provide some temporary flotation, but don't count on it. You'll need to get rid of them anyway if you have to swim. Non-swimming fishermen planning to do a lot of wading should figure on a vest with built-in flotation. Also available is a life preserver gadget that is worn and can be inflated in an emergency.

Footwear has special importance for fishermen working jetties, break-waters, sea walls and similar structures. Some of these have a flat, reasonably wide surface that is quite safe when dry. Those open to public fishing may even have a protective rail. Many others, however, are simply long heaps of boulders or chunks of concrete. On some you have to be part mountain goat. Such structures are tricky enough to negotiate when dry, and become downright dangerous when wet. Be especially wary of portions covered with aquatic vegetation and exposed at low water. This stuff can be as slippery as grease and very treacherous. Footing becomes doubly precarious on a jetty during the excitement of playing and landing a fish, a time when an angler is more likely to be concentrating on the action than where he's walking. Without proper footwear "jetty jockies" court a broken leg or arm — or worse.

Since some individuals are more active and/or careless than others, and maybe more excitable too, there is probably no footwear that offers an absolute guarantee against slipping. However, common sense and caution are the best preventives anyway, and non-skid footwear contributes an additional measure of insurance against calamities. It's cheap insurance too, considering what might happen otherwise. We advise against depending upon sneakers. They're fine on a dry deck, but on slippery rocks they could be bad news. Invest in footwear designed for jetty scrambling. There are shoes with non-skid soles of various materials, as well as "creepers" and similar non-slip devices that can be attached to ordinary shoes or boots. Specify its intended use when shopping for such footwear.

Fresh-water fishermen also should give thought to safety footwear. The beds of streams and rivers often are studded with large stones that are extremely slippery.

### Miscellaneous Items

1. Thermal underwear: These "longjohns" are a recommended investment for any kind of fishing in colder climes or even during the cooler phases of seasons. Thermal underwear provides warmth without bulk.

2. Hats: What can we say about these? A hat is a hat. Its sole function is to protect against sun, wind or cold. So long as it serves its purpose, the choice is the wearer's. Protection against sun is the most common use, and in warm climates this becomes important to guard against a bad burn or possibly sunstroke. For cold weather there are hats with ear flaps, but a hood is better because it protects the neck too and can't blow away.

Incidentally, there's a simple device — a short length of cord with a spring clip at each end — that can be clamped onto a hat to prevent its blowing off. It also can be used on eyeglasses and sunglasses.

Many anglers become attached to a certain hat for one reason or another and wear the fool thing until it becomes so ratty-looking you think they're kidding. (They're not.) Some will tell you solemnly that a particular hat is "lucky" for them. "I never caught a muskellunge until I wore this lid," a guy might say . . . or maybe his biggest striped bass, or when he won a fishing contest at Lake Pascudnick in 1960. They believe in that hat luck too, some of them. The writer had one experience with a "lucky" hat. Fishing a Long Island inlet, he hadn't caught a thing up to that point when here comes this sport-looking peaked cap, riding along with the tide. He snaked it out. It was new. After he dried it, someone advised, "Put it on. It'll change your luck." He did, and it didn't. A little later a breeze blew it back into the drink.

3. Sunglasses: These aren't clothing, but they're important enough to be considered an item or apparel — standard equipment for fishermen, that is. Good sunglasses not only protect the eyes against harmful rays and fatigue, they also screen out glare so the wearer can see below the surface, as when bringing a fish in for landing or scouting likely-looking places off a shore.

But accent the word "good." Cheap sunglasses aren't worth the wind to blow them off your nose. Their lenses may be too dark, forcing the eyes to strain for light. If the lenses aren't dark enough, their purpose is defeated. To these you can add defects in lenses, distortion and poorly constructed frames. Considering their life — you can't wear them out by looking through them — good sunglasses are a small investment. Particularly suited to fishing and boating are Polaroid lenses because of the way they cut water-surface glare and reflections. There are prescription-ground sunglasses for those who need them.

Frame styling is mainly a matter of appearance and vanity, not of practical importance. However, there is a practical wrap-around design that keeps out rays sneaking in from the sides. Overall weight is more important to fishermen than appearance. Skin oil and perspiration will cause heavy sunglasses to slide right off the nose, and maybe overboard. Reasonably light frames are the ticket, and there are plastic lenses for both prescription-ground and regular types to reduce weight further. (Plastic lenses do not break as readily as glass, but they are easier to scratch.) That gadget with its spring clips mentioned earlier will prevent glasses from being blown off by a breeze.

### General Memo on Fishing Garb

The United States is a mobile nation. Give us wheels, wings or a boat propeller, and we'll go anywhere. More and more fishermen are doing just that to sample the action elsewhere. When making inquiries beforehand about the action in unfamiliar regions they also should ask about the climate and request recommendations concerning clothing. Here are some of the reasons: (*1*) Rainy seasons. (*2*) Temperatures that are radically different than those at home during the same times of year. (*3*) A lot of angling, notably for trout, is done at higher altitudes where it becomes downright cold in the afternoon, even during the warmer months. (*4*) Similarly, even late spring can be chilly or cold offshore on the ocean. (*5*) Trickiest of all are areas with great temperature changes during the day, the thermometer dropping as much as 30 or 40 degrees in a few hours. (*6*) You also have to be prepared, clothing-wise, if you plan on shifting between low-and high-altitude areas, or between sheltered and wind-swept places.

## CLOTHING FOR FISHING

Anglers today are a lot more fortunate than even their immediately preceding generation. Not only is there a big selection of clothing and footwear for fishing, with a corresponding range of prices within reach of all, but modern garb is lighter, much less bulky, and, for the most part, warmer and more weatherproof. **Memo:** A key guideline in selecting jackets, parkas and the like should be **windproofing**, and for fishing footwear, **waterproofing.**

**Stearns Manufacturing Co., P.O. Box 1498, St. Cloud, Minn. 56301**

Clothing for all kinds of outdoor activities—fishing, hunting, boating, whatever—is the name of the game at Stearns.

**Deluxe Inflatable Angler's Vest, No. AV-41:** Lightweight, with pockets all over the place for fly boxes, other items, all with snaps, including a large back storage pouch. Urethane-coated nylon buoyant element. Instantly inflatable, by mouth or with CO2. In green, red or gold, sizes small (36-38), medium (40-42), large (44-46), extra-large (48-50). Approximate price, $50. CO2 cartridge, about $1.18.

**Stearns' Complete Drywear Suit, RW-102C:** A good investment for all fishermen, particularly those in open outboard boats and those wandering along remote streams. Water-repellent material helps reduce the chill factor due to wind, too. This **RW-102C** ensemble is of urethane-coated nylon, extremely light, electronically fused at the seams. Folds into a little take-anywhere package. Note snug drawstrings at hood and bottom of jacket. Pants feature zippered legs. For women and men, in high-visibility yellow or bright blue. Ladies' sizes, XS. Men's sizes, S, M, L, XL. Complete outfit, about $48. Jacket only, about $28. Pants only, about $20.

Stearns also has a collection of Coast Guard-approved, UL listed flotation vests for fishing, boating, hunting, water skiing, scuba diving (inflatable), canoe/kayak service. The brand name is Sans Souci. They come in a variety of colors and designs, peewee sizes for youngsters to nine years, and from small to magnum (size XXXL) for grownups, from about $17.50 (for peewees shown) to about $37.25 for magnum sizes.

**Rettinger Importing Co., 70 Caven Point Ave., Jersey City, N.J. 07305**

Under its brand name Retco this company markets a large assortment of outdoor sportswear that includes fishing vests, parkas, foul weather gear and footwear.

**Fishing vests: No. 104,** olive drab, has zipper closure, nylon net back, three large pockets and five small ones with snap closures, holders for license and hooks. **No. 318,** the deluxe version, is beige. 100 percent cotton poplin, zip front closure, ten expansion pockets, two large zip front pockets, zip pocket on back, snap closure on pockets. Both come in small, medium, large and extra-large sizes. Approximate prices: No. **104,** $6.98; No. 318, $12.98. Also Fishing Vest **No. 311,** in green, cotton poplin, zip closure, four roomy front pockets, metal net ring, detachable zip-off creel, about $9.98.

**Vulcanized rubber parka (No. 9000PK),** about $10.98, and bib-front pants (9000PTS), about $9.98. Both heavy rubber on fabric backing, in yellow. Parka has attached hood, zip front. Pants have adjustable suspenders. Sizes S to XL (XXL in pants, extra).

**Full-length Fishing Shirt, No. 6400:** Forest green, 100 percent nylon on coated rubber backing, zipper top opening, large front pocket, attached adjustable hood, 50" long, about $11.98.

In the large inventory of Retco sports footwear are numerous boots, waders and outdoorsmen's shoes. Some examples:

**Deluxe Nylon Chest Wader No. 50:** Double-texture top in heavy nylon, molded rubber boot, reinforced seams, in green, sizes 7-12, about $25.98 (suspenders extra). Also Deluxe Chest Wader, No. 13KG, heavy vulcanized rubber, with knee guard, large inside pocket, molded boot, steel arch, in olve drab, sizes 7-12, about $21.98 (suspenders additional). Catalog shows other chest-high waders.

**Hip boots:** No. 788, heavy cloth top, molded boot, with hard toe cap, cleated sole and heel, knee harness, belt strap, steel shank, adjustable thigh strap, olive drab, sizes 7-12, about $17.98. No. 733INS, foam-insulated, heavy lined, double knee, cleated sole and heel, steel arch, knee and waist harness, about $15.98. No. 75KG, deluxe hip boot, high quality rubber, vulcanized throughout, heavy lined, cleated sole and heel, steel arch, knee harness, waist straps, olive drab, sizes 7-12, about $16.98.

**Texas Water Crafters, Div. of Texas Recreation Corp., P.O. Box 539, Wichita Falls, Tex. 76307**

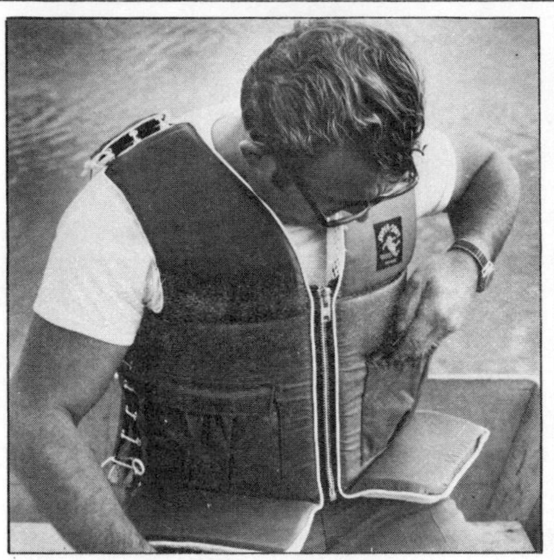

SZ Vest for fishermen, duck hunters, boasters: "SZ" stands for "Super-Soft, Zippered." In olive drag nylon, SZ Vest features two large flap pockets with elastic bands to hold contents securely—for small tackle items and tools, shotgun shells, and the like. Another feature is the modular front flaps that fold without binding while sitting. Modular construction throughout makes vest easy to fold for storage. SZ Vest is Coast Guard-approved as a Type III personal flotation device—soft, unicellular foam throughout for extra flotation. Other details: Heavy-duty, solid brass zipper closure, nylon net lining, flat inside pocket for sunglasses and fishing or hunting license, laces at shoulders and sides for 8" adjustment. In three sizes, about $28.95.

**Fishing vests from World Famous all in sizes S to XL: No. 6301** is a tan, water repellent cotton poplin with button closure. Has two chest pockets, two bellows (expanding) pockets, fly holder patch, rod holder. Sizes small, medium, large, extra-large. Price about $5.50. **No. 6308,** Custom Fishing Vest, is irridescent tan, water-repellent poplin, a full double vest with nylon zippers, fourteen outer bellows pockets, three zippered inner pockets, zippered inner pouch in black, rod holder, detachable nylon mesh creel. Costs about $15.00. **No. 6303** is the Deluxe Fishing Vest of water-repellent, green cotton poplin, with zipper front, twelve bellows pockets, fly holder patch, rod holder, detachable nylon mesh creel. Price about $9.00.

**Browning, Route No. 1, Morgan, Utah 84050**

Along with fishing tackle and hunting equipment, this well known company produces footwear that anglers—notably ice fishermen might want to look into.

**Ground Hugs, Model 3141M:** 100 percent waterproof rubber, really built to last, with a net lining and high-density foam insulation. Other details: Height, 12"; seamless toe; tough, dense-weave nylon bonded to upper 4" for added protection against snags and punctures, plus a strong binding around the top to discourage rips; tough steel shanks for comfort and arch support; all eyelets backed with canvas and metal-reinforced. In brown, M widths (equivalent to D width), sizes 6-13 (even sizes only), about $20.95.

**The Orvis Company, Inc., Manchester, Vt. 05254**

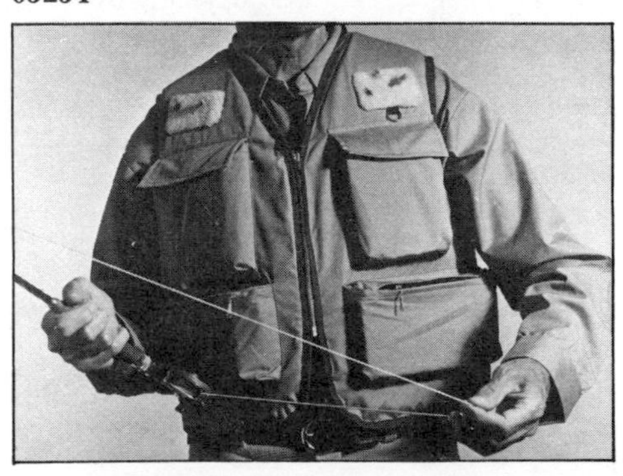

**Orvis Flotation Fishing Vest:** A fishing vest and a life jacket too, yet it's light, comfortable, not bulky. Positive flotation, buoyant foam built in—no inflation by cylinder or mouth. It's there instantly when need. With it you can't sink, says Orvis. Other features: two upper pockets, Velco-fastened; two roomy lower pockets, zippered; large all-across-the-back rear pocket for rain gear, lunch, etc; two fleece patches for flies; ring for a landing net in the back, top. Sizes S(36-38), M 40-42), L (44-46), XL (48-50), about $32.50.

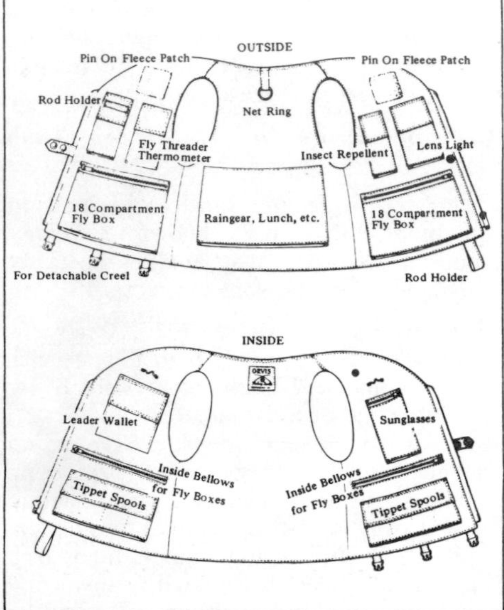


**Orvis Tac-L-Pack, a super-vest for serious fly fishermen:** 65 percent Dacron, 35 percent cotton, silicone-treated for water repellency, quick drying; two big waterproof front pockets to protect flies when wading deep; nineteen special compartments, plus tabs. Sizes S, M, L, XL. Price about $43. Detachable ArctiCreel, about $5.75.

## FISHING SUITS

Among the good ideas in angler's garb to come down the creek is the fishing suit, a one-piece overall with plenty of pockets in convenient locations. Most fishing suits are for warmer weather, being lightweight and having short sleeves, but there are winter-weight models too.

**Fred Arbogast Co.** (313 W. North St., Akron, Ohio 44303) offers the Dick Kotis All-Pocket Fishing Suit, designed by its angling president, for whom it was named. Specifications include: Special, finely woven cotton-polyester material—cool, tough, won't run if snagged; two-way front zipper; pleated back for bind-free action; permanently attached belt, adjustable; pockets all over the place, front and back, jacket and pants, sections, some with Velcro closures, for fly hoaxes, map, extra spools of line, or what-have-you; and it's machine washable. In green/blue, red or yellow, sizes small, medium regular, large regular and extra-large regular, about $29.95.

**The Garcia Corp.** (Special Order Dept., 320 Alfred Ave., Teaneck. N.J. 07666) has a lightweight fishing suit and a foam-insulated cold weather suit.

The former is machine washable, permanent press material (65 percent Dacron polyester, 35 percent cotton), lightweight and cool, has nine hold-everything well placed pockets, either with zipper or Velcro closure, short sleeves, two-way zipper front, elasticized waist with adjustable belt. In light blue, with bass patch on front pocket, Garcia patch on back. Sizes regular or tall for height, also S, M, L and XL. Price, about $19.95.

The winter-weight suit is light, strong and warm, and has a detachable hood. Its material is machine washable, doesn't need ironing, is made from a 50-50 mixture of Dacron polyester and combed cotton sateen, laminated to polyurethane foam insulation, lined in 100 percent nylon. Seven roomy pockets—three with zippers. Suit has two-way zipper front, elasticized waist for form fit, snap adjustment at wrists and ankles. In navy blue, with bass patch on front, Garcia patch on back, regular and tall lengths, sizes S, M, L, XL, about $29.95.

# Care of Equipment 12

## Rods

A rod bag provides good storage when it can be hung somewhere out of the way. Many rods come with a bag. It's a worthwhile investment for one that doesn't, because it protects in transit too. Fiberglass rods can be scratched. Lacking a container, a rod should lie flat, nothing on top of it to bend it or possibly damage its guides. Careful storage is particularly important with very skinny fly rods and other ultra-light models. For these there are protective tubular cases of aluminum or plastic. Some anglers store their rods at home in vertical or horizontal racks.

Before storage at the end of a season rods should be taken apart at the joints and both female and male ends of the ferrules cleaned. Some fishermen apply a thin coating of very light oil to the ferrules for long storage. A common practice is to leave rods disassembled when out of service for a period of time to prevent possible "seizing" of the ferrules. Actually they shouldn't seize if clean, and rods left assembled should have their ferrules cleaned first.

Except in flagrant misuse or abuse, rods are most likely to be damaged in transit. Careless handling is the usual villain. You'll see rods tossed into the rear section of a station wagon, and objects piled atop them: or literally jammed in among heavy sultcases in a bus's luggage compartment. After what has happened to some luggage, this writer winces at the thought of rods being subjected to the tender mercies of airlines baggage-maulers. On a flight one time a fellow writer foolishly checked his favorite fly rod as luggage. He thought it was safe in its aluminum container. The fallacy of that reasoning was proved when he got it back. Its container was badly dented, but luckily the rod was intact. Whenever possible, take a rod aboard with you as carry-on luggage. Same goes for long-range buses, which usually have an overhead luggage rack where a rod can lie safely.

A preseason tackle check has to include inspection of a rod's hardware. Accent the guides. They should be examined for grooving, cracks in the rings, rings that have broken away from their bases, and loose or broken wrappings. Roller guides should be checked for freedom of movement, cleanness and signs of corrosion. Look to the reel seat too. Make sure any locking rings and their threads are free of grit and corrosion and are freely functional. Neglected rings can "freeze" on their threads. Here again some anglers apply a thin coat of very light oil before storing. Ferrules also should be checked for signs of loosening, and looseness of fit (through wear).

## Reels

At intervals according to the amount of use they see, reels should be checked periodically for their state of health, and disassembled, cleaned and lubricated as needed. This servicing also should be done beforehand if they're to be stowed for the winter. Reels can pick up particles of sand, grit and other alien matter that may find its way inside to the gears or drag mechanism. Surf reels often are subjected to wind-blown sand.

At the time of servicing, reels also should be checked for badly worn parts that need replacing and for signs of rust and corrosion. If a reel has a level-wind device, it should be cleaned and lubricated if necessary. Sand, grit and gumminess will cause it to malfunction. Similar attention should be given to the clicker button, special clutches and anti-backlash mechanisms.

Often the manufacturer's instructions for disassembly, cleaning and lubricating are included, sometimes with a small reel wrench too. Manufacturer or dealer might also throw in a tube of recommended lubricant. You can get a reel wrench and the lubricant at a tackle shop, the latter usually in a handy applicator. There are three no-nos when servicing a reel: (*1*) Don't use screwdrivers that are too big or too small; you'll ruin screws' slots; (*2*) don't substitute pliers for a reel wrench — or, better yet, don't use pliers, period; and (*3*) don't get any lubricant on drag discs, otherwise you'll have a slipping brake.

Anodizing, baked enamel, plating, epoxy finishes and resistant metals protect modern reels against rust and corrosion, but it never does any harm to check them at intervals anyway. Particular attention should be given to fresh-water reels that double in salt water. Rust-preventive liquids are available.

**Important:** Never leave a reel with its drag on, even overnight. It can cause the mechanism to become sticky, "chattery" or even freeze tight. Leave the brake fully off.

## Lines

The same inherent qualities — notably imperviousness to water and toughness generally — that make synthetic lines superior to those of linen also offer another plus: Minimum maintenance. Linen lines require appreciable care to prolong their life. Because they absorb water, they're subject to mildew and rot. By rights they should be dry before spooling back on a reel. In conscientious care those fished in salt water are removed from their reels periodically for rinsing in fresh water. In the old days fishermen fashioned crude drum-like gadgets for drying their lines and storing them during off-seasons. And that was over and above the usual checking for wear and tear.

Gone are the rot and mildew headaches, but synthetic lines do neea a certain amount of attention.

Mostly this is periodic inspection for worn or frayed portions or otherwise suspicious-looking sections. Lines can become fatigued after long use. It goes without saying that it's better to discover these flaws beforehand, rather than have a fighting fish point them out. Lines should be checked prior to the start of each season, and any potentially weak sections removed and replaced. A line that is in doubtful or in generally poor health is better discarded entirely. If a line appears sound throughout, you can remove it from the reel and turn it around end for end to start with a fresh section. While you're respooling it back on a reel you can run it through a fold of cloth to clean it. If you happen to have a reel with a plastic spool, don't wind a synthetic line too tightly on it. Some synthetic lines build up a surprising pressure when tightly wound, enough to crack a plastic spool.

Notes on fly line care:

1. Burrs and other sharp projections on worn rod guides or a fly reel can ruin line quickly. Check those items at least three or four times during a season, and repair or replace any that are defective.

2. Cortland urges extra caution to prevent a fly line's surface from coming in contact with chemical substances that may harm the finish. Notable among these are the ingredients of some insect repellents, and the threat of line contamination is increased by the fact that fly fishermen often are in areas where insects are a nuisance. Apply a repellent with the *back* of the hand to eliminate contamination of the fingers and palm of the hand used to control the line.

3. Excessive heat can cause fast deterioration of a fly line's finish. Don't leave a reel filled with line in the sun's direct, hot rays. For the same reason, avoid transporting a line-filled reel on a car's dashboard or rear ledge, where the sun's rays are intensified by the glass.

4. Keep your fly lines clean. This is particularly important with floating types. They're bound to pick up minute particles of dirt and other debris present in most fishing waters. If not cleaned at intervals, floating lines eventually will accumulate a build-up that causes them to sink deeper in the surface film and then below it, defeating their purpose. Because of its thinner coating of buoyant finish material, the tip section of a tapered line will start sinking first, and that's your cue that the line needs cleaning. Some manufacturers include a cleaner with their lines, or it can be purchased separately. Frequent use is recommended to remove surface residue and lubricate the line for better passage through the guides. But avoid leaving an excess of cleaner on the line.

5. Give thought to storage during off-seasons. Avoid storing in places with extreme temperatures, high or low. Cortland recommends removing a fly line from its spool and hanging it in loose coils on a wooden peg.

**Hooks and Lures**

The chief detail of hook maintenance is keeping them sharp, needle-sharp. For this you can get a small honing stone, designed just for hooks, and carry it in your tackle box. Hooks have various finishes to retard it, but rusting is always an eventuality (except those made from stainless steel), particularly in damp climates. Keeping a tackle box in a dry place helps, but all hooks must be checked periodically for signs of rusting. This weakens them, dulls points and barbs. Hooks are cheap enough. Give rusty ones the deep six. Do the same to hooks that have been bent.

Today lure maintenance is chiefly hook care. Thanks to plastics technology, lure colors are permanent — impregnated, finishes are tougher and resistant to cracking, peeling and chipping; and the lures themselves are more resistant to assaults by fishes' teeth. There are exceptions, of course. Skirts of nylon or rubber can be shredded by fangs. Ditto soft plastic and rubber artificials such as worms, squid, etc. But those are calculated risks and simply are replaced when badly mangled.

In addition to hook maintenance, artificial flies require special care because they're delicate and small. Their hackles and other components have to be protected, especially when not in use. For this there are wallet-like carriers which protect and separated them.

# Human Aids to Fishing 13

Among a fisherman's greatest aids is another fisherman—provided the other guy knows what he's talking about, that is; otherwise it could be a compounding of ignorance. It's the old story: Two heads are better than one (so long as they're not on the same individual), especially when at least one of them is filled with hook-and-line lore.

If two heads are superior to one, a flock of them are better yet. And you'll find herds of heads in fishing clubs. Membership in such a group is strongly urged for *all* anglers, whatever their experience. Beginners can't help but benefit. No matter how wise a seasoned veteran may be, he can always learn something too.

### They Come in Gross Lots

For the simple reason that even an approximate census has never been taken, or is likely to be, we'll never know how many fishing clubs there are in the United States. There are uncountable thousands, fresh water and salt water, and many that are both fresh and salt water. Their sizes vary enormously.

### Advantages of Club Membership

There are multiple advantages in belonging to a fishing club. Group trips are one. Many clubs organize mass trips for members throughout the season. Sometimes — not always — it's possible to save each member a few bucks in the process. Sometimes it's possible for a club to arrange a junket that would not be available to members otherwise. Most important, trips are opportunities to get out with the bunch and relax. enjoy fishing and have a few laughs. Along the same lines, numerous clubs organize contests for members. Some also engineer public tournaments that can channel some coin of the realm into the treasury. And there are social affairs — awards dinners, dinner-dances during the off-season, barbecues, picnics and beer parties.

Still other advantages lie in the educational programs provided for members by many clubs. These programs assume many forms: Lectures by experts, including aquatic biologists, ecologists and professional environmentalists, with question-and-answer sessions afterward; motion pictures — there are many fishing films available rent-free; seminars led by specialists, with members joining in discussions; special meetings to discuss proposed legislation affecting the sport; and how-to demonstrations of the use of equipment, fly tying, etc.

### Locating a Club

Although there are local fishing clubs in profusion in the overall picture, it isn't always easy to find one, or to find one that is within practical traveling distance. Traveling distance is a factor because many groups meet on workweek nights.

So how do you go about locating a club? There are three routes. First and best is using your mouth. Ask around the local waterfront or lakeside. Buttonhole individual anglers. Odds are high that they have some affiliation. Their club might not be convenient for you, but they could offer suggestions. Inquire in local tackle shops too. They can be one of the best sources of information. Another route lies via local newspaper fishing columnists. Periodically they mention clubs. Better than watching their columns, write to them directly. (This writer is fishing columnist-editor of the New York Post, and has just such an inquiry on the desk now.) The third route is more devious and time-consuming and sometimes the least productive, but we'll mention it anyway. If the other two procedures fail, and it's doubtful, you'll have to contact a national fishermen's organization or try to find a regional federation of fishing clubs. The latter can be as difficult, if not more so, than tracking down a local club.

**If Worst Comes to Worst . . .**

You can always organize your own. Don't chuckle or throw up your hands. It's being done all the time. How do you suppose existing clubs got *their* start? If you *really* want to form a club, you can.

Only a tiny percentage of groups functioning as such with any regularity are so informal as to dispense with officers and governing documents. They have as much fun as the others, but any club worthy of the name should have the organization provided by officers, a constitution and by-laws. There should be leaders and rules to govern conduct. For the average fishing club a complex setup isn't necessary. They need only a president to conduct meetings and steer the group in its various functions, a vice president or second in command to take over in No. 1's absence, a treasurer to manage the club's pocketbook, and a secretary to handle correspondence and record minutes of meetings. If desired, a public relations officer can be added for liaison with other organizations and to prepare news releases about club activities for newspaper fishing columns. The panel of officers can be kept simple. Some small clubs are unnecessarily topheavy with officers — almost as many chiefs as Indians. Additional officers can always be added later as conditions dictate.

Constitution and by-laws also can be simple. The average club doesn't need an elaborate constitution. A document stating the organization's aims and purposes is its main point, to which may be added the titles of its officers. By-laws need be only simple rules of conduct, stating frequency of regular meetings, qualifications — if any — for prospective members, treatment of delinquent members, meeting procedures, etc.

To repeat something we said earlier because it's important, a meeting place for a newly formed club need not be a problem. A group's size is a factor, naturally, but it isn't an insurmountable hurdle. With effort a place can be found to accommodate even a large club. Many a fledgling group, while still of a size within reason, has got off the ground by gathering in members' homes, rotating so that everyone shares the responsibility. Local taverns and restaurants are distinct possibilities. The establishments get additional customers, the clubs have places to meet. If a group becomes a steady patron it's often possible to arrange for an alcove or private room.

Inquiries can reveal an elementary school or high school that will rent its cafeteria or a classroom, usually for a nominal fee. Also worth checking are the local headquarters of large organizations . . . and yacht clubs.

### National Fishermen's Organizations

There are several throughout the United States. In some, membership is solely on a national level — that is, not through regional chapters. In others, it's via local units of the parent organization. In still others, membership is through clubs affiliated with the association. All provide benefits because they're dedicated to members' interests. An annual membership fee is charged to fund their operations—combatting undesirable legislation, legal battles against pollution, assisting research projects, etc., but they're generally non-profit organizations. Most of them distribute their own magazine, house organ or periodic newsletter, included in the cost of dues, for liaison among affiliates. Most important, they're unions of anglers, large numbers of them, with communication. They can summon a loud voice when strong clout is needed.

Here are but some of them (addresses as last given to us):

1. American Casting Association, P.O. Box 51, Nashville, Tenn. 37202: Born in 1906 under another name. Its main objective is promotion of casting and angling in general as recreational activities. One might also add better casting as an ACA aim, because among its education projects is a Casting Instructor Certification Program to assure proper teaching. Other activities include sanctioning of approved regional and national flycasting, baitcasting and skish tournaments. It has member clubs in many states and Canada.

2. International Game Fish Association, 3000 E. Las Olas Blvd., Fort Lauderdale, Fla. 33316: Long-established and recognized around the globe as arbiter and custodian of official world records for marine game fishes. It is *the* organization hopefuls contact for recognition. For about thirty nine years IGFA membership was confined to bona fide clubs, but it now accepts individual memberships as well. Members receive *World Record Marine Fishes*, a booklet listing current records by species and line classes and containing IGFA rules, plus a newsletter and releases.

3. Trout Unlimited, national offices at 4260 E. Evans Ave., Denver, Colo. 80222: Incorporated in 1959 as a non-profit association, TU has mushroomed as a highly respected organization whose objectives, in a nutshell, are the preservation, protection and enhancement of trout fishing throughout the United States. It's what you might call a volunteer-action organization. Coordinated by national headquarters in Denver, TU's structure consists of local chapters in many states. For further coordination, three or more chapters in a state or region may form a Trout Unlimited council, also a functional part of the national setup. For members TU produces a fine magazine titled simply *Trout.*

4. Salt Water Fly Rodders of America, International, Box 304, Cape May Court House, N.J. 08210: This organization is to marine flyrodders what the IGFA is to wielders of conventional-type and spinning equipment. It's the

recognized arbiter and recorder of official world records set by fly fishermen in salt water. Already large and still expanding, it has members throughout the U.S. and abroad. Joining is recommended to all serious marine flyrodders. For each year the SWFRA issues a booklet listing its current world records, according to species and classes of tippets (6-pound, 10-pound, etc.).

5. Bass Anglers Sportsman Society of America — BASS for short, 1 Bell Rd., Montgomery, Ala. 36109: Although comparatively young as national anglers' associations go, BASS has exhibited phenomenal growth, with upwards of 160,000 members in more than 750 local chapters throughout the nation at last tally. Many of those local units, in turn, are united further in state Federations of BASS Chapters. The Society was created specifically for the sport of fresh-water black bass fishing and its *aficionados,* and is absorbed continously in looking after their interests. It backs its powerful voice with funds in fights against pollution and other detrimental conditions. Among membership benefits is an excellent magazine, Bassmaster.

BASS strongly links fisheries conservation with its promotion of angling. The Society conducts a series of regional tournaments during the year, culminating in a kind of fishing World Series, the Bass Masters Classic. Employing procedures developed by the organization, all fish caught in all BASS tourneys are released unharmed after weighing, and one of the Society's education programs is encouragement of similar measures in other contests.

6. International Women's Fishing Association, P.O. Box 2025, Palm Beach, Fla. 33480. Its name describes it, an organization solely for anglerettes. It maintains its own roster of marine and fresh water records set by women.

7. International Spin Fishing Association, P.O. Box 81, Downey, Cal. 90241: This organization came into being a long time ago to fill a great need. Spinfishermen rate an association that can determine and keep current world records for fishes caught on their type of tackle. The ISPA does just that, and issues periodic newsletters and bulletins to keep members apprised of developments.

8. All-American Bass Casters, 6 Churchill Rd., Chelmsford, Mass. 01824: Unless another one popped up in the last five minutes, this is the youngest outfit of the bunch. It too is dedicated to furthering the best interests of its adherents, but is unique in that its scope includes fresh water and marine basses — accent stripers for the latter. Members receive a fine bimonthly magazine.

9 and 10. Two outfits about, or from, which we haven't heard lately are, with their last known addresses: American Anglers Association, 8320 Gulf Freeway, Houston, Tex. 77017; and American Fishing Association, P.O.Box 62, Springdale, Ark. 72764.

Certain kinds are valued as people food—as in conch chowder.

**Cows:** A nickname for the females of some marine fishes, especially when the ladies tend to grow larger than the gents. You'll hear the heftier female cod and striped bass referred to as "cows."

**Creel:** A small wicker basket or cloth bag toted by fresh water fishermen to transport their catches. *See Stringer.*

**Crick:** A common regional colloquialism for "creek" or even a canal

**Crustaceans:** A term often appearing on lists of bait. It's applied to water creatures with a hard outer covering or exoskeleton (outer skeleton), in contrast with fishes and animals whose skeletons consist of bones and are worn respectably inside, out of sight. Crabs, lobsters and shrimp are crustaceans.

**Cuttyhunk:** Twisted linen line named for famed Cuttyhunk Island, Massachusetts, where it originated. The name still is seen occasionally on a spool of linen line.

**Dead Calm:** A relatively rare time on an ocean without wind, waves or appreciable tidal movement (as during a change of tides). Often an unproductive fishing time, although it aids greatly in sighting any surface-moving species such as tunas, swordfish and marlins.

**Deadfall:** A fresh-water area containing submerged trees, stumps, etc. Deadfalls can be productive of black basses and other game because they provide cover.

**Deep-Scattering Layer:** Familiarize yourself with this if you have a depth sounder. It's a sizable layer of small or minute organisms dense enough to "bounce back" a depth sounder's signals, giving an instrument reading similar to that for a bottom. It's called a false bottom.

**Dingdong:** Sound made by a bell buoy. In more practical use, a polite euphemism for some character in a fishing party you wish had stayed home. Comes in handy for speaking in front of ladies.

**Dorsal:** Pertaining to the back, like the uppermost surface of fishes. *See Fins.*

**Downrigger:** You might call it an underwater outrigger. Essentially it's a device for taking rigs 'way down in extra-deep trolling. You'll find it described elsewhere in these pages.

**Draft:** The minimum amount of water a boat requires to float properly. Specifically, the distance from the bottom of her keel to her waterline. Some outboard boats have their draft increased by their motor's lower unit.

**Drag:** (*1*) A reel's brake. (*2*) The frictional pull on a fishing line by water flowing past it.

**Dropline:** A simple handline—without a rod, that is. Not much fun.

**Dropper:** A short length of leader material tied into a fly leader for attaching another fly.

**Drop-Off:** A shelf or similar underwater area where depths change abruptly from shallow to deep. In the sea there are drop-offs plunging 1,000 fathoms and more. Drop-offs are important to marine and fresh water anglers because game fishes frequently prowl their edges when food shopping.

**Dry Fly:** A buoyant artificial intended to simulate a floating insect. *See Wet Fly.*

**Ecology:** The study of relations between and among animals and plants, and between them and their environment. (*Eco-* and *-logy* stem from old Greek words meaning "house" or "habitat" and "discourse on" or "study of," respectively.) An environment today is spoken of as an *ecosystem*.

**Eel Rig, Eelskin Rig:** Salt-water bait setups used for bluefish, striped bass, other gamesters. First employs a whole eel, armed with one or two hooks. Second utilizes only an eel's skin, relying on water flowing through it to inflate it to lifelike form and give it wiggle. Eelskins sometimes are rigged in combination with artificials. Both types get a big play in surfcasting.

**Epilimnion:** Fresh-water fishermen will encounter this term in literature. It's the upper, warmer layer of water in a lake.

**Estuary:** An area around a river's mouth where it empties into a larger body of water—a bay, sound, gulf or ocean. (Also applied, less commonly, to an inlet.) Since they can tolerate differences—up to a point, several marine and fresh-water may mingle within an estuarine area.

**Euphotic Zone:** A technical term, but of interest to you salt water anglers, since it applies to a belt in which you'll be doing much of your ocean fishing—from shore out to depths of about 30 to 40 fathoms.

**False Cast:** In fly fishing, a cast in which the line's forward progress is interrupted before the lure can hit the water, and followed by a back cast. A series of false casts will increase a line's speed and/or lengthen it for a true cast (one that is completed). False casts also are made to remove excess water from a dry fly to improve its flotation.

**Fathom:** Six feet.

**Fathometer:** Another name for a depth sounder.

**Feather:** An artificial lure with a skirt of feathers attached to a fairly heavy metal head, the hook riding in among the trailing feathers.

**Ferrule:** A joint in a rod, held together by friction. Ferrules permit disassembling for easier storage and transportation. Each consists of a male end, which is plug-like, and a female end or socket. Ferrules most commonly are made from metal, but several rods now have glass connectors.

**Fins:** These appendages serve fishes variously as propulsion equipment and stabilizers. A standard quota, which can be considered typical, is as follows: (*a*) A single dorsal fin on the back at about the middle of the body; (*b*) a pair of pectoral fins, one on either side, well down; (*c*) a pair of pelvic or ventral fins on the body's underside, usually forward; (*d*) a single anal fin, positioned on the underside near the tail's base; and (*e*) a single caudal fin or tail. There are the inevitable variations, of course: Two dorsal fins, exceptionally three (members of the cod family), two anal fins (uncommon), one ahead of the other, and so on.

**Fish Culture:** Artificial or hatchery propagation and rearing of fishing for angling sport or for food. Trout are a classic example of the former. Certain kinds of carp are among cultured food species. Breeding on a large scale for food has come to be called "fish farming," and chances are we'll see more and more of it. Fish culture also involves rearing of exotic species for home aquariums. Whatever the destiny of its products, fish culture employs experimentation and selective breeding to bring out the most desirable characteristics—size, hardiness, adaptability, etc.

**Fish-Finder:** (*1*) A rig (described elsewhere in this book) employed in surf bottom fishing. (*2*) An optimistic nickname given to a depth sounder.

**Fish Ladder:** A contrivance, which could be likened to an escalator, that enables river-migrating fishes to get around dams and other obstructions.

**Flasher:** (*1*) A shiny spoon or spinner blade tied just ahead of a bait or lure for added attraction. Sometimes multiple flashers are riggged. (*2*) A type of depth sounder.

**Flats:** (*1*) Expanses of sand, mud or marl with very shallow water. Depths depend upon areas' low tides. Some flats are partly or completely exposed at low water. A sand bar is a type of flat. (*2*) A shortening of the term "flatfish," applied to flounders.

**Flies** or **Artificial Flies:** Man-made lures concocted from bits of feathers, animal hairs, tinsel, colored thread and other materials to simulate aquatic insects or other small items on fresh water and marine sport fishes' menus. There are hundreds of patterns.

**Float:** Another name for a bobber (see definition).

**Float Fishing:** Casting from a boat as she drifts with a river's flow. A delightful way to fish, with scenery as a bonus.

**Fluke:** A marine sport fish. The word also means "by accident," a convenient explanation for use by disgruntled experienced anglers when they're out-fished by novices.

**Fly Book:** A flat, wallet-like container of leather or synthetic material, lined with felt or sheep's wool, to carry and protec delicate flies. Used for those that can lie flat safely.

**Fly Box:** A small, compartmented box, nowadays of transparent plastic, for toting flies. Protects and separates them, keeps them readily available.

**Flying Bridge** or **Fly Bridge:** Part of a boat's superstructure. Essentially it's the roof of a cruiser's cabin, wheelhouse or deck lounge, with a protective rail and outfitted with a control console, seats, other refinements. Some are open to the sky; others have a canvas shelter, with or without side curtains, against sun and rain. A flying bridge's prime advantage is the added visibility it affords, handy in navigating and in maneuvering when playing large game fishes.

**Flying Gaff:** A large, long-handled gaff for big game fishes, characterized by a head or hook which pulls free of its handle when it sinks into a fish. *See Straight Gaff.*

**Foul-Hooked:** A fish that has been hooked—snagged—anywhere but in the mouth or jaw.

**Forage Fishes:** Species which serve as food for larger fishes. They may or may not have sport or commercial value. Some, such as menhaden, are an important dietary item for bluefish and other marine gamesters, and also are used industrially. Many sport and market species—Atlantic mackerel and others—are forage fishes for larger battlers such as tunas and sharks. In any case, forage fishes are a vital link in the underwater food chain.

**Freeboard:** That portion of a boat's hull (proper) above water, not counting superstructure. The distance between a deck and the water.

**Fusiform:** Frequently used in technical descriptions of fishes. There it refers to body shape and means "spindle-like," or somewhat tapered at both ends.

**Game Fish** (also spelled as one word): Any species taken by angling methods—as opposed to commercial fishing techniques—and putting up spirited resistance when hooked. Since each angler's opinion as to what constitutes "spirited resistance" varies, the latter half of that definition is very elastic. For legal purposes, state fish and game departments may use the term to indicate a species reserved for recreational fishermen and excluded from commercial exploitation.

**Gang Hook:** A treble hook.

**Gimbal:** A swiveling metal socket in a fighting or fishing chair to receive the end of a rod butt. It helps support the tackle's weight in big-game fishing.

**Ginpole** (also spelled as two words): A sturdy vertical boom or hoist, with block and fall (pulley system) at its top, on a sport fishing boat for lifting heftier battlers clear of the water. A ginpole is standard gear on big-game boats. Made from wood or aluminum, square or round in cross-section, it's mounted next to a gunnel in the cockpit.

**Gonads:** The reproductive organs of fishes, either sex.

**Groundfish,** or as two words, optionally: A species that lives or spends most of its time on or near the bottom. Usually applied to marine fishes.

**Ground Swells:** The long, broad, widely spaced, leisurely moving and sometimes high waves encountered on open ocean. Not infrequently ground swells roll in on otherwise calm days. Unlike some other kinds of waves, they do not need wind to be maintained, but often are "fringe benefits" from storms far offshore. As they approach the progressively shallower water of a sloping

# Glossary

**Airboat:** A boat designed specifically for navigating very shallow water and marshy regions, such as Florida's Everlades saw-grass country. Commonly the hull is aluminum, typified by a flat bottom and little draft, with an aircraft-type engine and propeller for power. Used in fishing and hunting.

**Anadromous** and **Catadromous**: *Anadromous* is a term applied to fishes that spend much or most of their lives in salt water, but move into fresh-water rivers to spawn. Outstanding examples are striped bass, shad and Altantic salmon. *Catadromous* fishes operate in the reverse, spending much of their lives in fresh water, but traveling to sea to breed. A classic case is the American eel. Fishes that move freely between salt and fresh waters, but not to spawn, are called *amphidromous*. Tarpon and snook are but two.

**Anchor Ice:** That which forms on or close to the bottom in salt water. Requires really cold weather to produce.

**Angleworm:** Another name for the common earthworm, used as bait, chiefly in fresh-water fishing.

**Aquatic Insects:** Those developing and/or living in water. There are thousands of kinds. Many are food items for fishes, and so are important to anglers. Some winged forms develop from eggs laid in the water, later emerge to fly about and mate. (*See Hatch.*) Many kinds—caddisflies, mayflies, etc.—are models in both their immature stage (larva or nymph) and adulthood for artificial flies for trout and other finned game.

**Artificials:** *Any* man-made imitations of items of fishes' natural food, as opposed to the real thing.

**Astern:** Any area behind and outside a boat.

**Backing:** Line going on a reel spool ahead of line ordinarily used, to fill it properly and to accommodate long-running opponents. Examples: That preceding a fly line; and that spooled on a reel under wire line. Backing line may be Dacron, monofilament, etc.

**Backlash:** A snarl that occurs in casting with a revolving-spool reel when the spool overruns the outgoing line.

**Bait:** Broadly, anything used to attract a fish to a hook. Generally used to indicate a natural food, but sometimes the definition is expanded to include artificials.

**Baitcasting:** Casting an artificial lure with a revolving-spool reel. Originally baitcasting involved bait fishes such as minnows. Now it also involves plugs and other fakes designed to simulate those fishes.

**Bait Fishing:** Any angling employing natural food—worms, clams, pieces of crabs or crayfish, fish strips, etc.

**Barbels:** Fleshy appendages, like thick "whiskers," on the chins and around the mouths of some fresh water species (catfishes) and marine fishes (cod and others). They're sense organs aiding their owners to find food on the bottom.

**Bass Boat:** Originally an outboard craft created specifically for fresh-water bass angling, hence the name. Born in the South, *circa* the 1930s, subsequently developed there and in the Southwest. In those regions the boats still are considered primarily for bass fishing, in which field they're enormously popular because of their speed, maneuverability and stability (speed often is important to getting around on huge impoundments). But the definition of bass boats has broadened to include many open outboard models, up to about seventeen or eighteen feet long and often with the so-called trihedral hull configuration, used in both fresh water and salt water action in many parts of the U.S.A. A typical bass boat has the following: Squarish forward *deck*, doubling as a casting platform; roomy, unobstructed cockpit, sometimes with a raised section forward for casting; a rating for an outboard motor up to about 85 horsepower; a swiveling fishing chair forward; electric trolling motor for quiet maneuvering on bass grounds, mounted forward; flasher-type depth sounder; live bait well or equivalent; and rod racks and some under-seat storage for tackle. Many have their controls in a console. Some have "stick steering," an adaptation of an aircraft's "joy stick," mounted with the motor controls alongside the forward fishing chair. Because of their speed, bass boats also are coming in for increasing service as fast all-purpose craft and in water skiing.

**Bass Bug:** A buoyant artificial worked in fly fishing. Bass bugs are designed to imitate various aquatic and terrestrial creatures consumed by black basses—insects, frogs, mice, etc. Distinguished from regular dry (floating) flies by a bulky body of cork, hairs or plastic.

**Bass-Bugging Rod:** A stouter than usual fly rod with more than average muscle to "turn over" the heavier bass bugs in casting.

**Beach Buggy:** A vehicle—four-wheel drive favored—for negotiating soft sand to reach remote or otherwise inaccessible stretches of beach. Beach buggies have many forms—Jeeps, little "dune hoppers," converted panel trucks, small campers, and so on, according to the affluence and imagination of owners.

**Bilge:** Lowermost area long the keel inside a hull. With an exclamation point it means "hogwash," "nonsense," "baloney," "who're you tryin' to kid?"

**Billfish:** General term for any marine species characterized by a prominent bony extension of the upper jaw to form a "bill"—sailfishes, marlins, swordfish. Another general term occasionally seen is *spearfishes*, but this is undersirable because there are distinct species with that name.

**Bill-Wrapping:** A situation in which a billfish gets a few turns of a leader around the bill as a result of rolling at the surface, jumping, or some other combat maneuver. It's common in marlin fishing.

**Billy:** A short club, sometimes weighted with a lead core, for rapping more rambunctious fishes on the noggin to subdue them. A tranquilizer, you might say.

**Bimini Twist:** A rather intricate knot—usually takes two to tie it—employed in marine big-game fishing. It was developed as a non-slip, non-cutting knot for the double line frequently used next to a leader for hefty opponents. Particularly useful for a double line in monofilament or Dacron that can't be spliced.

**Black Bass (or Basses):** A catch-all term for several kinds of fresh-water basses, including the largemouth, smallmouth and spotted varieties. Actually, "bass" is a misnomer, because these critters belong to the sunfish family and are not related to the true basses. This detracts nothing from their popularity, however.

**Blue Water:** In fishing and boating dialogue it means the deeper ocean water well offshore, in which sense it may or not be blue. In angling, **blue water fishing** usually is taken to mean big-game action.

**Bobber:** A float—also called that—to suspend a baited rig at a desired level beneath the surface. Its bobbing signals nibbles.

**Brackish Water:** A mixture of salt and fresh, as in tidal rivers, estuaries and the like.

**Broaching-To:** A situation we hope you'll know about only through reading. It's a precarious situation in which a boat is caught in a wave trough and swung broadside to oncoming rollers. Very hairy . . . sometimes fatal.

**Broadbill:** Anglers' shortening of "broadbill swordfish," the gladiator's full common name.

**Bucketfish:** A pail of a short length of stout twine with a snap-swivel. For unsuspecting beginners and fishermen who doze in fighting chairs. Secretly snapped on a line, it slides downward to simulate a hit and a fighting fish. Guaranteed to bring any patsy to alertness. Just be sure his rod is in a holder first. Also used is a disc of metal, aluminum or brass, about 12 inches in diameter—very realistic in the water as the boat moves ahead slowly. For added levity when the victim sees what he has been fighting, put this legend on the disc in large red letters: *DID I HURT YOU, HONEY?*

**Bucktail:** An artificial fly with long wings of animal hairs, made to resemble a minnow or other forage fish. Also a skirt of such hairs affixed to some salt-water lures, like lead-headed jigs. So called because the hairs originally came from deer tails.

**Bugging Taper:** On a fly line intended for casting the larger bass bugs, a short, rather heavy portion in its forward section.

**Bunker:** Contraction of "mossbunker,"(see Mossbunker).

**Butt:** Lowermost, thickest section of a rod.

**Calcutta:** A kind of bamboo popular in U.S. rod building many years ago and imported from India. So called because most shipments were made from Calcutta. Later replaced largely by Tonkin cane.

**Catadromous:** Defined under *Anadromous*.

**Caudal Fin:** A fish's tail. *See Fins*.

**Caudal Peduncle:** A technical term you'll encounter in fish anatomy. It means the base of the tail, where it connects with the body proper.

**Charter Boat:** A sport fishing craft with professional crew, available for hire by one or two individuals or a small group on an exclusive basis. Sizes range from small skiffs to 40- to 50-foot cruisers, according to action and areas. Fee usually includes tackle, other fishing essentials. Charters can go anywhere from a half-day to a week or more, depending upon skippers. *See Party Boat*.

**Chinese Fire Drill:** Confusion -- any kind.

**Chumming:** Distribution of natural food in the water to attract fishes to waiting hooks. Used for chum are ground-up fish, small whole shrimp, clams, pieces of fish, and small whole fish. The stream of chum extending outward from a boat is variously called a chum line, chum streak or chum slick. That first is the best term. The other two give an impression that chum remains on the surface.

**Ciguatera:** Of Spanish derivation and native to the Caribbean, the term refers to a type of poisoning acquired by eating the toxic flesh of otherwise fresh fishes. It's not a poisoning caused by devouring "spoiled" flesh. Many different species, chiefly tropical, have been known to cause *ciguatera*, sometimes fatally. Although it has been theorized that fishes' diet (toxic plants or organisms) is the villain, the illness is not yet understood thoroughly. It's difficult to track down because a given species may be poisonous to eat in one region, but not in another, or be under suspicion at a particular season but not at other times. Unfortunately, a fish's appearance gives no warning of *ciguatera*.

**Coaming:** A low "wall" around the gunnels of a cockpit to lessen splashes from waves.

**Cold Kill:** A destruction of marine fishes, sometimes in wholesale lots, by sudden, sharp drops in water temperature to which they can't adjust. Commonly a cold kill occurs when such fishes are overtaken in shallow waters and have no chance to escape to deeper, warmer areas. Some species can adjust to appreciable drops in water temperature if the change is gradual. Others are particularly sensitive and can't. In fresh water such a mortality is called a winter kill (see definition). Intolerably warm water also can cause mass kills among certain fresh water and marine fishes.

**Compass Rose:** A diagram of the mariner's compass card, indicating the instruments' directional points and degrees throughout 360° of arc. Compass roses appear on navigation charts.

**Conchs:** Marine snails grouped with the order Mollusca, a vast tribe that also includes clams, oysters and, believe it or not, squids and octopuses. Conchs are cut into pieces as bait for some salt water fishes.

beach they have no place to go but up, and some become higher and break. They can create quite a surf. Their lazy elevator action on boats fishing at anchor is a motion some people find conducive to *mal de mer*.

**Habitat:** Fishes and animals call it home sweet home. The environment in which they find conditions most satisfactory.

**Hackle:** A component of an artificial fly. A feather, from the neck or back of a chicken or other fowl, incorporated in the lure in such a way that it gives an illusion of legs.

**Hair Bug:** A floating lure popular in fly fishing for fresh water basses. Fashioned completely from animal hairs (caribou, deer) to imitate assorted critters, moths to frogs and crayfish.

**Hatch:** In fly fishing lingo, the emergence of certain kinds of flies that have developed underwater—graduation time, nymph or larval stage to mature, winged insects. A hatch or emergence occurs when nymphs make their way to the surface and there, while floating or atop a convenient dry rock, break out of their "shucks" and unfold their brand new wings for the first time. During emergence they're especially vulnerable to attacks by predators, a fact that doesn't go unnoticed by trout and other fishes, and they attend the graduation ceremony as uninvited guests. When fishes prey upon the emerging insects it's a "rise."

**Haywire Twist:** A method of forming a strong terminal loop in a wire leader. Commonly employed in marine big-game fishing.

**Head Boat:** Another name for a party boat (*which see*). Term stems from charging fares on a per-head or per-person basis.

**Hellgrammite:** Larval form of the dobsonfly, a fresh-water bait.

**High-Low Rig:** In salt water fishing, a two-hook rig in which one is tied in close to the sinker for bottom-cruising customers and its mate, the high hook, attached at varying distances above for fishes at levels above bottom.

**Horse Mackerel:** A term of historic interest. An old alias for bluefin tuna, usually the big specimens. Seldom spoken anymore, but seen in print occasionally.

**Hypolimnion:** A $10 word (used to be $5, but inflation jacked it) for the colder bottom layer of water in a lake.

**Ichthyology:** The study of fishes. Ancient Greeks had two words for it: *Ichthyos*, "fish," and *-logy*, "a discourse on or study of."

**Impoundment:** A body of water backed up behind a dam. The U.S. is getting increasing numbers of impoundments, many gigantic, as a result of hydroelectric, flood control and irrigation projects. Although often controversial, the fact remains that stocking them with fishes is providing angling for thousands of Americans, many of them in areas where there was no fishing before. Similarly, development of shoreside facilities—marinas, accommodations, etc.—is furnishing outdoor recreation for still others

**Inboard:** Within a boat's hull, as an inboard engine. Also applies to something brought into a boat, like a gaffed fish being swung inboard.

**Inboard/Outboard**(commonly shortened to I/O): A type of boat propulsion in which the engine proper is mounted permanently inside the hull, while its drive unit and propeller are outside like an outboard motor's. Also seen in print as "sterndrive" and "outdrive."

**Inferior Mouth:** Among fishes, a mouth positioned on the underside of the head, as in the case of sturgeons.

**Inshore:** A flexible word meaning close to shore. Users have their own definitions as to what constitutes "close." To a surfcaster it might signify out to a couple of hundred yards from a beach. To a troller it might be distances out to a mile or so. To an offshore fisherman it could mean any water inside of five miles from the beach. And so on. *See Offshore.*

**Jacking,** also known as **Gigging:** Locating fish by sight in shallow water and spearing them by hand. Technically, there's a fine difference between jacking and gigging. In many areas, "jacking" implies gigging at night with a lantern. Rod-and-reelers frown on both tactics..

**Jig:** A type of artificial, described elsewhere in this book.

**Jigging:** An angling technique.

**Johnboat:** A small, flat-bottom boat with straight sides and squarish bow and stern, lengths up to 18 or 20 feet or so. A kind of overgrown rowboat, really. Called a skiff in some regions. Developed for use in shallow, quiet water.

**Jug Fishing:** A fresh-water method in which a baited rig is tied to a glass or plastic jug that is allowed to drift with a river's current, the angler following in a boat. Employed for big catfish in the South.

**Kidney Harness:** A broad belt of leather and canvas or other material with a strong connector at each end. Employed in big-game fishing from a fighting chair, its widest portion fits in the small of the back and its connectors snap onto special moorings on the reel. Helps the back and shoulders get into the act. Also helps support the tackle while under strain.

**Killy Car:** A small, wooden, floating container for keeping killies (mummichogs) and other small bait fishes alive until needed. Tied alongside the boat, access is through a hatch on top. A forerunner of the live-bait well.

**Kite Fishing:** A procedure in which a kite serves as a kind of aerial outrigger. Can be used in ocean big-game fishing at anchor or while drifting to have an extra rig out or to keep a bait well clear of the boat. Also can be employed in shoreside and surf fishing, when the wind is right, to take a rig out beyond casting range.

**Kype:** A strange word for a strange, hook-like projection of the jaws of male salmon during breeding periods.

**Landing Net:** A small net consisting of a meshed bag, held open at its top by a frame and closed on the bottom, with a handle for wielding. For clinching capture of hooked fishes as they're lifted from the water. Used in both fresh and salt water.

**Lateral Line:** You'll encounter this term frequently in description of fishes. Simply explained, it's a row of specialized sensory receptors, part of a fish's nervous system, that apprises its owner of obstructions, changes in current flow, presence of creatures, etc. There's a lateral line on each side of the body, running lengthwise.

**Leadheads:** Collective name for a family of salt and fresh water jigs characterized by stubby, heavy bodies of metal. Some are dressed with bits of bucktail or feathers.

**Lee:** Literally, "shelter." The side of a boat or land mass away from the wind or foul weather, a sheltered side. If a vessel has the wind on her port side, for example, that becomes the *windward or weather side*, and her starboard is the lee side.

**Line Dressing:** A compound applied to a fly line to make it float.

**Littoral:** Means "coastal" or "of the coast or shore," especially a seacoast. A zone extending approximately from the intertidal belt to close inshore.

**Live Bait:** As its name implies, an item of fish diet impaled on a hook which is still alive to take advantage of its movements and more natural appearance. Live bait includes worms, small fishes, little crabs. Some anglers also apply the term to fresh bait that is cut into strips or chunks on the spot.

**Live-Bait Well:** A receptacle incorporated in a boat's hull to keep small fishes, eels and other bait alive until needed. Ideally, a live-bait well will have some means of circulating water to keep it fresh, properly oxygenated and at a reasonable temperature. There are also portable wells and *bait buckets*.

**Live-lining:** Definitions may vary regionally, but one is for a technique in which a live bait, sometimes suspended from a float, is allowed to drift away from the boat, the angler lightly holding the line in his hand to feel for nibbles.

**Longline:** A hated word among sport fishermen. It's a mass-production commercial fishing outfit consisting of long lengths of buoyed and moored main line from which shorter lines carrying baited hooks are suspended. A longline system may be strung out for 20, 25 miles or more. Longlines are a favored gear of the ubiquitous Japanese commercial fishermen, with which they harvest marlins, tunas, swordfish, sharks, other species. Among sport fishermen it's a tossup as to which is worse, longlines or big nets.

**Long Rod:** Nickname for a fly rod.

**Low-Water Slack and High-Water Slack:** "Low water" and "high water" refer to the tides of the same names, of course. "Slack" refers to a relatively short period after a low tide ebbs its fullest and before rising water begins: also, after a high tide reaches its peak and before it starts to drop. Slack water is just that—little or no current motion.

**Luck:** In fishing, as elsewhere, a seemingly ever-present intangible that comes in two kinds, good and bad. But with this modification: When anglers do well, good luck isn't mentioned. The word is skill. When catches are poor, skill isn't mentioned. The words are bad luck.

**Lure:** Generally considered as referring to an artificial bait, to separate it from natural ones. In the broadest sense, though, anything that attacts a fish to a hook is a lure.

**Mandible and Maxillary:** The bones of a fish's lower and upper jaws, respectively.

**Marl:** A word encountered in literature about fishing the flats, notably bonefishing. It's a sediment blanketing many flats where bonefish are hunted. Off-white or grayish, marl consists chiefly of calcium carbonate from coral and disintegrating shells, plus material from certain plants. Little puffs or clouds of it in otherwise clear water on flats may betray the presence of feeding bonefish or permits, but it makes for difficult wading.

**Midge:** A tiny aquatic insect resembling a mosquito and an important food item for some fresh-water fishes. You may hear it nicknamed "punky," "gnat," "smut" or "no-see-um." Despite their small size, midges are imitated by artificial flies. Unlike mosquitoes, midges do not bite, but they pester streamside anglers by swarming around the head and face and dancing in front of the eyes.

**Milt:** The spermatic fluid of male fishes. At hatcheries it's "milked" from donors for adding to eggs in artificial propagation.

**Mossbunker:** The most often used common name of the menhaden, a member of the herring tribe and related, believe it or not, to the mighty tarpon. Extremely important in East Coast marine angling, where the flesh is used variously as chum and bait for several species. Menhaden oil and flesh have industrial applications too.

**Multiplying Reel:** As opposed to a single-action reel, one with a gear system that multiplies the turns of a revolving spool with each revolution of its crank. Gear ratios go 2½:1, 3:1 and more.

**Mudding:** Bonefish or other flats-feeding fishes stirring up clouds of marl.

**Mummies:** Short for "mummichogs," an American Indian name for small minnow-like, salt water fish employed as bait. "Killifish" and "killies" are other names.

**Native Trout:** Originally, a name given to brook trout in the Eastern U.S. to distinguish them from brown trout introduced from Europe in the late 1800s. Now 't's also a regional alias for cutthroat trout in the West. Sometimes it's applied to a species of trout native to a region to differentiate it from other kinds that have been introduced.

**New York Bight:** A spacious oceanic triangle

formed by the northern New Jersey coast as one side and the southern shore of New York's Long Island as the other. The triangle's apex is at Staten Island and Manhattan. Its broad base is the open Atlantic to the east. From the standpoint of sheer numbers of anglers enjoying it, New York Bight is one of the world's most important sport fishing regions.

**Nymph:** An underwater stage in the development of certain winged aquatic insects. Since nymphs are items of fish food, there are artificials to simulate them. Additionally some nymphs are used as natural bait.

**Offset Handle:** A recessing of a portion of a rod handle for better seating of certain baitcasting reels.

**Offshore:** On an ocean or a truly huge body of inland water, "offshore" usually is interpreted as meaning an appreciable distance off the beach, perhaps out of sighting of land. Where an inshore zone ends and offshore begins is largely a matter of individuals' definition. There's no set distance. Thus for one angler "offshore" may begin, say, a mile out, while for another the term conjures up distances of five or ten miles or more. For whatever it's worth, here's one old-time deep sea fisherman's explanation: Inshore, up to about three miles out; offshore, beyond that. *See Inshore.*

**Omnivorous:** Used in describing fishes' feeding habits. Means "eating everything."

**Open Boat:** Another name for a party boat. Doesn't refer to a lack of cabins, but to the fact that the boat is open to the public.

**Operculum:** Fancy name for a fish's gill cover.

**Outboard:** (1) Applied to anything extending outward from or located outside a boat, the opposite of Inboard. (2) Short for "outboard motor" and a boat so powered.

**Outriggers:** Two pole-like structures that can be extended outward, port and starboard, from a boat like skinny arms. Strictly for trolling: to allow putting out more rigs, or to keep lures and bait well clear of the craft or to prevent their interfering with other rigs.

**Palming** or **To Palm:** In baitcasting, grasping the reel by its sideplate in the palm of the hand.

**Panfishes:** In fresh-water angling a catch-all term to indicate species—bluegills, yellow perch, etc.—considered too small (frying pan size) to be considered game fishes.

**Parr:** Not the one named Jack, but a young salmon at a particular stage of development. Darkish bars or blotches appearing on the sides at this time are known as parr marks.

**Party Boat:** A public sport fishing vessel manned by a professional crew and accepting passengers on a first-come, first-served basis within her legal safe capacity, fares charged per person. Fare usually include bait, but not tackle, which can be rented at a modest fee aboard some boats. Because they carry more fishermen, most party boats are longer than the average charter boats. Lengths into the 60- to 70-foot bracket are not uncommon; some in the New Jersey-New York region reach 100 to 110 feet. Like their charter counterparts, well-maintained party boats are outfitted with electronic gear—depth sounders, radiotelephones, radar, even loran—for safety, navigation and efficiency. Among comfort refinements are heated cabins in winter and snack bars. Party boats in the San Francisco area have swivel seats around the rails, a feature not usually seen on their East Coast sisters. Besides charging on a per-head basis, party boats differ further from charter craft by leaving their docks at a set morning hour, or evening time when there's night fishing, then returning after a period of hours when captains figure they've given customers' their money's worth. Charter boats sail and return at hours mutually agreeable to clients and skippers. Millions of anglers enjoy party boats all along the U.S. coastal perimeter, from Maine to Florida, around the Gulf of Mexico's rim, and up the Pacific seaboard from California to Oregon and Washington.

**Pelagic:** Of or pertaining to the open sea, beyond the littoral belt. And at sea there's a pelagic zone, the uppermost layer extending to a depth to which light penetrates. "Pelagic" also is applied to fishes living in the open sea and/or its upper reaches.

**Pharyngeal Teeth:** Those in the throat, found among some fishes.

**Phytoplankton:** Plant forms of plankton. See plankton.

**Pintle:** The short, round, deck-mounted shaft on which the seat of a fighting chair swivels.

**Plankton:** From a Greek work, planktos, meaning "wandering." Collectively the term refers to many kinds of tiny, even microscopic, animals and plants residing in salt and fresh waters, often in upper levels. By and large they're free-wheeling organisms, floating and drifting at the whims of currents. Many forms are capable of commuting vertically between different layers of the sea by altering their specific gravity. Plankton are divided into two broad groups: Phytoplankton or plant forms, such as algae; and zooplankton or animal forms, which include minute worms and crustaceans. All together they comprise a vital first link in the underwater world's food chain, devoured by little fishes that are in turn eaten by larger ones, and so on up the scale. Many fishes are plankton-feeders, including, incongruously, the largest of all, the whale shark.

**Pod:** Definitions vary a bit, but "pod" commonly is interpreted as meaning a small group of fish, as opposed to a school.

**Point:** In fly angling, the tippet or outermost section of a tapered leader. When two flies are attached to the same leader, that tied directly to the tippet is a point fly, while the second fly, secured via a short length of leader material (a dropper), is called the dropper fly.

**Practice Plug:** A small dummy "plug" of rubber, without hooks, for practice casting.

**Predacious** or **Predatory:** Means "preying upon others." All flesh-eating creatures, including fishes, fit the adjective to one degree or another.

**Presentation:** In fly fishing, that finale phase of a cast in which the line straightens out and the lure lands on the water to be accepted or ignored. It's often the detail that separates duffers and aces.

**Progressive Taper:** Simplified, the tapering of a rod in such a way that its tip section bends sensitively with the lighter lures and bait, yet farther down has "spine" and power for casting heavier weights. A progressive taper, therefore, allows a wider range of casting weights than other rods.

**Quadrant Brake:** The most common form of brake adjustment on revolving-spool reels is the star drag. Some of the more expensive models substitute a lever for the star-shaped wheel. Mounted on the crank side, it moves forward and backward through 90 degrees of arc (hence the name "quadrant," one-quarter of a circle) to tighten or loosen the drag. Right under the lever is a tricolor band to show degrees of tightness. A quadrant brake's advantages over a star drag are its easier accessibility and the fact that it can be returned to previous settings more precisely.

**Race:** A stretch of water where a tide or current flows at a lively clip. Races can be productive fishing places because they tumble little fishes and other food that get seized by predators. They also can be rough, even dangerous for small boats, when especially swift or strong, or when there are colliding currents or a tide is battling a wind.

**RDF:** Short for "radio direction finder," described among electronic aids to fishing in this book.

**Redd:** A "nest" or shallow, saucer-shaped depression scooped out of the bottom, usually by female fishes with sweeping motions of their tails, as a repository for fertilized eggs during incubation. Several fresh water species build redds. Trout are noted for it. Among some fishes the males become security officers during incubation and hatching, fiercely guarding the nests against predators.

**Red Tide:** Expanses of discolored sea water, rusty-looking, caused by "blooms" or great population explosions of certain minute organisms. Those known as dinoflagellates are the most notorious producers of red tides, and chief among them is a kind called *Gymnodinium brevis*—Jim Brevis for short. Jim Brevis stands indicted as the cause of Florida's red tides. The organisms are tiny—25,000 strung out would measure only about an inch, but in a bloom they can be lethal to fishes in wholesale lots, due to a poison they release. During heavy blooms this substance sometimes finds its way into the air when the organisms break down. Carried about as a vapor or fine mist, it can be irritating to human eyes. "Tides" (blooms) can be yellow, black, green, blue or other color, according to the organisms involved. In fresh water a similar condition is caused by a green algae when they erupt in population explosions. It's reported that animals have died from drinking water so contaminated. Fortunately, not all dinoflagellates are toxic to fishes.

**Riffles:** Minor disturbances on the water's surface caused by wind or by a flow over submerged objects, commonly seen in shallow streams. At sea, from a distance, wind riffles can be mistaken for a ruckus generated by surface-feeding game fish. That's when binoculars come in handy to save fuel and time.

**Rip:** A fast-moving tidal current, usually marked by some turbulence and bubbly water. Tide rips frequently occur around a point of land or in an inlet or narrowing channel. Edges of rips are productive angling locations. Prowling game fishes hunt lesser neighbors seeking haven in quieter water. The rips themselves also produce. Techniques include anchoring to one side of a rip and casting a lure or letting a bait drift toward the edge, as well as trolling in the rip.

**Rocket Taper:** *See Weight-forward line.*

**Rod Belt,** also known as **Gimbal Belt:** A wide belt, of canvas and leather, with a reinforced cup or gimbal that accepts the end of a rod butt. Worn in stand-up arguments with opponents that are big enough to be ornery but not so large as to need a fighting chair. It helps support the tackle, taking some of the strain off the angler's arms and protecting the abdomen and sensitive parts of his or her anatomy against possibly painful jabs of the rod butt. As a charter skipper remarked, fighting a tough opponent without one could give you another bellybutton.

**Rod Holder:** A sleeve of metal or high-impact plastic for holding a rod when not in action. Rod holders are secured to a boat's coaming or gunnel. Some fishing craft have them already built in, flush-mounted in the deck alongside the cockpit. Fighting and fishing chairs come equipped with them.

**Roe:** A fish's eggs while still contained in the ovary. The roe of some species is edible. That of shad is considered a delicacy when fried. Sturgeons' roe is processed to become that expensive item known as caviar. In dramatic contrast, the roe of some species is poisonous when eaten. A noteworthy example is that of puffers and gars. Puffers include the mass-caught "blowfish" of the East Coast. A certain portion of that species' flesh is fine eating, marketed as "blowfish tails" and appearing on restaurant menus under such fancy aliases as "sea squab" and "chicken of the sea." But certain internal organs, especially the gonads and liver, are highly toxic to humans, possibly fatal. *And don't give them to pets.* The "treat" will kill them.

**Roiled Water:** That water clouded by mud or sand in suspension, as a river during spring run-off or the surf after a storm. It impairs the visibility of lures, often calls for larger or lighter-colored models, or those with sonic effects, to compensate.

**Salinity:** Degree of saltiness of water. It varies, even in sea water. Some fishes can tolerate or adapt to a broad range of salinity, even dilution in brackish water. Others are sensitive to relatively slight changes. Salinity may be a vital factor in the survival of eggs and infants among some fishes.

**Sandbugs,** also known as **Sand Fleas** and **Mole Crabs** (from their habit of burrowing): Neither bugs nor fleas, but a form of crustacean. Found along Atlantic and Pacific oceanfront beaches in wet sand, where they dig in. They're bait, alone or in combination with artificials, for some marine sport fishes, including pompano and striped bass.

**Sand Spike:** A rod holder with a pointed leg for thrusting into a beach or shore, a surf fishing accessory. Keeps a reel out of the sand during recesses.

**School Tuna:** Not a distinct species *per se*, but young bluefin tuna. The "school" refers to their habit of traveling in groups, often huge. Arbitrarily, the school-size classification goes up to about 100, 125 pounds. Bigger individuals enter a category labeled "giants," but here again cataloging is flexible, indefinite. To some fishermen, bluefins become giants at 300 pounds (their size potential goes to at least 1,000); to others, at 500. Strangely, there has never been a popular name for the size category between school and giant.

**Scrod:** A market and restaurant menu term for very small cod, usually those to about 3 or 4 pounds.

**Sea Anchor:** A cone of canvas put out to keep a vessel headed into the wind in foul weather and when drifting. Sea anchors have been improvised from tarpaulins. They function in water like a kite does in a breeze.

**Seizing:** A method of connecting two lengths of line, or a line and a leader, or with a double line, without knots. *It can't be used with monofilament.* It's a wrapping procedure. Dental floss can be used as seizing material, but it tends to slip. Dacron seizing on Dacron line definitely will slip. Best is a strand of linen fishing line, but *it should be no heavier than about 1/3 the strength of the line to be seized.* Seizing isn't difficult, but it must be done absolutely right. Then it will hold on lines through 130-pound test and pass through rod guides freely. It's as least as strong as a knot.

**Shoal:** (1) Regarding water depths: it means "shallow." (2) Also used, not so much in the U.S. but in British angling literature, as a synonym for "school" (of fish).

**Shooting Line:** The uniform-diameter section of a weight-forward fly line that follows the back taper.

**Shooting the Line:** In flycasting, releasing line previously hand-stripped from the reel, at the instant when momentum from a forward cast starts to pull. This momentum usually is sufficient to pull additional yardage from the reel. Its purpose is to lengthen a cast.

**Single-Action Reel:** A non-multiplying model. That is, it has no gears, so 1 turn of its crank = 1 revolution of its spool. Single-action reels are fly reels. (*See Multiplying Reel.*)

**Siphon:** The "neck" of certain clams, part of their mechanism for taking in or ejecting water. Used as bait for some marine fishes. Its flesh is tough, stays on a hook well.

**Skunked:** Coming back without fish.

**Snell:** A short length of gut, monofilament or tarred line already secured to a hook, usually with a loop for its attachment to a rig. Snelled hooks are without eyes, the snell being secured directly to the shank.

**Spawning:** Reproduction or breeding among fishes.

**Spearing** or **Sperling** (ichthyologists favor **Silversides**): A very small, silvery, salt water fish used as bait for fluke, young bluefish and other species on the Atlantic seaboard. Their much greater importance is in the sea's economy, where they are forage for many larger species. Fried, they're edible and are a component of a seafood platter known as whitebait.

**Spent-Wing:** A dry fly design in which hackle feathers are tied to extend horizontally and at right angles to the hook shank. The idea is to imitate a "spent" or dead mayfly or other flying insect.

**Spider:** Another artificial fly pattern, this one in dry and wet types. Characterized by hackles that are extra-long in relation to hook size. They imitate insects and usually are most effective on glassy or fairly calm surfaces.

**Spikes:** A term applied, often derisively, to undersized individuals of some marine species, notably Atlantic mackerel and northern weakfish.

**Sport Fisherman** (or as one word): You know its meaning. The purpose in including it here is to explain a difference between one- and two-word spellings. As two words it better differentiates between recreational and commercial fishermen, since the latter is always written as two. Further, as one word it also has come to mean a boat used for sport fishing.

**Spud:** A sharp-toothed device with a long handle for chopping holes in ice fishing. Many ice anglers prefer a specially designed auger, which drills a hole. There are also powered augers.

**Squidding:** Surfcasting metal artificials—squids—made to resemble various small bait fishes.

**Star Drag:** A Brake system on a revolving-spool reel. Adjustment—tightening or easing-off—of the drag is by a star-shaped wheel mounted on the crank's shaft. Most revolving-spool reels have this arrangement. (*See Quadrant Brake.*)

**Steamer:** A soft-shell clam used as bait when clams are indicated. Excellent eating when steamed and dunked in melted butter.

**Still-Fishing:** Angling at anchor.

**Stink Bait:** A repulsive name for an often repulsive bait (repulsive to humans, that is). It's awful-smelling stuff, but catfishes find it very tasty. Items include putrid meat, chicken guts, and cheese so strong it could tear holes in your shirt.

**Streamer Fly:** A type of artificial fly worked in both fresh and salt water, typified by a long feather or hair wing to simulate a minnow or other little bait fish.

**Strike:** (1) When a fish smacks a bait or lure. (2) Raising the rod tip to sink a hook in a fish.

**Straight Gaff:** Also called a fixed-head gaff. One whose hook or head is affixed to its handle, won't come free like that of a flying gaff.

**Stringer:** A length of stout twine or light rope to secure and transport a catch. The stringer is fed in through a fish's mouth and out under a gill cover.

**Stripe** and **Striper:** The first is short for striped marlin, the later for striped bass.

**Stripping Line:** In fly fishing, pulling line from the reel by hand prior to casting. In a few salt water techniques—none of them casting—a few yards of line may be hand-stripped from the reel to better present a bait.

**Sucker:** A kind of fresh water fish. Also a guy who buys junky tackle.

**Supralittoral:** That zone of a beach above the normal high tide line. (*See Littoral.*)

**Tagging:** Marking fishes with special tags to keep track of their movements and populations, a very important part of fisheries' research in which every angler can assist. One kind of tag is the so-called spaghetti type, a thin plastic tube with a metal end that is superficially planted in the flesh of the back of the fish. Another type can be clipped on a fin. Tags are neither harmful nor do they hinder their wearers.

**Tailrace:** A stretch of river or its channel just below a dam, a section into which an impoundment's water is released from time to time. Often good for trout and other species.

**Tapered Leaders, Tapered Lines:** Discussed in the section devoted to fly fishing equipment.

**Teleosts:** You won't see this word often, but you will run across it, so you might as well learn it. It's technical language for "bony fishes," a category that embraces just about all the finned creatures you'll ever hook. Bony fishes are those with—you guessed it—internal skeletons of bone. Sharks, by the way, are not teleosts. Their framework is of cartilage.

**Terminal Tackle:** Collectively, anything beyond the end of a line—leaders, swivels, hooks, sinkers, lures. Everything but the fish.

**Thumbing:** Lightly braking a revolving spool with the thumb during a cast, mainly to prevent backlashes. Not recommended as a means of braking when a fish runs—can give painful line burns.

**Tippet:** That portion of a fly leader nearest the lure, and—note this—frequently subject to the greatest wear.

**Trace:** (1) In marine angling, "trace" may refer to a wire leader: or, loosely used, any leader. In big-game fishing it can indicate a wire leader or a doubled line, or both, separately or as a unit. That use makes for confusion, which may be why you won't hear it too much anymore in that sense. (2) In baitcasting, a trace is the link between casting line and lure. It can be of wire, some kind of line, etc.

**Trash Fishes:** A commercial fishing term for any species without market value, ordinarily discarded. But they can be ground into pulp for chum, if you can contact a local netter.

**Trolling Blind:** Also known as "scratching." It's trolling without having sighted fish. Sometimes also a form of optimism.

**Trotline:** A stout main line from which short lines carrying baited hooks dangle every couple of feet. A trotline may be strung across a stream or be moored and buoyed in a strategic location. Trotlining is primarily a commercial method, used for catfishes and other species. Anglers generally frown on it as being unsporting. In some regions or for certain fishes it may be prohibited by law.

**Tuna Tower:** A skeletal structure of metal tubing with a small, railed-in platform rising above a sport fishing cruiser's flying bridge and accessible by ladder. Its advantage is the added visibility afforded by its height. Primarily for sighting marine game fishes at the surface, but it also can aid in navigation—for spotting buoys in the distance, etc. Towers come factory-installed or can be added later. The most elaborately outfitted tuna towers have steering and engine controls for maneuvering in combat with big gamesters.

**Tyee:** A U.S. Pacific Coast nickname for chinook or king salmon.

**Ultra-Light Tackle:** The very lightest gear, whatever its type. In this weight class you find the extremes. Ultra-light spinning tackle, for example, includes rods less than 3 ounces (total) and hair-thin lines under 3-pound test. Ultra-light status varies with the kinds of equipment. For instance, what would be called ultra-light in conventional gear would be heavier than its counterpart in fly fishing. In any case, it all is very sporty, but it imposes considerably greater demands on the wielder's skill. It also requires resignation to prospects of losing some fish, lures and line. It's not for novices.

**Unhooker** and **hook disgorger:** As their names imply, these are devices for getting hooks out of catches. They're handy when a hook has been very solidly planted or has been taken deep in the gullet, and doubly so when a fish has a mouthful of sharp dental work. They save time too. There are various hook-removers. Cheapest is a disgorger, a simple metal tool six inches or so long that is slid down along the line or leader to the hook to force it free. Costing a bit more but superior is a gadget that looks like a long pair of pliers with a pistol grip. With this you can seize a hook even deep in the throat and work it loose with the instrument's jaws, well clear of fish fangs. Many veteran anglers dispense with a disgorger or unhooker, and have bite scars to prove it.

**Variant:** A kind of dry fly characterized by larger than ordinary hackles but otherwise dressed in the manner of a standard pattern.

**Ventral:** Applied to the lowermost sides and "belly" of a fish, the opposite of dorsal.

**Vomerine Teeth:** A term encountered in angling literature. Vomerine teeth are those found on the roof of the mouth of some species.

**Weight-Forward Line:** A type of fly line. Synonyms are "forward-taper," "rocket head," "bass bug taper," "torpedo head."

**Wet Fly:** An artificial fly, usually sparsely dressed, designed to simulate a drowned insect or the larval form of some aquatic insect. Accordingly, it's fished below the surface.

**Whitebait:** A seafood platter conceived in England in the 1700s. Essentially it consists of up to half a dozen different kinds of very small or very young salt water fishes deep-fried to golden crispness. Smelt, sardines, herring and anchovies are among those cooked in U.S. versions. You may see them sold in fish markets under the name "whitebait."

**White Water:** Foamy, bubbly water caused by turbulence—tide rips, a rough surf, colliding currents, etc.

**Winter Kill:** Death by suffocation for fresh water fishes. What happens is this: Lakes and ponds get oxygen through contact with air. When they ice-over, that supply is cut off. However, if the ice is clear enough to let sunlight through, aquatic plants may be able to generate enough oxygen for the finned residents. But if the ice will not permit sunlight penetration, as when covered with snow, those plants die and decompose, and in so doing consume oxygen instead of releasing it. Oxygenation of the water then becomes so depleted that fishes die from suffocation. Shallow lakes and ponds with large fish populations are most prone to the calamity. Not all winter kills are calamities, however. Sometimes they serve a beneficial purpose by reducing overpopulations so that survivors have better feeding conditions.

**Wreck Buoy:** All buoys have significance for boat-navigating anglers, but this one can be special. Carrying red and black horizontal stripes, it marks a wreck that might just be productive of several kinds of fishes. This is especially true in salt water, where wreck-frequenting species include cod, sea bass, blackfish (tautogs) and porgies.

**X:** Used with a figure to indicate (a) wire diameters of hooks and (b) the diameter, and therefore the strength (with pounds-test equivalent) of leader material. By itself, the letter "X" doesn't represent a unit of measurement. When combined with a figure—2X, 3X, etc.—it represents a definite measurement in thousandths of an inch. Needless to say, for practical comparison purposes it's a lot easier to remember 2X, 3X, and so forth than thousandths of an inch.

**Y-Rig:** Coined name for a certain salt water bottom rig involving two snelled hooks. Hook No. 1 is attached to the line in the usual desired fashion, generally close to the sinker. Hook No. 2 then is bridled—tied—by its snell at about the middle of the first hook's snell, forming a Y-shaped rig. If necessary, a leader is used for No. 1, but never on No. 2. This rig's main service is in drifting. It's often favored for rocky floors, but is applicable to any bottom fishing.

**Zoogeography:** A study of the geographic distribution of fishes and animals, together with any special adaptations in regions.

**Zooplankton:** Those planktonic organisms that are classified as animal in nature, as opposed to plant forms or phytoplankton. Among zooplankton are minute crustaceans and worms, protozoa and other simple creatures.

# State Fish and Game Departments 15

These agencies are very good sources of information about angling in their respective states and they respond to requests with literature telling about available species and best seasons for same, often with suggestions as to areas, methods, lures and bait. Sometimes maps are included.

Rod-'n'-reelers planning to give other states a whirl should contact those fish and game departments *beforehand* to be apprised of additional details such as non-resident license fees, catch limits, open and closed seasons for certain species, and so on. They also will want to know about any special permits needed in addition to a regular fishing license.

**ALABAMA**
Department of Conservation and Natural Resources
64 N. Union Street
Montgomery 36104

**ALASKA**
Department of Fish and Game
Subport Building
Juneau 99801

**ARIZONA**
Game and Fish Department
2222 W. Greenway Rd.
Phoenix 85023

**ARKANSAS**
Game and Fish Commission
Game and Fish Building
State Capitol Grounds
Little Rock 72201

**CALIFORNIA**
Department of Fish and Game
1416 Ninth St.
Sacramento 95814

**COLORADO**
Fish and Game Department
6060 Broadway
Denver 80216

**CONNECTICUT**
Board of Fisheries and Game
State Office Building
Hartford 06115

**DELAWARE**
Department of Natural Resources and Environmental Control
Division of Fish and Wildlife
P.O. Box 457
Dover 19901

**FLORIDA**
(1) Game and Fresh Water Fish Commission
(fresh water information)
620 S. Meridian St.
Tallahassee 32304

(2) Florida's Department of Natural Resources
(salt water information)
Larson Building
Tallahassee 32304
(We suggest writing to both.)

**GEORGIA**
Game and Fish Commission
270 Washington St., S.W.
Atlanta 30334

**HAWAII**
Department of Land and Natural Resources
Division of Fish and Game
1179 Punchbowl St.
Honolulu
(Incidentally, Hawaii offers some fresh water fishing in addition to its famous salt water action. Ask for booklet.)

**IDAHO**
Fish and Game Department
600 S. Walnut St.
Boise 83707

**ILLINOIS**
**Department of Conservation**
**Division of Fisheries**
102 State Office Building
Springfield 62706

**INDIANA**
Department of Natural Resources
Division of Fish and Game
608 State Office Building
Indianapolis 46204

**IOWA**
State Conservation Commission
State Office Building
300 4th Street
Des Moines 50319

**KANSAS**
Forestry, Fish and Game Commission
Box 1028
Pratt 67124

**KENTUCKY**
Department of Fish and Wildlife Resources
State Office Building Annex
Frankfort 40601

**LOUISIANA**
Wild Life and Fisheries Commission
400 Royal St.
New Orleans 70130

**MAINE**
(1) Department of Sea and Shore Fisheries
State House Annex
Capitol Shopping Center
Augusta 04330
(2) Department of Inland Fisheries and Game
State House,
Augusta 04330

**MARYLAND**
Department of Natural Resources
Fish and Wildlife Administration
Tawes State Office Building
580 Taylor Avenue
Annapolis 21401

**MASSACHUSETTS**
Department of Natural Resources
Division of Fisheries and Game
100 Cambridge St.
Boston 02202

**MICHIGAN**
Department of Natural Resources
Stevens T. Mason Building
Lansing 48926

**MINNESOTA**
Department of Natural Resources
Division of Game and Fish
Centennial Office Building
658 Cedar St.
St. Paul 55101

**MISSISSIPPI**
Game and Fish Commission
Game and Fish Building
402 High St
Jackson 39205

**MISSOURI**
Missouri Department of Conservation
P. O. Box 180
Jefferson City 65101

**MONTANA**
Department of Fish and Game
Mitchell Building
Helena 59601

**NEBRASKA**
Game and Parks Commission
State Capitol Building
Lincoln 68509

**NEVADA**
Department of Fish and Game
P.O. Box 10678
Reno 89510

**NEW HAMPSHIRE**
Fish and Game Department
34 Bridge St.
Concord 03301

**NEW JERSEY**
Department of Environmental Protection
Division of Fish, Game and Shell Fisheries
P.O. Box 1809
Trenton 08625

**NEW MEXICO**
Department of Game and Fish
State Capitol
Santa Fe 87501

**NEW YORK**
Department of Environmental Conservation
Conservation Department Building
State Office Building Campus
50 Wolf Rd.
Albany 12201

**NORTH CAROLINA**
Wildlife Resources Commission
P.O. Box 2919
Raleigh 27602

**NORTH DAKOTA**
State Game and Fish Department
2121 Lovett Ave.
Bismark 58501

**OHIO**
Department of Natural Resources
907 Ohio Departments Building
Columbus 43215

**OKLAHOMA**
Department of Wildlife Conservation
Information and Education Division
1801 N. Lincoln
Oklahoma City 73105

**OREGON**
State Game Commission
P.O. Box 3503
Portland 97208

**PENNSYLVANIA**
Pennsylvania Fish Commission
P.O. Box 1070
Harrisburg 17120

**RHODE ISLAND**
Department of Natural Resources
Division of Fish and Wildlife
Veterans' Memorial Building
Providence 02903

**SOUTH CAROLINA**
(1) Department of Parks, Recreation and Tourism
P.O. Box 1358
Columbia 29202
(2) Division of Game and Freshwater Fisheries
P.O. Box 167
Columbia 29202

**SOUTH DAKOTA**
Department of Game, Fish and Parks
State Office Building
Pierre 57501

**TENNESSEE**
Game and Fish Commission
P.O. Box 40747
Nashville 37220

**TEXAS**
Parks and Wildlife Department
Information and Education Section
John H. Reagan Building
Austin 78701

**UTAH**
Fish and Game Division
1596 W. North Temple
Salt Lake City 84116

**VERMONT**
Vermont Fish and Game Department
Montpelier 05602

**VIRGINIA**
(1) Virginia Department of Conservation and Economic Development
Division of Public Relations and Advertising
811 State Office Building
Richmond 23219
(2) Commission of Game and Inland Fisheries
4010 W. Broad St.
Richmond 23230
(We suggest writing to both.)

**WASHINGTON**
Department of Game
Fishery Management Division
600 N. Capitol Way
Olympia 98504

**WEST VIRGINIA**
Department of Natural Resources
Division of Wildlife Resources
State Office Building No. 3
Charleston 25305

**WISCONSIN**
Department of Natural Resources
Division of Fisheries
Box 450
Madison 53701

**WYOMING**
Game and Fish Commission
Information and Education Division
Box 1589
Cheyenne 82001

**FEDERAL**
United States Fish and Wildlife Service
Department of the Interior
Washington, D.C. 20242

**AND IN THE OCEANS AND SEAS**

**Puerto Rico**
Department of Natural Resources
P.O. Box 11488
San Juan 00910
(We suggest writing Sport Fishing Information on the envelope.)

**U.S. Virgin Islands**
Department of Conservation and Cultural Affairs
Charlotte Amalie
St. Thomas 00801
(Here too it would be a good idea to write Sport Fishing Information on the envelope.)

**American Samoa**
Government of American Samoa
Department of Marine Resources
Office of Tourism
Pago Pago, Tutuila 96920

**Guam**
You're on your own here. You might try addressing the envelope like this (and lots of luck): Department of Tourism Information, Office of the Governor, Agana, Guam 96910. Failing to get a reply, try the U.S. Fish and Wildlife Service in Washington.

# Bibliography 16

There are many fine books about angling, fresh water and salt water; and more are coming out all the time. Collectively, they discuss every conceivable aspect of the sport. Individually, their coverage varies widely.

The list of titles we're about to suggest covers a broad spectrum. With it you can build an excellent library, and you can do it inexpensively by purchasing one book at a time. We've concentrated on volumes of more recent vintage because older books have a way of vanishing from the scene. All books are in hard covers unless otherwise specified.


*Angler's Guide to the Fresh Water Sport Fishes;* Edward C. Migdalski; The Ronald Press Co., New York, 1962; 431 pages.

*Angler's Guide to the Salt Water Game Fishes* (a companion volume to the above); Edward C. Migdalski; same publisher, 1958; 506 pages.

*Art Flick's New Streamside Guide to Naturals and Their Imitations;* Art Flick; Crown Publishers, New York, 1969; 173 pages.

[*The*] *ABC's of Fishing* (paper cover); Bob Zwirz; Digest Books, Northfield, Ill., 1974; 288 pages.

*A Fine Kettle of Fish Stories* (humor); Ed Zern; Winchester Press, New York, 1972; 122 pages.

[*The*] *Art of Tying the Wet Fly & Fishing the Flymph;* James E. Leisenrig and Vernon S. Hidy; Crown Publishers, New York, 1971; 160 pages.

*Anglers' Guide to the United States Atlantic Coast;* Bruce L. Freeman and Lionel Walford; 1974. In four sections, each with paper covers: Section I covers Passamaquoddy Bay, Me., to Cape Cod; Section II, Nantucket Shoals, Mass., to Long Island Sound; Section III, Block Island, R.I., to Cape May, N.J.; and Section IV, Delaware Bay to False Cape, Va. Thin books with huge pages (14 by 16½ inches), with charts, other useful information. For sale by the Superintendent of Documents, U.S. Government Printing Office, Washington, D.C. 20402.

*A Book of Trout Flies;* Preston J. Jennings; Crown Publishers, New York, 1970; 190 pages.

[*The*] *Art and Science of Fly Fishing;* Lenox H. Dick; Winchester Press, New York.

*Bait Tail Fishing;* Al Reinfelder; A. S. Barnes and Co., New York, 1969; 168 pages.

[*The*] *Blue Water Bait Book;* Capts. Samuel A. Earp and William J. Wildeman; Little, Brown and Co., Boston, 1974; 177 pages.

*Bonefishing;* Stanley M. Babson; Winchester Press, New York, 1973; 144 pages.

*Big Fish and Blue Water, Gamefishing in the Pacific;* Peter Goadby; Holt, Rinehart and Winston, New York, 1970; 334 pages.

*Complete Guide to Fishing Across North America* (fresh and salt water); Joe Brooks; Harper & Row, New York, 1970; 613 pages.

*Creative Fly Tying and Fly Fishing;* Rex Gerlach; Winchester Press, New York, 1974; 231 pages.

[*The*] *Compleat Brown Trout;* Cecil E. Heacox; Winchester Press, New York, 1974; 182 pages.

[*The*] *Complete Book of Fly Casting;* John Alden Knight and Richard Alden Knight; G. P. Putnam's Sons, New York, 1963; 192 pages.

*Fishing Made Easy* (fresh and salt water); Arthur L. Cone Jr.; The Macmillan Co., New York, 1968; 319 pages.

*Fishing for Beginners* (fresh and salt water); John Fabian; Atheneum Publishers, New York, 1974; 177 pages.

*Fly Casting with Lefty Kreh;* Lefty Kreh; J. B. Lippincott Co., Philadelphia and New York, 1974; 127 pages.

*Fishing Moments of Truth;* Eric Peper and Jim Rikhoff (eds.); Winchester Press, New York, 1973; 207 pages.

*Fly Fishing Digest* (paper cover); Bill Wallace; Follett Publishing Co., Chicago, 1973; 257 pages.

*Fishing for Bass;* A. D. Livingston; J. B. Lippincott Co., Philadelphia and New York, 1974; 256 pages.

*Flyfishing in Salt Water;*Lefty Kreh; Crown Publishers, New York, 1974; 252 pages.

*From Hook to Table, How to Clean and Cook Fish;* Vic Dunaway; Macmillan Publishing Co., New York, 1974; 150 pages.

*Fishing the Nymph;* Jim Quick; The Ronald Press Co., New York, 1960; 139 pages.

*Fishing for Fun and to Wash Your Soul;* Herbert Hoover; Random House, New York, 1963; 86 pages.

[*The*] *Flying Fisherman;* R. V. ("Gadabout") Gaddis; Trident Press, New York, 1967; 182 pages.

*Fisherman's Bounty;* Nick Lyons (ed.); Crown Publishers, New York, 1970; 352 pages.

*Fly-Fishing for Trout, a Guide for Adult Beginners;* Richard W. Talleur; Winchester Press, New York, 1974; 260 pages.

*Fishing Secrets of the Experts* (salt and fresh water); the writings of eighteen topflight anglers, selected and edited by one of them, Vlad Evanoff; Doubleday & Co., New York, 1962; 288 pages.

*How to Catch Salt-Water Fish;* Bill Wisner; Doubleday & Co., New York, 1973; 584 pages.

*How to Tie Freshwater Flies;* Kenneth E. Bay; Winchester Press, New York, 1974; 152 pages.

*How to Fish the Pacific Coast* (paper cover); Ray Cannon; Lane Books, Menlo Park, Cal., 1967; 160 pages.

*Kamloops, an Angler's Study of the Kamloops Trout;* Steven Raymond; Winchester Press, New York.

*Line Down! The Special World of Big-Game Fishing;* Jack Samson; Winchester Press, New York, 1973; 177 pages.

*McClane's New Standard Fishing Encyclopedia;* A. J. McClane (ed.); Holt, Rinehart and Winston, New York, 1974 (revised, enlarged edition); 1,176 pages.

*Don't Blame the Fish;* Bob Warner; Winchester Press, New York, 1974, 210 pages.

[*The*] *Experts' Book of Freshwater Fishing;* Steve Netherby (ed.); Simon & Schuster, New York, 1974; 317 pages.

*Fishing from Boats;* Milt Rosko; The Macmillan Co., New York, 1968; 272 pages.

*Fly Fishing the Lakes;* Rex Gerlach; Winchester Press, New York, 1972; 163 pages.

# Bibliography


*Modern Fresh and Salt Water Fly Fishing* (paper cover); Charles F. Waterman; Collier Books (division of Macmillan), New York, 1972; 368 pages.

*Modern Saltwater Sport Fishing;* Frank Woolner; Crown Publishers, New York, 1972; 319 pages.

*Modern Book of the Black Bass;* Byron Dalrymple; Winchester Press, New York.

*Modern Fishing Tackle;* Vlad Evanoff; A. S. Barnes, New York, 1961; 211 pages.

*Nymphs, a Complete Guide to Naturals and Imitations;* Ernest Schwiebert; Winchester Press, New York, 1973; 339 pages.

*Practical Fishing Knots;* Lefty Kreh and Mark Sosin; Crown Publishers, New York, 1972; 160 pages.

*Profiles in Saltwater Angling;* George Reiger; Prentice-Hall, Englewood Cliffs, N.J., 1973; 470 pages.

*Practical Fresh Water Fishing;* Francis E. Sell; The Robald Press Co., New York, 1960; 198 pages.

*Salt Water Fishing on the Pacific Coast;* J. Charles Davis II; A. S. Barnes & Co., New York, 1964; 259 pages.

*Salt Water Flies;* Kenneth E. Bay; J. B. Lippincott Co., Philadelphia and New York, 1972; 150 pages.

*Secrets of Striped Bass Fishing;* Milt Rosko; The Macmillan Co., New York, 1966; 238 pages.

*Song of the Outriggers, Big Game Fishing on the Ocean Surface;* Ralph R. Whitaker; Warren H. Green, Inc., St. Louis, 1968; 311 pages.

*Spinfishing, the System That Does It All;* Norman Strung and Milt Rosko; The Macmillan Publishing Co., New York, 1973; 339 pages.

*Steelhead;* Mel Marshall; Winchester Press, New York, 1973; 186 pages.

*Striped Bass & Other Cape Cod Fish* (paper cover); Paul Schwind; The Chatham Press, Riverside, Conn., 1972; 128 pages.

*Successful Bluefishing;* Henry ("Hal") Lyman; International Marine Publishing Co., Camden, Me., 1974; 112 pages.

*Successful Ocean Game Fishing;* Frank T. Moss, with chapters by nine other experts; International Marine Publishing Co., Camden, Me., 1971; 245 pages.

*Successful Striped Bass Fishing;* Frank T. Moss; International Marine Publishing Co., Camden, Me., 1974; 195 pages.

*Surf Fishing;* Vlad Evanoff; Harper & Row, New York, 1974; 195 pages.

*Teaching Your Children to Fish* (fresh water and salt); Jack Fallon; Winchester Press, New York, 1974; 189 pages.

*There's No Fishing Like Fly Rod Fishing;* ten experts contribute chapters, including one on salt water flyrodding; Richard's Rosen press, New York, 1972; 181 pages.

*The Trail of the Sharp Cup* (story of the fifth oldest trophy in international sports, this one for big-game tuna fishing); S. Kip Farrington Jr., famed big-game angler and originator of the International Tuna Cup Match in Nova Scotia; Dodd, Mead & Co., New York, 1974; 176 pages.

*The Trout, the Whole Trout and Nothing But the Trout;* John Shingleton; Winchester Press, New York, 1974; 143 pages.

[*The*] *Ways of Game Fish* (marine and fresh water); Russ Williams and Charles L. Cadieux; J. B. Ferguson Publishing Co., Chicago, 1972; 326 pages.

*Why Fish Bite and Why They Don't;* James Westmena; Prentice-Hall, Englewood Cliffs, N.J., 1961; 211 pages.

[*The*] *Way of a Trout;* R. P. Van Gytenbeek; J. B. Lippincott Co., Philadelphia and New York, 1972; 146 pages.

*Worming and Spinning for Trout;* Jerry Wood; A. S. Barnes and Co., New York, 1959; 156 pages.

[*The*] *101 Best Fishing Trips in Oregon* (paper cover); Don Holm; The Caxton Printers, Caldwell, Ida., 1970; 207 pages.

*1001 Fishing Tips and Tricks* (1966), 247 pages, and *Another 1001 Fishing Tips and Tricks* (1970), 206 pages, both covering fresh water and salt water; Vlad Evanoff; Harper & Row, New York.

## A PARTING WORD

Once upon a time we all fished away like crazy, carefree in a delusion that our oceans, bays, lakes and rivers are a bottomless cornucopia. "Why, more fish die from old age, or are eaten by each other, than man could ever catch," we told ourselves . . . and believed it.

We all were in for a terrible awakening.

The sea dealt us the most dramatic jolt because of its sheer size. For generations we thought of it as swarming with fishes. Biologists have shot down that idea with evidence indicating that an ocean is actually a vast watery "desert," with scattered populations of fishes as mobile "oases." Commercial exploitation has given substance to that concept by literally cleaning out several species in different regions. At one stage Atlantic salmon were being pushed to the brink of extinction. Netting has threatened bluefin tuna with the status of an endangered species. Declines in West Coast tuna, anchovies and sardines also underscore the point. On the East Coast, swordfish have demonstrated the impact of longlines, while nets still clobber menhaden for industrial uses and sometimes seem to be sweeping the Atlantic clean of haddock, porgies and other marketable fishes.

And that's only part of the dilemma. Who ever thought an ocean, with all its vastness, could be polluted to the detriment of marine life? Now we know that it can be, and it's frightening.

Our inland fisher resources have been beset by similar woes: Industrial, municipal and agricultural pollution; commercial over-exploitation in some instances; and ruining or elimination of fishes' environment by deforestation, road building and mushrooming residential communities.

Nor is that all. For reasons best known to itself, nature tosses wrenches into the machinery too. There are poor spawning years. Sometimes environments turn hostile to exact heavy tolls among fishes' eggs and young. Or a link in the food chain is weakened or destroyed, throwing an ecosystem out of kilter. And always there are predators. In the underwater world assassins lurk everywhere.

So we do not have a bottomless cornucopia. That will become even more evident as commercial and sport fishing pressures continue to increase. It's a bleak picture, but not one of doom — yet. A ray of hope shines from the realization, finally, that unless sensible conservation and management procedures are adopted *now*, we won't have fishery resources tomorrow.